SEPARATION OF POWERS AND ANTITRUST

Separation of powers and antitrust deal with power and occupy center stage in our challenging times, but their interactions have not yet been analyzed. This timely and groundbreaking book provides an innovative cross-disciplinary analysis of the potential convergence of these two fields. Notably, Vincent Martenet examines the concentration of politico-economic power in the hands of a few digital firms that have adopted private regulation, impacting an entire industry and society at large. He combines doctrinal method with historical developments, case studies, assessment of legislative proposals, and observations on the functioning of digital markets and democracy in the digital and artificial intelligence era. This book sketches important new axes of the separation of powers and suggests that antitrust may contribute, albeit in a limited way, to greater trust in both society and democracy. *Antitrust for trust*, or the ultimate apparent antitrust paradox.

Vincent Martenet is the Dean of the Faculty of Law, Criminal Sciences, and Public Administration at the University of Lausanne where he teaches Swiss and comparative constitutional law, as well as competition law. He has occupied various positions at the Swiss Competition Commission, which he chaired from July 2010 until December 2017, and is currently Deputy Justice at the Supreme Court of Switzerland. His fields of interest include constitutional law, comparative public law, and competition law.

ASCL STUDIES IN COMPARATIVE LAW

ASCL *Studies in Comparative Law* publishes monographs and collections that broaden theoretical and practical knowledge of the world's many legal systems. Published under the direction of the American Society of Comparative Law, the *ASCL Studies* examine legal problems in a comparative light to advance legal science, develop technical insights, and promote greater cooperation across jurisdictional and cultural boundaries. This book series serves legal practitioners and those seeking to improve law and justice by publishing in-depth comparative studies of specific legal problems in every area of law.

The series has two general editors. David Gerber is Distinguished Professor of Law and Co-Director of the Program in International and Comparative Law at Chicago-Kent College of Law, Illinois Institute of Technology. He is past President of the American Society of Comparative Law. Mortimer Sellers is Regents Professor of the University System of Maryland and Director of the Baltimore Center for International and Comparative Law. He is past President of the Internationale Vereinigung für Rechts-und Sozialphilosophie.

Separation of Powers and Antitrust

VINCENT MARTENET
University of Lausanne

CAMBRIDGE
UNIVERSITY PRESS

CAMBRIDGE
UNIVERSITY PRESS

Shaftesbury Road, Cambridge CB2 8EA, United Kingdom

One Liberty Plaza, 20th Floor, New York, NY 10006, USA

477 Williamstown Road, Port Melbourne, VIC 3207, Australia

314–321, 3rd Floor, Plot 3, Splendor Forum, Jasola District Centre, New Delhi – 110025, India

103 Penang Road, #05–06/07, Visioncrest Commercial, Singapore 238467

Cambridge University Press is part of Cambridge University Press & Assessment, a department of the University of Cambridge.

We share the University's mission to contribute to society through the pursuit of education, learning and research at the highest international levels of excellence.

www.cambridge.org
Information on this title: www.cambridge.org/9781009357258

DOI: 10.1017/9781009357265

© Vincent Martenet 2024

First published 2024

A catalogue record for this publication is available from the British Library

A Cataloging-in-Publication data record for this book is available from the Library of Congress

ISBN 978-1-009-35725-8 Hardback

To Patricia, Arnaud, and Cassandre

From the earliest years of our nation, Americans have understood that too great a concentration of economic power is fatal to democracy.

Jack M. Balkin, review of *The Anti-Oligarchy Constitution*

Competition is the most remarkable and ingenious instrument for reducing power known in history.

Franz Böhm, "Democracy and Economic Power," 279

The laws of circumstances are abolished by new circumstances.

Napoléon Bonaparte, *Maximes et pensées*, 110 (translation)

A monopoly is an autocracy in business clothes.

Dave Eggers, *The Every*, 354 (words of a fictional U.S. politician "running for small business. For free enterprise. For freedom. For president.")

Contents

Preface

This book investigates whether separation of powers and antitrust are – at least partly – based on common ground from a historical, comparative, and prospective point of view. Are we ultimately witnessing some actual or potential convergence between them? Both separation of powers and antitrust occupy center stage in our challenging, digital times, but their interactions have never been analyzed. Even though one relates first and foremost to state power and the other to economic power, they may interact with one another, especially in an era of unprecedented accumulation of economic and political power by a few firms in the digital and artificial intelligence era.

Both separation of powers and antitrust indeed deal with *power*. This timely book breaks new ground notably by examining the concentration of politico-economic power in the hands of a few firms which adopt private regulation that affects an entire industry and society at large, which are part of the digital infrastructure of democracy and which may exercise a significant influence on public decision-makers. It combines doctrinal method with historical developments, assessment of legislative proposals, case studies, and observations on the concrete functioning of digital markets and democracy in the digital and artificial intelligence era.

The approach followed in this book helps one to arrive at the tenet of some reinforced separation between political and economic powers or, put another way and actually more accurately, between governmental and platform powers. The book sketches new axes of the separation of powers – some of them involving antitrust – and concludes that the latter may contribute to trust within society and in democracy.

This book includes interdisciplinary and multidisciplinary perspectives, showing how constitutional and antitrust principles can interact. It provides readers with the keys to understanding the need for regulatory and antitrust reform to address the concentration of politico-economic power by a few digital platforms. It is aimed at being concise and, at the same time, insightful, as well as thought-provoking.

On a more personal note, this book represents the unique chance to combine my two main fields of interest and expertise, both as an academic and a public servant.

It has accompanied me for many years. Initially, I intended to write an article, but David J. Gerber encouraged me to develop the subject matter in a wider context and to write a monography. I have thought about it and decided to abide by his suggestion! I would like to thank him warmly for having convinced me to launch this adventure, as well as him and his co-editor, Mortimer Sellers, for having accepted to publish my book in the ASCL Studies in Comparative Law at Cambridge University Press. My deepest thanks also go to Tom Randall and Marianne Nield, former and current Commissioning Editors at Cambridge University Press, respectively, who followed this project in a very professional and supportive way.

I had the opportunity to discuss parts of the book with various colleagues whom I greatly respect and who have given me very useful feedback. In this regard, I am indebted to Odile Ammann, Marc Amstutz, Bruce J. Caldwell, Vikram Chand, Boi Faltings, Dana Foarta, David J. Gerber, Inge Graef, Andreas Heinemann, Martin Jaggi, Shaheeza Lalani, Catherine Larrère, Thierry Ménissier, Sylvain Métille, Jan-Werner Müller, Luka Nenadic, Kazuaki Nishioka, Peter Georg Picht, Edgar Philippin, Dominique Schnapper, and Heike Schweitzer for their helpful comments. I thank Clémence Demay, Julia Kamhi, Natalia Pérez, and Stéphanie Tumini from the University of Lausanne for their excellent research assistance, Derek Heath for his extremely valuable proofreading as well as Doriana Ferreira for her meticulous review of the bibliography and the index.

Finally, this book is dedicated to my wife and our children for illuminating my life.

Introduction

The separation of powers principle and antitrust both relate to power and, notably, deal with the concentration of power. However, they are usually conceptualized, analyzed, and promoted separately. Separation of powers primarily refers to the branches of government or the main functions of the state and, in this respect, to public or state power or powers, while the economic power of private or, to a lesser extent, public firms is at the core of antitrust. Though appealing, this distinction is not clear-cut. These powers interact with one another. The concentration of political power in one or a few hands may typically denote an authoritarian regime. By contrast, the same cannot automatically be said about the concentration of economic power. Still, the latter may facilitate the emergence or the strengthening of such a regime.[1] Accordingly, a correlation or even a cause may exist in this regard.

The separation of powers principle does not seem to have any economic content. Theorists of this principle often do not consider the concentration of economic power in the hands of one or a few persons or firms. On closer inspection, however, at least some of them see, in such a concentration, similar dangers to those that they attribute to the absence of separation or division of powers with respect to branches of government or state functions. Therefore, some connection – albeit implicit – may be established between separation of powers and antitrust.

Antitrust, for its part, seems to be focused on economic power – more precisely on market power. Nevertheless, from a historical perspective, antitrust had a political content or even purpose in several jurisdictions. Has this dimension of antitrust completely and permanently disappeared? This question must be assessed prospectively, in light of the digitalization of the economy and the challenges linked to it. One of the goals of this book is to investigate whether separation of powers and antitrust are – at least partly – based on common grounds from a historical and prospective perspective. Are we currently witnessing some actual or potential convergence or interactions between them in the digital era or in

---

[1]   See Crane, "Instrument of Democracy," 24–28.

the age of artificial intelligence?[2] This yet-to-be-examined question must first be addressed under the existing antitrust and competition laws. An unsatisfactory response possibly demonstrates the need for legislative reform. The next challenge is to determine which is more appropriate to deal with the politico-economic issues raised by the digitalization of the economy – antitrust or specific regulation.

The concentration of politico-economic power in one or a few hands also raises fundamental issues in a democracy. Although this book is not directly about the latter, it is partly underpinned by considerations on liberty, conflicts of interest, and, ultimately, democracy, so that the analysis includes developments upon them. The threat to democracy is duly considered and actually forms the backdrop of the book but is sometimes put to the forefront when and where it is appropriate. Currently, and in the future, special attention must be given to the fact that a few digital platforms contribute to the digital infrastructure of democracy, with the internet having been described as "the most powerful tool in human history"[3] and criticized for concentrating power, rather than dispersing it.[4] This continuing evolution needs to be addressed from a mingled separation of power and antitrust or regulatory perspective. In this regard, pieces of legislation recently adopted or proposed in several jurisdictions can be compared, as different democracies face, or may face, similar issues. This invites an analysis on how some of these issues are addressed by constitutional law, regulation, or antitrust from a comparative point of view.

The terms *antitrust* or *competition law and policy* are mostly used in this book interchangeably. *Competition law and policy* is broader and used in many jurisdictions, while *antitrust* is a term used mainly in the United States, where the interactions between political and economic powers have been explored probably more than in any other country. One should note, however, that this term can also be found in other jurisdictions, for instance in the European Union.[5] As this book explores the foundations of antitrust laws, the term *antitrust* reflects this and, therefore, is chosen in the title, though the analysis will actually encompass what is usually understood as *competition law and policy* and will also include illustrations or considerations on what would qualify as antimonopoly – and not just antitrust – legislation in the United States.

For its part, the term *digital platform*, widely used in the book, notably refers to the "major digital platforms that have drawn so much media and political attention"[6] – especially Alibaba, Amazon, Apple (mostly with respect to its app ecosystem),

---

[2]   The "Age of AI" (Kissinger, Schmidt & Huttenlocher, *Age of AI*) is itself digital, at least to a great extent. Issues specifically relating to artificial intelligence will also be addressed.

[3]   Hoffman, *Forces*, 35.

[4]   Narula, *Society*, 194–99; Fukuyama, *Liberalism*, 104–5 & 109.

[5]   In the European Union, see, for example, https://ec.europa.eu/competition-policy/antitrust_en. Regarding anticompetitive agreements and abuses of dominant position specifically, see Combe, *Concurrence*, 219. In the present book, merger control is included in a broad notion of *antitrust*.

[6]   Hovenkamp, "Antitrust and Platform Monopoly," 1956.

Facebook, and Google. Of course, other platforms such as Baidu, Instagram, KakaoTalk, LinkedIn, TikTok, X/Twitter, YouTube, WeChat, or WhatsApp and, more recently, developments relating to the gaming industry, artificial intelligence, or the metaverse will also be considered. The fact that several platforms belong to the same company – Facebook, Instagram, Messenger, and WhatsApp to Meta Platforms, Inc.; Google, Bard, and YouTube to Alphabet Inc.; Bing, LinkedIn, and the Microsoft Gaming division to Microsoft Corporation, not to mention its partnership with OpenAI; WeChat and Tencent Interactive Entertainment Group, with its subdivision Tencent Games, to Tencent Holdings Ltd. – also matters. The use of the term *digital platforms* in connection with all of these, and other, firms is widespread and well established.[7]

In a nutshell, digital platforms have the following main characteristics:

> Digital platforms bring together individuals and organizations so they can innovate or interact in ways not otherwise possible, using modern software, hardware, and networking technology [...]. Digital platforms aim to connect two or more market actors (market sides) and generate positive feedback loops among or across users in ways that bring increasing value to platform participants (network effects).[8]

As far as antitrust is concerned, the notion of *dominant digital platform* or *dominant platform* will be used throughout this book, as it is relevant in many jurisdictions,[9] including in the United States.[10] This book does not attempt to determine which firms have a dominant position in one or several digital markets. This question is currently the subject of numerous proceedings in many jurisdictions. Each market requires a careful analysis, and great caution is needed in this respect. This implies avoiding any abrupt and summarily reasoned conclusion as to the existence or not of a dominant position of a firm in a given market. When the adjective *dominant* is used in the book, it means, in principle, that the firm at stake has a dominant position

---

7 See, e.g., Jenny, "Digital Ecosystems," 1144–46; Cusumano, Gawer & Yoffie, "Self-Regulation," 1260–62; Parker, Petropoulos & Van Alstyne, "Platform Mergers," 1310–22. Regarding the United States, see, for instance, U.S. House of Representatives – Subcommittee on Antitrust, Commercial and Administrative Law, *Digital Markets*, 132–376 (qualifying Facebook, Google, Amazon, and Apple as dominant online platforms). Regarding Germany, see, for instance, Monopolkommission, *Wettbewerb 2020*, 22–51 (with a summary in English on pp. 25–26). For a narrower approach, see Schrepel, "Platforms or Aggregators," 1–3 (arguing that Google.com, Facebook.com, Twitter.com, Amazon.com, Netflix, Uber and Airbnb are aggregators, not platforms, and that "only cases dealing with platforms [and not with aggregators] should point towards reduced consumer choice to signal anticompetitive practices" [quotation from p. 2]). However, if an "aggregator" provides its users with partial information, is the latter's choice not *de facto* reduced?

8 Cusumano, Gawer & Yoffie, "Self-Regulation," 1260 (quotation) and *Business of Platforms*, 13. Regarding "platforms," see OECD, *Handbook*, 10 ("Platforms are firms that provide different services to different groups of interconnected consumers"). Regarding "network platforms," see Kissinger, Schmidt & Huttenlocher, *Age of AI*, 94 ("[D]igital services that provide value to their users by aggregating those users in large numbers, often at a transnational and global scale").

9 See OECD, *Ex Ante Regulation*, 9–10; UNCTAD, *Digital Era*, 2–5 & 10.

10 See, e.g., Hovenkamp, "Monopolizing," 1680–81.

within the meaning of, for example, Article 102 of the Treaty on the Functioning of the European Union (TFEU) or may fall under, for instance, Section 2 of the Sherman Act in the United States.

The methodology followed in the book can be qualified as doctrinal. Indeed, it is based on the study of – and reflections on – the foundations of both the separation of powers principle and antitrust; it intends to investigate whether they historically and contemporaneously share some common ground. Methodologically, after having (re)examined the foundations on which the separations of powers principle and antitrust rest, and from which they can evolve, the book evaluates the interactions between them as well as their actual and possible convergence. The interactions are carefully analyzed through the lens of both the separation of powers principle and antitrust. The analysis is not, however, a purely abstract exercise. On the contrary, historical developments, assessments of legislative proposals, case studies, and observations on the concrete functioning of digital markets and democracy in the digital and artificial intelligence era supplement and support the doctrinal method. In other words, this study takes a theoretical approach, but, at the same time, it is based on practical considerations and addresses current issues on antitrust and regulatory matters. These issues are delineated from numerous legislative proposals, reports, books, scholarly and press articles, and other publications such as entries in specialized blogs relating to digital platforms. This set of generally accessible data, gathered over several years and quoted throughout the book, allows defining some contours of a new separation of powers in the digital era and in the age of artificial intelligence while identifying or synthetizing the actual or potential contribution – if any – of specific regulations or antitrust in this regard.

By contrast, this book does not primarily deal with checks and balances in antitrust enforcement and to the related institutional choices, as abundant literature[11] and numerous reports on that subject currently exist or are forthcoming, for instance, from the Organisation for Economic Co-operation and Development (OECD).[12] However, some comments on the institutional aspect of antitrust or regulatory agencies will have a place in the last chapter. Neither does this book specifically question, from an institutional perspective, the sweeping language used in several key antitrust provisions in the United States,[13] Europe,[14] or elsewhere. Granted, too much leeway or discretion for antitrust agencies and courts can raise rule of law and separation of powers concerns.[15] Before changing this paradigm of antitrust, from the onset, a note of caution is warranted: all things considered, but without further elaboration,

---

[11] See, e.g., Sokol & Guzman (eds.), *Antitrust Procedural Fairness*; Nihoul & Skoczny (eds.), *Procedural Fairness*.
[12] See, e.g., OECD, *Standard of Review* and *Procedural Fairness and Transparency*.
[13] See Khan, "Antitrust History," 1677–82.
[14] See, e.g., Lévêque, *Entreprises hyperpuissantes*, 111–12.
[15] See, e.g., Tucker, "Antitrust" ("[T]he equilibrium is vague statutes that allow bureaucrats and judges to shift high policy while virtuously claiming fidelity to the law"); Crane, "Antitrust and Democracy," 8.

the openness, flexibility, and transversality across sectors and industries, as well as the adaptability of antitrust,[16] should not be sacrificed before a thorough examination of an alternative, more convincing regime. Napoléon Bonaparte warned that "[t]he laws of circumstances are abolished by new circumstances."[17]

This book is divided into three parts. Part I focuses on the foundations of antitrust and the separation of powers principle, not only from a historical viewpoint but also from a contemporary one in the digital and artificial intelligence era. Democracy serves, to a certain extent, as a backdrop to the analysis, since the concentration of politico-economic power is often viewed as a threat to it. Part II evaluates the actual or possible convergence – if any – of the separation of powers principle and antitrust *de lege lata*, as well as the interactions between them. The approach taken is rather unique, as it shows that two of the main instruments against concentration of powers – the separation of powers and antitrust – share a common basis and may interact in both ways in the digital and artificial intelligence era. This leads, in Part III, to a new view on the separation of powers principle and to a reflection on the potential contribution of antitrust *de lege ferenda* – or at least significantly reinterpreted – and specific regulation to it. The new separation of powers implies a multidimensional appraisal of this principle that takes account of the politico-economic power of digital platforms and the ways to regulate them through constitutional law, antitrust, or specific regulations, as Jamie Susskind also envisioned.[18] From the perspectives of the separation of powers principle and antitrust in the digital era or in the age of artificial intelligence, the approach followed helps one to arrive at the tenet of some reinforced separation between political and economic powers or, put another way, between governmental and platform powers. Platform power, as used throughout the book, relates to the multidimensional power of digital platforms, especially in democratic regimes. As highlighted in the Conclusion, antitrust may actually contribute to separation of powers in a digital and artificial intelligence era, as well as, ultimately, to trust within society and in democracy.

---

[16] See, for instance, Hovenkamp, "Antitrust and Platform Monopoly," 2050 ("Competition problems in digital platforms present some novel challenges, but most are within reach of antitrust law's capacity to handle them"); see also Jean, *Algorithmes*, 21 & 142–44.

[17] Bonaparte, *Maximes et pensées*, 110 (translation).

[18] Susskind, *Future Politics*, 358–59 and *Digital Republic*, 175–210 ("Counterpower") & 245–47.

PART I

Foundations

This first part of the book focuses on the foundations of the separation of powers principle and those of antitrust. Chapter 1 emphasizes that both notions refer to questions of power(s). Chapter 2 demonstrates that a few theorists of separation of powers and other authors have also based some of their analyses on economic considerations. Chapters 3 and 4 highlight the historical and prospective political content of antitrust and lead to the fundamental observation that the digital infrastructure of democracy is – at least partly – in private hands and, more precisely, in those of firms subject to antitrust and competition laws.

1

Power

The separation of powers principle and antitrust both relate to power – a multidimensional, multifactorial, contextual, and evolutive notion (Section 1.1) – and notably deal with the concentration or the abuse of power (Section 1.2). The separation of powers principle primarily relates to the branches of government and state functions (Section 1.3). For its part, antitrust is linked to economic power (Section 1.4).

1.1 A MULTIFACTORIAL, MULTIDIMENSIONAL, CONTEXTUAL, AND EVOLUTIVE NOTION

Power should always be understood in its context and based on the specificities of the system at hand. Separation of powers and antitrust usually address different issues relating to power, even though they may sometimes share similar concerns or even overlap. Therefore, they should not merge.

A general theory of power seems out of reach and would inevitably be fragmented into several components, aspects, or dimensions. The search for a universally satisfactory definition of power also constitutes a herculean task.[1] The noun *power* has many meanings – forty according to the *Oxford English Dictionary*.[2] It primarily pertains to ability, control, strength, authority, or influence.[3]

Power is exercised over institutions, authorities, persons, or firms, but the locution "power over" only partially covers the notion at stake, since power is also understood

---

[1]   Regarding the "conceptual problem of power," see already White, "Problem of Power," 479–90 (concluding, on p. 490, that "no universally satisfactory account of *the* meaning of power is possible").

[2]   See *Oxford English Dictionary*, which lists forty meanings for the noun *power*.

[3]   See *Cambridge English Dictionary*, first four meanings of power; *Oxford English Dictionary*, first seven meanings of power (meanings I.1.a and b; I.2.a, b, c, d, and e). Regarding ability, see, for instance, Morriss, *Power*, 13 & 48–106. Regarding influence, see, for instance, Castelfranchi, "Constitution of Power," 225–28; Wrong, *Power*, 23–24; Dahl, "Power," 201–15. For a critical account of Dahl's evolving view of power, see, e.g., Lukes, "Dahl on Power," 261–71 (concluding, on p. 270, that "[b]y conflating power and influence, it fails to see power as dispositional and thus not needing to be activated to have significant effects").

as an ability or a capacity to effect outcomes ("power to").[4] These two forms of power are, to a large extent, connected and involved in a complex dialectic.[5] Furthermore, power changes the real and virtual environment faced by every person, every firm, every government, etc.[6] When power is – directly or indirectly, through circumstance, for example – relative to others,[7] the idea of absolute power can, to a wide extent, be regarded as an oxymoron. Indeed, power is usually caught in a web of interactions.

Several main characteristics of power can be highlighted in the issue at hand. First, power is multifactorial[8] – or, in other words, multisource and multicausal – and multidimensional, as it is a complex and protean phenomenon. State and economic powers can be distinguished, even though they interact one with another and are, to some extent, interdependent. In the words of Milton Friedman, "economic power can be a check to political power instead of an addition to it."[9] The reverse is certainly also true. It is therefore important not only to adopt an encompassing vision of power but also to clearly determine the dimensions[10] and characteristics of the power one is benefiting, facing, or simply analyzing. Moreover, the source of power may be of a different nature than its manifestation. A dominant firm's economic power may, for instance, generate societal or political power. From this perspective, power potentially has a transformative effect.[11] In addition to this, the power held by some digital firms can be characterized as politico-economic because its economic and political dimensions are actually – at least for a good part – meshed together.[12]

Second, power is contextual.[13] The circumstances in which power is exercised or simply being felt considerably matter. The relevant constitutional and statutory framework may significantly or enormously differ from one country to another, but

---

[4] See Morriss, *Power*, 32–35. For an exchange on this issue, see Pansardi, "Power," 73–89 (arguing that both *power over* and *power to* refer to social relations); Morriss, "Response to Pansardi," 91–99; Pansardi, "Reply to Morriss," 493–97.

[5] See, for instance, Hearn, *Power*, 6–7 & 16–17.

[6] See, e.g., Popitz, *Phenomena of Power*, 15–18 (noting, on p. 17, that "[w]e are affected by power via technical action because we are bound to an artificially modified world of objects, which has always been entirely or partly produced by others").

[7] See, e.g., Benkler, "Freedom, Power," 19 ("By *power*, I mean the capacity of an entity to alter the behaviors, beliefs, outcomes, or configurations of some other entity").

[8] Regarding "platform power," see Busch, Graef, Hofmann & Gawer, *Platform Power*, 5–14.

[9] Friedman, "Capitalism and Freedom," 7 (quotation) and *Capitalism and Freedom*, 15.

[10] From a sociological perspective, see Lukes, "Power and Economics," 20–25.

[11] See, e.g., Ezrachi & Stucke, *Barons*, 130; Stucke, *Breaking Away*, 243; Susskind, *Digital Republic*, 238; Fishkin & Forbath, *Constitution*, 230 ("Capitalist wealth has an inevitable tendency to convert economic into political domination"), 314 (quoting Wendell Berge, who served as head of the Antitrust Division of the U.S. Department of Justice from 1943 to 1947), 413–14, 422, 436–37 & 475; Eifert, Metzger, Schweitzer & Wagner, "Taming the Giants," 991; Steinbaum & Stucke, "Standard," 603.

[12] See *infra* Chapter 4.

[13] See, for instance, Castelfranchi, "Constitution of Power," 235–36.

the study of a governmental body's or a firm's power should go beyond this framework and look at the whole context in which this power operates or produces its influence. This comment relates, in particular, to governmental or, more broadly, state power and to economic power.

Third, power is evolutive,[14] as the influence or perception of a given power – of religious or economic nature, for instance – can vary considerably over time. A government body or a firm can see their power increase or decrease in a changing political or economic environment. Power may prove stable or, on the contrary, unstable. The dynamics of a given power or between powers is of special interest in this context.[15] The potentialities of power – in a way, the power of power – should therefore be integrated into the analysis.

These various characteristics can relate either to the power or powers at the core of the separation of powers principle or at the one of antitrust. Indeed, both refer to a multidimensional, multifactorial, contextual, and evolutive conception of power. Separation of powers and antitrust have greatly evolved since the times of Montesquieu or Senator Sherman, but some of the fundamental issues they addressed are timeless and have stood the test of time, such as the risks of abuse associated with the concentration of political or economic power.

1.2 CONCENTRATION AND ABUSE

Power as such is an institutional, economic, social, or – without any claim of completeness – interpersonal phenomenon. It is subject to multiple types and forms of regulation. One of the law's functions is to regulate power in countless settings or situations and for different purposes. More precisely, the purpose of many international, constitutional, or statutory norms, as well as fundamental principles, aims, among other things, at avoiding the concentration or the abuse of power.[16] In other words, power is also viewed as a threat or a danger, notably because it does not tend to balance, but rather to concentrate and, potentially, lead to inequality.[17] Accordingly, it should be framed and constrained by law.

Moreover, the concentration of power can also threaten individual freedom and, ultimately, democracy or even the rule of law, including when a vast amount of politico-economic power lies in private hands, as stressed in the Executive Order on Promoting Competition in the American Economy adopted by U.S. President Joe Biden on 9 July 2021:

[14] Regarding "platform power," see Busch, Graef, Hofmann & Gawer, *Platform Power*, 6–7.
[15] See, for instance, Castelfranchi, "Constitution of Power," 236–37.
[16] Regarding platform industries in the United States, see, e.g., Sitaraman, "Foreign Platforms," 1141 ("Sectoral regulations in platform industries have often been adopted to prevent the abuse of economic and political power").
[17] Castelfranchi, "Constitution of Power," 261.

A fair, open, and competitive marketplace has long been a cornerstone of the American economy, while excessive market concentration threatens basic economic liberties, democratic accountability, and the welfare of workers, farmers, small businesses, startups, and consumers.[18]

Freedom itself is multidimensional and includes – among other – political, social, and economic dimensions. Besides, power and freedom form a complex relationship with one another,[19] though they are neither identical nor opposite concepts. On the one hand, freedom is necessary in order to be able to utilize one's own powers to achieve one's own purposes.[20] On the other hand, the exercise of power usually restricts others' freedom. However, it can be misleading to claim that "[a]ll exercise of power is a limitation of freedom."[21] Power may actually be used to protect the effective freedom of many, especially vulnerable persons. Furthermore, one can neither theoretically nor empirically demonstrate that the more power is concentrated, the less effective individual freedom is in all circumstances, and vice versa.[22] The last part of this assertion should probably be reformulated to state that the more power is concentrated, the greater is, *ceteris paribus*, the risk to freedom, at least from a significant level of power concentration.[23] In the same vein, competition in politics, in cultural life or in economic relations can be regarded as a fundamental prerequisite of freedom.[24]

In sum, the more economic power is concentrated, the less its regulation can be left, *ceteris paribus*, to the market,[25] and the more countering power or powers

---

[18] President Joseph R. Biden Jr., *Executive Order on Promoting Competition in the American Economy*, The White House, 9 July 2021, Section 1 *in initio*. On this order, see Hovenkamp, "Executive Order," 386–87 (noting that the order is "hardly an endorsement of the proposition that antitrust should ignore economic concerns in favor of political ones" [quotation from p. 387]). See also U.S. House of Representatives – Subcommittee on Antitrust, Commercial and Administrative Law, *Digital Markets*, 20 & 391–92 (recommending to reassert the anti-monopoly goals of the antitrust laws and "their centrality to ensuring a healthy and vibrant democracy"). Regarding Facebook, see Simons & Ghosh, *Utilities for Democracy*, 6–8 ("Because Facebook has unilateral control over so much of the algorithmic infrastructure of our public sphere, Facebook can simply impose its own approach to the design of our public sphere, free from any obligation to reflect or represent deep disagreements about the governance of public debate. Without regulatory oversight or democratic accountability, regardless of the particular algorithms or policies Facebook develops, that kind of unilateral control over important social infrastructure is, in a democracy, objectionable on its own" [quotation from p. 6]).

[19] See, for instance, Morriss, *Power*, 116–22.

[20] Beetham, *Legitimation of Power*, 43.

[21] Popitz, *Phenomena of Power*, 6.

[22] See Susskind, *Digital Republic*, 245.

[23] Simons & Ghosh, *Utilities for Democracy*, 7 & 11 ("antitrust protects competition not just for narrow economic reasons of consumer welfare and market efficiency, but also for reasons of political liberty and self-government, because private powers which control important forms of public infrastructure should be subject to clear structures of accountability" [quotation from p. 7]).

[24] Andriychuk, *Foundations*, 260.

[25] See already Galbraith, *Power*, 120 & 182 (noting, on p. 182, that "[t]he concentration of industrial power can be seen in the mere handful of huge organizations that now dominate modern economic activity [...]. This is in overwhelming contrast to the wide distribution of economic activity in the

are needed.[26] Competition and regulation contribute to limit or channel and, at the same time, to legitimize, power. This consideration relates not only to political power but also to economic power.[27] Power gained through fair competition and regulated by appropriate rules, which are also perceived as such, may indeed be viewed as legitimate or, at least, as acceptable by the general public.[28]

Power, whether heavily concentrated or not, can lead to abuse. Abuses, or more exactly, the risks of abuses, explain the existence of international, constitutional, or statutory norms that govern the functioning of governments, institutions, markets, or public and private firms. The purpose of these norms consists in preventing, mitigating, sanctioning, or repairing abuse. From this perspective, any legal reflection on power often considers the risk of its abuse. Both separation of powers (Section 1.3) and antitrust (Section 1.4) can be, at least partly, approached through these lenses.

1.3 SEPARATION OF POWERS

The separation of powers principle is an elusive principle; its interpretation depends on many factors. As its name suggests, it deals with power, or more exactly, with powers. To gain a better sense of the possible interactions between separation of powers and antitrust, it seems indispensable to begin by identifying the core values and fundamental purpose or purposes of the first principle.

The separation or division of powers relates primarily to the legislative, executive and judiciary branches of government, or from a functional angle, to state functions. Charles-Louis de Secondat, Baron de La Brède et de Montesquieu, is usually associated with this approach ultimately based on liberty:

> When legislative power is united with executive power in a single person or in a single body of the magistracy, there is no liberty [...]. Nor is there liberty if the power of judging is not separate from legislative power and from executive power [...]. All would be lost if the same man or the same body of principal men, either of nobles, or of the people, exercised these three powers: that of making the laws, that of executing public resolutions, and that of judging the crimes and the disputes of individuals.[29]

earlier age of market capitalism [...]. The only thing that now disguises this concentration of economic power (and then not well) is the increasingly obsolescent conditioning that asserts the continued power-dissolving subordination of the firm to the classical market").

[26] See Galbraith, *Power*, 189.

[27] Regarding competition, see Hearn, *Power*, 148 (highlighting "the absolute centrality of competition to the operations, authority and legitimacy of our two great institutions: state and economy" and insisting that "[b]oth are validated by power being won through forms of competition that have been institutionally channelled and regulated").

[28] For an analysis based on the consent to limitations of freedom – i.e., in this respect, rules – by the "subordinate," see Beetham, *Legitimation of Power*, 60–63; see also Baker, *Antitrust Paradigm*, 32–62.

[29] Montesquieu, *Spirit of the Laws*, 157.

Though they differ on several issues relating to the separation or division of powers, Montesquieu's and James Madison's thoughts are built on similar foundations, as the latter emphasizes the risks related to the accumulation of power and the need to preserve or promote liberty:

> The accumulation of all powers, legislative, executive, and judiciary, in the same hands, whether of one, a few, or many, and whether hereditary, self-appointed, or elective, may justly be pronounced the very definition of tyranny.[30]
>
> In order to lay a due foundation for that separate and distinct exercise of the different powers of government, which to a certain extent is admitted on all hands to be essential to the preservation of liberty, it is evident that each department should have a will of its own […].[31]

John Locke, for his part, mentions "[t]he legislative, executive and federative powers of the commonwealth"[32] but does not single out a specific judiciary function or power. Immanuel Kant alludes to "three distinct authorities 1. Legislative, 2. Executive and 3. Judicial by which a state has its autonomy, that is, by which it forms and preserves itself in accordance with laws of freedom."[33] Benjamin Constant distinguishes, in a constitutional monarchy, "five distinct powers: (1) royal power (2) executive power (3) representative power of long duration [the hereditary assembly] (4) representative power of public opinion [the elective assembly] (5) judicial power," with the idea to have some balance of powers that the monarch, as head of state, is charged to preserve and restore.[34] The protection of liberty underpins the approach followed by Constant.[35] Hence, he sees the concentration of power as a source of arbitrariness, tyranny, despotism, or even dictatorship.[36] Alexis de Tocqueville does not elaborate much on separation of powers but makes an illuminating comment on the existence of different powers in a state as a way to avoid tyranny:

> Suppose […] a legislative body composed in such a manner that it represents the majority without necessarily being the slave of its passions; an executive power with a force that is its own and a judicial power independent of the other two powers; you will still have democratic government, but there will be almost no more chance of tyranny.[37]

This list of authors could go on and on. They may disagree on several issues, but they share some key understandings of the separation or the division – or even the

---

[30] Madison, *The Federalist No. 47*, 239.
[31] Madison, *The Federalist No. 51*, 256. For a nuanced view on *The Federalist No. 51* in this regard, see Amar, *Constitution*, 60.
[32] Locke, *Second Treatise of Government*, chapter 12.
[33] Kant, *Metaphysics of Morals*, part II (Public Right), chapter I (The Right of a State), § 49.
[34] Constant, *Principles of Politics*, 184–85.
[35] Constant, *Principles of Politics*, 186–87. See, e.g., Burnand, *Constant*, 156–57 & 264.
[36] Constant, *Principles of Politics*, 185–86. See, e.g., Burnand, *Constant*, 108, 157, 255 & 264.
[37] Tocqueville, *Democracy*, volume 1, 242.

balance – of powers.[38] This principle relates to the branches of government's powers or to the state's main functions. It aims to preserve freedom or liberty and to avoid the conflation,[39] concentration or accumulation[40] of power(s) leading to autocracy,[41] despotism,[42] tyranny,[43] arbitrariness, or abuse.[44] Although seemingly convincing, the arguments in favor of separation of powers are nevertheless, at best, scarce.[45] Finally, the concentration of economic power in private hands did not belong – at least not explicitly – to the framework of thought at that time.

In the late nineteenth and the twentieth centuries, those key arguments remain the core of the separation of powers principle. Albert Dicey focuses on the rule of law rather than on the separation of powers principle. On the basis of the rule of law, and fearing the arbitrary exercise of – executive – power,[46] he points out that government officials must obey the rules enacted by the Parliament and that this should be ensured by the courts having jurisdiction to enforce legal limits governing the exercise of executive power.[47] Maurice Vile identifies a "pure doctrine" of separation of powers, which is based on the division of the government into three branches, which he then criticizes.[48] While he briefly addresses the issue of social justice whose achievement meant, *inter alia*, the control of monopolies,[49] he devotes the epilogue of his book to the administrative state and its impact on separation of powers.[50] Friedrich A. (von) Hayek regards this principle as protecting liberty:

---

[38] Separation and division of powers may be distinguished (see Waldron, "Separation of Powers," 438–43). However, the two principles are overlapping to a significant extent (*id.*, at 440). The broader and most well-known understanding is used in this book to reflect issues that actually relate more to the division of powers. In particular, the "concern about undifferentiated governance" (*id.*, at 467) is linked by Jeremy Waldron to separation of powers (*id.*) but also relates to the division of powers. The same can be said of the relevant – and beautiful – definition of the separation of powers that he adopts: *"articulated government through successive phases of governance each of which maintains its own integrity"* (*id.*).

[39] On Montesquieu, see Troper, "Separation of Powers," para. 27 ("What should be avoided is very simple the conflation of powers or the gathering of powers in the hands of one man alone").

[40] Madison, *The Federalist No.* 47, 239.

[41] See *Myers* v. *United States*, 272 U.S. 52, 293 (1926) (Brandeis, J., dissenting) ("The doctrine of the separation of powers was adopted by the convention of 1787 not to promote efficiency, but to preclude the exercise of arbitrary power. The purpose was not to avoid friction but, by means of the inevitable friction incident to the distribution of the governmental powers among three departments, to save the people from autocracy").

[42] Montesquieu, *Spirit of the Laws*, 157–59 & 162.

[43] Montesquieu, *Spirit of the Laws*, 157 & 162; Blackstone, *Commentaries*, book 1, chapter 2; Madison, *The Federalist No.* 47, 239; Constant, *Principles of Politics*, 186; Tocqueville, *Democracy*, volume 1, 242.

[44] Montesquieu, *Spirit of the Laws*, 155; Madison, *The Federalist No.* 51, 257–58.

[45] On Montesquieu, see, e.g., Waldron, "Separation of Powers," 453–54 ("[Montesquieu] announced several times that unless the different powers of government are separated, tyranny would result, but he never explained why." [quotation from p. 453]); Troper, "Separation of Powers," paras. 25–44.

[46] Dicey, *Constitution*, 110–11 & 120.

[47] Dicey, *Constitution*, 120–22, 259 & 271–73. See, e.g., Meyerson, "Rule of Law," 1–6.

[48] Vile, *Constitutionalism*, 14 & 346–84.

[49] Vile, *Constitutionalism*, 382.

[50] Vile, *Constitutionalism*, 385–420.

The principle of separation of powers must not be interpreted to mean that in its dealing with the private citizen, the administration is not always subject to the rules laid down by the legislature and applied by independent courts.[51]

In his criticism of the theory, or more specifically, of the theories of separation of powers, Michel Troper rejects the idea of equilibrium or balance of powers[52] while acknowledging that these theories are based on the concern of avoiding the concentration of political power.[53]

In the late twentieth and the twenty-first centuries, separation of powers remains an elusive and evolving principle. In his seminal article on "The New Separation of Powers," Bruce Ackerman outlines what he calls the "new separationism" with several institutional proposals[54] and emphasizes – without, however, evoking the concentration of power in private hands – what he sees as three great challenges of the modern age:

> to make the ideal of popular sovereignty a credible reality in modern government, to redeem the ideal of bureaucratic expertise and integrity on an ongoing basis, and to safeguard fundamental liberal rights by guaranteeing basic resources for self-development to each and every citizen.[55]

Daryl Levinson and Richard Pildes plead, in the United States at least, for the reorientation of the system of separation of powers around parties, that is, non-state – though political – actors.[56] Eoin Carolan elaborates a theory of the modern state and calls for a new separation of powers.[57] Concluding that "[t]he administrative bodies of today's state are just too diverse to be convincingly corralled within Montesquieu's original trinity of functions,"[58] he also retains a tripartite division of powers – namely courts, political bodies, and the administration[59] – and insists on the participatory and collaborative inter- or multi-institutional process of exercising public power.[60]

---

[51] Hayek, *Constitution of Liberty*, 319. See, e.g., Kethledge, "Hayek," 212. On this issue, see Waldron, "Separation of Powers," 459–60 ("The Separation of Powers requires not just that the legislature and the judiciary and the executive concur in the use of power against some particular person, X. [...] The Separation of Powers Principle holds that these respective tasks have, each of them, an integrity of their own, which is contaminated when executive or judicial considerations affect the way in which legislation is carried out, which is contaminated when legislative and executive considerations affect the way the judicial function is performed, and which is contaminated when the tasks specific to the executive are tangled up with the tasks of law-making and adjudication").

[52] Troper, *Séparation des pouvoirs*, 208 and "Nouvelles séparations des pouvoirs," 28–35.

[53] See Troper, "Nouvelles séparations des pouvoirs," 35.

[54] Ackerman, "Separation of Powers," 727–28.

[55] Ackerman, "Separation of Powers," 729.

[56] Levinson & Pildes, "Separation of Parties," 2347–86. See also Troper, "Separation of Powers," para. 47 and "Nouvelles séparations des pouvoirs," 35.

[57] Carolan, *Separation of Powers*.

[58] Carolan, *Separation of Powers*, 257.

[59] Carolan, *Separation of Powers*, 128–34 & 258.

[60] Carolan, *Separation of Powers*, 135 & 265–66.

This division and process must ensure the nonarbitrariness of the state power.[61] However, he does not address issues resulting from the concentration of power in private hands.

Toward the end of his book on the subject, Christoph Möllers envisages a "separation of powers beyond the state," giving special regard to the "internationalized constitutional state," European integration and the developments of international law and organizations.[62] In this context, he also deals with private law-making, especially with *lex mercatoria* and the law of standardization.[63] He mentions that competition law may impose limits to *lex mercatoria*.[64] Furthermore, the legal system "responds to the privatization of state duties – among which standard-setting can be seen – by imposing organizational and procedural duties on private companies resembling those for public organizations."[65] On a related point, but more precisely, Mauro Barberis mentions "large private companies, multinational corporations with budgets more substantial than the sum of the budgets of several states combined" and sees in the blurring of old boundaries between state and society new and more serious dangers for rights and liberties.[66] Jeremy Waldron seems to crystallize his approach to the subject with the terms "articulated government through successive phases of governance each of which maintains its own integrity."[67] Interestingly, he refers to individual liberty[68] and to people's control of political power[69] as a means of justification for his approach. Aileen Kavanagh emphasizes "the necessary interdependence, interaction, and interconnections between the branches"[70] of government while acknowledging that "a good governmental structure will also require that there are mechanisms in place to curb potential abuse of [government] power."[71] In *Architecture of Powers*, the author of the present book devotes several sections to private actors and civil society while analyzing challenges and consequences of the coexistence of powers at the level of a state, a union of states – especially the European Union – and the United Nations.[72] Competition law is integrated in the analysis as a mean to control non-state entities in a position of power.[73]

---

[61] Carolan, *Separation of Powers*, 118–34 & 256–58.
[62] Möllers, *Three Branches*, 150–226; see also Möllers, "Separation of Powers," 250–56.
[63] Möllers, *Three Branches*, 223–26.
[64] Möllers, *Three Branches*, 225.
[65] Möllers, *Three Branches*, 226.
[66] Barberis, "Séparation des pouvoirs," 730 (quote translated by the author of the present book).
[67] Waldron, "Separation of Powers," 467.
[68] Waldron, "Separation of Powers," 459 ("The legislature, the judiciary, and the executive – each must have its separate say before power impacts on the individuals").
[69] Waldron, "Separation of Powers," 466 (referring to "a common scheme of government that enables people to confront political power in a differentiated way"). We would also add the judiciary in this perspective.
[70] Kavanagh, "Separation of Powers," 237.
[71] Kavanagh, "Separation of Powers," 234.
[72] Martenet, *Architecture des pouvoirs*, 164–78, 219–25 & 253–60.
[73] Martenet, *Architecture des pouvoirs*, 256–58.

In sum, the dangers – theoretically or empirically funded – associated with the concentration of power in the hands of one or a few persons or of a branch of government continue to underpin the separation of powers principle, the contours of which may greatly differ from one country to another. Incidentally, power may be used in the singular, typically to refer to state power in general, or in the plural, usually with respect to the various branches of government or functions of the state. The submission of the administration, among others, to the law and the independence of the judiciary are common features of many approaches to the separation of powers principle, but here, concepts such as the rule of law or the "État de droit" ("Rechtsstaat" in German), just as for other aspects of separation of powers,[74] also come into play and usually occupy center stage. The private sector is, in principle, not – or at most only peripherally and recently – integrated in new models of this separation. When it is considered, reference is then usually – though not exclusively – made to competition law and policy or to antitrust.

1.4 ANTITRUST

The goal or goals of antitrust are widely debated. Although discussions and uncertainty remain in this regard, one can reasonably affirm that antitrust is focused on power. Indeed, antitrust or competition law and policy is eminently linked to economic power.[75] Competition itself has been described by Franz Böhm, one of the founders of the Freiburg School of Ordoliberalism, as "the most remarkable and ingenious instrument for reducing power known in history."[76] Emmanuel Combe, former Vice-President of the French Competition Authority, considers that competition is akin a form of economic democracy.[77]

Antitrust or competition law safeguards, protects, or, depending on the context, restores the competitive process or at least part of it. In a way, "[a]ntitrust is about unleashing the power of competition"[78] in order to reduce… power! According to its current chair, Lina M. Khan, the U.S. Federal Trade Commission needs, as a first policy priority, "to address rampant consolidation and the dominance that it has enabled across markets," under the following strategic approach:

> Focusing on power asymmetries and the unlawful practices those imbalances enable will help to ensure our efforts are geared towards tackling the most significant harms across markets, including those directed at marginalized communities.[79]

---

[74] See, e.g., Allan, "The Rule of Law," 211–15; Waldron, "Separation of Powers," 457–59; Troper, "Separation of Powers," para. 45; Bingham, *Rule of Law*, 48–54 & 91–92; Hayek, *Constitution of Liberty*, 319–20.

[75] See, e.g., Schweitzer, "Macht," 448 & 473.

[76] Böhm, "Democracy and Economic Power," 279; see also Kühling, "Herausforderungen," 522–24; Tepper with Hearn, *Capitalism*, 242 ("Competition is a critical element of capitalism because it promotes the diffusion of economic power and political freedom").

[77] Combe, *Concurrence*, 231.

[78] Devlin, *Antitrust*, 299.

[79] Memorandum from Chair Lina M. Khan to Commission Staff and Commissioners Regarding the Vision and Priorities for the FTC, Washington D.C., 22 September 2021, 1–2.

Moreover, antitrust has an important role to play not only in the functioning of competition but also "in ensuring that government responses to public pressure points do not overlook or override the contribution that competition can make to addressing" many concerns in a market economy.[80] In other words, competition must be taken seriously and, when properly functioning, can be referred to, *ex ante*, for counteracting the adoption of excessive legislative or regulatory proposals[81] and, *ex post*, for restrictively interpreting enacted laws and regulations.

Yet, few major material antitrust provisions contain the term "power." In the United States, the Sherman Antitrust Act and the Clayton Antitrust Act do not use this language.[82] The same can be said, for instance, about the material provisions of the Argentinian Law of Defense of Competition, except for the very end of Article 6 (Dominant Position),[83] Chapter II of Title V of the Brazilian Competition Act,[84] the Canadian Competition Act[85] except with respect to "the exertion of buying power outside Canada,"[86] all except one of the provisions of the Chilean Law Decree Establishing Rules for the Defense of Free Competition,[87] the Egyptian Competition Law,[88] Articles 101 and 102 of the Treaty on the Functioning of the European Union (TFEU),[89] the relevant articles of the French Commercial Code,[90] all except one of the material provisions of the German Act against Restraints of Competition,[91] the relevant sections of the Indian Competition Act,[92] the material provisions of the Indonesian, except for the reference to the concentration or centralization of "economic power" in Article 1 (General Provisions),[93] the Italian Competition

---

[80] Beaton-Wells, "Antitrust's Neglected Question," 192.

[81] See, e.g., Lemley, "Contradictions," 335–36.

[82] See Hovenkamp, "Antitrust Text," 4 & 8 (regarding the "market power requirement").

[83] Law No. 27442, 2018, www.enacom.gob.ar/multimedia/normativas/2018/Ley%2027442.pdf (in Spanish).

[84] Law No. 12.529, 2011, translation at http://en.cade.gov.br/topics/legislation/laws/law-no-12529-2011-english-version-from-18-05-2012.pdf/view.

[85] Competition Act, R.S.C, 1985, c. C-34 (last amended on 23 June 2022), https://laws.justice.gc.ca/PDF/C-34.pdf.

[86] Section 84.

[87] Law Decree No. 211, 1973, amended several times, translation at www.fne.gob.cl/wp-content/uploads/2018/09/DL_211_English.pdf.

[88] Law No. 3 on the Protection of Competition and the Prohibition of Monopolistic Practices, 2005, translation at www.gafi.gov.eg/English/StartaBusiness/Laws-and-Regulations/PublishingImages/Pages/TradeLaws/Law%20No%203%20of%202005%20Promulgating%20the%20law%20on%20Protection%20of%20Competition%20and%20Prohibition%20of%20Monopolistic%20Practices.pdf.

[89] Consolidated Version of the Treaty on the Functioning of the European Union, 2012, OJ C 326, 26 November 2021, 47-390 [hereinafter TFEU].

[90] Code de commerce [Commercial Code], Articles L. 420–1 to L. 420–7 and L. 430–1 to L. 430–10, translation in *The French Commercial Code in English, 2021–2022 ed.* (Philip Raworth trans., Toronto: Thomson-Reuters, 2021.)

[91] Gesetz gegen Wettbewerbsbeschränkungen [GWB] [Act against Restraints of Competition], 1957, translation at www.gesetze-im-internet.de/englisch_gwb/englisch_gwb.pdf.

[92] The Competition Act, 2002, www.cci.gov.in/sites/default/files/cci_pdf/ competitionact2012.pdf.

[93] Law No. 5 Concerning the Prohibition of Monopoly Practices and Unfair Business Conditions, translation at https://eng.kppu.go.id/wp-content/uploads/2016/11/law_5_year_1999_.pdf.

Law, but for a mention of "economic and financial power" in Article 6(1) (Control of Concentrations),[94] all except one of the material provisions of the Japanese Antimonopoly Act,[95] the Russian Law about the Protection of Competition,[96] the Competition Law of Saudi Arabia,[97] the material provisions of the Spanish Competition Act,[98] the material provisions of the South-African Competition Act,[99] the relevant sections of the Competition Act of the United Kingdom,[100] and Article 88 of the Amended Treaty of the West African Economic and Monetary Union.[101]

Section 20 (Prohibited Conduct of Undertakings with Relative or Superior Market Power) of the aforementioned German Act represents one of the exceptions in this regard. Another exception can be found in Article 9 of the Japanese Act mentioned above, which deals with the excessive concentration of economic power, a concept also mentioned in Article 1 of this Act. However, none of these competition law provisions form the core of *public* antitrust enforcement in these two countries.[102]

By contrast, some key or less central antitrust provisions expressly use the notion of "market power," or a similar concept, and therefore constitute real counterexamples to the above. Thus, sections 46 and 46A of the Australian Competition and Consumer Act[103] are about the "misuse of market power." A reference to market power ("poder de mercado") can also be found in Article 3(a) of the aforementioned Chilean Law Decree Establishing Rules for the Defense of Free Competition, which relates to some concerted agreement "conferring market power." In Iran, dominant economic condition is defined as "a market situation in which one or several legal or real entities have the power to determine prices, set supply or demand limits for goods or services or lay down conditions of a contract."[104] Israel Economic

---

[94] Law No. 287, 1990, www.agcm.it/chi-siamo/normativa/legge-10-ottobre-1990-n-287-norme-per-la-tutela-della-concorrenza-e-del-mercato (in Italian).

[95] Act No. 54 on Prohibition of Private Monopolization and Maintenance of Fair Trade, 1947, translation at www.jftc.go.jp/en/legislation_gls/amended_amao9/index.html.

[96] Federal Law of the Russian Federation about the Protection of Competition, 2006, No. 135-FZ, translation at https://cis-legislation.com/document.fwx?rgn=13747.

[97] Competition Law issued by Royal Decree No. M/75 of 29/06/1440H, 1999, translation at https://wipolex.wipo.int/en/text/566148.

[98] Competition Act 15/2007 of 3 July 2007, translation at www.cnmc.es/file/64176/download.

[99] The Competition Act No. 89, 1998, www.compcom.co.za/wp-content/uploads/2021/03/Competition-Act-A6.pdf.

[100] Competition Act 1998, www.legislation.gov.uk/ukpga/1998/41/contents.

[101] See, in French, www.uemoa.int/fr/system/files/fichier_article/traitreviseuemoa.pdf.

[102] Regarding Section 20 of the German Act against Restraints of Competition, which plays a significant role in private enforcement, see, e.g., Kathrin Westermann, "§ 20 GWB" [§ 20 ARC], in Säcker & Meier-Beck (eds.), *Wettbewerbsrecht 2*, 236–82, 240, para 11; Jörg Nothdurft, "§ 20 GWB" [§ 20 ARC], in Bunte (ed.), *Kartellrecht 1*, 781–850, 787, para. 5. Regarding Article 9 of the Japanese Antimonopoly Act, see, e.g., Wakui, *Antimonopoly Law*, 135 & 137.

[103] Competition and Consumer Act 2010, www.legislation.gov.au/Details/C2021C00151.

[104] Article 1 the Law on Implementation of General Principles of Article 44 of the Constitution of Iran, translation at www.nicc.gov.ir/asl-44-correction/2-uncategorised/1022-law-on-implementation-of-general-policies-of-principle-44-of-the-constitution.html.

Competition Law[105] refers to "significant market power" in one of its two definitions of a "monopolist."[106] The Mexican Economic Competition Law[107] repeatedly uses the notion of "substantial market power."[108] In the Netherlands, the word "power" appears in the legal definition of "dominant position."[109] In Nigeria, the notion of "dominant position of market power" is used in the Competition and Consumer Protection Act.[110] In Turkey, "dominant position" is defined as the "power of one or more undertakings in a particular market to determine economic parameters such as price, supply, the amount of production and distribution, by acting independently of their competitors and customer."[111] A more limited counterexample is *prima facie* given by the Spanish provision listing the criteria of the substantive assessment of an economic concentration, according to which the National Markets and Competition Commission must, among several criteria, take the "economic and financial power" of the undertakings at stake into account.[112] On close inspection, however, this official translation is not optimal, since the word used in Spanish – "fortaleza" and not "poder" – means "strength." Finally, part of the Chinese Anti-Monopoly Law[113] is based on the specific concept of "abuse of administrative power."[114] The notion of "controlling power" also appears in the law.[115]

This book does not attempt to trace the evolution of the relationship between, on one hand, antitrust or competition law and its enforcement and, on the other hand, economic power. While *per se* prohibitions remain applicable in many jurisdictions,[116] *market power* – the ability of a firm to profitably raise the market price of a good or service over marginal cost – currently lies at the heart of competition law

---

[105] Economic Competition Law, 1988, 5748-1988, translation at www.gov.il/BlobFolder/legalinfo/competitionlaw/en/englishsite_Economic%20Competition%20Law.pdf.

[106] Section 26(a)(2).

[107] Federal Economic Competition Law, 2014, translation at www.cofece.mx/cofece/images/Documentos_Micrositios/Federal_Economic_Competition_Law.pdf.

[108] Articles 59–60, 64, 70, 85 & 96.

[109] Article 1 (1) of the Dutch Competition Act, 1997, translation at www.dutchcivillaw.com/legislation/competitionact.htm.

[110] Sections 1(d), 18(3)(d) & 70(2) of the Federal Competition and Consumer Protection Act, 2018, www.africa-laws.org/Nigeria/Consumer%20Law/Federal%20Competition%20and%20Consumer%20Protection%20Act,%202019.pdf.

[111] Article 3 of the Act No. 4054 on the Protection of Competition, 1994, translation at www.rekabet.gov.tr/en/Sayfa/Legislation/act-no-4054.

[112] Article 10 Section 1/b.

[113] Anti-Monopoly Law of the People's Republic of China, 2007, translation at www.icao.int/sustainability/Documents/Compendium_FairCompetition/China/Anti-monopoly-Law_China.pdf. For the latest amendments, see Arendse Huld, "What Has Changed in China's Amended Anti-Monopoly Law?," *China Briefing*, 11 July 2022, www.china-briefing.com/news/what-has-changed-in-chinas-amended-anti-monopoly-law/.

[114] Articles 8, 32–37, 40, 51, 54 & 66.

[115] Article 27(1) (control of concentrations).

[116] Regarding the United States, see *National Collegiate Athletic Assn.* v. *Alston*, 594 U. S. ___ (2021), 141 S. Ct. 2141, 2156 (2021) ("[S]ome agreements among competitors so obviously threaten to reduce output and raise prices that they might be condemned as unlawful *per se* or rejected after only a quick look").

and policy throughout the world,[117] notwithstanding or, perhaps because of, its fluidity and its multifaceted nature, thoroughly analyzed by Louis Kaplow:

> Taken together, the analysis demonstrates that there are many channels by which market power can be relevant, that its relevance varies greatly across channels and contexts, that the relevant notion of market power varies as well, and that different components of a given notion of market power can have different effects.[118]

Antitrust policy is indeed "concerned with exercises of market power," as synthetized by Herbert Hovenkamp.[119] In the United States for instance, most restraints challenged under the Sherman Act are subject to the rule of reason, which requires a court to "conduct a fact-specific assessment of market power and market structure" in order to evaluate a challenged restraint's "actual effect on competition."[120] *Per se* cases, where market power is not required, still exist in the United States, but the assessment of damages may nevertheless lead to an analysis of market power.[121] In the European Union, the latter is also placed at the core of antitrust enforcement for the actual or, at least, presumed benefit for customers, as emphasized by Margrethe Vestager, speaking in her current capacity as Executive Vice-President of the European Commission for a Europe fit for the Digital Age and Commissioner for Competition:

> The problem comes when customers' choice gets so limited that their suppliers no longer have to care about what those customers want. Because the effects of market power like that are – and always have been – very bad for customers. For them, it means higher prices, less innovation, less choice. Because more market power means more dependence for customers. That's why dealing with market power is at the core of what we do; and why the champions we need are those that are still sufficiently challenged, not taking anything for granted, but always working to serve their customers better.[122]

---

[117] See, e.g., Areeda & Hovenkamp, *Antitrust Law*, para. 501; Hovenkamp, "Consumer Welfare Principle," 123 & 128 ("If properly applied, […] the one thing that it [the consumer welfare principle] should not tolerate is ever increasing amount of market power in the economy" [quotation from p. 128]); Baker, *Antitrust Paradigm*, 11–31 & 206–09; Gerbrandy, "Competition Law," 129; Whish & Bailey, *Competition Law*, 22; Schweitzer, "Macht," 472; Kaplow, "Market Power," 1304–05 & 1405.

[118] Kaplow, "Market Power," 1406.

[119] Hovenkamp, "Antitrust and Platform Monopoly," 1958.

[120] See *Ohio v. American Express Co.*, 585 U. S. ___ (2018), 138 S. Ct. 2274, 2284 (2018); *National Collegiate Athletic Assn. v. Alston*, 594 U. S. ___ (2021), 141 S. Ct. 2141, 2151 & 2155 (2021).

[121] Hovenkamp, *Principles of Antitrust*, 63–64 ("[A]lthough market power is not a requirement in most *per se* cases, such as price fixing, a consumer plaintiff seeking damages must generally show that there has been an 'overcharge,' which may require a showing of the defendants' collective market power"). From a historical perspective, see Fox, "Soul of Antitrust," 920–22.

[122] Margrethe Vestager, Speech to the Danish Competition and Consumer Authority for the 2021 Competition Day: "What Is Competition For?," 4 November 2021, https://ec.europa.eu/commission/commissioners/2019-2024/vestager/announcements/speech-evp-margrethe-vestager-danish-competition-and-consumer-authority-2021-competition-day-what_en.

To a large extent, antitrust is now about power and its "underlying political concern is that private economic power, like all absolute power, is subject to abuse and injurious to public welfare."[123] New developments of antitrust in the digital economy continue to be focused on power – sometimes, and, actually, more and more frequently, with references to platform or data power.[124] Thus, the notion of power seems to remain unavoidable. The more market power is concentrated within a firm or a few firms, the more relevant, *ceteris paribus*, competition law and policy may become, as made clear by Lina M. Khan, in her current capacity as chair of the U.S. Federal Trade Commission:

> Growing evidence suggests that market power now looks to be an increasingly systemic problem across the economy, so we should generally focus our resources on the most significant actors, where our enforcement actions can have the greatest impact on the everyday lives of Americans.[125]

Finally, antitrust contributes to preserve or restore freedom not only of actual or potential competitors, but also of individuals. From an ordoliberal or neo-ordoliberal perspective, competition policy is even primarily oriented toward the goal of individual freedom of action or, as it is more usually referred to, freedom to compete.[126] Such an approach also existed in the United States when the Sherman Act was elaborated and enacted.[127] Although it does not reflect the current state of competition law enforcement in most of the jurisdictions, it can – at least indirectly – contribute to individual economic freedom,[128] including the freedom to compete and some freedom of choice.[129] Moreover, economic freedom possesses not only an economic

---

[123] Stucke, "Data-opolies," 313; see also Podszun, "Market Definition," 81 ("Yet, for many schools of thought, competition law is more than just lowering prices. It is the fundamental set of rules that preserves economic freedom by fighting excesses").

[124] See, e.g., Mazzucato, Entsminger & Kattel, "Reshaping Markets," 21–23 ("From market power to platform power"); Hovenkamp, "Antitrust and Platform Monopoly," 1958–67; Fukuyama, Richman & Goel, "Democracy," 99–102; Naughton, "Platform Power," 381–84. On this question, see Part II, Chapter 6, Section 6.1.

[125] Memorandum from Chair Lina M. Khan to Commission Staff and Commissioners Regarding the Vision and Priorities for the FTC, Washington D.C., 22 September 2021, 2.

[126] See, e.g., Mestmäcker, "Macht," 39–42; Möschel, "Competition Policy," 142 ("[C]ompetition policy is primarily oriented to the goal of securing individual freedom of action, from which the goal of economic efficiency is merely derived [...]"); Herrera Anchustegui, "Competition Law," 152–55 & 159–61.

[127] See, e.g., Fishkin & Forbath, *Constitution*, 213 ("Antitrust aimed to protect constitutional freedoms of trade and enterprise; it did this by blocking the coercive business practices of monopolists").

[128] Regarding Switzerland, see Martenet, "Liberté," 964–69.

[129] On this question, see General Court of the European Union, *Google and Alphabet v Commission (Google Shopping)*, 10 November 2021, T-612/17, ECLI:EU:T:2021:763, paras. 566 & 588 (dominant undertaking favoring the display of results from its own specialized search service, with the likely effect to reduce consumer choice with regard to comparison shopping services). Regarding consumers freedom of choice from a German and European perspective, see Schweitzer, "Missbrauch," 19–27. On the debate as to whether consumers actually want a wide choice, see, from a fictional and prospective perspective, Eggers, *The Every*, 233–34 & 553–72.

dimension, but also societal and even political dimensions.[130] The latter two result from the fact that individual freedom, when effective and actually utilized, can help destabilize or at least reduce the politico-economic power of, for instance, major firms of the digital industry. For instance, the freedom to quit a social network, to choose between competitors, or to challenge excessive business conditions with chances of success can be invigorated by competition law enforcement and, some-how, help check and balance these firms' politico-economic power. Ultimately, political and economic freedoms are intrinsically linked together,[131] as beautifully put by President Franklin D. Roosevelt or by Milton and Rose Friedman:

> Today we stand committed to the proposition that freedom is no half-and-half affair. If the average citizen is guaranteed equal opportunity in the polling place, he must have equal opportunity in the market place.[132]
> Economic freedom is an essential requisite for political freedom.[133]

In conclusion, the concentration of power or powers and the related risks justify both the separation of powers principle and antitrust. However, at least at first glance, the nature of the power concerned differs: political or – more broadly, in order to include, for instance, the judiciary – public or state power in one case, and economic or, more precisely, market power in the other. The next step of the analysis aims at verifying whether these two types of power can be strictly and neatly separated, or whether they actually interact with one another and are sometimes interdependent, like political and economic freedoms. It starts with the search for an eventual economic content of the separation of powers theories.

---

[130] From a historical perspective, see, regarding the United States, Fishkin & Forbath, *Constitution*, 173, 208 & 253.

[131] See, e.g., Stucke, "Goals," 624 ("In reconsidering the goals of competition as a means to secure politi-cal, economic, and individual freedoms, antitrust can be more responsive to citizens' concerns about promoting well-being. With a blended goal approach incorporated in better legal standards, antitrust, in the next policy cycle, will be harder to marginalize"); see also Rahman, "Economic Freedom," 327–29; Foer, *World*, 188 ("We feared concentrations of corporate power would inhibit freedom and make a mockery of democracy").

[132] Franklin D. Roosevelt, *Acceptance Speech to the Democratic National Convention*, 27 June 1936, avail-able at https://teachingamericanhistory.org/document/acceptance-speech-at-the-democratic-national-convention-1936/. See Fishkin & Forbath, *Constitution*, 252–53. From a broader perspective, see also *International Association of Machinists v. Street*, 367 U.S. 740, 814–15 (Frankfurter, J., dissenting) ("The notion that economic and political concerns are separable is pre-Victorian [...]. It is not true in life that political protection is irrelevant to, and insulated from, economic interests. It is not true for industry or finance. Neither is it true for labor").

[133] Friedman & Friedman, *Free to Choose*, 2; see also Tepper with Hearn, *Capitalism*, 237–38 & 242.

2

Economic Content of the Separation of Powers Theories?

The content of separation of powers is neither defined in constitutions, which usually do not explicitly guarantee this principle,[1] nor in other legal texts. Its content cannot be circumscribed with precision. Several influential authors have dealt extensively with separation of powers. However, few of them were constitutional *and* economic thinkers. After careful analysis, but without claiming to be exhaustive, three major names stand out. The connection between reflections by Montesquieu (Section 2.1) and Hayek (Section 2.2) on the concentration of state power on one hand, and on economic concentration on the other hand, is illuminating and fascinating but has never before been established. Aron (Section 2.3) also deserves a special mention in this regard, as he notably dealt with democracy and totalitarianism as well as competition in the same breath throughout some major parts of his work.

2.1 MONTESQUIEU

From an institutional and functional perspective, Montesquieu was focused on the legislative and executive powers, the judiciary being "in some fashion, null."[2] Although Montesquieu does not use these terms, the separation or division of powers – more precisely, the distribution of powers that limits abuses and prevents the conflation of them – was conceived and promoted in the name of political liberty. In addition, Montesquieu was also an economic thinker, the "real French equivalent of Adam Smith, the greatest of [French] economists" according to John Maynard Keynes[3] and "one of the most influential thinkers of all time" "though his economics is insignificant – without originality, force, or scholarship" according to Joseph Schumpeter![4] Montesquieu was notably interested in commerce and trade and considered that:

---

[1]   Regarding the United States, see Manning, "Separation of Powers," 2005–40. Regarding Switzerland, see Martenet, "Séparation des pouvoirs," 1007–8.
[2]   Montesquieu, *Spirit of the Laws*, 160.
[3]   Keynes, *Employment, Interest, and Money*, preface to the French edition.
[4]   Schumpeter, *History of Economic Analysis*, 135–36, n. 22.

[t]he laws must also prohibit nobles from engaging in commerce; merchants with such rank would set up all sorts of monopolies. Commerce is the profession of equal people, and the [most miserable of] despotic states are those whose prince is a merchant.[5]

He went on to consider that "a prince should not engage in commerce" and, in this context, asked rhetorically, speaking for Emperor Theophilus, "[w]ho can curb us if we make monopolies?"[6] Montesquieu made a similar point when he spoke about banks "in countries governed by one alone"[7] and pleaded for a separation between economic activities and political power in monarchies. Montesquieu's approach differs, for instance, from Machiavelli's one, for whom the political power holder is also an entrepreneur, generating a confusion between public and private affairs.[8] In a republic, however, according to Montesquieu, "private wealth and public power may be properly entwined since every citizen participates in the exercise of public power."[9] This probably presupposes that such a republic is organized along the principle of separation of powers.

Since the separation of powers is supposed to preserve political liberty,[10] one cannot simply conclude that, for Montesquieu, the separation between political power and commerce or trade, where applicable, protects the liberty of commerce[11] or trade only. Montesquieu does not delineate strictly between these two types of separation. Indeed, his economic thoughts and views on commerce and trade also include a political dimension,[12] as made clear *inter alia* by the reference to "despotic states [...] whose prince is a merchant."[13] Some parallel can be drawn here between Montesquieu and Tocqueville, as the latter warns that "[i]n this [XIXth] century, to

---

[5] Montesquieu, *Spirit of the Laws*, 53 (the correction is based on Philipp Stewart's new translation, see *Spirit of Law*, http://montesquieu.ens-lyon.fr/spip.php?article2625 [2018]).

[6] See Montesquieu, *Spirit of the Laws*, 349 (Philip Stewart proposes a better translation of this passage of book XX, which is used here, see *Spirit of Law*, http://montesquieu.ens-lyon.fr/spip.php?article2924 [2018, updated to 1 October 2021]).

[7] Montesquieu, *Spirit of the Laws*, 344 (Philip Stewart proposes a better translation of this passage of book XX, see *Spirit of Law*, http://montesquieu.ens-lyon.fr/spip.php?article2916 [2018, updated to 1 October 2021]). See, e.g., Larrère, "Montesquieu," 338 & 348–49.

[8] See Ménissier, "Nouvelles figures du Prince," 98.

[9] Larrère, "Montesquieu," 349 (regarding Montesquieu on economics and commerce).

[10] See Montesquieu, *Spirit of the Laws*, 154–57. See, e.g., Troper, "Separation of Powers," para. 26.

[11] See Montesquieu, *Spirit of the Laws*, 345.

[12] See Spector, "Commerce," para 16 ("In *The Spirit of Law* the critique of monopolies also regards the use of political or social privileges in the economy. Such is the reason for which the nobility must be forbidden to trade in aristocracies [...]"). See also Larrère, "Montesquieu," 347–50; Spector, *Montesquieu*, 228 ("[C]ommerce, because of its *mobility*, is source of freedom: it contributes to external security (against the policy of conquest) and internal security (against abuses of power)" [translation by the author of the present book]).

[13] Montesquieu, *Spirit of the Laws*, 53 & 416–17. See, e.g., Krause, "Despotism," 242–43; Larrère, "Montesquieu," 337–38 & 348–49 ("In monarchies, political and economic functions must be kept well apart. Confusing wealth and power as would be the case if the nobility were allowed to engage in commerce would lead to despotism, and a despotic government whose prince is a merchant is the worst kind of despotism" [quotation from p. 349]).

hand over the direction of industry to the government is to hand over the very heart of the next generations."[14]

However, Montesquieu does not merge his thoughts on separation of powers and separation between political power and commerce or trade, where applicable, into a single model or scheme. Still, commerce is, according to him, related to the constitution.[15] One could venture to say that, in the spirit of Montesquieu, any political system that does not "separate powers" should at least "separate" political power and commerce.[16] In this last case, one should avoid referring to powers in the plural, as Montesquieu describes money resulting from commerce or trade as "the means of everything without any power."[17] In his eyes, this last word relates first and foremost to political power.[18] Nevertheless, both types of "separation" – that is, the separation between the branches of government, on one hand, and, when applicable, the separation between political power and commerce, on the other – share common grounds, namely, the protection of liberty and the goal of avoiding despotism and tyranny.[19] Tocqueville refers to Montesquieu on this issue when he emphasizes the relationship between liberty and commerce: "[i]t is said that the commercial spirit naturally gives human beings the spirit of liberty."[20]

2.2 HAYEK

In *The Road to Serfdom*, Hayek thought about power in a rather general way and warned against the concentration of all the means of production and its impact on power over individuals:

> It is only because the control of the means of production is divided among many people acting independently that nobody has complete power over us, that we as individuals can decide what to do with ourselves. If all the means of production were vested in a single hand, whether it be nominally that of "society" as a whole or that of a dictator, whoever exercises this control has complete power over us.[21]

[14] Alexis de Tocqueville, "Letter to Pierre-Paul Royer-Collard," 6 April 1838 (excerpt published in Mélonio & Manzini, *Abécédaire de Tocqueville*, 90 [translation by the author of the present book]).
[15] See, e.g., Bibby, *Montesquieu*, 22–24.
[16] The verb "separate" has two meanings here. Regarding the political system, it must be understood as the antonym of "conflate" or "combine" (see Troper, "Separation of Powers," paras. 27–28); regarding the relationship between political power and commerce, it implies "to put apart, set asunder" (Oxford English Dictionary, under "separate, v").
[17] Montesquieu, *Spirit of the Laws*, 344.
[18] Montesquieu, *Spirit of the Laws*, 43 (Philip Stewart proposes a better translation of this passage of book V, see *Spirit of Law*, http://montesquieu.ens-lyon.fr/spip.php?article2620 [2018, updated to 1 October 2021]). While speaking of wealth, Montesquieu uses the term "puissance," which implies strength and capacity, rather than the term "pouvoir."
[19] See Bertrand, "Conception du commerce," 275–80.
[20] Alexis de Tocqueville, "Voyage en Irlande" [Travel in Irland], 1835 (excerpt published in Mélonio & Manzini, *Abécédaire de Tocqueville*, 54 [translation by the author of the present book]).
[21] Hayek, *Serfdom*, 108.

Hayek wrote much more about the various means to limit power in the political process than about antitrust and similar policies. One might indeed read *The Constitution of Liberty* as expressly addressing such concerns in the political realm.[22] By contrast, Hayek wrote quite little about economic power abuses by large firms or cartels. However, he did not ignore these issues, and his position was actually nuanced.

In Hayek's system of thought, separation of power and antitrust are successively analyzed. In the *Political Order of a Free People*, the third volume of *Law, Legislation and Liberty*,[23] the chapter on the division of democratic powers is followed by the chapter on the public sector and the private sector, and then the chapter on government policy and the market.[24] Notably, in this last chapter, the "problem of anti-monopoly legislation"[25] is addressed. Liberty, though protean, is a common thread of these chapters and, more generally, of the book,[26] and the proper functioning and the promotion of competition may require state intervention.[27]

Hayek makes several links between economic power and political power. He acknowledges the "political aspects of economic power"[28] and the influence of the latter on government:

> [i]n so far as corporations have power to benefit groups of individuals, mere size will also become a source of influencing government, and thus beget power of a very objectionable kind. [...] such influence, much more serious when it is exerted by the organized interests of groups than when exerted by the largest single enterprise, can be guarded against only by depriving government of the power of benefiting particular groups.[29]

In principle, such an influence does not occur against the will of the government, according to Hayek, but with its help and assistance.[30] This meshing of the "power of [the] government" and the "power of the organized group interests"[31] is seen as detrimental to important groups such as "the consumers in general, the taxpayers,

---

[22] See Hayek, *Constitution of Liberty*, part II.

[23] See Hayek, *Law, Legislation and Liberty*.

[24] Hayek, *Political Order of a Free People*, 20–97.

[25] Hayek, *Political Order of a Free People*, 85–88. See, e.g., Schrepel, "Hayek's Contribution to Antitrust," 208–12.

[26] See, e.g., Kusunoki, "Hayek and Antitrust," 65 ("One major characteristic of Hayek's economic theory is that it is connected to his legal theory and *vice versa*. More accurately, his theory of liberty is based on his economics and his legal theory or his theory of the rule of law is based on his theory of liberty[...]. Hayek's antitrust doctrine exists at the 'crossroads' of his economic and legal thought and is the fruit of the border transgression of these fields").

[27] See Gamble, "Hayek," 128.

[28] Hayek, *Political Order of a Free People*, 80–83.

[29] Hayek, *Political Order of a Free People*, 82.

[30] Hayek, *Political Order of a Free People*, 97 and *Constitution of Liberty*, 383 ("[T]here will always be inevitable monopolies whose transitory and temporary character is often turned into a permanent one by the solicitude of the government"). On this aspect of Hayek's thought, see Frankel Paul, "Hayek on Monopoly and Antitrust," 175 ("Turning transitory monopolies into permanent ones is the artifice of government").

[31] Hayek, *Political Order of a Free People*, 97.

the women, the aged, and many others who together constitute a very substantial part of the population."[32] In other words, bigness as such was less worrisome than the preferential treatment of powerful organized groups by governments.

Hayek concludes that "[a]ll these [non-organized] groups are bound to suffer from the power of organized group interests,"[33] and pleads, if not for strict separation, at least for distance between such economic power and political power. This distance will not primarily be achieved by the means of "anti-monopoly legislation."[34] However, this legislation may still be relevant if and when it protects "the individuals against group pressure,"[35] that is, against a collective expression of private power possibly having a significant or, as the case may be, decisive impact on government.

2.3 ARON

Raymond Aron, one of France's most prominent thinkers of the twentieth century, had several areas of intellectual interest, especially in sociology, philosophy, democracy, economics, and geopolitics. He promoted and defended liberalism, while maintaining a moderate and "temperate" approach in this regard throughout his life.

For Aron, western democracies are notably characterized by the separation between political power and economic power, including from an individual perspective.[36] By contrast, such a separation typically does not exist in totalitarian regimes. In this respect, Aron names five signs of totalitarianism: One party has a monopoly on political activity; an ideology upheld by the ruling party "becomes the official truth of the state"; the state reserves for itself the monopoly for the means of coercion and persuasion – radio, television, and press being directed and commanded by the state and its representatives; "[m]ost economic and professional activities are subject to the state and become, in a way, part of the state itself"; and all the possible crimes of individuals are politicized and subject to ideological transfiguration, leading to police and ideological terror.[37]

The importance of the separation between political power and economic power in a democracy had already been highlighted, for instance, by Maurice Hauriou, the great administrative and constitutional lawyer, philosopher, and dean of the Law Faculty at the University of Toulouse in France.[38] In the same vein, Carl J. Friedrich and Zbigniew K. Brzezinski suggested that the modern totalitarian regimes

---

[32] Hayek, *Political Order of a Free People*, 97.

[33] Hayek, *Political Order of a Free People*, 97. From this perspective, see also Hovenkamp, "Monopolists or Cartels."

[34] On the role of anti-monopoly legislation according to Hayek, see Hayek, *Political Order of a Free People*, 86.

[35] From a broader perspective, see Hayek, *Political Order of a Free People*, 96.

[36] See Châton, *Aron*, 36.

[37] Aron, *Democracy and Totalitarianism*, 193–94; see also Kjeldahl, "Aron and Totalitarianism," 122–23 & 138–39.

[38] Hauriou, *Principes*, vii and 438–39. See Beaud, "Multiplication des pouvoirs," 48–50. From a general and contemporary perspective, see Obertone, *Game Over*, 111–24.

"have subordinated the industrial machine to the requirements of the regime" and concluded that "[w]hat is decisive is the overpowering reality of totalitarian central control by the dictator and his party."[39] Aron's thinking is therefore not new in this regard. It is nevertheless interesting and, to a certain extent, original, as Aron directly links the absence of such separation, among a few other elements, to totalitarianism.[40]

Aron is also interested in competition and mentions economic competition and political competition in the same breath. As Georg Simmel made an analogy between a merchant and an elected official in 1903,[41] Aron compares political competition with economic competition:

> In the political order, as in the economic one, the problem is how [scarce goods] are to be shared out. Not everyone can become a deputy or a minister. The competition for political benefits can be compared to the competition for wealth.[42]

In sum, Aron shows that power and competition for it have political and economic dimensions and considers them globally.[43] Ultimately, he links democracy to political and economic competition. Moreover, the separation between political power and economic power is seen as a factor of diversity among the ruling classes.[44] By contrast, unity characterizes totalitarian or authoritarian regimes. For him, all the authoritarian revolutions of the twentieth century appear as "attempts to restore unity: unity of the supreme truth, unity of the social classes in a single party, unity of the Society and the State."[45] Even if Aron does not use these words, he probably considers that this separation and this diversity generate some form of checks and balances in a democracy.[46]

Like Montesquieu and Hayek, Aron warns against the concentration of political and economic powers. Political and economic competition is intrinsically linked with a non-totalitarian, democratic regime. Such an approach may explain, and help support, the political content of antitrust from a historical perspective.

---

[39] Friedrich & Brzezinski, *Dictatorship and Autocracy*, 244.
[40] See, for instance, Mahoney, "Aron on Ideology and Totalitarianism," 142.
[41] Simmel, "Sociology of Competition," 962; see also Helle, "Soziologie der Konkurrenz," 945–56.
[42] Aron, *Democracy and Totalitarianism*, 233 (translation corrected by the author of the present book). For a similar approach, see, more recently, Hearn, *Power*, 147–48.
[43] See Aron, *Philosophie politique*, 133 ("[W]hen there is this total concentration of economic and political powers in the same hands, one can have fun holding elections, but these elections are emptied of their meaning." [translation by the author of the present book]).
[44] Aron, *Lutte de classes*, 1094–98. See Audier, "Conception of Democracy," 153; Châton, *Aron*, 36.
[45] Aron, *Lutte de classes*, 1094 (translation by the author of the present book).
[46] See Audier, "Conception of Democracy," 157 ("[I]f economic and political powers are merged and there are no relatively independent groups capable of providing a counterweight and competition – as is the case in communist regimes – then elections are devoid of any meaning" [footnote omitted]).

3

Political Content of Antitrust from
a Historical Perspective

In several jurisdictions, antitrust or competition laws are deemed as having a political content, at least from a historical perspective. A link is further made between antitrust and democracy. Here, the focus is put on *separation of powers-type arguments* explaining and supporting the adoption of antitrust or competition laws in the United States (Section 3.1), in Germany (Section 3.2), in Japan (Section 3.3), and in the European Union (Section 3.4).

3.1 UNITED STATES

In the United States, much has been said, but also remains to be said, about the political content of antitrust from a historical perspective.[1] Until the late 1970s, antitrust was, according to Eleanor Fox, "*against* high concentration and abuses of power."[2] In his seminal article on this subject, Robert Pitofsky warned not to ignore political considerations at the origin of antitrust legislation.[3] Several authors have followed and quoted legislative records and press accounts, articles, or books of the late nineteenth and the twentieth centuries, mentioning the risk that the concentration of economic power poses for democracy.[4] A careful reading of legislative

---

[1] Regarding the creation of the FTC, see, e.g., Berk, *Brandeis*, 103–4 ("[Senator Francis Newlands] assured Republican progressives that the commission was intended to regulate, not destroy, large corporations. [Senator Albert] Cummins responded patiently to populist concerns about economic power. He assured them that the FTC was meant to prevent corporate power before it undermined economic initiative and democracy. Together, they turned the Federal Trade Commission Act into a law with multiple, yet precise, meanings"). On the events having shaped antitrust law in the United States, see Werden, *Foundations*, 1–135.

[2] Fox, "Against Goals," 2158; see also Gerber, *Competition Law and Antitrust*, 27.

[3] Pitofsky, "Political Content," 1051–75. For a different understanding of the intentions of the Congress, see, e.g., Bork, *Antitrust Paradox*, 50–71 ("The conventional indicia of legislative intent overwhelmingly support the conclusion that the antitrust laws should be interpreted as designed for the sole purpose of forwarding consumer welfare" [quotation from p. 71]).

[4] See, for instance, Fishkin & Forbath, *Constitution*, 210–50, 311–18, 376–78 & 471–77; Robertson, "Antitrust, Big Tech, and Democracy," 262–63; Teachout, "Monopoly," 52–59; Katz, "Chicago School," 418–29 & 457; Khan, "Antitrust History," 1662; Weber Waller, "Antitrust and Democracy,"

31

records, articles, and books on this issue shows that separation of powers-type concerns were actually raised,[5] sometimes prominently. A statement by Senator John Sherman goes in this direction, albeit rather implicitly:

> If we will not endure a king as a political power, we should not endure a king over the production, transportation, and sale of any of the necessities of life. If we would not submit to an emperor, we should not submit to an autocrat of trade, with power to prevent competition and to fix the price of any commodity.[6]

A statement by Senator C. Estes Kefauver, one of the two leading sponsors of a bill that eventually became the amended section 7 of the Clayton Act, and the aforementioned article of Robert Pitofsky provide more explicit references to separation of powers, checks, and balances or similar principles:

> I am not an alarmist, but the history of what has taken place in other nations where mergers and concentrations have placed economic control in the hands of a very few people is too clear to pass over easily. A point is eventually reached, and we are rapidly reaching that point in this country, where the public steps in to take over when concentration and monopoly gain too much power. The taking over by the public through its government [...] either results in a Fascist state or the nationalization of industries and thereafter a Socialist or Communist state.[7]
>
> Congress has in its antitrust enactments – most clearly when it amended section 7 of the Clayton Act in 1950 – exhibited a clear concern that an economic order dominated by a few corporate giants could, during a time of domestic stress or disorder, facilitate the overthrow of democratic institutions and the installation of a totalitarian regime. That concern about economic power and the desire that it be dispersed complements the general American governmental preference for a system of checks and balances and distribution of authority to prevent abusive actions by the state.[8]

808–16; Stoller, *Goliath*; Wu, *Curse of Bigness*, 24–82; Fox, "Antitrust and Democracy," 319–21; Stucke, "Goals," 559–62; see also Hawley, *Tyranny*, 27–37 & 147–52. For a synthesis, see, e.g., Eskridge & Ferejohn, *Republic of Statutes*, 123–45 & 159–60.

[5] See, e.g., Horton, "Values," 238–40 ("American courts and enforcers have lost sight of the fundamental values balanced and blended by Congress for more than 100 years to create a set of regulatory checks and balances designed to protect our economic system from undue concentrations and exercises of economic power and their 'destructive consequences in a free society.' In so doing, they have precipitated a 'destructive alienation' of antitrust from our most fundamental and essential historic American social, political, moral, and economic values" [quotation from pp. 239–40, footnotes omitted]); Kaysen & Turner, *Antitrust Policy*, 17 (arguing that the goal of antitrust was a "proper distribution of power" in the economic sphere). On this approach, see Teachout & Khan, "Taxonomy of Power," 64–65.

[6] 21 *Congressional Records* 2455, 2457 (1890). See Millon, "Sherman Act," 1220 & 1275–92 (arguing that the Sherman Act grew out of a long "tradition that aimed to control political power through decentralization of economic power" [quotation from p. 1220]).

[7] 96 *Congressional Records* 16,452 (1950). Regarding the representativeness of the views of Senator C. Estes Kefauver and Representative Emanuel Celler for "a broad segment of the majority voting in favor of the bill," see Pitofsky, "Political Content," 1064; see also Wu, *Curse of Bigness*, 81; Crane, "Fascism and Monopoly," 1323–26.

[8] Pitofsky, "Political Content," 1053–54 (footnote omitted).

Before them, Louis Brandeis did not invoke separation of powers but drew a parallel between the preservation of liberty and the regulation of competition.[9] As seen in the first chapter,[10] liberty underpins separation of powers. Brandeis also believed in the importance of countervailing powers, including within society and business,[11] notably as he wrote that "[t]he American people have as little need of oligarchy in business as in politics."[12]

During the same period, a famous cartoon depicted a Standard Oil tank as an octopus with numerous tentacles stretched around not only steel, copper, and shipping industries but also the U.S. Capitol and a state house, one tentacle reaching for the White House.[13] The power of Standard Oil, evoked in this cartoon, was supposed to affect not only the "separation" between the government and the economy but also the one between the legislative and the executive branches, as they would both fall under the thumb of the octopus.

A causal link between the concentration of economic power and a totalitarian regime, that is, without separation of powers, is often emphasized and feared,[14] but neither carefully analyzed nor indisputably established, as noted by Daniel A. Crane:

> On a scholarly basis, much work remains to be done to establish the general proposition that extreme concentration of economic power tends to facilitate extreme concentrations of political power [...]. The idea that concentrated economic power breeds concentrated political power has much rhetorical appeal, but documenting the relationship historically, exploring the variations and mechanisms, and prescribing the particular antidotes remains a largely incomplete project.[15]

Accordingly, the link may or may not be empirically founded.[16] The absence of explanation or valid foundation for this link does not necessarily preclude its

---

[9] Brandeis, "Regulation of Competition," 109. See, e.g., Stoller, *Goliath*, 456 ("The real question is not whether commerce is good or bad. It is how we are to do commerce, to serve concentrated power or to free ourselves from concentrated power. This is the choice that has always confronted the American people, liberty for all or a small aristocracy governing our commerce and ourselves"); Khan, "New Brandeis Movement," 131 ("Brandeis feared that autocratic structures in the commercial sphere – such as when one or a few private corporations call all the shots – can preclude the experience of liberty, threatening democracy in our civic sphere"); Teachout & Khan, "Taxonomy of Power," 72 ("Decentralization of economic power in most areas of commerce is an essential underpinning of political freedom").

[10] See *supra* Chapter 1, Section 1.3.

[11] See, e.g., Foer, *World*, 194; Susskind, *Digital Republic*, 239–40.

[12] Brandeis, *People*, 207–8.

[13] Joseph Keppler Jr., "Next!" *Puck* (1904).

[14] See, e.g., Tepper with Hearn, *Capitalism*, 239 ("Monopolies, effectively, represent an economic tyranny") & 242.

[15] Crane, "Fascism and Monopoly," 1370 (quotation) and "Instrument of Democracy," 24–28; see also Baker, "Reformers," 735–40 ("A view of today's politics as turning primarily on the economic interests of large firms does not credit the significance of social and cultural concerns as independent motivators of political positions" [quotation from p. 738]); Crane, "Antitrust and Democracy," 4–5; Tepper with Hearn, *Capitalism*, 137–66.

[16] Regarding the German industrial concentration and the Nazi regime, see Crane, "Fascism and Monopoly," 1333–69 (concluding that "the historical record reveals that German monopolies and cartels

consideration if and when the political dimension of antitrust is reflected in the law, or leads, among other concerns, to the adoption of legislation, provided, in the latter case, that non-textual sources can validly influence statute interpretation in a jurisdiction.[17] From a historical perspective, the interpretation of U.S. antitrust laws, in particular the original provisions of the Sherman Act and Section 7 of the Clayton Act, does not immediately support the complete exclusion of all noneconomic concerns in antitrust enforcement. It is even maintained by Spencer Weber Waller and Jacob E. Morse that "[a]ntitrust has always been political in nature."[18]

3.2 GERMANY

In Western Germany after World War II, the Allied forces pushed for the enactment of competition legislation. They were concerned by the political risks posed by the concentration of economic power and aimed at the decartelization of the German economy. On 12 February 1947, the U.S. Military Government enacted Law No. 56, entitled "Prohibition of Excessive Concentration of German Economic Power."[19] This law, though seldom applied,[20] aimed, *inter alia*, at laying "the groundwork for building a healthy and democratic German economy."[21] In other words, decartelization and unbundling were linked to democracy.[22] Similar pieces of legislation were adopted by the British Military Government[23] and the French High Command.[24] By 1948, "decartelization and deconcentration had unmistakably evolved towards antitrust legislation in the American sense of the term," as observed by Marie-Laure Djelic, now Salles.[25]

played an important role in consolidating Hitler's power and carrying out his policies even apart from the directly military functions" and that the "application of consumer welfare-oriented antitrust principles would have prevented the path that the German economy took to concentration and monopoly in 1933 and beyond" [quotation from pp. 1364 & 1369]). From an empirical perspective on the impact of antitrust law on democracy and economic growth, see Petersen, "Antitrust," 604–21 (suggesting that existing antitrust laws have no significant effect on the level of democracy, and that this might be due to the design of these laws to promote economic efficiency rather than to prevent economic concentration).

[17] On the legislative history of the Sherman Act and subsequent acts, see, e.g., Pitofsky, "Political Content," 1060–65.

[18] Weber Waller & Morse, "Political Face," 95.

[19] U.S. Department of State, *Germany 1947–1949*, 344. See, e.g., Djelic, *American Model*, 80 & 105–7; Thorsten Käseberg, "Einleitung to GWB" [Introduction to ARC], in Bunte (ed.), *Kartellrecht* 1, 1–70, 4, paras. 5–6.

[20] See, e.g., Käseberg, "Einleitung to GWB," 4, para. 6; Stedman, "German Decartelization," 443–56.

[21] Preamble of Law No. 56.

[22] See, e.g., Gerber, "Prisms," 798 ("[I]n the years after World War II, U.S. representatives promoted American antitrust around the world as a democratic antidote to the consolidation of power in Germany and Japan that was thought to have contributed to the forces of Nazism and Japanese militarism that led to the devastations of that war." [one footnote omitted]). For an in-depth analysis of these developments, see Gerber, *Global Competition*, 168–69 & 211–13.

[23] British Military Government Ordinance No. 78.

[24] Ordinance No. 96 of the French High Command.

[25] Djelic, *American Model*, 163.

   This legislation was ultimately replaced by the German Act against Restraints of Competition, which entered into force on 1 January 1958. The U.S. approach to antitrust[26] and the ordoliberalism of the Freiburg School[27] influenced the content of this Act, which notably prohibited cartels, albeit with some important exceptions, as well as some abuse of economic power by market dominating companies.[28] However, the German legislator never fully adopted the ordoliberal thought.[29] The power to order the break-up of a company was discussed, for instance, but never put into law.[30] Merger control came later, in 1973.[31]

   From a historical perspective, economic and political dangers – rightly or wrongly – associated with the concentration of economic power may partly explain the existence of a strong competition legislation in Germany.[32] Interestingly, the concentration of economic power was viewed by both the Ordoliberals[33] and the Americans consulted or referred to during the German legislative process[34] as a danger for democracy, liberty – both economic and political[35] – and the rule of law, which could be addressed by competition law, as emphasized by Franz Böhm, one of the founders of the Freiburg School of Ordoliberalism:

> [P]rivate power does not in any way fit into a constitutional democracy. It has no legitimate standing either in the system of government or the system of society of a constitutional democracy. Our system of government cannot tolerate it, because it knows no other than constitutionally assigned power with a political purpose.[36]

Walter Eucken, another founder of the Freiburg School of Ordoliberalism, developed the idea of the "interdependence of economic order and state order," relating in particular to the close relationship between the economic and the political systems.[37] Furthermore, a rule-based, competitive economic playing field was deemed

---

[26] See, e.g., Djelic, *American Model*, 169–70, 174 & 235; Gerber, *Europe*, 275–77.

[27] See, e.g., Gerber, *Europe*, 270–80. See, however, Maier-Rigaud, "Foundations," 152–61 & 167 (minimizing the ordoliberal influence on the German Act against Restraints of Competition).

[28] See Shapiro, "German Law," 9–46.

[29] See, e.g., Nettesheim & Thomas, *Entflechtung*, 12; see also Maier-Rigaud, "Foundations," 152 & 159–61.

[30] See Maier-Rigaud, "Foundations," 159; Nettesheim & Thomas, *Entflechtung*, 10–13.

[31] See Kühling, "Herausforderungen," 522.

[32] See Gerber, *Europe*, 240 & 251 ("Having witnessed the use of private economic power to destroy political and social institutions during the Weimar period, the ordoliberals emphasized the need to protect society from the misuse of such power […]. It also led them to demand the dispersion of not only political power, but economic power as well" [quotation from p. 240, one footnote omitted]).

[33] See Böhm, "Democracy and Economic Power," 273–80; Eucken, *Wirtschaftspolitik*, 52–53, 304–8 & 334–36. On the ordoliberals and democracy, see, e.g., Deutscher & Makris, "Ordoliberal Paradigm," 183 & 186–95; Maier-Rigaud, "Foundations," 142–43 & 163–65.

[34] See, e.g., Gerber, *Global Competition*, 168–69 and *Europe*, 275–77.

[35] See Tepper with Hearn, *Capitalism*, 153.

[36] Böhm, "Democracy and Economic Power," 271.

[37] Eucken, *Wirtschaftspolitik*, 332–4. See, e.g., Bönker & Wagener, "Hayek and Eucken," 192; Sally, *Classical Liberalism*, 109–11; Schweitzer, "Macht," 452–53. On the issue of "adequacy of economic

to fulfill a peace function.[38] From this perspective, a link can be established between separation of power and competition, as pointed out by Frédéric Marty:

> A direct link was established between the dispersion of economic power – a condition for freedom of access to the market – and that of political power – a condition for the exercise of individual freedom. For the ordo-liberals, the constitutional framework must establish a system of powers and checks and balances to guarantee freedoms. Competition is therefore a tool for dispersing power and exercising freedom.[39]

However, issues involving the combination of concentrated economic power and concentrated political power were not clearly addressed during the debate on the German Act against Restraints of Competition, and separation of powers-type arguments were not explicitly – at least neither prominently nor openly – made.

3.3 JAPAN

For some of the same reasons it influenced competition law in Germany after World War II, the United States considerably influenced competition law in Japan.[40] The overall purpose of the Japanese Antimonopoly Act consists, still today, in promoting "the democratic and wholesome development of the national economy" as well as securing "the interests of general consumers" by different measures, including the prevention of "excessive concentration of economic power."[41] Thus, a link is explicitly made between antitrust and democracy.[42]

Article 9 of the Antimonopoly Act is devoted to excessive concentration of economic power. The concentration of industries prior to World War II in Japan was, at least retrospectively, seen as a danger for the economy[43] and, more broadly, for peace and democracy.[44] Nowadays, this provision is applied to a "company group"

---

and political order," see Schmidt & Haucap, *Wettbewerbspolitik*, 38–39; Klump & Wörsdörfer, "Ordoliberal Interpretation of Smith," 36–37 (noting that "Smith and Eucken are not only concerned with *economic* freedom (i.e., economic liberalism); *ethical* and *political* freedom (i.e., ethical-political liberalism) are at least as much as essential as economic freedom").

[38] See Podszun, "Ordnungspolitik."

[39] Marty, "Politiques européennes de concurrence," 345 (translation by the author of the present book); see also Klump & Wörsdörfer, "Ordoliberal Interpretation of Smith," 41 ("In order to secure consumer's sovereignty and personal liberty, Smith's (and the Ordoliberal's) aim has to be seen in making government as little dependent as possible on individuals and special interest groups. A clear, precise and general (rule of) law is necessary as well as institutionalized (and republican) checks and balances (i.e., most importantly separation of powers and competition minimizing all forms of economic oppression (i.e., monopolistic privileges; [...]))" [two references to Eucken's books omitted]).

[40] See, e.g., Gerber, *Global Competition*, 211–12; Haley, *Antitrust*, 30–42; Iyori, "Comparison," 64–67.

[41] Article 1 of the Japanese Act on Prohibition of Private Monopolization and Maintenance of Fair Trade.

[42] See, e.g., Vande Walle, "Competition," 123–26; Gerber, *Global Competition*, 212; Ohara, "Japanese Antimonopoly Act," 6–9.

[43] See, e.g., Matsushita, "Antimonopoly Law," 178 & 181.

[44] See, e.g., Wakui, *Antimonopoly Law*, 135.

that "has big influence over the national economy" and "obstructs enhancement of the fair and free competition."[45] However, neither excessive political influence nor a threat to democracy are aspects considered by the Japan Fair Trade Commission when it enforces the Antimonopoly Act.

The U.S. proponents of the new legislation in Japan immediately after World War II, and members of the National Diet, did not explicitly establish a connection between risks posed by excessive concentration of economic power and those arising from the concentration of public or state powers. This may have come to mind at the time, as a new constitution was adopted in Japan. The 1946 Constitution of Japan is indeed based on the separation of powers, however, with a close relationship between the legislative and executive branches due to the parliamentary nature of the political system.[46]

3.4 EUROPEAN UNION

At its origin, European competition law was influenced, *inter alia*, by ordoliberalism, though the actual impact of the ordoliberals on the relevant provisions of the Treaty of Rome remains disputed.[47] U.S. antitrust laws also played a role in the aftermath of World War II.[48] The protection and strengthening of democracy helped justify the inclusion of competition law rules in the first treaties of the European Communities, which ultimately became the European Union.[49] These rules pursued, in particular, the politico-juridical-economic goal of integration, as illuminatingly emphasized by David J. Gerber:

> The goal of a unified market dominated the process of constructing the competition law system, because it was *the* central impetus for the "new Europe."[50]

---

[45] Japan Fair Trade Commission, *Excessive Concentration of Economic Power*, 2–3.

[46] See, e.g., Jones & Ravitch, *System*, 173; Matsui, "Separation of Powers," 387–410.

[47] See, e.g., Deutscher & Makris, "Ordoliberal Paradigm," 182–83; Patel & Schweitzer, "Introduction," 7–10; Schweitzer, "Efficiency and Freedom," 179–81; Gerber, *Europe*, 263–65 & 338–40 ("While the prohibition of cartel agreements had analogues in US antitrust law, the concept of prohibiting abuse of a market-dominating position was an important new development that was particularly closely associated with ordoliberal and German competition law thought and very different from the discourse of US law" [quotation from p. 264]). See, however, Akman, "Freedom," 183–213 & "Soul," 267–303 (raising serious doubts concerning the validity of the "conventional ordoliberal-influence thesis"); Maier-Rigaud, "Foundations," 152, 160 & 167 (minimizing the ordoliberal influence on the Treaty of Rome); Marty, "Politiques européennes de concurrence," 351–62 (also minimizing the ordoliberal influence on the Treaty of Rome, but considering that the Court of justice was significantly affected by this influence, notably in the 1960s).

[48] See, e.g., Talbot, "Ordoliberalism," 268–69; Djelic, *American Model*, 156 ("[A]rticles 60 and 61 of the ECSC [European Coal and Steel Community] treaty laid the foundation of antitrust legislation for the common European market. Such antitrust legislation was clearly foreign to European industrial traditions and had direct and unmistakable American origins"); Gerber, *Europe*, 338–39.

[49] See, e.g., Robertson, "Antitrust, Big Tech, and Democracy," 263–65; Gerbrandy, "Rethinking Competition Law," 133; Wu, *Curse of Bigness*, 82; Talbot, "Ordoliberalism," 266–73.

[50] Gerber, *Europe*, 343 & 347–48 (quotation from p. 347). See also Petit, *Droit européen de la concurrence*, 90–4; Talbot, "Ordoliberalism," 268 & 286–88.

Competition policy, according to the ordoliberal conception, is primarily oriented toward the goal of individual freedom, gives a strong role to the state in preserving the basic parameters of the competition system, is shaped by the rule of law, that is, a more rule-based system, and is embedded in "the economic order of a free and open society."[51] The state could, and should, intervene in cases of excessive concentration of power among a few private entities.[52] These characteristics can also be attributed, *mutatis mutandis*, to separation of powers. Indeed, a system of separation of powers aims to protect liberty, supposes an important role for state bodies – parliaments and courts, for instance – to ensure its preservation and is based on rules and helps to foster a free and open society. However, ordoliberals did not conceptualize separation of powers and competition policy in one single scheme.

In the end, the link between separation of powers and competition law is rather implicit in the European Union, but it indicates that both share some common ground. One reaches a similar conclusion for the United States, Germany, and Japan. The concentration of economic power – some economic disorder from an ordoliberal standpoint – may translate into concentration of political power, leading to interactions or even to a symbiosis between the two types of power. This claim was made in the United States, Germany, and Japan[53] and, from an individual perspective, notably by Brandeis and Hayek – and even by Montesquieu and Aron, who feared the potential fusion of economic and political powers. As we shall see in the next chapter, it may, to some extent, also apply nowadays in the digital and artificial intelligence era. Antitrust plays a role in this context, bearing in mind that separation of powers as such, that is, in a classical sense, does not usually fall within its – direct – goals. Nevertheless, the first may contribute to preserve the second.

---

[51] Möschel, "Competition Policy," 142; see also Maher, "Story of European Competition Law," 164; Gerber, *Europe*, 239–50; Mestmäcker, "Macht," 39–42; Eucken, *Wirtschaftspolitik*, 250.

[52] See Nettesheim & Thomas, *Entflechtung*, 12; Eucken, *Wirtschaftspolitik*, 334–36.

[53] Regarding post-War antitrust regimes in Europe and the United States, see Crane, "Fascism and Monopoly," 1369–70.

4

Political Content of Antitrust in the Digital and Artificial Intelligence Era

The foundations of the separation of powers principle and those of antitrust have become the subject of an actual and renewed interest, as we are currently witnessing a resurgence of noneconomic concerns in the antitrust literature.[1] This observation especially relates to the United States, but many issues raised in this country are also relevant in other jurisdictions. Several key provisions of antitrust national laws or European treaties are rather vague, leaving broad room for interpretation,[2] and have remained unchanged in substance for decades, which may open a connection between the political content of antitrust viewed historically and prospectively; to a certain extent, the ball is now in the court of agencies and courts.[3] Here, again, the focus will be placed on the separation of powers-type arguments which might reveal common ground, and even foundations, between such separation and antitrust. The concentration of power in the digital and artificial intelligence era constitutes the starting point of the analysis (Section 4.1), which continues with the observation that some digital platforms have significant political power (Section 4.2) and ends with the idea that such platforms have become important or even fundamental parts of the digital infrastructure of democracy (Section 4.3).

4.1 CONCENTRATION OF POWER

The current accumulation of power by a few firms of the digital economy seems unprecedented.[4] Due *inter alia* to their shares of the relevant markets, their

---

[1] See, e.g., Wu, *Curse of Bigness*, 18–19, 133 & 138–39; Khan, "Amazon," 739–46; Khan & Vaheesan, "Market Power and Inequality," 277–79; First & Weber Waller, "Deficit," 2544.

[2] Regarding the Treaty of Rome, see Talbot, "Ordoliberalism," 271. Regarding U.S. law, see Hovenkamp, *Federal Antitrust Policy*, 69 (referring to antitrust statutes as "vague and malleable").

[3] Regarding the United States, see Jacob M. Schlesinger, "The Return of the Trustbusters: A New Generation of Regulators Inspired by Louis Brandeis Hopes to Overturn the Light-touch Approach to Antitrust Shaped by Robert Bork," *Wall Street Journal*, 28 August 2021, C.1 ("While the neo-Brandeisians are influential in the legislative and executive branches, they will struggle unless they also win over the judiciary").

[4] See, e.g., Acemoglu & Johnson, *Power and Progress*, 276–77; Kissinger, Schmidt & Huttenlocher, *Age of AI*, 51 ("Corporations, having become collectors and aggregators of users' data, now wield more

capitalization, their profits,[5] their cash flow, their products and services, the amount of data they possess, control, process, or have access to – their data and platform power in a sense, as (part of) their market power[6] –, the codes, algorithms, rules, and standards they write,[7] tipping and network effects,[8] the importance of scale,[9] the gatekeeper and gateway function of their platforms,[10] their control of ecosystems,[11] their ability to buy companies and hire talent,[12] their capacity to stifle disruptive innovations,[13] some markets' winner-take-all-or-most tendency,[14] and the "networks of influence and investment,"[15] as well as "consumer inertia"[16] and "data gravity,"[17] these few firms hold considerable power that could significantly increase in the future, according to a special report published by *The Economist* in 2020:

power and influence than many sovereign states"), 96 & 101; Naughton, "Platform Power," 391–92; Cusumano, Gawer & Yoffie, *Business of Platforms*, 235–36; see also Deutscher, "Reshaping Digital Competition," 313; Dunne, "Pro-competition Regulation," 343–45.

[5] See, e.g., Lévêque, *Entreprises hyperpuissantes*, 39–41.

[6] See, e.g., OECD, *Ex Ante Regulation*, 40. On the concept of "data power" as already covered by German competition law, see Schweitzer, Haucap, Kerber & Welker, *Modernisierung*, section C.IV.4. For an English summary of this study, see Budzinski & Stöhr, "Competition Policy Reform," 40–44. On the competitive value of a "data advantage," see UK CMA, *Online Platforms*, 5 ("Both Google and Facebook grew by offering better products than their rivals. However, they are now protected by such strong incumbency advantages – including network effects, economies of scale and unmatchable access to user data – that potential rivals can no longer compete on equal terms"); Stucke, *Breaking Away*, 13–22; Ezrachi & Stucke, *Virtual Competition*, 20–21 and *Barons*, 97.

[7] See, e.g., Susskind, *Digital Republic*, 70.

[8] See, e.g., Stucke, *Breaking Away*, 7–12; Mäihäniemi, *Competition Law*, 60–64; Rubinfeld & Gal, "Access Barriers," 377.

[9] See, e.g., Stucke, *Breaking Away*, 5–6.

[10] See, e.g., Eifert, Metzger, Schweitzer & Wagner, "Taming the Giants," 991; Klobuchar, *Antitrust*, 15–16.

[11] See, e.g., Ezrachi & Stucke, *Barons*, 42–60.

[12] Howard Yu & Jialu Shan, "How Apple and Amazon Are Winning through the COVID-19 Fallout," *Forbes*, 1 May 2020, www.forbes.com/sites/howardhyu/2020/05/01/how-tech-giants-are-winning-the-covid-19-fallout-even-apple/#692c2f616b86 ("[...] the biggest tech platforms will not only dominate in size but in functionalities as well as experience. Nearly all tech companies are lavishing fortunes on hiring the best. They have to — and are willing to — pay millions to experts in the fields of self-driving cars, robotics, health care, and artificial intelligence to name a few. Given this trend, what was difficult for smaller players to do is now impossible"); see also Ezrachi & Stucke, *Barons*, 97.

[13] See Ezrachi & Stucke, *Barons*, 41–139.

[14] See, e.g., Stucke, *Breaking Away*, 22–23; Ezrachi & Stucke, "Antitrust Enforcement," 232–35 (mentioning several data-driven network effects); Parker, Van Alstyne & Choudary, *Platform Revolution*, 224–27; Cusumano, Gawer & Yoffie, *Business of Platforms*, 29–61.

[15] O'Mara, *Code*, 399.

[16] See, e.g., Busch, Graef, Hofmann & Gawer, *Platform Power*, 8; Mäihäniemi, *Competition Law*, 299; see also Stucke, *Breaking Away*, 40–41.

[17] "The Data Economy," Special Report, *The Economist*, 22 February 2020, 7 ("Now, more and more data flow into the big computing factories operated by AWS [Amazon Web Services], but also its main competitors, Microsoft Azure, Alibaba Cloud and Google Cloud [...]. AWS and other big cloud-computing providers are striving mightily to deepen this centralization [...]. Data attract more data, because different sets are most profitably mined together — a phenomenon known as 'data gravity'").

The big tech firms' supersized valuations suggest their profits will double or so in the next decade, causing far greater economic tremors in rich countries and an alarming concentration of economic and political power.[18]

Moreover, companies such as Alphabet Inc. (Alphabet), Amazon.com Inc. (Amazon), Apple Inc. (Apple), Meta Platforms, Inc. (Meta Platforms), and Microsoft Corporation (Microsoft) may emerge stronger and more powerful from a downturn, as "analysts, investors and economists predict that the world's largest companies will widen their lead in their respective markets."[19] From this perspective, their position and, as the case may be, their dominance in markets, such as social media, premium smartphones, e-commerce, cloud computing, and search, will possibly get stronger.[20]

The power at stake is not only of economic but also of political and societal nature. What is meant here does not simply relate to the influence – through different activities and channels and by various means – of powerful firms on policies, on politicians or on the agenda of political parties, or, directly, of the government.[21] Adam Smith had already warned against "the insolent outrage of furious and disappointed monopolists" when members of parliament oppose proposals strengthening them or are able to thwart them.[22] This observation remains fully valid, but the issue has taken on new dimensions. Furthermore, social networks are "as old as *Homo sapiens* as a species," to quote Niall Ferguson,[23] but technology and various factors have made some networks enormous.[24]

[18] "Big Tech's \$2trn Bull Run," *The Economist*, 22 February 2020, 7; see also, e.g., Klobuchar, *Antitrust*, 252–58. However, see, regarding Amazon's rivals that have emerged in both e-commerce and the cloud, "The Genius of Amazon" & "And on the Second Day…," *The Economist*, 20 June 2020.

[19] Tripp Mickle, "Big Tech Greets Markets' Slide with a Shrug," *New York Times*, 21 May 2022, A1.

[20] Tripp Mickle, "Big Tech Greets Markets' Slide with a Shrug," *New York Times*, 21 May 2022, A1; see also Akash Pasricha, "The Briefing: Robinhood Isn't Out of the Woods Just Yet," *The Information*, 22 September 2022, www.theinformation.com/articles/robinhood-isn-t-out-of-the-woods-just-yet; Martin Peers, "The Briefing: What Shopify and Snap Have in Common," *The Information*, 1 September 2022, www.theinformation.com/articles/what-shopify-and-snap-have-in-common.

[21] On this issue, from the antitrust perspective, see, e.g., Lévêque, *Entreprises hyperpuissantes*, 104–7; Klobuchar, *Antitrust*, 176, 207–10 & 269; Hawley, *Tyranny*, 129–32; Wu, *Curse of Bigness*, 54–58; Khan, "New Brandeis Movement," 131; Ezrachi & Stucke, *Virtual Competition*, 244–46 ("The problem is the combination of concentrated economic power, weakened limits on corporate political spending, and an amorphous legal standard, such as the Supreme Court's 'rule of reason' legal standard for most antitrust violations" [quotation from page 246, footnotes omitted]); Zingales, *Capitalism for the People*, 38–39 & 157 (arguing that "antitrust law reduces the political power of firms" [quotation from p. 38]); Teachout & Khan, "Taxonomy of Power," 42–53 (listing the "Power through Campaign Funding," the "Power through Staffing and Recruiting from Government," the "Power through Creating Information," the "Power to Direct the Politics of Employees and Contractors," and "Too Big to Fail"); Böhm, "Democracy and Economic Power," 273. From a broader perspective, see, e.g., Boix, *Democratic Capitalism*, 197 ("[D]emocratic elections are not likely at risk any time soon. But democratic accountability could be in the immediate future"); Teachout, *Corruption*, 189; Kuhner, "Separation," 2378–91. From a historical perspective, see Lamoreaux, "Problem of Bigness," 97–98 & 112–13.

[22] Smith, *Wealth of Nations*, Book 4, Chapter 2, para. 43, p. 471.

[23] Ferguson, *Square and Tower*, 355.

[24] Ferguson, *Square and Tower*, 358.

When, for instance, firms possess, control, process, or have access to data that may help a person get elected or reelected, or that may frame the political agenda, they become part of the electoral and democratic process,[25] part of the digital infrastructure of democracy.[26] The concentration of this multidimensional and protean power may thus be seen as a danger for self-government,[27] democracy or the democratic process,[28] and the republic of the common person, in the words of U.S. Senator Josh Hawley.[29] From this perspective, the regulation of the ownership, control, processing, and use of data "may well be the most important political question of our era," for Yuval Noah Harari.[30] Indeed, a very small number of firms "have at their disposal new means of manipulation and control that are unprecedented in human history," as observed by Robert Epstein.[31] Rohit Chopra, former Commissioner of the Federal Trade Commission and current Director of the Consumer Financial Protection Bureau, noted in 2019 that "[t]he case against Facebook is about more than just privacy – it is also about the power to control and manipulate."[32]

Even though internal checks and balances exist in large firms, one may wonder whether they are sufficient.[33] The power of firms like Meta Platforms or Alphabet

---

[25] See, e.g., Stigler Committee, *Final Report*, 14–15 ("Digital platforms are uniquely powerful political actors: Google and Facebook may be the most powerful political agents of our time [...]. This concentration of economic, media, data, and political power is potentially dangerous for our democracies" [Boldface type omitted]); Susskind, *Digital Republic*, 294–99; Narula, *Society*, 138 (regarding Twitter); Sitaraman, "Foreign Platforms," 1086; van Dijck, Nieborg & Poell, "Platform Power," 9–11; Tavoillot, *Peuple-roi*, 195–96; Drexl, "Economic Efficiency," 243–51 & 266–67; Stucke & Grunes, *Big Data*, 275 & 335. See also "Big Tech's $2trn Bull Run," *The Economist*, 22 February 2020, 7 ("Big tech's role in politics is already toxic; social media and videos influence elections from Minnesota to Myanmar"); Bradshaw & Howard, *Global Disinformation Order*, 2 ("We found evidence of organised social media manipulation campaigns in 70 countries, up from 48 countries in 2018 and 28 countries in 2017. Some of this growth comes from new entrants who are experimenting with the tools and techniques of computational propaganda during elections or as a new tool of information control [...]. Despite there being more platforms than ever, Facebook remains the dominant platform for cyber troop activity").

[26] See Section 4.3 in the present chapter.

[27] Foer, *World*, 192.

[28] See, e.g., UNCTAD, *Digital Economy*, para. 46; U.S. House of Representatives – Subcommittee on Antitrust, Commercial and Administrative Law, *Digital Markets*, 75–77. See also Ezrachi & Stucke, *Barons*, 5, 130–34 & 214; Susskind, *Digital Republic*, 70 & 138–41; Fishkin & Forbath, *Constitution*, 1, 8; Fukuyama, Richman & Goel, "Democracy," 98–104 & 109–10; Klobuchar, *Antitrust*, 214 ("If Americans are to rebalance our democracy, we must recapture the spirit of the antitrust movement"); Fukuyama *et al.*, *Platform Scale*, 2–9; Fukuyama, "Loaded Weapon"; Stoller, *Goliath*, 449–51; Lessig, *They Don't Represent Us*, 118–25 ("[T]he platforms of modern media and communication may well be rendering us incapable as citizens. Democracy is made poor so that Facebook can be rich" [quotation from p. 125]); Tambini, "Social Media Power," 281–88 (focusing on Facebook); Foer, *World*, 201–4.

[29] Hawley, *Tyranny*, 3, 147 & 152.

[30] Harari, *21 Lessons*, 80 (making this comment in relation to the question "how do you regulate the ownership of data?").

[31] Epstein, "Manipulating Minds," 300–13 (quotation from page 313); see also Helberger, "Power," 850.

[32] Dissenting Statement of Commissioner Rohit Chopra in *Facebook, Inc.*, Commission File No. 1823109 (24 July 2019).

[33] See Frenkel & Kang, *Truth*, 300 ("One thing is certain. Even if the company undergoes a radical transformation in the coming years, that change is unlikely to come from within. The algorithm that

should, therefore, be balanced by countervailing power.[34] It is suggested that the latter can be provided by other social media companies.[35] However, a firm like Facebook or its parent organization, Meta Platforms, may be dominant in the relevant market,[36] and any countervailing power from other social media companies may appear insufficient. Eventually, TikTok could increasingly play this countervailing role, though the need for checks and balances remains.

Furthermore, the concentration of power also has an individual dimension. Jeff Bezos has a major influence on Amazon.com, Inc., although power at this firm is gradually shifting to public shareholders[37]; Mark Zuckerberg owns the majority of the voting rights to Meta Platforms, Inc., the parent organization of Facebook, Instagram, and WhatsApp; and Larry Page and Sergey Brin hold more than 50 percent

serves as Facebook's beating heart is too powerful and too lucrative"). In October 2019, hundreds of Facebook employees signed a letter to Mr. Zuckerberg and other leaders of the company, decrying the decision to allow politicians to post advertisements including false claims on the platform (see *New York Times*, online edition, 28 October 2019, www.nytimes.com/2019/10/28/technology/facebook-mark-zuckerberg-letter.html). This letter claims that Facebook's policy "allows politicians to weaponize our platform by targeting people who believe that content posted by political figures is trustworthy." Initially, Facebook had not fundamentally changed its policy in this regard (see Mike Isaac, Sheera Frenkel & Cecilia Klang, "Mark Zuckerberg Goes It Alone," *New York Times*, 17 May 2020, BU1 (indicating that "Mr. Zuckerberg resolved to take control of the global superpower in which he already dominated the voting" and "said he would be making more decisions on his own, based on his instincts and vision for the company," as well as quoting Mark Zuckerberg: "[t]his is not a democracy")). More recently, however, it has decided to allow people to opt out of seeing political ads on their Facebook or Instagram feeds (see Mike Isaac, "Hate Political Ads? Opt Out, Facebook Says," *New York Times*, 17 June 2020, B3).

[34] See, e.g., Acemoglu & Johnson, *Power and Progress*, 396–402; Fukuyama, Richman & Goel, "Democracy," 103 ("Digital platforms' concentrated economic and political power is like a loaded weapon sitting on a table [...]. No liberal democracy is content to entrust concentrated political power to individuals based on assumptions about their good intentions. That is why the United States places checks and balances on that power"). Regarding Facebook, see Tambini, "Social Media Power," 287–88; see also Tambini & Moore, "Dominance," 398.

[35] See Tambini, "Social Media Power," 287.

[36] Regarding Germany, see Bundesgerichtshof, Case KVR 69/19, 23 June 2020, paras. 24–57. For a different viewpoint, see, e.g., Hovenkamp, "Slogans and Goals," 144 ("Considering today's large digital platforms, they are generally not monopolies in most of the markets in which they operate. There are some exceptions. Google Search has a dominant share (exceeding 90%) of the consumer search market. Amazon has a dominant position in ebooks, assuming that ebooks are a distinct market from print books. But neither Facebook nor Amazon have anything close to monopoly power in the vast number of individual products and services that they sell" [one footnote omitted]).

[37] See Martin Peers, "The Briefing: Amazon's Public Shareholders Show Their Hand," *The Information*, 1 April 2022, www.theinformation.com/articles/amazon-s-public-shareholders-show-their-hand ("As of February [2022], Bezos had the right to vote just 12.7% of Amazon stock, including shares owned by his ex-wife, MacKenzie Scott. A decade ago, Bezos could vote 19.5%. Back in 1998, shortly after Amazon went public, he owned 41%. Perhaps just as meaningful: This year the combined stakes of two big institutional holders, Vanguard and BlackRock, is almost equal to his. And remember, Amazon doesn't have a class of supervoting shares guaranteeing its founder control regardless of his ownership, unlike firms such as Alphabet and Meta Platforms. What this means is that power at Amazon is gradually shifting to public shareholders. That's going to continue as Bezos and Scott steadily sell stock. You can foresee a day not too far from now where Bezos will have a relatively small vote compared to institutional investors").

voting shares of Alphabet Inc., the parent company of Google LLC. Although these four persons are subject to numerous legal and economic constraints, their power remains considerable, potentially unprecedented, not just from an economic point of view.[38] Furthermore, some of these individuals can by no means be regarded as passive shareholders. Mark Zuckerberg, for instance, accumulates considerable – not to say autocratic – power within Meta Platforms and Facebook, according to the investigation conducted by Sheera Frenkel and Cecilia Kang:

> Zuckerberg's affinity for the first Roman emperor, Caesar Augustus, [...] was well known. Up to this point [around July 2018], Zuckerberg's governance had been analogous to that of the Roman Republic. There was a clear leader, but his power was backed by a Senate of sorts that deliberated over big decisions and policies. What he was outlining now looked more like Rome's move from a republic to an empire. Zuckerberg was establishing rule by one.[39]

This concentration of power, also combined with the development of artificial intelligence based on data,[40] is examined and sometimes criticized through the lens of democracy.[41] Some authors more specifically raise separation of powers-type concerns and refer to the foundations of both the separation of powers principle and antitrust. Tim Wu, former special assistant to the President of the United States for technology and competition policy, reaches the following conclusion:

---

[38] See, e.g., Stigler Committee, *Final Report*, 15; Josh Hawley, "Too Much Power in Too Few Hands," *Wall Street Journal*, online edition, 29 October 2021, www.wsj.com/articles/how-to-fix-social-media-11635526928 ("Three billion people use the Facebook suite of apps, yet just one person wields final authority over everything. Google, ultimately controlled by just two people, is no better"). From a broader perspective, see Acemoglu & Robinson, "Persistence," 287 ("[E]lites that have fewer members, that can benefit more from controlling economic institutions, and that are more forwardlooking are more likely to dominate politics").

[39] Frenkel & Kang, *Truth*, 193 & 220 (quotation from p. 193). Regarding Sheryl Sandberg's resignation as Chief Operating Officer of Meta Platforms, see "Leaning Out: A Shake-Up at Meta," *The Economist*, 4 June 2022, 55 ("The exit of Mr Zuckerberg's adult supervisor seems to alarm investors [...] and it leaves his firm looking like a one-man show. He is the only founder still calling the shots at one of America's tech giants. Reports were already swirling that his management style had become more iron-fisted, taking big decisions with less counsel. Without his long-term partner, he may start to cut an even more solitary figure").

[40] On the link between data and artificial intelligence or machine learning, see Kissinger, Schmidt & Huttenlocher, *Age of AI*, 57 ("AIs 'learn' by consuming data, then drawing observations and conclusions based on the data") & 79 ("Machine learning requires data, without which AIs cannot learn good models"); Hoffman, *Forces*, 133–94 & 225–30; Crawford, *Atlas of AI*, 114 ("Machine learning models require ongoing flows of data to become more accurate"); Digital Competition Expert Panel, *Digital Competition*, 4 ("[T]o the degree that the next technological revolution centres around artificial intelligence and machine learning, then the companies most able to take advantage of it may well be the existing large companies because of the importance of data for the successful use of these tools").

[41] See, e.g., Fukuyama, Richman & Goel, "Democracy," 98–104 & 109–10; Klobuchar, *Antitrust*, 214; Zuboff, *Surveillance Capitalism*, 192 ("[T]he pioneer surveillance capitalists at Google and Facebook evaded the disciplines of corporate governance and rejected the disciplines of democracy, protecting their claims with financial influence and political relationships"); Stoller, *Goliath*, 449–56.

The English Magna Carta, the Constitution of the United States, and other foundational laws of democracies around the world were all created with the idea that power should be limited — that it should be distributed, decentralized, checked, and balanced, so that no person or institution could enjoy unaccountable influence. Yet this vision has always had a major loophole. Written as a reaction to government tyranny, it did not contemplate the possibility of a concentrated private power that might come to rival the public's, of businesspeople with more influence than government officials, and of an artificial creature of law, the corporation, that would grow to have political protection exceeding that of actual humans. That's why the struggle for democracy now and in the progressive era must be one centered on private power — in both its influence over, and union with, government. […] By providing checks on monopoly and limiting private concentration of economic power, the antitrust law can maintain and support a different economic structure than the one we have now.[42]

In her seminal note, Lina Khan, now chair of the U.S. Federal Trade Commission, refers, *inter alia*, to "legislative intent, which makes clear that Congress passed antitrust laws to safeguard against excessive concentrations of economic power" as well as to disperse "political and economic control."[43] In order to capture the anticompetitive concerns arising from Amazon's business strategies and current market dominance, she concludes that "we should replace the consumer welfare framework with an approach oriented around preserving a competitive process and market structure."[44] In an editorial, she makes an analogy between the Constitution and antimonopoly:

In much the same way that the Constitution disperses power among different branches and tiers of government, antimonopoly aims to create a system of checks and balances in the commercial and economic spheres. Antitrust law is just one tool in the antimonopoly toolbox.[45]

Jonathan Kanter, Assistant Attorney General for the Antitrust Division within the U.S. Department of Justice, makes a relatively straightforward link between competition and democracy when he says, for instance, that "[c]ompetitively healthy markets offer more economic opportunity and less risk of corporate power dominating our democratic and social wellbeing."[46] Josh Simons and Dipayan Ghosh insist that "[a]ntitrust affirms a commitment to the idea that economic regulation has political aims, because untrammelled corporate power threatens the balance of power that

[42] Wu, *Curse of Bigness*, 138–39.
[43] Khan, "Amazon," 743 (footnotes omitted).
[44] Khan, "Amazon," 803.
[45] Khan, "New Brandeis Movement," 131; see also Khan, "Antitrust History," 1681–82. The present book focuses on the "antitrust tool."
[46] Remarks delivered at New York City Bar Association's Milton Handler Lecture, New York, 18 May 2022, available at www.justice.gov/opa/speech/assistant-attorney-general-jonathan-kanter-delivers-remarks-new-york-city-bar-association.

underpins democracy."[47] Finally, without pretending to be exhaustive, U.S. Senator Amy Klobuchar mentions separation of powers and antitrust in the same breadth:

> Americans have never been ones to tolerate too much consolidated power. America's founders and framers insisted on economic competition and separation of powers, assigning different powers to the legislative, executive, and judicial branches. They opposed monopolies, and they divided power between the federal government and the states while reserving rights and power to the people themselves. The U.S. Bill of Rights and the American republic's system of checks and balances were, like the antitrust laws, specifically designed to ensure that too much power would never be placed in the hands of a ruling few.[48]

Now, do separation of powers and antitrust really share common ground? Is antitrust the appropriate tool to avoid politico-economic concentration of power in the digital and artificial intelligence era? If yes, to what extent? Before addressing these fundamental questions in the second and third parts of this book, it seems important to put them into context with a few words on the political power of digital platforms (Section 4.2) and the digital infrastructure of democracy (Section 4.3).

4.2 POLITICAL POWER OF DIGITAL PLATFORMS

Digital platforms – social media and search platforms especially – fulfill many roles, including a political one. They connect, for instance, elected officials and public authorities with citizens. They may or may not diffuse political advertisements. Due to the number of users and the data to which platforms have access and process, they have become an important tool to influence individuals and, among them, voters.[49] In other words, the power of firms such as Meta Platforms or Google is not only economic but also social and political,[50] even if these firms do not necessarily set out to influence an election or a referendum.[51] A platform such as Facebook exercises

---

[47] Simons & Ghosh, *Utilities for Democracy*, 8.

[48] Klobuchar, *Antitrust*, 61. From a historical perspective, see, e.g., Hawk, *Monopoly*, 169–70.

[49] See, e.g., Stigler Committee, *Final Report*, 18–19 (proposing solutions for reducing the political power of digital platforms); Stucke, *Breaking Away*, 24; Zuboff, *Surveillance Capitalism*, 277–81; see also Landemore, *Open Democracy*, 217.

[50] Fukuyama, Richman & Goel, "Democracy," 98–103 & 109–10; Buchmann, "Demokratie und Öffentlichkeit," 21; Dolata, "Platform Regulation," 461–62; Simons & Ghosh, *Utilities for Democracy*, 2; Helberger, "Power," 845–50; Tambini & Moore, "Dominance," 398–99; Stucke, "Data-opolies," 312–20; O'Mara, *Code*, 404. See also Sitaraman, "Foreign Platforms," 1102–3; Crawford, *Atlas of AI*, 211 ("The entire practice of harvesting data, categorizing and labeling it, and then using it to train systems is a form of politics"); Pollicino & De Gregorio, "Constitutional Law," 15 & 22. From a historical perspective, see, regarding the United States, Fishkin & Forbath, *Constitution*, 216 & 230–32.

[51] See Read, "Chaos" ("As has been repeatedly demonstrated over the last two decades, Mark Zuckerberg and his peers have almost no clue what is happening on, or because of, the platforms they've built"); Naughton, "Platform Power," 381 ("The leaders of Google and Facebook did not set out to influence the course of the Brexit referendum or of the US presidential election. And yet the activities that their platforms enabled did influence the campaigns – and perhaps the outcomes – in each case"); see also Fukuyama, Richman & Goel, "Democracy," 102; Wagner, "Free Expression," 226–28.

quasi-public powers, for instance, when it designs the rules of content moderation and enforces them.[52] This concentration of power poses "not just an economic, social, or political problem but a *constitutional* problem," as emphasized by Joseph Fishkin and William E. Forbath[53] or by Jürgen Habermas.[54] Moreover, the role of large or, *a fortiori*, dominant platforms in a democracy directly questions the role of constitutions – to take up the questioning of Oreste Pollicino and Giovanni De Gregorio:

> [T]he original mission of constitutionalism was to set some mechanisms to restrict government power through self-binding principles, including by providing different forms of separation of powers and constitutional review. To reach this goal, it is crucial to focus on the exploration of the most disruptive challenges which the emergence of private powers has posed to the modern constitutional state and the various policy options for facing said transformations. This requires questioning the role that constitutions play in the information society and leads one to investigate whether constitutions can and should do something in light of the emergence of new powers other than those exercised by public authorities.[55]

This power also has an individual dimension, since the majority of the voting rights in Meta Platforms and Google is in the hands of one or two persons.[56] Thierry Ménissier goes one step further and convincingly argues that, with reference to Machiavelli's *magnum opus*, the new Princes of today are the bosses of Alphabet/Google, Apple, Meta Platforms/Facebook, Amazon, Microsoft, and, he adds, Tesla.[57] This power also has an interindividual dimension, since persons controlling the company owning a large or, *a fortiori*, dominant digital platform may interact and even collude with powerful office holders, as accurately warned by Jan-Werner Müller:

> Concentrated power means that unaccountable individuals could influence elections, but it could also permit governments to exert pressure on individuals who will tweak their politics so as to preserve the platforms' profits. A Trump and a Zuckerberg are individually perilous for democracy; all the ways they might use each other significantly compound the dangers.[58]

The data that large or, *a fortiori*, dominant digital firms possess, control, process, or have access to have an economic *and* political value. These politico-economic data and the number of their users not only make some platforms particularly attractive

---

[52] De Gregorio & Pollicino, "Constitutional Road," 17.

[53] Fishkin & Forbath, *Constitution*, 3 & 474 (quotation from p. 3); see also Pollicino, *Fundamental Rights*, 184–211; Pollicino & De Gregorio, "Constitutional Law," 6 & 15–24; Steinbaum & Stucke, "Standard," 622; Wu, *Curse of Bigness*, 54.

[54] Habermas, *Strukturwandel*, 67.

[55] Pollicino & De Gregorio, "Constitutional Law," 6, 14–15 & 21–22 (quotation from p. 15); see also Pollicino, *Fundamental Rights*, 191 & 200–7.

[56] See Section 4.1 in the present Chapter.

[57] Ménissier, "Nouvelles figures du Prince," 96–100.

[58] Müller, *Democracy Rules*, 128.

but also raise very sensitive issues in a democracy. These issues may be appropriately addressed and regulated by special rules on election, media, privacy, data protection, or other laws. However, it is possible that no such rules exist in a given country or that the rules in force do not measure up to the stakes.[59] Moreover, if a large or, *a fortiori*, dominant platform advantages a political party, this may have an implication on all three branches of government in presidential, semi-presidential, or parliamentary regimes, at least where judges are chosen by members of the political branches. In sum, some digital platforms may enjoy increased politico-economic power, potentially threatening democracy and, at least *de facto*, separation of powers. Specific regulation addressing this fundamental issue is advisable, but it is at best scarce until now.[60] This gap between the challenges and dangers posed by the concentration of politico-economic powers within a few firms on one hand and the lack of regulation addressing them on the other may increase the interest in antitrust. Eric Posner and Glen Weyl, for instance, consider that antitrust has a role to play in "preventing the excessive concentration of political power" to the detriment of democracy.[61] Franklin Foer also connects antitrust with democracy,[62] after having noted that "[o]ne of the most sacrosanct obligations of the data-driven firms is that they don't abuse their power to undermine democracy."[63]

Antitrust or competition laws have a general and broad scope. They are here and, most probably, here to stay. Social networks, search engines, generative artificial intelligence platforms, and other platforms at least fall under these laws that can address – eventually after having been partially reinterpreted – politico-economic risks or harms caused by the rise of dominant platforms.[64] The fact that their products and services may be used by governments or politicians running for election should not lead, from the outset, to the inapplicability of antitrust laws in this context,[65] if only because the activity of social networks and other platforms is of an economic nature. In some cases, antitrust can even be regarded as a legislation of last resort.[66] This should by no means be interpreted as a plea in favor of the subsidiarity of antitrust laws. Election, privacy, data protection, consumer protection,

---

[59] See, e.g., Stucke & Grunes, *Big Data*, 254–55 & 274–76. See also Part II, Chapter 5, Section 5.2.3.
[60] See Part III, Chapters 8 & 9.
[61] Posner & Weyl, *Radical Markets*, 203; see also Economic Security Project, *Antimonopoly Fund*, 9, 11, 38, 40 & 44 (insisting on the need to broaden the popular understanding of antimonopoly beyond antitrust exclusively); Fukuyama, *Liberalism*, 149; Susskind, *Digital Republic*, 245–46; Fishkin & Forbath, *Constitution*, 471–77 ("Antitrust is a mechanism — not the only one, but a very important one — of blocking the concentration of too much economic and political power in too few hands" [quotation from p. 473]); Cohen & Fung, "Democracy," 45–46.
[62] Foer, *World*, 201–4.
[63] Foer, *World*, 201. See, however, Habermas, *Strukturwandel*, 66.
[64] See, e.g., Baker, *Antitrust Paradigm*, 18–20 & 119–49; see also Stucke & Grunes, *Big Data*, 302–12.
[65] See Part II, Chapter 6.
[66] See, however, Shapiro, "Protecting Competition," 90 ("Stronger antitrust enforcement, while needed, is not a substitute for badly needed regulations directed at reducing the political influence of corporations, protecting privacy and data security, and limiting the spread of disinformation").

or sectoral laws on the one hand, and antitrust laws on the other, may be jointly applicable in some instances,[67] although through different procedures and enforcement mechanisms.

Election, privacy, data or consumer protection, or sectoral laws and regulations may be the most appropriate tools to address certain issues raised by the existence of platforms in the data economy.[68] For instance, questions relating to hate speech, to the consent of individuals for a platform to use personal data, or to the correction of erroneous data, as well as those relating to political mis- or disinformation, fall within the scope of criminal, data protection, privacy, media, or election laws.[69] Antitrust may still come into play but will most probably not be placed at center stage. By contrast, issues clearly connected to the concentration of "data power" or "platform power" may put antitrust – but not necessarily on its own – in the forefront,[70] including when the digital infrastructure of democracy is at stake.

4.3 DIGITAL INFRASTRUCTURE OF DEMOCRACY

Some digital platforms not only enjoy significant politico-economic power but also have grown into important or even fundamental parts of the digital infrastructure of democracy. It does not mean that they, in the aggregate, positively affect the latter. In reality, large and, *a fortiori*, dominant digital platforms have an ambivalent

---

[67] See Klobuchar, *Antitrust*, 353; Simons & Ghosh, *Utilities for Democracy*, 7; Rahman, "New Utilities," 1678–80; Stucke & Grunes, *Big Data*, 275 ("[C]ompetition authorities should not assume that competition policy and privacy are distinct, unrelated concepts"). See also Gökçe Dessemond, "Restoring Competition," 25 ("Governments should have in place all the relevant policies and legal frameworks [...] to overcome different challenges of the platform economy. These may include competition, consumer protection and privacy policies and legislation").

[68] See, e.g., Shapiro, "Protecting Competition," 79, 86 & 90; Ohlhausen & Okuliar, "Competition," 150–56 (concluding that "[a]lthough privacy can be (and is today) a dimension of competition, the more direct route to protecting privacy as a norm lies in the consumer protection laws"); Petit, *Big Tech*, 238–56; Wiggers, Struijlaart & Dibbits, *Digital Competition Law*, 134–35. See also, from a general perspective, *Verizon v. Trinko*, 540 U.S. 398, 412 (2004) ("One factor of particular importance is the existence of a regulatory structure designed to deter and remedy anticompetitive harm. Where such a structure exists, the additional benefit to competition provided by antitrust enforcement will tend to be small, and it will be less plausible that the antitrust laws contemplate such additional scrutiny").

[69] See, e.g., Shapiro, "Protecting Competition," 86 & 90; Stucke & Grunes, *Big Data*, 335 ("[One] cannot assume that antitrust is a panacea for every privacy and consumer protection concern"); Wheeler, Verveer & Kimmelman, *New Digital Realities*, 25 ("It's not realistic to expect antitrust to have an important influence on privacy, data security, hate speech, imminent incitements to violence, malign foreign influence, or misinformation. Amelioration of these and other similar problems will have to come, if at all, from other sources [...]"); Petit, *Big Tech*, 255–56.

[70] Coming from a different perspective but reaching a similar conclusion, see Botta & Wiedemann, "Exploitative Conducts," 472–73 ("Data protection law is oftentimes not suitable to solve these issues [limiting the number of data collected by online platforms] in modern digital markets, since, for example, it still mostly relies on the concept of consent"). See also Baker, "Reformers," 750 ("[A]ntitrust needs to address the economy-wide growth of market power and novel antitrust issues raised by large digital platforms").

relationship with democracy, as they generate interactions and information that can enhance or detract it. In this last case, these platforms may be part of the digital infrastructure of a struggling, sickened, ill or endangered – hopefully not dying – democracy.[71] In the notion of *digital infrastructure of democracy*, the latter is not qualified in an unproblematic way.

In addition, some of these platforms belong to groups that offer plenty of services and have strategic infrastructures either in the cloud or with a range of satellites. In South Korea, KakaoTalk messaging app has 47.6 million monthly users – equal to over 90% of the South Korean population – and is pervasive in the country for both personal and business communications; its accounts can also be linked to many other services, from payments to ride-hailing – Kakao T controls around 90% of this market – and GPS.[72] The eventual combination of activities between X/Twitter, Neuralink, and Starlink – a satellite internet constellation operated by Space Exploration Technologies Corp. (SpaceX) – could generate tremendous power in the hands of Elon Musk if he keeps control over these companies.[73]

Google's and Facebook's platforms and algorithms especially "have become part of the infrastructure of our public sphere"[74] and "provide important public goods,"[75] as also recently made clear in the war between Russia and Ukraine. Digital infrastructure must not necessarily be understood in a technical way, but rather as a substructure[76] on the basis of which democracy actually functions – or disfunctions[77] – and which allows citizens and other persons to obtain political information or to reach each other.[78] In this context, Ethan Zuckerman notes that "[d]igital infrastructures can be social as well as economic or technical."[79]

For at least two reasons, the notion of *digital infrastructure of democracy* and not just *of public sphere* is used here, although both notions are linked and could

---

[71] See, e.g., Habermas, *Strukturwandel*, 29 & 61–67; Cohen, *Homo numericus*, 114–22 & 181–82.

[72] See Kotaro Hosokawa, "South Korean Super App Kakao's Outage Reveal Growing Pains," *Nikkei Asia*, 20 November 2022, https://asia.nikkei.com/Business/Technology/South-Korean-super-app-Kakao-s-outage-reveals-growing-pains.

[73] See Christian Weisflog, "Elon Musk wird Washington zu mächtig" [Elon Musk Becomes Too Powerful for Washington], *Neue Zürcher Zeitung*, 24 October 2022, 2; see also Durand, "Musk," 29–30.

[74] Simons & Ghosh, *Utilities for Democracy*, 3; Cohen & Fung, "Democracy," 36 ("[A] few firms dominate the infrastructure of the digital public sphere"); van Dijck, Nieborg & Poell, "Platform Power," 9–11 ("From platform markets to societal infrastructures"); Balkin, "Regulate," 74–78. See also Schrape, "Plattformöffentlichkeit," 118–29; Landemore, *Open Democracy*, 216–17; Nemitz & Pfeffer, "Future," 284 ("Because the GAFAM networks and the search engines themselves aggregate political news and disseminate it tailored to personal profiles accumulated by them, they themselves have become key actors of the electronic public sphere"); Langlois & Elmer, "Impersonal Subjectivation," 239–42.

[75] Wagner, "Free Expression," 236; see also Candeub, "Bargaining for Free Speech," 396, 400, 406 & 433.

[76] See *Oxford English Dictionary*, under "Infrastructure."

[77] See, e.g., Ezrachi & Stucke, *Barons*, 130–34 ("The surveillance economy is fundamentally anti-democratic" [quotation from p. 133]); Fukuyama, *Liberalism*, 105 & 109.

[78] See Müller, "Infrastructure," 269–82; Simons & Ghosh, *Utilities for Democracy*, 3–6; Zuckerman, *Infrastructure*, 4–8; Busch, Graef, Hofmann & Gawer, *Platform Power*, 20–23.

[79] Zuckerman, *Infrastructure*, 8.

partially merge into a notion such as *digital infrastructure of the public sphere of democracy*.[80] First, public sphere usually refers to an area in social life where ideas and information are exchanged.[81] Digital platforms fulfill this role, but they are also used, for instance, simply to unilaterally gather or disseminate information. Furthermore, a debate on the nature of the Internet and, more concretely, of its most used platforms as public spheres or not[82] is avoided here. Second, the issues raised by some digital platforms do not simply relate to the digital public sphere but to democracy itself[83] and, more specifically, to the electoral or democratic process. When many people search information through Google or, in the future maybe, through OpenAI's ChatGPT or Bing enhanced by the latter before an election or a referendum and participate to the democratic debate at large through Facebook, Instagram, KakaoTalk, X/Twitter, WhatsApp, or, more recently, TikTok, they implicitly indicate that these platforms contribute to structuring the – good or bad – functioning of democracy[84] and to shaping public opinion[85] from a digital perspective.

---

[80] See Buchmann, "Demokratie und Öffentlichkeit," 18 (using the notion of "democratic public spheres").

[81] See Wikipedia, *Public Sphere*, https://en.wikipedia.org/wiki/Public_sphere (26 June 2023).

[82] See, e.g., Caplan, "Private Speech Governance," 172 ("Platforms themselves are moving away from an embrace of the idea that they are the digital public sphere and toward an approach of the more private, 'curated community,' which acknowledges a common set of rules and standards by which users must abide to remain inside" [one footnote omitted]); Schäfer, "Digital Public Sphere," 327.

[83] See, e.g., Gerard de Graaf, "Die EU muss sich nicht dafür rechtfertigen, dass sie das Internet reguliert" [The EU Does Not Have to Justify Itself for Regulating the Internet], interview with Marie-Astrid Langer, *Neue Zürcher Zeitung*, 15 September 2022, 22, English translation at www.nzz.ch/english/ gerard-de-graaf-is-the-new-eu-ambassador-to-silicon-valley-ld.1701947 ("The Big Tech […] have realized they have an important influence now on our democratic systems"); Shoshana Zuboff, "The EU Has Fired the Starting Gun in the Fightback Against Big Tech," *Financial Times*, online edition, 2 May 2022, www.ft.com/content/31f49915-0f85-48b0-bf81-131960318967 ("With the DSA [Digital Services Act], the EU has declared that digital spaces belong to society and are mission-critical to a healthy democracy. The digital must live in democracy's house, not as an adversary, but as a productive family member"); Tingyang, "Democracy" ("[T]he real beneficiaries of democracy are the powerful groups who have the ability to manipulate the market and public opinion"); Landemore, *Open Democracy*, 216 and "Open Democracy and Digital Technologies," 65 & 71–84 (arguing that digital technologies and, more concretely, a platform on which every citizen would be registered at birth, and which could be used as a safe and secure space for deliberation may "support and deploy a new and better kind of democracy" [quotation from p. 84]); Nosthoff & Maschewski, "Big Data," 5–6 ("GAFAM have expanded what we call *infrastructural power* that is power that essentially circumvents or avoids concrete political deliberation or regulation, with the aim of establishing a new, universal standard or norm"); Balkin, "Regulate," 77–78, 92 & 96; Patino, *Civilisation*, 135; Susskind, *Future Politics*, 356–60.

[84] See Müller, "Infrastructure," 273 & 279 ("[I]ntermediary institutions have a choice in how they present and structure conflicts" [quotation from p. 273]); Pasquale, *Laws of Robotics*, 115 ("[F]or better and worse, vast conglomerates like Facebook and Google effectively take on the role of global communications regulators"); Simons & Ghosh, *Utilities for Democracy*, 11; van Dijck, Nieborg & Poell, "Platform Power," 5 & 9–11; Candeub, "Bargaining for Free Speech," 398, 400, 406 & 433. From a general perspective, see Coleman, "Digital Democracy," 311–14.

[85] Ezrachi & Stucke, *Barons*, 130–34; Kissinger, Schmidt & Huttenlocher, *Age of AI*, 219. Regarding ChatGPT, see Dominique Nora, "La guerre de l'IA est déclarée" [The AI War Is Declared], *L'Obs*, 2 February 2023, 30–35, 34–35.

Many observations in this respect have been made in several jurisdictions, for instance, in Brazil as summed up by Jan-Werner Müller:

> During the 2018 presidential election in Brazil, WhatsApp served as the (free) messenger of choice for a massive disinformation campaign funded by corporations pushing for the far-right candidate Jair Bolsonaro. WhatsApp is used by 120 million out of 210 million citizens in a country where internet access is very expensive for households and where mobile plans tend not to include unlimited data: The result is that Brazilians use messaging apps heavily but do not necessarily have any link to the World Wide Web as such, let alone media that could serve as a check on disinformation. Because WhatsApp (which is owned by Facebook) primarily connects friends and family, "information" shared on it seems automatically more credible, since those who transmit it are more trusted.[86]

In other words, Google, Facebook, and other major platforms function as gatekeepers and gateways to find, receive, and exchange political information or to debate. This translates into political and social power,[87] even though the gates are or seem widely open. According to a survey of Pew Research Center, based on data collected in 2021 and 2022, about a third of adults in the United States (31%) regularly got news on Facebook in 2021 and 2022.[88] WhatsApp (15.8%), Instagram (14.3%), and Facebook (14.2%), which are all subsidiaries of Meta Platforms, are the top-three favorite social media platforms of global internet users aged 16–64.[89] Facebook (2.958 billion monthly global active users), WhatsApp (2 billion), and Instagram (2 billion) are ranked first, third, and fourth, respectively, in a recent list of the world's most-used social platforms, YouTube (2.514 billion) – owned by Google – being second.[90]

This may not necessarily be relevant for the application of antitrust and competition laws but shows the need for *public* regulation and supervision,[91] as well as for checks and balances.[92] The fact remains that antitrust and competitions laws apply to such firms,[93] which may be dominant or have monopoly power, and that a good portion of the digital infrastructure of democracy is in a few private hands.[94] In such a case, some of their behaviors, including those relating to their gatekeeping

---

[86] Müller, *Democracy Rules*, 121–22 (footnotes omitted); see also Ruediger & Grassi, "Polarization Presidentialism," 285–86, 290, 294 & 296.

[87] Pohle & Voelsen, "Centrality and Power," 21–22; Farrell & Schwartzberg, "New Public Sphere," 203.

[88] Liedke & Matsa, *Social Media*, 2–3; Walker & Matsa, *News*, 4. See also Stucke, *Breaking Away*, 236–37; Cusumano, Gawer & Yoffie, *Business of Platforms*, 187–89.

[89] We Are Social/Meltwater, *Digital 2023*, 113; We Are Social/Hootsuite, *Digital 2022*, 103.

[90] We Are Social/Meltwater, *Digital 2023*, 111; We Are Social/Hootsuite, *Digital 2022*, 99. See also Stucke, *Breaking Away*, 227–29.

[91] See, e.g., Dolata, "Platform Regulation," 474.

[92] Narula, *Society*, 195. From a broader perspective, see Zuboff, *Surveillance Capitalism*, 519 & 524; see also Sturn, "Digital Transformation," 428–29 (using the notion of "techno-oligarchy").

[93] See, e.g., Persily, "Platform Power," 210.

[94] See, e.g., Dolata, "Platform Regulation," 459 & 462–63; Dixon, "Decentralization."

function, may prove abusive within the meaning of said laws. Granted, antitrust does not directly aim at protecting democracy.[95] Nevertheless, there may be points of juncture between them.[96] Abusive discrimination performed by a dominant firm can, for instance, fall under competition or antitrust laws.[97] Accordingly, antitrust should not, as a matter of principle, be left out of the picture.

One step further leads to qualify Google and Facebook, especially, as utilities of and for – or against – democracy[98] or, more simply, as public utilities[99] or new digital commons.[100] For Thomas Piketty, systemic platforms used by a significant fraction of the population should even be treated as quasi-public service.[101] From these perspectives, "[p]rivate powers who shape the fundamental terms of citizens' common life should be held accountable to the public good," according to Josh Simons and Dipayan Ghosh.[102] However, one may wonder whether the concept of public utility or the one of public service are necessary or simply useful in this context.[103] Public utilities have historically been considered as natural monopolies and are subject to forms of public control or to extensive regulation. Access to the infrastructure, including its pricing, and rates or profits would typically be regulated. Is this approach appropriate for Google and Facebook?[104] Is it adequate to talk about natural monopolies?[105] Treating dominant platforms as public utilities may further raise constitutional issues in certain jurisdictions.[106]

---

[95] See, e.g., Crane, "Instrument of Democracy," 23 & 40; Schweitzer, "Macht," 453; Petersen, "Antitrust," 604–21.

[96] See Crane, "Instrument of Democracy," 24–40.

[97] See Part II, Chapter 6, Section 6.4.

[98] Simons & Ghosh, *Utilities for Democracy*, 9–15; see also Ghosh, "Facebook" ("The economic design of the United States rightly gives the capitalistic market free sway to innovate — but when such commercialization breeds exploitation of the individual, our nation has always taken action to protect our democratic interests ahead of the freedom of markets"). See, however, Stucke, *Breaking Away*, 236–41 ("[T]he behavioral advertising model rewards 'echo chambers' and 'filter bubbles,' while society bears the cost from the increase in conspiracy theories, rancor, polarization, and extremism. This also degrades public deliberation, a foundation for democracies, juries, and civic engagement" [quotation from p. 237]).

[99] See, for instance, Rahman, "New Utilities," 1666–89; Bagnoli, "Digital Platforms," 903–5. See also Guggenberger, "Platforms," 314. From a historical perspective, see, regarding the United States, Fishkin & Forbath, *Constitution*, 219–20.

[100] Narula, *Society*, 190.

[101] Piketty, *Égalité*, 152, n. 1; see also Durand, "Musk," 31.

[102] Simons & Ghosh, *Utilities for Democracy*, 15.

[103] For a rather negative answer, see Balkin, "Regulate," 86–87.

[104] For a rather negative answer, see Tirole, "Google and Facebook"; Petit, *Big Tech*, 253–54 ("[U]tilities regulation creates opportunities for inefficient rivals to engage in rent seeking. Appeal to public authorities and courts provides a route to reverse-engineer market outcomes. This in turn chills successful firms' incentives to innovate, and negates the very principle of competition on the merits" [quotation from p. 254]); see also Akcigit *et al.*, *Market Power*, 25–26, para. 43.

[105] For a negative answer, see Portuese, "Robust Antitrust," 248–49.

[106] Regarding the United States, see Lakier, *Limits*, 6–8 ("There is, nevertheless, a serious problem with the idea of turning platform companies like Facebook and Google into public utilities and requiring them to provide nondiscriminatory access to consumers: doing so would almost certainly be considered a violation of their First Amendment rights." [quotation from p. 7]).

Utilities or not, regulation is probably needed anyway. The existence of a natural monopoly does not usually condition governmental intervention and regulation. Access may actually be an issue dealt with by special regulation or, potentially and to a limited extent, by antitrust.[107] Additionally, checks and balances within a firm or, partially, outside of it may contribute to or, as the case may be, prove indispensable for the proper functioning of democracy from a digital perspective.

Suitable regulation may or may not come. Either way, antitrust does not disappear from the picture. In the absence of specific regulation, antitrust – thanks to its transversal nature – sets minimal limits to Google, Meta Platforms, or Microsoft, for instance, which may indirectly benefit the proper function of democracy.[108] The existence of specific regulation does not exclude antitrust, either, as the latter also affects regulated industries.[109] As a rule, regulation and antitrust may complement each other in important respects, as Philip E. Areeda made clear long ago.[110]

In sum, some digital platforms raise issues pertaining notably to democracy, separation of powers, and antitrust – all three sharing some common ground or even foundations and facing some similar questioning and threats. The second part of this book will then focus on the interactions between separation of powers and antitrust *de lege lata* in the contemporary context, that is, in the digital and artificial intelligence era, with democracy serving, to a wide extent, as a backdrop for this analysis.

---

[107] See *infra* Parts II and III.

[108] On this rather indirect impact, see Crane, "Instrument of Democracy," 23, 26–27 & 39–40.

[109] See, for instance, Bostoen, "Digital Markets Act," 304–05 (concluding that the Digital Markets Act "is in now way competition law's curtain's call" [quotation from p. 305]); Klobuchar, *Antitrust*, 353 ("Reasonable regulations work in tandem with antitrust laws to protect against abuses of power"); Simons & Ghosh, *Utilities for Democracy*, 7; Rahman, "New Utilities," 1678–80; Graef, "When Data Evolves into Market Power," 93–94.

[110] See, regarding the United States, Areeda, "Antitrust and Regulation," 44–57.

PART II

Interactions

This second part of the book evaluates the interactions between the separation of powers principle and antitrust, as well as the actual or possible convergence of them. Chapter 5 investigates whether separation of powers-type considerations may be used in antitrust matters. Chapter 6 shows that some risks posed by dominant firms are possibly addressed by competition and antitrust laws *de lege lata*, which may thus be integrated into a broader scheme of separation of powers. Building upon this, but broadening the reflection, the third and last part of this book will attempt to define some contours of the new separation of powers in the digital era and in the age of artificial intelligence, while identifying or synthetizing the potential contribution, if any, of specific regulations or antitrust *de lege ferenda* – or at least significantly reinterpreted – in this regard.

5

Separation of Powers in Antitrust

Firms are not organized in a monolithic way; their organizations include checks and balances imposed by various sources (Section 5.1). Separation of powers may be used, by analogy, in antitrust matters (Section 5.2), especially to define organizational remedies or commitments (Section 5.3). It may also be raised as an argument or a defense to avoid or reduce sanctions and to get a merger approved (Section 5.4).

5.1 VARIOUS SOURCES IMPOSING CHECKS AND BALANCES TO A FIRM

To a large extent, firms decide how they organize themselves. However, their freedom is not unlimited. Various legal and other sources restrict it. Some of them actually impose checks and balances to firms and address the risks posed by the concentration of power in one or a few hands. At least three main categories of sources come into play.

First, corporate law and governance have a deep impact on a firm's organization. Notably, they impose or recommend various checks and balances to firms. The distinctive roles for shareholders, directors, and officers/management provide for some separation and specialization of functions in a firm, even though officers and managers usually make most corporate decisions.[1] In particular, the relationship between the Shareholders' General Meeting and the Board of Directors is of obvious interest in this context. An analogy with the separation of powers principle[2] would probably be exaggerated and artificial, if not completely misplaced. Nevertheless, corporate law and governance provide for the distribution of power

---

[1] Regarding the United States, see Thompson, "Power of Shareholders," 443.

[2] For such an analogy, see, regarding Israel, Lurie & Frenkel, "Corporate Governance," 275–83 (concluding that "the new Israeli company law has adopted, in general terms, the democratic model and the principle of separation of powers for the governance of corporations, based on the view that a corporation is like a quasi-state, and thus should have a policy of checks and balances" [quotation from p. 282]); see also, regarding the United States, Thompson, "Anti-Primacy," 402–3; Coglianese, "Legitimacy," 163–64.

between various bodies as well as the establishment of control mechanisms, as K. Sabeel Rahman coins it:

> [C]orporate governance as a strategy for legal reform emerged from the same intellectual roots as the Brandeisian critiques of bigness — and at its heart was focused on defusing the dangers of unchecked concentrated private power in an industrializing economy.[3]

Recent corporate governance reforms impose or reinforce checks and balances within firms, "mimicking traditional institutional forms of public politics like election and the separation of powers."[4] In the words of Cary Coglianese, "[p]erhaps more than ever before, corporate governance reforms bear a much closer resemblance to institutional mechanisms typically found in government."[5] Market and regulatory changes have made separation and balance more salient as a governance approach for many corporations; such an evolution is reflected *inter alia* in the nomination of independent directors, the expanded role for internal controls or the greater use of independent auditors and lawyers, as well as in a more public – and not just private – view of governance.[6] In the United States, for example, the Sarbanes–Oxley Act of 2002[7] has a profound impact on corporate governance, as it notably requires public companies to strengthen audit committees or to perform internal control tests.[8]

A firm's bylaws and other governing documents will reflect these legal requirements and, where deemed appropriate, these principles of governance. Corporate Social Responsibility, Responsible Business Conduct, and other types of self-regulations or guidelines may also play a role in the future, but for the time being they are not focused on checks and balances as such within a firm.[9] Finally, for now, the attempt to define a judicial power within or related to a firm *prima facie* leads to a dead end, but recent developments, such as the creation of an Oversight Board by Meta Platforms[10] in charge of reviewing difficult content decisions on Facebook or Instagram, call for a nuanced approach even in this regard.

---

[3] Rahman, "New Utilities," 1631.
[4] Rahman, "New Utilities," 1682 (footnote omitted); see also Grace, Prendergast & Koski-Grafer, "Board Oversight" ("It is both timely and good business for boards to put in place systems of substantive checks and balances that start with the CEO, senior management, and the board itself, and then proceed through the entire organization. Improving board and organizational oversight and governance can not only lower the risk of failures and problems in the organization, but can also bring sustainable operating benefits to a company and its shareholders"); Greenfield, "Corporate Law," 21–23 (noting that for all its limitations, corporate governance has one uniquely important feature of regulating private power not through external oversight of firm conduct, but instead by building in checks and balances within the firm itself to systematically induce firms to serve the public good).
[5] Coglianese, "Legitimacy," 161–67 (quotation from p. 161).
[6] Regarding the United States, see, e.g., Thompson, "Anti-Primacy," 402–3; Sale, "Corporation," 140–41.
[7] Public Law 107–204, Approved July 30, 2002, 116 Stat. 745, as Amended through P.L. 116–222, Enacted 18 December 2020, www.govinfo.gov/content/pkg/COMPS-1883/pdf/COMPS-1883.pdf.
[8] From the perspective of the separation of powers principle, see Coglianese, "Legitimacy," 163–65.
[9] See, e.g., United Nations, *Principles*, 16–26; OECD, *Multinational Enterprises*, 19–20.
[10] See *infra* Section 5.3 in the present Chapter.

Second, regulations, either transversal or sectoral, also partially determine or influence a firm's organization. Specific rules in this respect may, for instance, exist in data protection law, which transversally apply to all economic sectors. In the European Union, the General Data Protection Regulation contains rules regarding the designation, position, and tasks of the data protection officer within a firm.[11] Sectoral regulation in the financial or the telecommunications sectors, for instance, may contain other rules affecting a firm's organization. In the United States, for example, specific requirements relating to audit and other committees apply to regulated banks.[12]

Thirdly, antitrust does not usually influence the internal organization of firms. Compliance duties in this field certainly have an impact on the latter, but firms autonomously – at least, to a wide extent – determine their compliance mechanisms. Nevertheless, antitrust deals with the concentration of economic power. It may lead to the creation of checks and balances within or with respect to a dominant firm. This third source specifically will be investigated in this Chapter.

5.2 SEARCH FOR AN ANALOGY BETWEEN SEPARATION OF POWERS AND ANTITRUST

The search for an analogy between separation of powers and antitrust starts intuitively with the power of an agency or court to break up or unbundle a firm (5.2.1) and naturally follows with merger control (5.2.2). A more promising avenue for analogy, though, resides in the fact that firms sometimes possess, *de facto*, regulatory powers in an industry, raising concerns *inter alia* on their organization (5.2.3).

5.2.1 *Breaking Up or Unbundling Firms*

Breaking up or unbundling dominant digital companies or some of their key activities is requested or advocated by agencies,[13] politicians or even ministries,[14]

---

[11] See, for instance, Articles 37–39 of Regulation (EU) 2016/679 of the European Parliament and of the Council of 27 April 2016 on the protection of natural persons with regard to the processing of personal data and on the free movement of such data, and repealing Directive 95/46/EC (General Data Protection Regulation, OJ L 119, 4.5.2016, pp. 1–88).

[12] Code of Federal Regulations, Title XII, Chapter XII, Subchapter B, §§ 1239.5 & 1239.32.

[13] In the United States, the FTC is currently suing Facebook and is seeking a permanent injunction in federal court that could, *inter alia*, require divestitures of assets, including Instagram and WhatsApp (First amended complaint for injunctive and other equitable relief, 19 August 2021, www.ftc.gov/system/files/documents/cases/ecf_75-1_ftc_v_facebook_public_redacted_fac.pdf).

[14] Regarding Google and Facebook, see, for instance, Hawley, *Tyranny*, 150. Regarding Amazon, Facebook and Google, see Elizabeth Warren, see, for instance, Elizabeth Warren, "Here's How We Can Break Up Big Tech," *medium.com*, 8 March 2019, https://medium.com/@teamwarren/heres-how-we-can-break-up-big-tech-9ad9e0da324c and some of her tweets ("It's time to break up Facebook & finally hold them accountable," 31 October 2021, https://twitter.com/SenWarren/status/1454908911870435333). In Germany, see Bundesregierung [Federal Government], *Entwurf eines Gesetzes zur Änderung des Gesetzes gegen Wettbewerbsbeschränkungen und anderer Gesetze* [Draft

and scholars.[15] It seems difficult to draw an analogy with the separation of powers principle, as different companies – and not simply different parts of a common scheme – would result from the deconcentration of power. Of course, independent companies are, together, part of the "economic order" in ordoliberal terms, but states are also part of an "order": an international or world order. Functional separation is also envisaged in certain cases[16] and is to be differentiated from ownership separation, as separate companies are not created.

Breaking up a company into separate parts because it holds too much power might be likened to the splitting of a state regarded as too powerful but that has lost a war. The point here is not to draw an analogy. On the contrary, any separation of powers analogy would – partly, at least – be rather misleading in this context.

That said, the fact remains that breaking up or unbundling dominant digital companies or some of their key activities could deconcentrate politico-economic power, though the decision to break up companies or to unbundle commercial activities raises at least four major difficulties. They should be carefully considered before taking – or simply advocating for – such fundamental steps.

First, competition agencies, courts, or other bodies are not entitled to break up companies or unbundle commercial activities in many jurisdictions, where this antimonopoly tool simply does not exist. In other jurisdictions, it remains unclear whether it exists or when it can be used. In the European Union, for instance, a consensus on the exact contours of the possibility for the European Commission to take divestiture decisions amounting to breaking up or unbundling a firm is lacking.[17] In any event, the sole concentration of power within a firm would not suffice, as an

Act Amending the Act against Restraints of Competition and Other Laws] (Berlin: Bundesregierung, 5 April 2023), proposed Section 32f(4); Bundesministerium für Wirtschaft und Klimaschutz, *Wettbewerbspolitische Agenda*, point 9 ("In the long term, we advocate an abuse-independent unbundling option at European level as a last resort in entrenched markets." [unofficial translation]; see Kühling, "Herausforderungen," 524).

[15] See, e.g., Acemoglu & Johnson, *Power and Progress*, 405–06; (see also Thomas Fuster, "Technologieriesen sollten zerschlagen werden" [Technology Giants Should Be Broken Up], *Neue Zürcher Zeitung*, 18 February 2023, 23, quoting Daron Acemoglu); Khan & Vaheesan, "Market Power and Inequality," 291; Foer, *World*, 203–4. Regarding Amazon, for instance, see Khan, "Separation," 973–1098. See, however, Hovenkamp, "Consumer Welfare Principle," 123 ("One of the more damaging proposals directed at vertical integration is the suggestion that large platforms should choose between selling their own products or the products of others, but not be permitted to do both on the same site" [footnote omitted]). For a more nuanced approach, see Crémer, de Montjoye & Schweitzer, *Competition Policy*, 67–68 ("While there may be cases in which full platform unbundling is called for, this remedy should not be the generalised answer to the finding of an abusive self-preferencing. Less restrictive ways to effectively preclude self-preferencing may exist"). For an overview of various proposals, see UNCTAD, *Digital Economy*, paras. 31–34 & 45.

[16] See, e.g., Geradin & Katsifis, "Apple App Store," 584–85 (evoking "some form of 'functional separation' between the management of the App Store and Apple's other divisions, most notably product development" [quotation from p. 584]).

[17] See, for instance, Michael Bauer, "Art. 7 VO (EG) 1/2003" [Art. 7 of Regulation (EC) 1/2003], in Säcker, Bien, Meier-Beck & Montag (eds.), *Wettbewerbsrecht 1*, 2163–75, 2167–68, para. 22 (concluding that "[t] he break-up of dominant companies, familiar from other jurisdictions, [...] is also not permissible also

abuse resulting from the concentration in the sense of Article 102 TFEU would have to be established.[18] This task may prove herculean.

Second, a decision to break up companies or to unbundle commercial activities must comply with applicable fundamental rights, both procedural and substantive. Due process, property rights, economic freedom or equal protection especially come to mind. The need for checks and balances in the decision-making process is particularly pressing for such drastic measures.[19] All these limits and constraints form very high hedges, perhaps impassable in some jurisdictions. In Germany, for instance, breaking up companies over competition concerns due to an excessive concentration of power does not belong to the toolbox of the Federal Cartel Office, other bodies of the executive branch, or courts. A legislative reform of the German legislation in this respect[20] could run afoul of the constitutional guarantee of property and occupational freedom, depending on the case at hand.[21]

Third, proceedings for breaking up a firm is long, costly, and complex.[22] The battle in court can last for years.[23] Such a length of time creates a very uncertain economic environment, not just for the firms involved and their shareholders, but also for workers, users, consumers, business partners, or creditors, without any claim of completeness.

---

under the new cartel procedure law" [translation by the author of the present book]). For a different interpretation of this provision of regulation 1/2003, see Dorothe Dalheimer, "Art. 7 VO 1/2003," in Dalheimer, Feddersen & Miersch (eds.), *EU-Kartellverfahrensverordnung*, 56–57, paras. 13–14 (admitting that the European Commission may decide to unbundle existing dominant companies).

[18] See Article 7 of the Council Regulation (EC) No 1/2003 of 16 December 2002 on the Implementation of the Rules on Competition Laid down in Articles 81 and 82 of the Treaty (Text with EEA relevance), consolidated text. For an illustration, see European Commission, *Statement of Objections on Google's Practices in Online Advertising Technology*, 14 June 2023. Regarding EU and German law, see Franck & Peitz, "Big Tech," 88 ("Neither in the EU nor in Germany can divestiture be ordered as an (objective) instrument of market regulation"); Jochen Anweiler, "Art. 7 VerfVO" [Art. 7 of Regulation (EC) 1/2003], in Loewenheim, Meessen, Riesenkampff, Kersting & Meyer-Lindemann (eds.), *Kartellrecht*, 1149–69, 1167, para. 60.

[19] See, e.g., Marco Colino, "Incursion of Antitrust," 256–57.

[20] See Bundesregierung [Federal Government], *Entwurf eines Gesetzes zur Änderung des Gesetzes gegen Wettbewerbsbeschränkungen und anderer Gesetze* [Draft Act Amending the Act against Restraints of Competition and Other Laws] (Berlin: Bundesregierung, 5 April 2023), proposed Section 32f(4); Kühling, "Herausforderungen," 524. See *infra* Part III, Chapter 8, Section 8.3.

[21] Articles 14 and 12 of the German Basic Law, translation at www.gesetze-im-internet.de/englisch_gg/englisch_gg.html#p0064. See Nettesheim & Thomas, *Entflechtung*, 85–139.

[22] See, e.g., Usman, "Breaking Up Big Tech," 545–47; Fukuyama, "Loaded Weapon." Regarding Facebook, see Frenkel & Kang, *Truth*, 300 ("Zuckerberg and Sandberg built a business that has become an unstoppable profit-making machine that could prove too powerful to break up"). See, however, Van Loo, "Breakups," 1995–98 ("Costly Breakups May Increase Deterrence").

[23] See, e.g., Fukuyama, "Internet Safe for Democracy," 40. Regarding the Federal Trade Commission's antitrust lawsuit against Facebook Inc., now Meta Platforms (Civil Action No. 20-3590 before the United States District Court for the District of Columbia), see Martin Peers, "The Briefing: What FTC's Meta Victory Means," *The Information*, 11 January 2022, www.theinformation.com/articles/what-ftc-s-meta-victory-means (making the following comment after the Court denied on 11 January 2022 Facebook's motion to dismiss the case: "The FTC's ultimate goal is to force Meta to divest Instagram and/or WhatsApp in what would effectively be a breakup of the tech giant. We're a long way from there, of course […]. The government still has to prove that acquisitions of Instagram and WhatsApp harmed competition and led to poor services for consumers. The substantive part of the case isn't likely to be heard for years. Let the real battle begin").

The final decision may come too late or not address the fundamental issues at stake,[24] possibly at a time where the industry and the competition concerns have changed.[25] Moreover, breaking up firms like Microsoft, Meta Platforms, Amazon, and Alphabet or solely Google may only slightly reduce their political influence and power,[26] and the problems identified could be perpetuated within their ecosystems or with other firms.[27]

Fourth, the consequences and benefits for consumers[28] or other stakeholders[29] and, more broadly, for society and even democracy[30] of such a decision remain

---

[24] See Moore & Tambini, "Holistic Vision," 342 ("Legal action will take years, involve tortuous nego-tiation, and eventually result in complex compromise. The companies that emerge at the end of it will be the products of legal process, not democratic design"); Lakier, *Limits*, 3–5; see also Stucke, *Breaking Away*, 107–9.

[25] Regarding Facebook, see Josh Sisco, "Decision on Facebook Breakup Likely Won't Come Until 2025," *The Information*, 3 March 2022, www.theinformation.com/briefings/decision-on-facebook-breakup-likely-wont-come-until-2025?utm_source=sg&utm_medium=email&utm_campaign=article_email&utm_content=article-7378; Martin Peers, "The Briefing: Why Disney's Ad-Streaming Move Would Be a Big Deal," *The Information*, 3 March 2022, www.theinformation.com/articles/why-disney-s-ad-streaming-move-would-be-a-big-deal ("By the time this case is decided, we might even know what the meta-verse is!"). Regarding the acquisition of Giphy by Meta Platforms, see Martin Peers, "The Briefing: Microstrategy's All-or-Nothing Bitcoin Bet," *The Information*, 29 March 2022, www.theinformation.com/articles/microstrategy-s-all-or-nothing-bitcoin-bet ("TikTok today unveiled a new tool featuring content from Giphy that people can use to jazz up their videos. This deal is *exactly* what Britain's Competition and Markets Authority argued would not happen if Meta was allowed to keep Giphy […]. Maybe Meta struck this deal just to prove the CMA wrong. Or maybe the CMA was just wrong. Either way, its argu-ments no longer hold much water. But regulators being regulators, you can bet it will waste more money fighting a legal action to try to force the unwinding of a now two-year-old acquisition"). On 14 June 2022, the Competition Appeal Tribunal ruled, on a procedural ground, in favor of Meta Platforms in its appeal against the CMA's order demanding that Meta sells GIF, but did not reject CMA's finding that the deal could harm competition ([2022] CAT 26, Case No. 1429/4/12/21; see, e.g., Smith, "Meta/Giphy"). See also Winston, "Antitrust," 274. On 18 October 2022, the CMA published its final report on the case remitted by the Competition Appeal Tribunal and decided again to require the full divestiture of Giphy (see https://assets.publishing.service.gov.uk/media/635017428fa8f53463dcb9f2/Final_Report_Meta.GIPHY.pdf). Meta accepted the ruling (see James Vincent, "Meta Says It Will Sell Off Giphy Following Order from UK Competition Watchdog," *The Verge*, 18 October 2022, www.theverge.com/2022/10/18/23410487/meta-sell-off-giphy-following-uk-cma-competition-ruling) and sold Giphy in 2023.

[26] Acemoglu & Johnson, *Power and Progress*, 405–06; Lakier, *Limits*, 4–5; see also Fukuyama, "Internet Safe for Democracy," 40.

[27] Ezrachi & Stucke, *Barons*, 176 ("So even if Facebook were broken up and displaced by TikTok, would we benefit? Yes, in some ways […]. If TikTok builds out its ecosystem on behavioral advertising, the toxic competition and toxic innovation will continue") & 193–96.

[28] See Hovenkamp, "Consumer Welfare Principle," 123 and "Antitrust and Platform Monopoly," 2010 ("Breaking up any platform subject to significant economies of scale threatens to be socially costly. It would force ineffi-ciencies on all postbreakup constituents as well as cause consumer harm"); Jenny, "Digital Ecosystems," 1150 ("A challenge for competition authorities is to prevent quality degradation due to the increased market power of platforms while keeping the quality benefits due to the size of the platform. Deconcentration measures may simultaneously affect both dimensions, thus leading to uncertain results for users' welfare").

[29] See Hovenkamp, "Abuse of Dominance" ("Simply breaking them [very large firms] up hurts not only consumers, who will pay higher prices and face lower quality and less innovation, but it also harms workers, whose output is proportional to product output. The better approach is to scrutinize the conduct of dominant firms carefully"); see also Stucke, "Relationship," 17 ("[…] Nor will breaking [data-opolies] apart necessarily promote our privacy, autonomy, and well-being").

[30] See Cohen & Fung, "Democracy," 45–47.

extremely uncertain. Any decision is highly speculative and constitutes a bet. Overall, history has not – always – been kind to decisions to break up companies, notably in the United States.[31] This should lead to a very thorough analysis of all the markets at stake and to an extreme caution before using this tool,[32] even in *ultima ratio*. In the digital and artificial intelligence era, firms with bundled activities may offer products with substantial added value to consumers and businesses.[33] Moreover, breaking up highly integrated platforms may prove enormously difficult, if not impossible.[34]

All things considered, breaking up dominant digital companies or unbundling some of their key activities should not be presented as a miracle tool or as a sort of *deus ex machina*. Herbert Hovenkamp, for instance, is generally skeptical on divestiture, structural breakup, line-of-business restrictions, or breaking apart assets or units with respect to digital platforms.[35] The intervention of antitrust or regulatory agencies must be more focused and subtle. In other words, the contribution of governmental agencies or courts to break up companies or to unbundle their key activities to the deconcentration of political-economic power in private hands may prove chimerical. Breaking up companies cannot be the core of a sound and reliable competition policy in the digital and artificial intelligence era, while it may be justified on very rare occasions, in extraordinary circumstances. Otherwise, antitrust agencies would run the risk of riding the horse of Don Quixote going to fight against windmills.

5.2.2 *Merger Control and Politico-Economic Power*

An analogy between merger control and separation of powers would also be based on a partially truncated perception of the foundations of the two. As properly understood, the latter is concerned with checks and balances between "powers." By contrast, merger control usually aims at avoiding the substantial lessening of competition or significant impediment of effective competition.

---

[31] Hovenkamp, "Antitrust and Platform Monopoly," 2008; O'Donoghue & Padilla, *Article 102 TFEU*, 1201; Kovacic, "Failed Expectations," 1105–50. For a positive assessment, see Kwoka & Valletti, "Unscrambling the Eggs," 1292–99; Van Loo, "Breakups," 1961–94.

[32] See, e.g., Bernhardt & Voges, "Kartellrechtsdurchsetzung," 651–56; Geradin, Katsifis & Karanikioti, "Google," 680 ("[S]eparation remedies are particularly drastic and may result in inefficient market outcomes, or even send the wrong policy signals to companies, potentially freezing innovation, hence they should be used with caution. Even so, we do not see why under certain conditions (such as when antitrust concerns cannot be effectively addressed through less intrusive means) regulators should not have recourse to such tools"); see also Akcigit *et al.*, *Market Power*, 25–26, para. 43.

[33] Priest, "Monopolies"; Hovenkamp, "Antitrust and Platform Monopoly," 2010; see also Crane, "Antitrust and Democracy," 9; Susskind, *Digital Republic*, 243; Durand, *Techno-féodalisme*, 228–29.

[34] Hovenkamp, "Antitrust and Platform Monopoly," 2010; see also Philippon, *Reversal*, 276.

[35] Hovenkamp, "Antitrust and Platform Monopoly," 2007–16, 2039 & 2050 ("As the long history of antitrust shows, breaking apart assets can be dangerous because it threatens losses of beneficial economies of scale or scope" [quotation from p. 2050]); see also Shapiro, "Antitrust," 42–43 ("More fundamentally, breaking up monopolies and oligopolies on a 'no-fault' basis would be fighting against powerful, underlying economic forces associated with economies of scale and scope that are a pervasive feature of advanced economies around the world").

However, they share the common goal of averting excessive concentration of power. As such, antitrust and competition laws focus on economic power and widely disregard political power. This limit is certainly debatable, but there are strong arguments for competition agencies and courts to remain economically focused, at least in this context.[36] One may indeed skeptically view the idea that an antitrust authority or a court could block a merger or break up a company solely on the basis of the excessive political influence the latter may gain or have. Empirical data and methods are lacking on this subject,[37] and neither an antitrust authority nor a court possess the tools to assess whether a company has or would gain excessive political influence in a given jurisdiction.[38] Of course, tools may be developed in the future,[39] and cases of abusive discrimination are another story,[40] but, all things considered, the balancing of fundamentally political considerations is probably better left out of the hands of such an authority or court, as emphasized by Carl Shapiro:

> Asking the DOJ, the FTC to evaluate mergers and business conduct based on the political power of the firms involved would invite corruption by allowing the executive branch to punish its enemies and reward its allies through the antitrust cases brought, or not brought, by antitrust enforcers. On top of that, asking the courts to approve or block mergers based on the political power of the merging firms would undermine the rule of law while inevitably drawing the judicial branch into deeply political considerations. Let me be clear: the corrupting power of money in politics in the United States is perhaps the gravest threat facing democracy in America. But this profound threat to democracy and to equality of opportunity is far better addressed through campaign finance reform, increased transparency, and anti-corruption rules than by antitrust.[41]

However, the problem is broader and does not only lie in the "corrupting power of money in politics." The concentration of politico-economic power in the digital era raises democratic concerns since the digital infrastructure of democracy[42] and

[36] Baker, *Antitrust Paradigm*, 59–61; see also Hovenkamp, "Slogans and Goals," 106 ("Most statements of antitrust's purpose are economic, consistent with the language of the statutes"). From a historical perspective, see Posner, *Antitrust*, 35. Regarding President Biden's Executive Order on Promoting Competition in the American Economy of 9 July 2021, see Hovenkamp, "Executive Order," 386–87. For a different view on this matter, see Susskind, *Digital Republic*, 245–46; Foroohar, *Don't Be Evil*, 190 (calling for "citizen welfare" to replace "consumer welfare" as the test for merger control).
[37] See, e.g., Shapiro, "Populism," 716; Maier-Rigaud, "Foundations," 165–66.
[38] Katz, "Chicago School," 450.
[39] Katz, "Chicago School," 450–54; see also Robertson, "Antitrust, Big Tech, and Democracy," 260, 273 & 278 ("There still is a considerable way to go before it is possible to assess whether democracy-related harm is, indeed, a justiciable antitrust harm" [quotation from p. 278]); Posner & Weyl, *Radical Markets*, 203. For an integrated model deemed to capture the circularity between political decisions and market competition, see Callander, Foarta & Sugaya, "Market Competition and Political Influence," 2750 ("[I]f a proposed merger would create a clear market leader that, following the logic of our model, would have the power to win protection from an industry regulator, the prospect of capture of that regulator should be factored into merger reviews by the antitrust authority").
[40] See *infra* Chapter 6, Section 6.4.
[41] Shapiro, "Populism," 716 & 745–46 (quotation from p. 716, footnote omitted); see also Werden, *Foundations*, 333–4; Hovenkamp, "Consumer Welfare Principle," 125–30; Fukuyama, "Loaded Weapon."
[42] See *supra* Part I, Chapter 4, Section 4.3.

possibly private regulatory power[43] are at stake. That said, the contribution of anti-trust *de lege lata* to avoid excessive concentration of political power is, at best, lim-ited and, in any case, indirect. The recurring question that runs through this book remains, though: What if there is no appropriate regulation?

With regard to merger control, deeply democratic considerations may still come into play. There may indeed be a case for a political interdiction that would follow an authorization of a given merger or acquisition by the relevant competition author-ity, especially when a merger poses a threat to democracy. The risks posed by such a procedure should be carefully assessed before reforming the applicable laws in a given country or union of states like the European Union. Such a procedure does not seem to exist in any democratic jurisdiction until now, so that this issue will be examined separately from a *de lege ferenda* perspective in the last part of this book.[44]

For now, and in the short to medium term, merger control, as performed by com-petition agencies and courts, remains, and will most probably remain, economi-cally focused. This does not mean that it should not evolve. The so-called killer acquisitions or, more broadly, the acquisitions of innovative, potentially disruptive, start-ups – as pure killer acquisitions are reportedly rare[45] – are especially of concern in the digital economy.[46] A change in the practice – at least a higher scrutiny – of antitrust agencies, or even in the policy,[47] may be justified in this respect, bearing in mind the "heightened uncertainty in nascent mergers."[48] Acquisitions of nascent firms by incumbent dominant companies should be investigated rigorously and blocked where necessary.[49] However, such a change would not directly aim at pre-venting the concentration of power, but rather to preserve innovation and future competition.[50] In this respect, an analogy with the separation of powers principle, even envisaged broadly, would be a rather far stretch in this context as well.

---

[43] See *infra* 3 & Section 5.3 in this chapter.

[44] See *infra* Part III, Chapter 10, Section 10.1.

[45] Witt, "Conglomerate Mergers," 230–31; Crémer, de Montjoye & Schweitzer, *Competition Policy*, 117.

[46] See, e.g., Ezrachi & Stucke, *Barons*, 38, 82–83 & 86–90.

[47] OECD, *Start-ups*, 49 ("[S]ome agencies have used the flexibility of their legal and analytical frame-works to quickly move to begin to enforce merger control in this previously neglected field. However, for others it is more difficult, and indeed even those that have moved quickly may face setbacks along the way, therefore policy change may be necessary to be confident that agencies can successfully chal-lenge the anticompetitive nascent acquisitions that need to be challenged to fulfil agencies' duty to protect competition and consumers from harm"). See also Stucke, *Breaking Away*, 32, 38–39 & 69–70; Baker & Comanor, "Antitrust Agenda," 69; Cunningham, Ederer & Ma, "Killer Acquisitions," 696–97; Salop, "Dominant Digital Platforms," 578–86; Mackenzie, Goeteyn, Mantine & Westrup, "Metaverse"; Philippon, *Reversal*, 274. Regarding the United States, see *infra* Part III, Chapter 8, Section 8.8.

[48] OECD, *Start-ups*, 49; see also Yun, "Potential Competition," 675–78.

[49] OECD, *Start-ups*, 49; Ezrachi & Stucke, *Barons*, 162–63 & 186–87.

[50] See Summers, "Policy" ("[W]e need to recognize when we address technology companies, that if we prevent startup companies from ever being purchased by larger companies, we may interfere with competition by discouraging startup companies who no longer have the exit route of acquisition. So there are very difficult balances that need to be struck").

5.2.3 *Public or Private Regulation and Antitrust*

A more convincing and relevant analogy comes to mind when a company remains intact, but its organization is modified to address the issue of concentration or abuse of power.[51] The changes would not simply reflect the requirements of the applicable corporate or sectoral laws and of governance and best-practice rules but would be based upon antitrust and competition laws and would seek to prevent and remedy abuses of power. Depending on the situation, separation of powers-type arguments would be used by analogy.

The most salient example relates to the role of platforms as *regulators*. Alibaba Group Holding Limited (Alibaba), Alphabet Inc. (Alphabet), Amazon.com, Inc. (Amazon), Apple Inc. (Apple), Baidu, Inc. (Baidu), ByteDance Ltd. (ByteDance), Kakao Corporation (Kakao), Meta Platforms, Inc. (Meta Platforms), Microsoft Corporation (Microsoft), and Tencent Holdings Ltd. (Tencent), for instance, or some of their subsidiaries may indeed exercise *de facto* regulatory functions. When they adopt important rules relating to the functioning of their platforms and their ecosystems, they may face fundamental conflicts of interests because they are usually active in other markets. On 17 July 2019, the European Commission decided to initiate antitrust proceedings on Amazon's use of commercially sensitive information available to Amazon's marketplace operations, particularly regarding third party sellers, products listed by third party sellers, or transactions with third party sellers on Amazon's marketplace for the purposes of Amazon's retail activities in the European Economic Area.[52] As emphasized in the press release, "Amazon has a dual role as a platform: (i) it sells products on its website as a retailer; and (ii) it provides a marketplace where independent sellers can sell products directly to consumers."[53] On 10 November 2020, the Commission sent a Statement of Objections to Amazon for the use of nonpublic seller data and opened a second investigation on possible preferential treatment of Amazon's retail business or of the sellers that use Amazon's logistics and delivery services.[54] On 14 July 2022, the European Commission invited comments on commitments offered by Amazon to address competition concerns, notably over its use of nonpublic marketplace seller data.[55] In December 2022, the European Commission made commitments offered by Amazon legally binding under EU competition rules; the commitments will ensure, among other things,

---

[51] See, by analogy, Müller, "Infrastructure," 277 (underlining "the need for intermediary powers within Intermediary powers" such as political parties or media).

[52] Case AT.40462 Amazon Marketplace.

[53] Opening of Proceedings and Press Release, 17 July 2019, https://ec.europa.eu/competition/elojade/isef/case_details.cfm?proc_code=1_40462). Regarding Apple's and Google's "dual role," see Budzinski & Stöhr, "Competition Policy Reform," 48. On the elimination of conflicts of interests as a policy motivation and a functional goal of structural separations, see Khan, "Separation," 1052–55.

[54] Press Release, 10 November 2022, see also the press release relating to the Statement of Objections sent to Amazon, 10 November 2020, https://ec.europa.eu/commission/presscorner/detail/en/ip_20_2077.

[55] Press Release, 14 July 2022, https://ec.europa.eu/commission/presscorner/detail/en/ip_22_4522.

that Amazon does not use nonpublic marketplace seller data for its own retail operations.[56]

Furthermore, norms adopted by certain digital firms, such as community guidelines or standards,[57] can set standards for the rest of the industry.[58] This regulatory function is not subject to checks and balances like the ones faced by a public body adopting regulations, adding to the concentration of power within the hands of a few firms, as noted by the Organisation for Economic Co-operation and Development or by Damien Geradin, Dimitrios Katsifis, and Theano Karanikioti:

> The impact on the market and the negotiating position vis-a-vis users can reach a point where a gatekeeper platform amounts to a sort of private regulator, which is able to set rules on the market whilst being subject neither to accountability through democratic checks and balances (like public regulators) nor to market discipline.[59]
>
> [I]n contrast to public regulators whose decisions are adopted after lengthy processes and are subject to judicial review, *de facto* privacy regulators are not constrained in any meaningful way in the exercise of their power (lest an affected company succeeds in obtaining an injunction in court), nor are they subject to any democratic oversight. In the context of online advertising, Google and Apple get to decide for everyone the "right" trade-off between privacy, competition and efficiency, and impose their value judgment on all ecosystem participants. Despite such power, these companies are not held accountable for their decisions, even though these affect millions of businesses and may fundamentally reshape whole industries.[60]

In the words of Tom Wheeler, Phil Verveer, and Gene Kimmelman, "the dominant digital platforms have become governments unto themselves with the ability to

---

[56] Press Release, 20 December 2022, https://ec.europa.eu/commission/presscorner/detail/en/ip_22_7777. See Javier Espinoza, "Amazon Agrees Final Deal to Close EU Antitrust Probes," *Financial Times*, online edition, 6 December 2022, www.ft.com/content/86ae600a-0000-420c-b193-ba2bc6of6f03.

[57] See, e.g., Kissinger, Schmidt & Huttenlocher, *Age of AI*, 97 ("Although in principle most network platforms are content-agnostic, in some situations their community standards become as influential as national laws"); Busch, "Self-Regulation," 118–19.

[58] See Teachout & Khan, "Taxonomy of Power," 53–55. Regarding Amazon, see Stoller, *Goliath*, 444 ("Today, Amazon is an infrastructure and data conglomerate that is well on its way to becoming the intermediary of all commerce. It is a gatekeeper to online buying, with roughly half of all online retail coming through Amazon. This means that Amazon can impose conditions on any merchant that seeks to sell online, and it does so with abandon"); Stacy Mitchell, "Amazon Doesn't Just Want to Dominate the Market — It Wants to Become the Market," *The Nation*, 15 February 2018, www.thenation.com/article/archive/amazon-doesnt-just-want-to-dominate-the-market-it-wants-to-become-the-market/ ("[Amazon] can set the terms by which other companies have access to these pipelines, while also levying, through the fees it charges, a tax on their trade. In other words, it's moving us away from a democratic political economy, in which commerce takes place in open markets governed by public rules, and toward a future in which the exchange of goods occurs in a private arena governed by Amazon").

[59] OECD, *Ex Ante Regulation*, 10.

[60] Geradin, Katsifis & Karanikioti, "Google," 620 & 643–48 (calling tech platforms *de facto* privacy regulators [quotation from p. 645]).

impose their own set of rules on economic activities and consumer choices."[61] They possess norm-setting power,[62] and – to quote Damian Tambini and Martin Moore – "when platforms write rules they in fact write laws."[63] They especially assume the role of private regulators when they enjoy a gatekeeper position.[64] More generally, "they are taking on configurations that are increasingly similar to the state and other public authorities," as observed by Andrea Simoncini and Erik Longo.[65]

From a historical perspective at least, regulatory powers in private hands[66] can trigger the application of antitrust laws, as Thomas B. Nachbar and Ariel Katz opportunely remind us:

> Although it does protect against harms to efficiency, antitrust also protects interests similar to those protected by the public/private distinction in constitutional law. Not merely a rule of economic regulation, antitrust is a rule against private regulation […]. Although regulation is essential to the operation of a free society, centuries of constitutional tradition demand that such regulation come from public rather than private sources. Private regulation is anathema to our system of ordered liberty, and the antitrust laws are a part of a larger constitutional structure that polices such improper restrictions on liberty.[67]
>
> Ensuring that private actors do not assume regulatory powers – the grant and exercise of which is the province of the state – has been an important goal of antitrust.[68]

The private origin of important norms is not specific to platforms. *Lex mercatoria* and standards, like ISO norms, have already been mentioned in Chapter 1.[69] However, these norms were, or are, elaborated by many stakeholders. Amazon's, Facebook's/Meta Platforms' or Google's/Alphabet's standards, codes of conduct, guidelines, or rules[70] are prepared and adopted within one firm, over which – we may recall – one or two individuals ultimately have controlling voting power or *de facto* enormous influence. The role

---

[61] Wheeler, Verveer & Kimmelman, *New Digital Realities*, 6; see also Tepper with Hearn, *Capitalism*, 109 ("The power of platforms makes them a different class of companies. They set the rules that govern their world. We simply live in it").

[62] Wagner, "Free Expression," 230–31; see also Stucke, *Breaking Away*, 90–91 ("Google and Facebook have become the 'de facto regulators' of online advertising, and we pay the price" [quotation from p. 90; one footnote omitted]) & 170 ("Under their quasi-regulatory regime, the data-opolies will continue to set the rules around surveillance and data sharing not just within their ecosystems but for other market participants").

[63] Tambini & Moore, "Dominance," 406.

[64] Schweitzer, "Digitale Plattformen," 4–7; Busch, Graef, Hofmann & Gawer, *Platform Power*, 5–6; see also Busch, "Self-Regulation," 117–20.

[65] Simoncini & Longo, "Fundamental Rights and the Rule of Law," 33.

[66] See, e.g., Dolata, "Platform Regulation," 467–72.

[67] Nachbar, "Antitrust Constitution," 69, 88–93 & 114 (quotation from pp. 69 & 114); see also, from a historical (U.S.) perspective, Fishkin & Forbath, *Constitution*, 140 & 164–65. From an ordoliberal perspective, see Böhm, "Problem der privaten Macht," 58 and "Democracy and Economic Power," 271 & 279.

[68] Katz, "Chicago School," 423–28 (quotation from p. 423); see also, from a German and European perspective, Persch, "Fundamental Rights," 556.

[69] See *supra* Part I, Chapter 1, Section 1.3.

[70] On the distinction between standards and rules, see Kahneman, Sibony & Sunstein, *Noise*, 250–60 (with respect to Facebook, see pp. 353–54).

of Elon Musk within X/Twitter is evolving... Alibaba's, notwithstanding the recent decision to split into six independent business units,[71] Baidu's, or Tencent's principles, codes, or rules seem to be, at least tacitly, controlled by the Chinese Government.[72] In the future, Microsoft and OpenAI may together define fundamental rules regarding generative artificial intelligence. On the basis of antitrust, dominant platforms may actually face specific obligations relating to the rule-setting function they exercise, as outlined in the highly influential report prepared by Jacques Crémer, Yves-Alexandre de Montjoye, and Heike Schweitzer for the European Commission:

> [M]any platforms, in particular marketplaces, actually act as regulators, setting up the rules and institutions through which their users interact. [...] [B]ecause of this function as regulators, the operators of dominant platforms have a responsibility to ensure that competition on their platforms is fair, unbiased, and pro-users. [...] [D]ominant platforms have a responsibility to ensure that the rules they choose do not impede free, undistorted and vigorous competition without objective justification.[73]

Additionally, transparency may also be a competition policy issue. According to the democratic participation principle of the Montréal Declaration for a Responsible Development of Artificial Intelligence, "[t]he code for algorithms, whether public or private, must always be accessible to the relevant public authorities and stakeholders

---

[71] See "A Six-way Bet," *The Economist*, 1 April 2023, 56 ("The main unspoken goal may be to decentralize decision-making, not least by disassociating Alibaba further from its founder").

[72] "Big Tech's $2trn Bull Run," *The Economist*, 22 February 2020, 7 ("China keeps its internet giants under tacit state control") & "Alibaba and the 40 Officials," *The Economist*, 7 May 2022, 56–57 ("The entrepreneurs behind China's biggest tech successes have come to a grim reckoning: that because of government meddling they will be unable to innovate, and may even become boring" [quotation from p. 56]); see also Lévêque, *Entreprises hyperpuissantes*, 152–55. The State Administration for Market Regulation communicated, on 24 December 2020, that it had opened an investigation into whether Alibaba has engaged in monopolistic practices, such as restricting vendors from selling merchandise on other platforms (see Raymond Zhong, "Beijing Reins in Tech Behemoths It Let Run Free," *New York Times*, 25 December 2020, A1). From a broader perspective, see Juro Osawa & Shai Oster, "How China Broke Up with Its Internet Companies," *The Information*, 14 October 2021, www.theinformation.com/articles/the-end-of-a-fare-why-china-broke-up-with-didi?utm_source=sg&utm_medium=email&utm_campaign=article_email&utm_content=article-6899; Jeanne Whalen, "Chinese Government Acquires Stake in Domestic Unit of TikTok Owner ByteDance in Another Sign of Tech Crackdown: Government also Took One of Three Board Seats at the Subsidiary, Which Controls a Similar App inside China," *Washington Post*, online edition, 17 August 2021, www.washingtonpost.com/technology/2021/08/17/chinese-government-bytedance-tiktok/ ("China's move comes amid a months-long push by Beijing to assert more control over a domestic technology sector that has spawned a variety of successful and powerful companies active in social media, music streaming, online shopping and mobile payments").

[73] Crémer, de Montjoye & Schweitzer, *Competition Policy*, 60–62; see also David Streitfeld, "As Amazon Rises, So Does the Opposition," *New York Times*, 19 April 2020, BU1 (quoting Stacy Mitchell: "If we don't regulate Amazon, we are effectively allowing it to regulate us"). In the European Union, see Regulation (EU) 2019/1150 of the European Parliament and of the Council of 20 June 2019 on Promoting Fairness and Transparency for Business Users of Online Intermediation Services (OJ L 186, 11 July 2019, 57).

for verification and control purposes."[74] Through the lack of transparency of its rules or the way in which it applies the latter, a dominant platform may distort competition and, thus, infringe antitrust or competition laws.[75] Transparency – probably not full, due to the protection of privacy and business secrets, for instance[76] – in this regard, and more importantly, explicability could allow better assessments of whether algorithms produce anticompetitive – and, by the way, possibly antidemocratic – effects in the relevant market.[77] More generally, transparency, explainability, and interpretability in artificial intelligence[78] also help elaborate and enact appropriate legislation and regulation.[79] Explainability and interpretability are supposed to determine whether humans are able to accurately explain and interpret the results of, for instance, an algorithm. From a political perspective, the opacity of complex algorithms may distort the electoral or democratic process when the platform at stake structures public debate and access to information. A duty to transparency may be justified from this perspective as well.[80]

Now, how do you make sure that the rules and institutions involved meet these standards? For instance, does the management of Alibaba, Alphabet, Amazon, Apple, Baidu, ByteDance, Kakao, Meta Platforms, Microsoft, or Tencent provide sufficient guarantees that they will adopt fair, unbiased, transparent, and pro-user rules, bearing in mind that these companies are active in several markets?[81] The answers to these questions may trigger organizational issues. In this respect, the *ex post* control by competition

---

[74] *Montréal Declaration for a Responsible Development of Artificial Intelligence*, principle 5 ("Democratic participation principle"), para. 3.

[75] Regarding EU competition law, see Crémer, de Montjoye & Schweitzer, *Competition Policy*, 63–65; see also Botta & Wiedemann, "Exploitative Conducts," 472 & 475. From a broader perspective, see Stigler Committee, *Final Report*, 187–90 (recommending increasing the transparency of digital platforms); see also Rose-Ackerman, *Democracy*, 120–21 ("Private standard-setters and regulators may engage in self-serving behavior either in setting standards or in limiting entry. Whenever their actions affect the public interest, even if only indirectly, the law should require them to carry out open and transparent processes and to make their standards and rules freely available to the public"). See, however, Mäihäniemi, *Competition Law*, 297.

[76] See, e.g., Jean, *Algorithmes*, 132–33.

[77] See, e.g., Lovdahl Gormsen, "Consumer Choice," 83–84; Susskind, *Future Politics*, 364–56.

[78] On these notions, see, e.g., Jean, *Algorithmes*, 125–40, 176, 211–12 & 215 (concluding that "the search for explainability of an algorithm is, in most cases, much more relevant than its transparency" [quotation from p. 133; translation by the author of the present book]); see also Nemitz, "Constitutional Democracy," 13 ("[T]he claim of tech giants that explanations of how AI functions and how it has arrived at decisions are not possible must be rejected").

[79] See, e.g., Cai & Wang, "Middle Ground," 252; Jean, *Algorithmes*, 24. See, however, Le Cun, *Machine*, 352.

[80] See Simons & Ghosh, *Utilities for Democracy*, 12–13 ("Democratic utilities [such as Facebook and Google] should be required to explain how their systems are designed and articulate the principles that underpin them, and develop consistent approaches to publish data that sheds greater light on the impact they have on public debate" [quotation from p. 13]); see also Buchmann, "Demokratie und Öffentlichkeit," 21; Chavalarias, *Data*, 263–64; Ménissier, "Moment machiavélien," 72–73 & 78; Patino, *Civilisation*, 138.

[81] See, e.g., Ezrachi & Stucke, *Barons*, 138 (rhetorically asking "Are the Tech Barons' interests aligned with our interests?").

authorities may prove too slow and come too late, even with interim measures.[82] "Too little, too late" is a criticism that is often levelled at competition and antitrust agencies with regard to their interventions against large digital platforms.[83] *Ex ante* public regulation could be an answer,[84] but such regulation would need to be based on laws according to the rule of law. This raises three difficult problems.

First, government and parliament may not be willing to adopt appropriate rules – and leave, consciously or unconsciously, the matter to antitrust[85] – or may not know what kind of rules would be adequate, as noted by Daniel Kahneman, Olivier Sibony, and Cass R. Sunstein.[86] Regulation is often discussed and called for but, like *Godot*, may never come,[87] which is, by the way, sometimes

---

[82] See, for instance, CMA, *Mobile Ecosystems*, 350 ("Our current powers are important, but they can be too slow for fast-moving digital markets, and are focused on fixing problems after the fact, rather than preventing them before they arise. While they work well across the economy, they are less well suited to some of the specific challenges we see in digital markets today and are much less well suited to tackling ongoing and evolving concerns in markets"); Ezrachi & Stucke, *Barons*, 173–75 (concluding that "even if the Tech Barons eventually lose the antitrust battles, they still win" [quotation from p. 175]); Witt, "Taming Tech Giants," 187; Eifert, Metzger, Schweitzer & Wagner, "Taming the Giants," 1025; Veljanovski, "Algorithmic Antitrust," 62; Wheeler, Verveer & Kimmelman, *New Digital Realities*, 29 & 36. See also Javier Espinoza, "How Big Tech Lost the Antitrust Battle with Europe," *Financial Times*, online edition, 21 March 2022, www.ft.com/content/cbb1fe40-860d-4013-bfcf-b75ee6e30206, and "EU to Unveil Landmark Legislation to Tackle Market Power of Big Tech," *Financial Times*, online edition, 23 March 2022, www.ft.com/content/1c66027d-717f-4d71-b76b-34077721a678 (quoting Thierry Breton, the EU's internal market commissioner: "We have tried in the past to address gatekeeper issues through competition cases. But these cases can take years and in the meantime the harm to SMEs and innovators is done"); Amelia Fletcher, "Big Tech: How Can We Promote Competition in Digital Platform Markets?" *Economics Observatory*, 16 June 2021.

[83] See, e.g., Kühling, "Herausforderungen," 528.

[84] See, e.g., UNCTAD, *Digital Economy*, para. 30. From a broader perspective, see Crémer, de Montjoye & Schweitzer, *Competition Policy*, 52–53 ("In some situations, [...] some issues are closely related to the existence of market power, but arise frequently and systematically enough that a new regulatory regime is warranted. In other situations, the case-by-case approach of competition law will be found to remain the most appropriate legal framework"); see also Patino, *Civilisation*, 147–48.

[85] From a broader perspective, see Crane, "Antitrust's Unconventional Politics," 135 ("From the Sherman Act forward, [...] it is certain that antitrust has often been deployed as a foil to more interventionist forms of regulation"); see also Budzinski & Stöhr, "Competition Policy Reform," 54 ("If antitrust policy does not 'tame the tech titans', other regulation, which is less driven by free-market ideas, becomes more probable").

[86] Kahneman, Sibony & Sunstein, *Noise*, 352–53 & 355; see also Tamke, "Big Data," 383 ("[T]he rapid developments of digital markets could be better taken into account by applying the corrective measures of competition law rather than introducing less flexible ex ante regulation").

[87] Regarding this problem, see, e.g., Hovenkamp, "Antitrust Duty to Deal," 1556; Editorial Board of the Washington Post, "Holding Facebook Accountable," *Washington Post*, 18 May 2020, A20 (regarding, for example, privacy harms or insufficient disclosure obligations in elections messaging and advertising: "Governments ought to set rules of their own, and this country's legislature has fallen short"); see also Brooke Masters, "Apple Has Too Much Power over Its Rivals," *Financial Times*, online edition, 1 November 2021, www.ft.com/content/94d9f964-10d8-4ff3-9781-821f3fc9ee3a ("Big Tech has opened up new markets while amassing immense power in a previously ungoverned area [...]. Regulators need to catch up. We need a Cyberspace Commerce Commission to start setting boundaries. And we need it soon"). Regarding the United States, see Martin Peers, "The Briefing: Why Elizabeth Holmes

preferable![88] Moreover, regulation may prove *ex ante* in theory, but *ex post* in practice, as it is rightfully based on market experience or consumers' behavior but arrives when the to-be-solved problems have vanished and new ones are arising.[89] In additions to this, it may have unintended consequences.[90] In any event, how do you determine whether a rule promotes fair, unbiased, or pro-user competition in evolving markets?

Second, when regulation exists, it may be influenced by lobbies and potentially not serve the interests of consumers or users appropriately. The list of ineffective or even counterproductive regulations – often adopted after intense lobbying from various stakeholders – is long, unfortunately.[91] Due to its transversal and general nature, antitrust is probably, *ceteris paribus*, less subject to the decisive influence or even capture by a given economic actor or sector.[92] Furthermore, Section 2 of the Sherman Act, Article 102 TFEU or similar provisions in other jurisdictions are placed in the hands of antitrust or competition authorities – that is, nonpolitical bodies that are supposed to act independently in many countries, including in the United States, at least with respect to the Federal Trade Commission – and courts.[93]

Third, the issues raised by digital platforms are not specific to a given country[94] but are, regrettably, often addressed at national level – the European Union is

---

Shouldn't Go to Prison," *The Information*, 3 January 2022, www.theinformation.com/articles/why-elizabeth-holmes-shouldn-t-go-to-prison ("Congress could act, but does anyone expect anything substantive out of Washington nowadays? Wall Street is probably right to disregard all the noise about antitrust investigations. We should believe big changes to Apple's rigid App Store rules only when we see them. If Apple shares hit a speed bump, it won't be because of worries about regulators"); Fukuyama, "Internet Safe for Democracy," 41 ("Regulation […] seems to be a dead end in the United States at the present moment"); Fukuyama, Richman & Goel, "Democracy," 103 ("Although regulation may still be possible in some democracies with a high degree of social consensus, it is unlikely to work in a country as polarized as the United States"). For a warning on "how sectoral regulations sold to the public as simple, clear, and cheap can go awry" and an implicit plea against regulation, see Wilson & Klovers, "Nostalgia," 10–29.

[88] On some contradictions of platform regulation proposals, see Lemley, "Contradictions," 305–36.

[89] See, e.g., Stucke, *Breaking Away*, 59–60.

[90] Regarding a bill put together by a bipartisan group of U.S. Senators to force Google to divest its ad tech operations, see Martin Peers, "The Briefing: The Dangers of War Against Google's Ad Tech," *The Information*, 28 January 2022, www.theinformation.com/articles/the-dangers-of-war-against-google-s-ad-tech.

[91] See, for instance, Corporate Europe Observatory & LobbyControl, *Lobby Network*, 7 ("The aim of Big Tech and its intermediaries seems to make sure there are as few hard regulations as possible — for example those that tackle issues around privacy, disinformation, and market distortion — to preserve their profit margins and business model. If new rules can't be blocked, then they aim to at least water them down. In recent years these firms started embracing regulation in public, yet continue pushing back against behind closed doors").

[92] See, e.g., Lévêque, *Entreprises hyperpuissantes*, 112.

[93] See *infra* Part III.

[94] See, e.g., World Economic Forum, *Competition Policy*, 15 ("Global businesses in global markets require global responses"); Fukuyama, "Internet Safe for Democracy," 44.

an exception here[95] – with a myriad of solutions, partly contradictory, being possible.[96] Internal – between agencies in charge of competition, privacy, consumer protection, and other domains in a given jurisdiction[97] – as well as international cooperation and the search for some convergence or, at least, some coordination are therefore important and should be promoted with regard to legislation or regulation and enforcement.[98] In this regard, antitrust or, more broadly, competition law and policy could prove more advanced than the laws and regulations in many sectors due to the UNCTAD, the OECD, the International Competition Network (ICN), or, in the European Union, the European Competition Network (ECN). True, some regulation can *de facto* have an extra-territorial scope, like the European General Data Protection Regulation,[99] but it does not seem the case for a specific regulation relating to platforms – for now at least.[100] It remains to be seen whether, for instance, the new Digital Markets Act or the future Artificial Intelligence Act[101] will also benefit from this "Brussels Effect" – to use the expression coined by Anu Bradford.[102]

A final comment relating to both antitrust and regulation seems justified in this context. One should not lose sight of the preventive or disciplining effect of antitrust and its possible enforcement as well as of actual or potential regulation and its

[95] See, e.g., Rubinfeld & Gal, "Access Barriers," 380; see, however, Drexl, "Economic Efficiency," 259 ("[M]easures [based on competition law] can be taken on the supranational level of the EU, while sector-specific regulation would typically be placed on the national level").

[96] See OECD, *Ex Ante Regulation*, 53; Graef, "Essential Facilities," 65 ("Failure of competition law to act may also provide room for EU or national legislators to intervene in a way that does more harm than good, for instance due to lobbying by corporate giants trying to adjust new regimes in a way that furthers their interests. Competition enforcement is generally less perceptive to such forces"); Tamke, "Big Data," 385.

[97] See, e.g., CMA, *Mobile Ecosystems*, 351–53; Akcigit *et al.*, *Market Power*, 26, para. 44.

[98] OECD, *Ex Ante Regulation*, 53; CMA, *Mobile Ecosystems*, 353–55; Bernhardt & Voges, "Kartellrechtsdurchsetzung," 659; Baker & Comanor, "Antitrust Agenda," 70; de Streel *et al.*, "DMA" (calling for the establishment of a "global forum for Big Tech regulation"); Bayer, Holznagel, Korpisaari & Woods, "Regulatory Responses," 582; Wiggers, Struijlaart & Dibbits, *Digital Competition Law*, 138–39. Regarding the United States and China, see Cai & Wang, "Middle Ground," 259–60. Regarding competition law enforcement, see also UNCTAD, *Digital Era*, 14.

[99] See, e.g., Akcigit *et al.*, *Market Power*, 27–28, paras. 47–49; Bradford, *Effect*, 132–55.

[100] Regarding the Digital Services Act and the Digital Markets Act proposed by the European Commission (on these acts, see *infra* Part III, Chapter 8, Section 8.2), see Eifert, Metzger, Schweitzer & Wagner, "Taming the Giants," 1025–28 (concluding, on the basis of several assumptions, that "[t]he two legislative proposals would set the stage for the internal market only" [quotation from p. 1028]).

[101] See *infra* Part III, Chapter 8, Section 8.2.

[102] See, e.g., Gerard de Graaf, "Die EU muss sich nicht dafür rechtfertigen, dass sie das Internet reguliert" [The EU Does Not Have to Justify Itself for Regulating the Internet], interview with Marie-Astrid Langer, *Neue Zürcher Zeitung*, 15 September 2022, 22, English translation at www.nzz.ch/english/gerard-de-graaf-is-the-new-eu-ambassador-to-silicon-valley-ld.1701947 ("Quite a number of the bills on the Hill contain language that is literally copied from European legislation from the DSA and DMA. What we do see around the world is the Brussels effect. A lot of countries are asking the same questions. The European Union is a source of inspiration for them"); Adam Satariano, "E.U. Takes Aim at Big Tech's Power with Landmark Digital Act," *New York Times*, online edition, 24 March 2022, www.nytimes.com/2022/03/24/technology/eu-regulation-apple-meta-google.html?. On the "Brussels Effect," see Bradford, *Effect*.

enforcement. The measure of effectiveness should focus more on the adherence to applicable laws and regulations, rather than on the number of decisions rendered. Of course, this adherence also depends on the fact that antitrust and regulation are actually enforced[103] and their rules have not become dead letters. Furthermore, legislatures should have a respectable track record in terms of adoption of appropriate pieces of legislation in economic matters.[104] Otherwise, the preventive or disciplining effect would be insufficient or not play out at all.

In sum, the concentration of power in a few digital firms should be addressed through antitrust *and* specific – public – regulation.[105] However, the latter will most probably not exhaust the matter, and private regulation by large or dominant digital platforms will likely remain a reality in the future. This issue calls for potential changes in the organization of firms possessing important regulatory powers in an industry. From a procedural perspective, this can lead to organizational remedies or commitments.

5.3 ORGANIZATIONAL REMEDIES OR COMMITMENTS

The reflection on organizational remedies or commitments is premised on the need for additional checks and balances within or on dominant firms whose platforms have a significant impact on society or democracy (5.3.1). It may ultimately lead to the creation of platform assemblies or parliaments (5.3.2).

---

[103] See Khan, "Antitrust Statutes" ("If the antitrust agencies look at the market and think that there's a law violation and the current law might make it difficult to reach, there's a huge benefit to still trying, especially with some of the bigger companies, some of the more high-profile cases. Because if you don't try, the message that sends out to the world is that the enforcers don't think there's a problem in the market"); Lemley, "Contradictions," 335; Baker, *Market Power*, 1–4 & 11. On this issue, see also Martin Peers, "The Briefing: Why Elizabeth Holmes Shouldn't Go to Prison," *The Information*, 3 January 2022, www.theinformation.com/articles/why-elizabeth-holmes-shouldn-t-go-to-prison ("Investors really don't care about antitrust investigations. That's one takeaway from the latest rally in Apple stock, which lifted Apple's market capitalization briefly above $3 trillion today. It came the same day as India's antitrust regulator was reported to be investigating Apple's App Store, a major source of the company's profits. But India's regulatory folks will have to get in line, as seemingly every major regulator on the planet is doing the same thing [...]. The U.S. Justice Department, for instance, hasn't even decided whether to sue Apple yet, and one factor it has to keep in mind in its decision is the cost of a lawsuit").

[104] See, e.g., Klobuchar, *Antitrust*, 320 ("Anticompetitive conducts will not stop if actions — including antitrust cases — are not taken to stop that conduct, and that also means meaningful remedies and passing new legislation to better regulate the companies going forward").

[105] See, e.g., Kühling, "Herausforderungen," 528; Parker, Petropoulos & Van Alstyne, "Platform Mergers," 1322–34; Salop, "Dominant Digital Platforms," 586; Mazzucato, *Mission Economy*, 196–97; Klobuchar, *Antitrust*, 353; Simons & Ghosh, *Utilities for Democracy*, 7; Rahman, "New Utilities," 1678–80. On this alternative, see, e.g., Witt, "Platform Regulation," 700–1; Colangelo & Borgogno, "Apple-Google." From a broader perspective, see Tepper with Hearn, *Capitalism*, 244 ("Antimonopoly is more than antitrust. [...] Law and regulation must be geared toward preventing dominant companies from preventing new entrants"). For the rest, see Part III, Chapters 8, 9, and 10.

5.3.1 *Additional Checks and Balances*

The importance of antitrust or regulatory laws and their enforcement has been stressed, but firms also face some fundamental duties, especially in concentrated industries having a significant impact on society or democracy. Firms in general and these ones in particular are not just economic but also social institutions with multiples constituencies or stakeholders that provide value for the firms and, possibly, for society.[106]

In a highly concentrated industry, and in the absence of adequate public regulation, separation of powers-type arguments may indeed come into play in antitrust cases, albeit by analogy. Remedies may be decided by antitrust authorities in order to create additional checks and balances in the functioning and decision-making of a company.[107] Antitrust authorities usually enjoy a wide freedom to define remedies in merger control or in monopolization or abuse of dominance cases.[108]

In the United States, the FTC has already issued orders affecting the structure of a powerful company. On 24 July 2019, it approved a 5-billion-dollar settlement with Facebook, Inc. (Facebook), based, however, on data privacy and not on antitrust concerns.[109] This 20-year settlement order establishes an Independent Privacy Committee to review decisions affecting privacy. Members must be independent and are appointed by an Independent Nominating Committee. Furthermore, the order requires Facebook to designate compliance officers to oversee a privacy program, to undergo regular privacy audits and to appoint an independent third-party assessor to monitor the handling of data. In its press release, the FTC linked the creation of the Independent Privacy Committee with the removal of "unfettered control by Facebook's CEO Mark Zuckerberg over decisions affecting user privacy."[110] In other words, separation, or more precisely, restriction of powers-type arguments were used by the FTC to impose some checks and balances on Facebook relating to its core business. The flexibility of antitrust laws in the United States or in other

---

[106] See, e.g., Deakin, "Corporation," 377–81; McGaughey, "Codetermination," 145–46; see also Mazzucato, *Mission Economy*, 194 ("Stakeholder value brings purpose to the interaction of different economic actors and the creation of value in support of a common good").

[107] Regarding "pro-democratic antitrust remedies," see, by analogy, Robertson, "Antitrust, Big Tech, and Democracy," 277–78; see also Acemoglu & Johnson, *Power and Progress*, 393 ("One does not need to be an AI expert to have a say about the direction of progress and the future of our society forged by these [digital] technologies").

[108] Regarding Articles 101 and 102 TFEU, see Article 7 of Council Regulation (EC) No 1/2003 of 16 December 2002 on the implementation of the rules on competition laid down in Articles 81 and 82 of the Treaty (hereinafter: Regulation 1/2003), Jan. 4, 2003 O.J. (L 1) 1. See, e.g., Ward, Bourke & Kristoff, "Enforcement and Procedure," 1204–7. For a summary typology of measures, see Këllezi, *Mesures Correctives*, 75–105.

[109] Stipulated Order for Civil Penalty, Monetary Judgment and Injunctive Relief, 24 July 2019, www.ftc.gov/system/files/documents/cases/182_3109_facebook_order_filed_7-24-19.pdf; Plaintiffs' Consent Motion for Entry of Stipulated Order for Civil Penalty, Monetary Judgment, and Injunctive Relief, 24 July 2019, www.ftc.gov/system/files/documents/cases/182_3109_facebook_consent_motion_filed_7-24-19.pdf.

[110] FTC, "FTC Imposes $5 Billion Penalty and Sweeping New Privacy Restrictions on Facebook," *Press Release*, 24 July 2019, www.ftc.gov/news-events/press-releases/2019/07/ftc-imposes-5-billion-penalty-sweeping-new-privacy-restrictions.

countries or jurisdictions[111] would usually permit an agency to impose analogous remedies to eradicate or reduce antitrust concerns.[112]

More important measures and remedies might be envisaged. Facebook has created an Oversight Board whose purpose is "to protect free expression by making principled, independent decisions about important pieces of content and by issuing policy advisory opinions on Facebook's [and Instagram's] content policies."[113] The Oversight Board's most talked about decision concerns Facebook's decision, taken on 7 January 2021, to restrict then-U.S. President Donald J. Trump's access to posting content on his Facebook page and Instagram account.[114] Reportedly, Facebook is also considering forming an Election Commission to proactively provide guidance.[115] This evolution in the organization of Facebook and Meta Platforms is not constrained by antitrust concerns but still relates to the concentration of politico-economic power in one firm.

The proposition is also made that so-called "utilities for democracies,"[116] such as Facebook or Google, should establish firewalls separating the various functions of their platforms, and that their governance should, according to Josh Simons and Dipayan Ghosh, "involve legitimate and participatory processes that enable the expression of competing interests and disagreements."[117] The commercial imperatives of digital advertising should be separated from other functions, such as the governance of public debate.[118] Additionally, mechanisms of democratic governance, such as citizen juries, mini-publics or platform or social media councils, implying

[111] From a global perspective, see, e.g., World Economic Forum, *Competition Policy*, 16 ("Competition authorities should become more creative in their approach to enforcement tools and remedies"); see also de Streel, "Antitrust," 4.

[112] Regarding the United States, see, by analogy, Hovenkamp, "Antitrust and Platform Monopoly," 2039 ("We should be paying more attention to remedies that permit firms to perform better rather than worse, but in more competitive environments. One possibility is to transfer firms' internal decision making to groups of participants that can be subjected to antitrust control under section 1 of the Sherman Act").

[113] Oversight Board Charter, fourth recital (second sentence) of the Preamble, www.oversightboard.com/governance/. On the Oversight Board, see Klonick, "Facebook Oversight Board," 2418–99 (concluding that "five years ago, few would have thought it possible that a private corporation would voluntarily divest itself of part of its power in order to create an independent oversight body" [quotation from p. 2499]).

[114] Case decision 2021–001-FB-FBR, 5 May 2021 (upholding Facebook's decision to restrict access, but holding that "it was not appropriate for Facebook to impose the indeterminate and standardless penalty of indefinite suspension").

[115] Ryan Mac, Mike Isaac & Sheera Frenkel, "Facebook Said to Consider Forming an Election Commission," *New York Times*, online edition, 25 August 2021, www.nytimes.com/2021/08/25/technology/facebook-election-commission.html ("Mark Zuckerberg, Facebook's chief executive, does not want to be seen as the sole decision maker on political content, two of the people [with knowledge of the matter] said").

[116] For a critical appraisal of this notion, see *supra* Part I, Chapter 4, Section 4.3.

[117] See Simons & Ghosh, *Utilities for Democracy*, 13–14. From a general perspective, see Landemore, *Open Democracy*, 217–18 (arguing for democratizing firm governance).

[118] Simons & Ghosh, *Utilities for Democracy*, 13. For a different view on this issue, see Alexiadis & de Streel, "Standard," 39–40 ("a remedy of structural or functional separation should not be adopted because many of the benefits and efficiencies generated by digital platforms might be lost if their businesses were to be separated").

structured processes of governance, have been advocated for,[119] with the idea that "the public has the ultimate authority to shape how the algorithmic infrastructure of the public sphere is designed and controlled."[120] In that same vein, platform or social media councils may address the preoccupation that platforms set the rules for communication spaces that are crucial for opinion aggregation and articulation, largely without democratic control,[121] and only with very selective judicial correction.[122]

From a perspective more focused on antitrust, a board of, for instance, active Amazon participants is evoked by Herbert Hovenkamp, one of the most influential antitrust scholars worldwide:

> Suppose a court required Amazon to turn important commercial decisions over to a board of active Amazon participants who made their own sales on the platform, purchased from Amazon, or dealt with it for ancillary services. Acting collaboratively, they could control product selection, distribution and customer agreements, advertising, internal product development, and pricing of Amazon's own products. Their decisions would be subject to antitrust scrutiny under section 1 of the Sherman Act. Such an approach could be particularly useful in situations involving refusals to deal [...]. The number and diversity of participants could vary, but they should be sufficiently numerous and diverse to make anticompetitive collusion unlikely. That could include individual merchants who sell on Amazon, principal shareholders, and perhaps customers and others. The Board should be subject to rules setting objective standards for product selection.[123]

In this context, a discussion may exist between the notion of *user* or *consumer* and the one of *citizen*.[124] However, a lot, if not most, of the citizens in many countries are users of Google and Facebook or consumers on Amazon. Moreover, consumers also act as citizens in digital and other markets.[125] Furthermore, measures taken by a platform may impact users both as consumers and citizens, without a clear distinction in this respect.[126] The notion of *users-citizens* or *citizen-users* reflects this duality.

---

[119] Simons & Ghosh, *Utilities for Democracy*, 14. Regarding "deliberative mini-publics," see Susskind, *Digital Republic*, 160. Regarding "juries or random people," see especially Jonathan Zittrain, "A Jury of Random People Can Do Wonders for Facebook," *The Atlantic*, 14 November 2019.

[120] Simons & Ghosh, *Utilities for Democracy*, 15.

[121] Regarding Facebook, see Acemoglu & Johnson, *Power and Progress*, 27–28 & 359–62.

[122] See Kettemann & Fertmann, *Democracy*; see also Bernhard Pörksen, "Soziale Netzwerke müssen reguliert werden" [Social Networks Must Be Regulated], *Neue Zürcher Zeitung* [New Zurich Gazette], 21 January 2021, 18. From a general perspective relating to "global law," see, e.g., Benyekhlef, "Droit global," 19–22.

[123] Hovenkamp, "Antitrust and Platform Monopoly," 2029–32, 2039 & 2050 (quotation from pp. 2029–30).

[124] See Rahman, "New Utilities," 1679 ("[...] what we want as consumers or investors is not necessarily the same thing as what we want as a public."); see also Lévêque, *Entreprises hyperpuissantes*, 116 ("[Competition law] is only concerned with consumers, not citizens, let alone voters" [translation by the author of the present book]).

[125] See Beaton-Wells, "Antitrust's Neglected Question," 181–83 & 189–92.

[126] See Bayer, "Rights and Duties," 38 ("The market power and monopoly status of a service provider have a crucial impact on users not only as consumers but also as citizens"); see also Chalmers, *Reality+*, 360.

The need to specifically and distinctly involve or protect non-users or non-consumers as such with regard to the rule-setting function exercised by these platforms does not seem to be sufficiently established, at least for now.

5.3.2 *Platform Assemblies or Parliaments*

From an organizational perspective, the next step of the reflection would be to focus on the quasi-legislative function assumed by some large or, *a fortiori*, dominant firms controlling a digital platform. In this regard, an assembly of consumers or users could decide on certain matters. Such a reform would contribute to the (re)empowerment of users.[127] Assemblies of users or similar bodies may already exist, but their members are usually designated by the firm itself – in principle by its management. The novelty would be to let users and other external stakeholders, such as advertisers, sellers or developers choose their representatives within a body with substantial decision-making powers, not just consulting ones.

A parliament for Amazon, Apple (with respect to its apps ecosystem),[128] Facebook, Google, or KakaoTalk may even come to mind. A specific parliament for Facebook – and not only for Meta Platforms – or for Google – and not only for Alphabet – would probably be preferable, considering the power amassed by these platforms. Microsoft is also relevant here, notably with respect to operating systems and, possibly in the future, to Bing enhanced by OpenAI's ChatGPT, professional networking (LinkedIn), or the gaming ecosystem. Its regulatory power, combined with data and platform power, though, is probably less consolidated than one of the aforementioned firms. Some of these platforms may however become dominant in their relevant markets. X/Twitter, for its part, does not have the economic power of these firms, but a reform of its governance seems unavoidable to provide for more principled decision-making. In Autumn 2022, Elon Musk polled Twitter users on several occasions in a very unstructured, uncontrolled, and problematic way.[129] Of course, Chinese conglomerates such as Alibaba, Baidu, ByteDance, or Tencent are not on principle excluded from this institutional reflection, but the political regime in China implies another level of analysis which is beyond the scope of this book.

These envisaged bodies could be called *platform assemblies* or *platform parliaments*. The term "parliament" may be seen as exaggerated, but it has a symbolic value and would reflect the weight given to it by the firms at stake and the very idea

---

[127] On the disempowerment of users, see Narula, *Society*, 198–99.

[128] On 16 June 2020, the Commission of the European Union opened an investigation into Apple's App Store rules (see Press Release, June 16, 2020, https://ec.europa.eu/commission/presscorner/detail/en/ip_20_1073). In the United States, the Coalition for App Fairness promotes ten "App Store Principles" (https://appfairness.org/our-vision/).

[129] See, e.g., Durand, "Musk," 30; Clare Duffy, "After Twitter Users Voted to Oust Elon Musk as CEO, He Wants to Change How Polls Work," *CNN* online, 20 December 2022, https://edition.cnn .com/2022/12/20/tech/elon-musk-twitter-polls/index.html.

of checks and balances.[130] Besides, states or unions of states do not have a monopoly on it.[131] The use of the noun *platform* does not mean that a given assembly or parliament would not address issues relating to the entire relevant ecosystem.[132] In some ways, these bodies would be *ecosystem assemblies* or *ecosystem parliaments*.

Such an assembly or parliament would first and foremost concern large or, *a fortiori*, dominant platforms[133] which perform *de facto*-legislative functions, especially because they adopt rules that potentially distort competition and, at the same time, govern an industry and cover important areas of economic, political, and social life. It would be created due to, among other things, antitrust concerns and would therefore be at least partially based on antitrust. It would vote on the principles, rules, or codes where the concentration of power poses a threat for competition and, indirectly, for society. A second justification for such an assembly or parliament could lie in the fact that some platforms contribute to form the digital infrastructure of democracy.[134] Facebook and Google especially, as well as possibly X/Twitter, come to mind in this regard. Jamie Susskind refers to the view that "Facebook shouldn't be able to change functionalities that affect liberty, democracy, and justice without the permission of the people affected by that change."[135] Here, again, specific statutes and regulations are certainly preferable to regulate these platforms, but they may prove lacking, flawed or significantly incomplete.

Platform assemblies or parliaments would adopt principles, rules, or codes and, thus, perform a kind of legislative – though private – task. By contrast, an entity such as Facebook's or Meta's Oversight Board performs functions of a rather judicial nature.[136] Indeed, the Oversight Board appeals process allows people to challenge content decisions on Facebook or Instagram.[137] More concretely, members of a platform assembly or parliament would debate and vote on limits to the extraction, collection or use of personal data, on other privacy issues, on surveillance practices that may damage competition, on general business conditions affecting competition or on methods of competition of the firm's digital marketplace. As the case may be, this could include the definition of limits for algorithms or artificial intelligence tools used by the platform or for the collection and use of data.

---

[130] On this issue, see, by analogy, Boyer, "Process or Revolution," 1203.

[131] Regarding international parliaments, see Schimmelfennig *et al.*, *International Parliaments*.

[132] On the necessity to consider entire ecosystems, not just particular markets or platforms, see Ezrachi & Stucke, *Barons*, 169–73, 176–78, 183 & 197.

[133] As mentioned in the Introduction, this book does not purport to assess whether a given firm has dominant or monopoly power.

[134] See *supra* Part I, Chapter 4, Section 4.3.

[135] Susskind, *Future Politics*, 359.

[136] See, e.g., Susskind, *Digital Republic*, 180–81; Frenkel & Kang, *Truth*, 293–94.

[137] See Oversight Board Charter, Art. 2, www.oversightboard.com/governance/; see also Klonick, "Facebook Oversight Board," 2476–77 ("The analogy to courts is valuable, but also imperfect" [quotation from p. 2476]); Editorial Board of the Washington Post, "Holding Facebook Accountable," *Washington Post*, 18 May 2020, A20 (describing the Oversight Board as "Facebook's high court").

A platform assembly or parliament would be composed of various types of stake-holders, such as end consumers or users – or delegates from their organizations – independent sellers, advertisers, app and other developers and other stakeholders – or delegates from their respective business associations, if any – as well as, perhaps, representatives of the firm at stake. Another solution could consist in only allowing the firm's representatives to propose drafts and participate in parliamentary discussions without being members of the latter, that is, without voting rights. End consumers or users could hold a (vast) majority of votes in the platform assembly or parliament of these firms or, at least, in one chamber of a bicameral parliament. Accordingly, members of such a body would be part of civil society[138] and close to the actual issues raised by platforms and to the market. The empowerment of non-shareholders[139] is not unknown in the corporate world. In Germany, federal legislation reallocates some substantial corporate power to unions and work councils through quasi-parity code-termination and co-decision rights in supervisory boards of companies with over 2,000 employees; for companies with 500–2,000 employees, one third of the supervisory board must be elected by workers.[140] Similar rules exist in other Nordic or Germanic countries in Europe, and co-decision rights in boards or even in general meetings are advocated for or envisaged by renowned authors such as Isabelle Ferreras, Thomas Piketty, Joseph Fishkin, and William E. Forbath.[141] A platform assembly or parliament would replace neither the Board of Directors nor a similar body composed of work-ers' representatives in certain jurisdictions, nor the General Meeting of Shareholders. They would all coexist. The latter body may also be considered as a kind of "parlia-ment," however it relates to the firm itself, while the platform assembly or parliament would be linked to the platform and ecosystem at stake. In any event, each firm should choose the terminology with which it feels the most comfortable.

A firm could establish a bicameral assembly[142] or parliament. One chamber for each side of the market would excessively simplify the situation, as in reality plat-forms have many sides. That said, end users or consumers – or members of their

---

[138] On the legitimacy of the involvement of society in the governance of Big Tech firms, see Durand, "Musk," 31.

[139] See Hovenkamp, "Antitrust and Platform Monopoly," 2031.

[140] For an overview in English, see, e.g., Enriques, Hansmann, Kraakman & Pargendler, "Basic Governance Structure," 79; McGaughey, "Codetermination," 164–76; Doellgast, "Labor Power," 1209–10.

[141] See Ferreras, *Firms*, 127–88 (proposing a model of bicameral governance with a capital investors' house of representatives and a labor investors' house of representatives); Piketty, *Égalité*, 166–75 & 238 and *Capital and Ideology*, 972–75 (advocating for a 50–50 split of voting rights between employees and shareholders [within the body responsible for setting the overall direction of the company, i.e., the board of directors or, in certain jurisdictions for all or certain companies, the management council or the oversight committee] and for a strict limitation of voting rights of individual shareholders depend-ing on the size of the company); Fishkin & Forbath, *Constitution*, 478–79. See also Mazzucato, *Mission Economy*, 194.

[142] Regarding a proposal based on a model of bicameral governance of a capital investors' house of representa-tives and a labor investors' house of representatives, see Ferreras, *Firms*, 127–88. The proposal made in the present book would not replace the General Meeting of Shareholders but instead would coexist with it.

representative organizations – could sit in one chamber; advertisers, sellers, or developers – or members of their representative organizations or business associations – as well as other stakeholders could sit in the other. In this second chamber, especially, interactions between members and the decision-making process would of course have to comply with applicable antitrust and competition laws. This would probably limit the subject matters submitted to the platform assembly or parliament or, at least, to its second chamber. Speaking about an envisaged board of active Amazon participants, Herbert Hovenkamp draws the following line:

> Price fixing or unjustified limitations on output would be strongly suspect. On the other hand, rules establishing uniform practices governing distribution and resolution of customer complaints could certainly be reasonable and thus lawful. Concerted refusals to deal can cover a range of practices from naked boycotts motivated by price (per se unlawful) to reasonable standard setting (rule of reason), and should be addressed accordingly.[143]

The power of the two chambers, hypothetically of the same size,[144] would in principle be symmetrical, except if certain matters fall within the competence of only one chamber. Decisions would be made by a majority vote in each chamber on exactly the same text. A "shuttle" could take place between them in order to find a compromise. In case of persistent deadlock between the two chambers,[145] they could eventually convene, deliberate,[146] and vote together by a single and simple majority vote. Another solution could be that the reform is not accepted if the vote is not favorable in both chambers, provided that both are competent.

Furthermore, a firm could have veto power against decisions of the platform assembly or parliament. Veto would, for instance, be decided by the Board of Directors and would require a ratification by the General Meeting of Shareholders, voting at a qualified majority. This majority would have to be rather high, like three-quarters of the voting shares, considering the accumulation of voting shares by a few individuals in some of the firms at stake.[147] The veto would have to be reasoned and explained to the public in a transparent manner. These requirements would probably *ex ante* discourage a firm to follow this path, at least in most instances. Moreover, a firm could lose the benefit of attributing the decision to an assembly or parliament it does not control,[148] including from an antitrust perspective. Finally, the platform assembly or the parliament could, or could not, override the veto by a vote at a qualified majority – two-thirds vote, for example. Qualified majority would have to be reached in each of its chambers when the body is bicameral.

---

[143] Hovenkamp, "Antitrust and Platform Monopoly," 2030–32, 2039 & 2050 (quotations from pp. 2031–32, footnotes omitted).

[144] See, by analogy, Ferreras, *Firms*, 145.

[145] On this issue, see, by analogy, Boyer, "Process or Revolution," 1205.

[146] See, by analogy, Rebérioux, "Worker Involvement," 1212.

[147] See *supra* Part I, Chapter 4, Section 4.1.

[148] Regarding Facebook Oversight Board, see, by analogy, Frenkel & Kang, *Truth*, 294.

A platform assembly or parliament would be independent and financed by minimal fees on transactions, advertising, or commissions or by an independent trust and would decide on its internal organization or functioning and hire its own staff. Its members would be elected through a fully transparent process controlled by independent auditors. They would be subject to transparency requirements and would need to comply with ethical rules as well as with anti-corruption and other obligations, under the control of independent auditors, themselves financed by the aforementioned fees or trust. One may object that antitrust is supposed to protect the functioning of competition as a decentralized coordination mechanism based on individual preferences.[149] Yet, an assembly or a parliament is a collective body in which decision-making is governed by rules and procedures. But platforms are multisided and based on rules set – for the most part – by firms, and are, by nature, collective tools. A platform assembly or parliament would further not completely dismiss criticism that regulation would somehow remain private.[150] Thus, it must be regarded as a solution that considers the fact that public regulation will most probably not exhaust the matter in many, if not all, jurisdictions, and that private regulation will remain a reality in the years to come.

Of course, the representativeness of such an assembly or parliament constitutes a major challenge, and it is possible that no satisfactory solution can be found in this regard. It is worth noting, *en passant*, that the representativeness of national or federal parliaments themselves is also challenged in many countries.[151] Paradoxically, the constituency of a member of a platform assembly or parliament, understood as the group of voters who would elect this person, may be broader than the one of a national or federal parliament's member, as, for instance, the platform users would be voters regardless of their citizenship. As a lot, or even most, of the citizens in many countries are users of Google and Facebook, few, if not none, of the various main social categories of persons would be left outside the electoral process, subject to voting age limits and to age limits to be elected.

Furthermore, the applicable legislation and regulation would inevitably differ from one country to another, affecting the framework in which principles, rules, or codes could be elaborated and adopted by the platform assembly or parliament. Two responses to these concerns come to mind. First, all decisions would have to respect any applicable laws and would be subject to them. Second, it may be necessary to create regional or even national platform assemblies or parliaments, reflecting diversity across societies,[152] which would decide on matters for the relevant jurisdiction and would elect and send

---

[149] See, e.g., Künzler, "Economic Content," 203–5.
[150] On this issue, see *supra* Section 5.2.3 in the present Chapter.
[151] On the crisis of representative democracy, see, regarding France, Rouban, *Démocratie representative*; regarding the United States, see, e.g., Lessig, *They Don't Represent Us*. From a general perspective, see Landemore, *Open Democracy*, 25–52.
[152] Regarding diversity across societies and AI algorithms, see Kissinger, Schmidt & Huttenlocher, *Age of AI*, 221.

their delegates to an international or interparliamentary assembly that could decide on general matters – the adjective "universal" being too presumptuous at this stage. Some uniform or global rules may then be adopted and have a worldwide scope, something that neither national and regional parliaments, like the European Parliament, nor national and regional platform assemblies or parliaments can achieve.[153]

Obviously, the risk of manipulation of the platform assembly's or parliament's work by the firm's management or by competitors or even governments should not be underestimated. Transparency in this context would be of paramount importance. Equally important, these firms would be aware that any manipulation or undue influence on the parliamentary work could endanger the credibility and legitimacy of this work and expose them to increased antitrust or regulatory scrutiny.

The creation of platform assemblies or parliaments would not prevent states or unions of states, like the European Union, from voting on laws regulating platforms. Laws and regulations would supersede acts of these bodies in the relevant jurisdiction. At any time, states or unions of states could indeed regulate further the matter at hand. Acts of platform assemblies or parliaments would nevertheless be useful in jurisdictions where the applicable laws and regulations do not exist or prove insufficient due to their many loopholes. Various stakeholders close to the economic and social reality – that is, people who really understand the issues at stake and deeply know what they are talking about – would creatively debate on the rules governing platforms and then vote. Accordingly, these platform assemblies or parliaments could possibly become laboratories of governance and regulation.

The cooperation, consent, and unavoidable involvement of the relevant firm, in order to create such an assembly of users or parliament, would be indispensable. A commitment decision[154] may thus close a formal procedure. It may not be irrational for Amazon, Apple, Facebook/Meta Platforms, Google/Alphabet, Kakao, or even Microsoft and X/Twitter to grant power to an assembly of users or to a platform parliament consisting of various stakeholders, especially of users. Medium to long term, the decisions of such an entity could have a positive impact on their business based upon its attractiveness to users or consumers[155] and also contribute to the shareholder value creation.[156] Furthermore, the feared alternatives may be less appealing, with risks such as the breakup of the company or the requirement to comply with new, stronger regulations.

---

[153] From a general perspective relating to "global law," see, e.g., Frydman, "Droit global," 11–19.

[154] In the European Union, *see* Article 9 of Regulation 1/2003.

[155] See, e.g., Dolata, "Platform Regulation," 472. Regarding the transfer of firms' — Amazon's in particular — internal decision making to groups of participants that can be subjected to antitrust control under section 1 of the Sherman Act, see Hovenkamp, "Antitrust and Platform Monopoly," 2039 ("[M]aking Amazon's internal commercial structure more competitive would not likely place it at a disadvantage against competitors"); see also Ball, *Metaverse*, 235 ("[O]ne of the central lessons of the computing era is that the platforms that best serve developers and users will win").

[156] On this issue, see, by analogy, Boyer, "Process or Revolution," 1204; see also Rahman & Thelen, "Platform Business Model," 193 ("Companies such as Amazon and Uber [...] never cease to emphasize the benefits offered consumers in the form of better service and, at least for Amazon, lower prices").

Preemptive self-regulation or, in this context, self-organization measures may prove the better strategy from the firm's perspective.[157] Such measures have the potential to influence how legislatures, governments, and agencies perceive the need for legislative, regulatory, or enforcement action. To clarify, it is not necessarily advocated here for platform assemblies or parliaments, but the point is made that some "separation of powers" by analogy could reduce antitrust and other regulatory concerns.

5.4 ARGUMENT OR DEFENSE IN ANTITRUST MATTERS

The foregoing could also be invoked, for instance, as a defensive argument or, depending on the case and the applicable laws, as a formal or material defense – the "separation of powers defense," so to speak.[158] Firms would, upfront, adopt some separation of powers by analogy-type measures and, for instance, create an assembly of users or even a platform or ecosystem parliament with substantial powers. In other words, they would assess the antitrust and regulatory risks of their business model and adapt their internal or external organization in order to mitigate or suppress the risks posed by the power they concentrate.

The term "external organization" is also used here to reflect the fact that some institutional settings and some checks and balances may not belong to the pure internal organization of a firm. A platform assembly of users or a parliament would have an external dimension, notably because some or all[159] of its members would neither hold shares in the company at stake nor qualify as employees thereof, nor be part of the Board of Directors.

If antitrust proceedings are then launched against behaviors related to the concentration of power, the companies would argue and try to prove that the risks theoretically associated with this concentration, in particular the danger that rules detrimental to pro-user competition would be adopted, are mitigated by the organizational measures taken. The antitrust agency or the competent court would then have to assess the relevance of this argument or defense and its actual impact on the proceedings. In any event, the existence of such an assembly of users or platform parliament should not allow the relevant firm to simply obtain, in advance, antitrust immunity. The possible effect of such a body is still too uncertain, at least for the time being. It should therefore be assessed.

The appeal to consumers does more than insulate these firms against potential antitrust enforcement; it also creates a broader sense of social legitimacy and even active political support for these companies against government regulation").

[157] Regarding self-regulation by platforms in general, see Cusumano, Gawer & Yoffie, *Business of Platforms*, 199–207 & 235–36.

[158] Such a defense in civil or administrative proceedings and criminal prosecutions may be debated, including with respect to its nature, or may not even exist in many jurisdictions. Therefore, the softer notion of "defensive argument" is also mentioned and, actually, preferred in this book.

[159] There could be a policy making incompatible the membership and the holding of shares, including for Amazon's, Apple's, Facebook's, Google's, Kakao's, or Microsoft's representatives.

6

Antitrust in Separation of Powers

As seen in Chapter 5, separation of powers arguments may play a role in antitrust. The opposite is also true, as antitrust may influence the separation of powers envisaged in a broad – political and economic – perspective. Indeed, the concentration of power by a few companies of the digital economy reveals data, platform, and politico-economic powers (Section 6.1), which may lead to a rethinking of our understanding of separation of powers and let us question the role of antitrust *de lege lata* in this regard. One of the difficult tasks posed by antitrust typically consists of defining the relevant markets (Section 6.2), often a key element of antitrust analysis and enforcement. Once the markets are defined, data access, portability, sharing, and interoperability (Section 6.3), as well as the interdiction of abusive discrimination (Section 6.4), raise fundamental issues from a politico-economic perspective on the separation of powers principle and antitrust.

6.1 DATA, PLATFORM, AND POLITICO-ECONOMIC POWERS

The role of antitrust *de lege lata* in a broad scheme of separation of powers is probably limited. The data – including brain-derived data, which may prove increasingly significant in artificial intelligence[1] – owned, controlled, processed, or used by large or, *a fortiori*, dominant digital platforms may nevertheless become more and more important in the development of public policy or for elections or referenda, especially when the data allow for improved targeting of citizens. This *data power*, as (part of) market power, would be considered – and would probably be crucial – in the assessment of these firms' dominance or monopoly. For example, at some point in the future, candidates running for office may not have a choice of which social network to use.[2]

---

[1] See Hoffman, *Forces*, 15–21.

[2] See, by analogy, Botta & Wiedemann, "Exploitative Conducts," 475 ("[U]sers do not have a choice of which social network to use"); see also O'Donoghue & Padilla, *Article 102 TFEU*, 997–98. In Germany, an important decision of the Federal Court of Justice, rendered in summary proceedings, is explicitly based on the lack of choice for Facebook users (Bundesgerichtshof [Federal Court of Justice], decision KVR 69/19, 23 June 2020).

Firms whose social networks, search engines, generative artificial intelligence platforms, or other platforms have become the principal gateways for citizens to obtain or exchange political information are political actors *and* subject to antitrust[3] and, if any, to consumer protection, privacy, or data protection laws, as well as other laws. Because digital platforms are concerned, data power is linked to *platform power*[4] or *infrastructural power*,[5] as the power at stake depends to a variable – and often large – extent, among other things, on the data the platform owns, controls, has access to, processes, is able to monetize, or simply uses,[6] the related infrastructure[7] and eco-system as well as the platform's gatekeeper and/or gateway function[8] and norm or standard-setting power.[9] One should, however, bear in mind that the existence and the intensity of market power must be assessed on a case-by-case basis.[10]

---

[3] See, e.g., Drexl, "Economic Efficiency," 259–60 (noting however that "[a]part from the difficulties in showing monopoly power or dominance, it is also quite questionable whether the specific conduct of disseminating populist or ideological views, including conspiracy theories, can be considered as anticompetitive" [quotation from page 260]). Regarding Facebook and, more specifically, Mr. Zuckerberg, see Deepa Seetharaman & Emily Glazer, "Washington's New Power Broker," *Wall Street Journal*, 17 October 2020 ("Mr. Zuckerberg is now an active political operator").

[4] See Robertson, "Digital Markets," 438–39; Mazzucato, Entsminger & Kattel, "Reshaping Markets," 21–23; Narula, *Society*, 185–86, 188 & 202; Hovenkamp, "Antitrust and Platform Monopoly," 1958–67; Busch, Graef, Hofmann & Gawer, *Platform Power*, 10–11 & 20; Fukuyama, Richman & Goel, "Democracy," 99–102 (noting however, on p. 100, that "the coin of the realm is data"); Fukuyama *et al.*, *Platform Scale*, 10 ("Data as a Key Asset"); Naughton, "Platform Power," 381–84.

[5] Nosthoff & Maschewski, "Big Data," 5–6.

[6] See, e.g., Autorité de la concurrence, *Enjeux numériques*, 5–8 & 11; Mazzucato, Entsminger & Kattel, "Reshaping Markets," 31 ("[Platforms] function as primary controllers of data aggregation and data flows"); Lancieri & Sakowski, "Competition," 82–88; Busch, Graef, Hofmann & Gawer, *Platform Power*, 10–11 ("Data as a source of power"); Patino, *Civilisation*, 62; Kathuria & Globocnik, "Exclusionary Conduct," 533 ("Data-driven platforms are continuously vying for the user data that forms the core architecture upon which their success depends"); Naughton, "Platform Power," 373 ("Possession of these hoards of user data is what really marks the 'pure digital corporations' from conventional companies"); Mäihäniemi, *Competition Law*, 81–82 & 87; UNCTAD, *Digital Economy*, para. 16 ("Market power assessment in the context of digital platforms requires analyzing different criteria. Access to and control of data is crucial and confers market power, and this feature is further reinforced by network effects"); Foer, *World*, 187; Graef, "Market Definition and Market Power," 504 ("Although good engineering resources and a well-functioning algorithm are also needed to successfully operate an online platform, data remains an important input of production for the delivery of good quality and relevant services to users and advertisers"); see also Australian Competition & Consumer Commission, *Digital Platforms*, 11. In its current investigation against Amazon, the European Commission is focusing on the use of non-public independent seller data (Press Release relating to the Statement of Objection sent to Amazon, 10 November 2020, https://ec.europa.eu/commission/presscorner/detail/en/ip_20_2077 ["The Commission's preliminary view, outlined in its Statement of Objections, is that the use of non-public marketplace seller data allows Amazon to avoid the normal risks of retail competition and to leverage its dominance in the market for the provision of marketplace services in France and Germany – the biggest markets for Amazon in the EU"]).

[7] See, e.g., Dolata, "Platform Regulation," 466 (using the notion of "infrastructural power").

[8] See, e.g., Podszun, "Regulierung," 57; Narula, *Society*, 188; Busch, Graef, Hofmann & Gawer, *Platform Power*, 5–6; van Dijck, Nieborg & Poell, "Platform Power," 3 & 12.

[9] Nosthoff & Maschewski, "Big Data," 5–6.

[10] Akcigit *et al.*, *Market Power*, 25, para. 41; Graef, "When Data Evolves into Market Power," 88.

The concentration of data and platform power in the hands of a few firms matters from an antitrust viewpoint. At the same time, the politico-economic power that results from this concentration potentially impacts democracy and, thus, matters from a democratic viewpoint as well. In other words, the issue lies at the junction of antitrust, separation of powers, and democracy. Granted, antitrust enforcement and the preservation of democracy should not be confused, but one cannot rule out that the former helps the latter. In contributing to the reduction or, at least, to the check of data and platform power of some dominant firms and, as the case may be, to some deconcentration of such power, antitrust may help, if not to separate powers these firms hold, then at least to check and balance them. From this perspective, the analysis therefore relates to the separation of powers in a broad sense.

The focus here is on competition, with separation of powers and democracy in the background. Indeed, some core issues of data and platform power relate to competition and, thus, to antitrust and competition laws.[11] When these laws apply in the relevant markets (Section 6.2), at least two main interrelated issues in this regard – data access, portability, sharing, or interoperability (Section 6.3), and abusive discrimination (Section 6.4) – come to mind as far as the separation of powers, broadly understood, is concerned.

6.2 SOME CONSIDERATIONS ON MARKET DEFINITION

Market definition plays an important role in competition law and policy. Digital markets raise many challenges for antitrust agencies and courts. Two of them are especially relevant with respect to the politico-economic power of digital firms through their platforms. The first one relates to zero monetary price products or services in multisided platforms (6.2.1) and the second one to competition for an election or a referendum (6.2.2).

6.2.1 *Zero Monetary Price Products or Services in Multisided Platforms*

An election or a referendum is traditionally – and rightfully – not viewed as a (main) relevant market within the meaning of antitrust and competition laws. Accordingly, the concentration of power in the hands of one or a few firms that may significantly influence the outcome of an election or a referendum is not directly a matter for antitrust. For this reason, the contribution of antitrust to a broader separation of powers principle that takes into account the politico-economic power of firms whose platforms have become an important or, *a fortiori*, fundamental part of the

---

[11] See, for instance, Amelia Fletcher, "Big Tech: How Can We Promote Competition in Digital Platform Markets?," *Economics Observatory*, 16 June 2021 ("Competition law certainly has an important role to play, in relation to the core issue of platform market power and also in relation to wider competition concerns, such as algorithmic collusion").

electoral or democratic process and of the digital infrastructure of democracy is indirect and, at best, quite limited.

As the main relevant market within the meaning of antitrust and competition laws is economic in nature, its definition is based on economic methods and considerations – not on political ones. Competition and antitrust agencies and, subsequently, courts should not, for instance, primarily measure whether the political influence of a given firm can be regarded as substitutable to the influence of another firm by the citizens, office holders, or other stakeholders and, thus, belong to the same market. In other words, the definition of the main relevant market implies using economic tools in order to identify and combine the product market and the geographic market.

Platforms such as Facebook and Google should be carefully considered in this context, if only because of their current or potential contribution to the digital infrastructure of democracy.[12] Facebook and Google are multisided, nontransactional[13] platforms with immense data, platform, and political powers, at the heart of which are zero monetary price products or services. A difficult question relates to the definition of the main relevant market from the end users' or consumers' perspective. A fully convincing methodology is still lacking and thus has yet to be found,[14] as the end users or consumers do not monetarily pay for all or some services offered by many platforms, yet they still pay for the vast majority of them through their personal data and their attention.[15] Non-transaction platforms in the digital sphere, such as online search or social networking, are more likely to be considered as gathering several different markets – and not a single market – and, thus, remain deemed, in principle, as multi-markets.[16]

For zero monetary price products or services, market definition cannot be based on monetary price as the relevant competition parameter.[17] A more complex qualitative or quantitative analysis must be performed. The reference to data and

---

[12] See *supra* Part I, Chapter 4, Section 4.3.

[13] On the distinction between a transaction platform (with observable transactions between different sides of the platform) and a non-transaction platform (without simultaneous transactions between market sides), see Eben & Robertson, "Digital Market Definition," 434; see also Hovenkamp, "Platform Antitrust," 724–25.

[14] See, e.g., Esayas, "Data Privacy," 170; Frank Montag & Andreas von Bonin, "Art. 2 FKVO" [Art. 2 EU Merger Regulation], in Säcker, Bien, Meier-Beck & Montag (eds.), *Wettbewerbsrecht* 1, 2607–766, 2638, para. 88; Podszun, "Market Definition," 72 & 76–78; Podszun & Franz, "Was ist ein Markt?" 126–27. See also European Commission, *Evaluation of the Notice on the Definition of Relevant Market*, 38 & 50.

[15] See, e.g., Eben & Robertson, "Digital Market Definition," 428–30; Steinbaum, "Establishing Market and Monopoly Power," 137; Lancieri & Sakowski, "Competition," 88–89; O'Donoghue & Padilla, *Article 102 TFEU*, 1097; Newman, "Antitrust," 1558–60 ("Consumers do pay for the vast majority of zero-price products: they exchange attention to advertisements, personal information, the rights to creative labor, and more in order to access zero-price products" [quotation from p. 1558; one footnote omitted]); Esayas, "Data Privacy," 167 & 181; Deutscher, "Privacy-related Consumer Harm," 191–94.

[16] See, e.g., Eben & Robertson, "Digital Market Definition," 442–48 & 454.

[17] See, e.g., Ezrachi & Stucke, *Barons*, 169–73; O'Donoghue & Padilla, *Article 102 TFEU*, 1096.

cross-jurisdictional dialogue seems particularly opportune in this regard, as underlined by Magali Eben and Viktoria H.S.E. Robertson:

> Enforcers have shown a willingness to consider data or quality as parameters in quantitative tests. Though progress is being made, these tests are not yet fully operational, meaning decision-makers tend to resort to qualitative analysis. It seems likely that quantitative tests will be refined in the future [...]. Achieving a workable, robust set of quantitative tools does not seem far off and would probably be achieved faster if there were cross-jurisdictional dialogue.[18]

In the future, a test called *Small but significant and non-transitory decrease in privacy (SSNDP)*,[19] derived from the *Small but significant and non-transitory increase in price (SSNIP)* test,[20] may have to be elaborated. A test called *Small but significant and non-transitory decrease in quality (SSNDQ)* is also mentioned, as an alternative to the SSNIP test,[21] bearing in mind that the notion of quality and its parameters are extremely vague and that its appreciation "involves subjectivity, which undermines predictability and legal certainty."[22]

The SSNDP test and, less directly, the SSNDQ test would recognize that data privacy has become a significant non-price competition parameter,[23] noting that privacy is not the only factor affecting quality.[24] The usefulness of the SSNDP test would depend especially upon not only the relevance of data in a given market but also on consumers' or users' awareness and understanding of data privacy issues,[25] as well as their care thereof.[26] It must be a market where personal data play an important role for users and not, for example, simply a pure attention market. This supposes that a vast majority of users must really care for their privacy and act accordingly.[27] Otherwise, an analogy with price increase would not be possible.

---

[18] Eben & Robertson, "Digital Market Definition," 453–54 (regarding the European Union, the United States and Brazil); see also Robertson, "Digital Markets," 436–37.

[19] See Deutscher, "Privacy-related Consumer Harm," 194; see also Jenny, "Digital Ecosystems," 1152 ("degradation of privacy as a reduction of consumer choice"); Esayas, "Data Privacy," 173 & 181; Oxera, *Market Power*, 5 (noting that "[i]n practice, the data required to undertake this analysis, and the inevitable cognitive biases among consumers when making the trade-off, makes this approach complicated").

[20] For an overview of the SSNIP test, see, e.g., Hovenkamp, *Principles of Antitrust*, 67–69.

[21] See, e.g., OECD, *Quality Considerations*, 20 & 49 and *Handbook*, 10; European Commission, *Evaluation of the Notice on the Definition of Relevant Market*, 38; Hutchinson, "Abuses," 454.

[22] O'Donoghue & Padilla, *Article 102 TFEU*, 1099.

[23] See, e.g., Stucke, *Breaking Away*, 61–62 and "Relationship," 5–11; Comanor & Baker, "Consumer Welfare," 20–21; Deutscher, "Privacy-related Consumer Harm," 187–97; Esayas, "Data Privacy," 181; Philippon, *Reversal*, 278 & 296.

[24] Comanor & Baker, "Consumer Welfare," 22.

[25] See Esayas, "Data Privacy," 174 & 176.

[26] On this issue, see, e.g., Coyle, "Platform Dominance," 60–61; see also Esayas, "Data Privacy," 177 & 180; O'Donoghue & Padilla, *Article 102 TFEU*, 1097 ("[I]t is well established under competition law that privacy may be an important parameter of competition and driver of customer choice in various multi-sided platform markets" [one footnote omitted]).

[27] On this issue, from an evolutive perspective, see Casadesus-Masanell & Hervas-Drane, "Competing with Privacy," 239–43; see also Cooper, "Antitrust and Privacy," 1197–201; Eben & Robertson, "Digital

Moreover, competition on privacy must reflect the functioning of the market, which implies a careful analysis of the market participants' incentives and of the dynamics of the entire ecosystem.[28] For the time being, digital markets, where revenues depend on behavioral advertising, may push firms to hoard as much data as possible.[29] Furthermore, privacy-focus start-ups seem to have had a difficult time, as they menace the business-model of major or, *a fortiori*, dominant firms controlling a powerful digital ecosystem.[30] Finally, a case-by-case approach seems unavoidable in this context[31] in order to determine when privacy elasticity can adequately be measured. Should that be the case, due to significative modifications of the behaviors of *both* the users and the digital platforms, the market could see platforms competing to protect privacy.[32] In this regard, "[c]ompetition can also help improve privacy," as envisaged by Thomas Philippon.[33] But we are not there yet…

The application of the SSNDP or SSNDQ test would, notably, consist of interviewing consumers or users regarding their decisions to use a platform or to become members of a network and determining whether a firm would profit from a small but significant and non-transitory decrease in privacy due, for instance, to additional extraction, aggregation, request, or use of the consumers' or users' personal data for its platform or from other reductions of data privacy level.[34] Empirical studies would also make sense. If sufficient numbers of consumers or users are likely to switch to one or more alternative platforms and the lost data would make the additional restriction of privacy unprofitable, then all these platforms compete, at least in principle, on the same relevant market. In the reverse hypothesis, the relevant market would probably have to be defined more narrowly. Of course, additional work needs to be performed to determine whether such a test makes sense[35] and, in case of a positive answer, to precisely define the contours of this new test and the applicable

---

Market Definition," 432 ("The challenge […] lies in identifying the characteristics of products, which truly influence purchase decisions and exercise competitive constraints, rather than focusing on parameters, which hardly matter to customers or matter solely to customers whose number is too small to influence an undertaking's conduct" [one footnote omitted]); Esayas, "Data Privacy," 173 & 177 (mentioning the concept of "consumer cynism").

[28] See Ezrachi & Stucke, *Barons*, 169–73 & 176–78.

[29] See Stucke, *Breaking Away*, 80–109, 117–30, 135–36 & 173–89.

[30] See Ezrachi & Stucke, *Barons*, 81–82.

[31] See Oxera, *Market Power*, 6.

[32] From this perspective, see Stucke, *Breaking Away*, 171 & 190–91 and "Competition Alone" ("Currently, the thinking among policymakers is with more competition, privacy and well-being will be restored. But that is true only when firms compete to protect privacy").

[33] Philippon, *Reversal*, 278.

[34] See Esayas, "Data Privacy," 180 ("[U]sers' valuation of privacy as a quality parameter is not limited to how much personal data is collected but also includes other dimensions such as users' ability to control their data and make informed decisions"); see also Falcon & Ragheb, "International Digital Competition" (insisting on the need to give "privacy-conscious platforms the ability to compete on a level playing field with big platforms").

[35] For a note of caution in this respect, see OECD, *Quality Considerations*, 22 ("Privacy can be quantified in some cases, although the degree to which it is quantifiable is limited by the lack of meaningful

methodology. In particular, the size of a platform and the associated network effects may impact the consumers' or users' decisions.[36] This should be considered either in the market definition or in the assessment of monopoly power or dominance. A rather fluid approach seems recommendable in this respect, leading, for instance, to say that the network effects contribute to create dominance or monopoly power,[37] irrespective of whether other platforms are included in the same market. Finally, interoperability may render a SSNDP test or, more broadly, a SSNDQ test particularly attractive, as it would suppress or reduce the entry barriers resulting from network effects.[38]

6.2.2 *Competition for an Election or a Referendum*

Once the main relevant market is defined, a second difficult question consists of determining whether the competition for an election or a referendum can be relevant when an impact on competition or a competitive disadvantage – foreseen by Article 102 Section 2(c) TFEU, for instance – is required by the applicable antitrust and competition laws.[39] It especially relates to behaviors of dominant firms granting access to data to certain candidates but not to others or discriminating between candidates or political parties and movements. In these situations, the electoral and, more generally, democratic process may be affected. Is this a matter for antitrust?

Favoring candidates or office holders by distorting economic and political competition cannot be a valid source of efficiency gains for a dominant company and does not reflect competition on the merits.[40] Was prohibiting such politico-economic behavior not what antitrust was initially meant to counter in several jurisdictions? A

---

measures from a consumer and competition perspective. Consumer surveys could be used to gauge the confidence that consumers have in a firm's privacy arrangements, although these perceptions may not match reality. Categorisations based on the completeness and length of privacy disclosure may similarly be misleading, since they should also be considered in the context of ease of reading and comprehension.").

[36] See Stucke, *Breaking Away*, 127–30; Esayas, "Data Privacy," 172–73; see also, regarding network effects, Podszun & Franz, "Was ist ein Markt?," 127.

[37] See Stucke, *Breaking Away*, 128–29.

[38] For a broader perspective, not based on a specific test, see Kades & Scott Morton, "Interoperability," 18–21 ("With interoperability [...], a user could choose the social network she preferred to join according to its features, user interface, privacy policies and more" [quotation from p. 18]).

[39] On this issue from a general perspective, see, e.g., Tamke, "Big Data," 374 ("[I]t is not excluded that terms and conditions of dominant market players allowing them to collect data might be scrutinised in dominance proceedings if they (also) have an effect on competition").

[40] See Persily, "Platform Power," 207 ("[P]latforms of a given size cannot use their monopoly position to intentionally favor or disfavor a candidate or party without some other community-standard enforcement reason for doing so"). On these aspects from a general perspective, see Ibáñez Colomo, "Discrimination," 160–61 & 163. On the lack of increase in efficiency as a necessary condition for conduct of a dominant undertaking to be abusive under Article 102 TFEU, see Akman, *Abuse*, 265 & 316–19. Regarding competition on the merits, see also, by analogy, Autorité de la concurrence, Decision No. 14-D-06 *(Cogedim)*, 8 July 2014, paras. 235.

positive answer eventually comes to mind, with respect to the United States at least, considering the history of antitrust that Naomi R. Lamoreaux reminds us:

> The New Brandeisians are raising concerns about the threat that monopoly power poses to the economy and our democracy. These concerns are not new. Indeed, they echo fears aroused by the rise of the Standard Oil Trust and other big businesses at the turn of the last century. Then, as now, the fears were not only about — nor even primarily about — the effect of monopoly on consumers but rather about the exclusion of competitors from the market and the manipulation of the political system for economic ends.[41]

From a historical perspective at least, the door of the application of antitrust laws should not stay irremediably closed. As previously seen, the concentration of economic and political power has now become unprecedented,[42] and certain firms pose a threat to both competition and democracy – the two factors being intertwined. Should the door of antitrust remain, at the very least, ajar in the present digital and artificial intellingence era, the danger of politicizing antitrust enforcement or the risk of destabilizing said laws[43] would seem remote, if not null, as long as enforcement is strictly framed and does not result in a general battle against any excessive political influence by dominant firms.

In this regard, some flexibility in the application of antitrust or competition laws may consider the stakes at play. If the primary or main market is clearly of an economic nature, which is usually the case in the digital economy, for example, as products and services are sold or granted to candidates running for office, and if the dominant firm treats like situations differently,[44] the political nature of the neighboring market at stake – the "electoral market"[45] – or, more exactly, of the competitive disadvantage, should not as such irremediably prevent the application of these laws.[46] In the European Union, the concept of "competitive disadvantage" is used in Article 102 Section 2(c) TFEU; of course, it is, in principle, supposed to be of an

---

[41] Lamoreaux, "Problem of Bigness," 113. See also Fishkin & Forbath, *Constitution*, 210–50, 311–18, 376–78 & 474–77; Hawk, *Monopoly*, 10, 165 & 169 ("[A]s in earlier times, the 19th century antitrust movement was motivated in part by the perceived political and social harms that come with monopoly privileges" [quotation from p. 165]; Hawley, *Tyranny*, 152 ("[T]he curse of bigness is back, and antitrust enforcement must come back with it, updated to perform its original, republican function: protecting the independence of the American people from oligarchic control"); Khan & Vaheesan, "Market Power and Inequality," 265–67; Tarbell, *Standard Oil*, 144–53.

[42] See *supra* Part I, Chapter 4, Section 4.1.

[43] On this risk, see, from a general perspective, Schrepel, "Antitrust without Romance," 391–400 & 430.

[44] See, e.g., O'Donoghue & Padilla, *Article 102 TFEU*, 974–75.

[45] Hovenkamp, "Consumer Welfare Principle," 130 (also using those words, but in another context).

[46] For a different view on this issue, see Drexl, "Economic Efficiency," 261–22; see also O'Donoghue & Padilla, *Article 102 TFEU*, 1055–56 & 1058–59 ("It is difficult for example to imagine what Article 102 TFEU could do about concerns as regards the impact of multi-sided platforms on democratic elections and other events, or media plurality more generally [...]. Instead, the role of Article 102 TFEU should be firmly anchored in concerns around the abuse of market power that limit output to the prejudice of consumers or involve some other harm to consumer welfare or impact on the structure

economic nature,[47] but the case law considers "costs, profits and any other relevant interest" in this respect.[48]

With this in mind, two main interrelated issues may belong to antitrust and separation of powers envisaged in a broad – politico-economic – sense: data access, portability, sharing, or interoperability (Section 6.3), and abusive discrimination with respect to data and related services (Section 6.4).

6.3 DATA ACCESS, PORTABILITY, SHARING, AND INTEROPERABILITY

Data access, portability, sharing, and interoperability raise major issues in the digital and artificial intelligence era. Rules in this regard have been adopted or proposed in several jurisdictions like the European Union or the United States.[49] They usually are in the interest of consumers or users but do not tackle, as such, the immense concentration of politico-economic power within the hands of a few digital firms, even though they may contribute to some deconcentration of this power. Data portability and interoperability grant more effective freedom and – countervailing – power to consumers and users toward these firms, and thus may have pro-competitive effects.[50] Interoperable platforms would indeed be more likely to intensively compete among themselves on features that matter for users, like quality or privacy.[51] Further, switching costs as well network effects would be reduced or even minimized.[52] However, prudence is advisable here, as data portability and interoperability do not necessarily promote competition and actually may even produce opposite

---

of competition" [quotations from pp. 1058–59]); Guggenberger, "Platforms," 317–18 (taking examples of commercial discriminations from an U.S. law perspective).

[47] See, e.g., Whish & Bailey, *Competition Law*, 803–4.

[48] See Court of Justice, *MEO – Serviços de Comunicações e Multimédia SA v Autoridade da Concorrência*, 19 April 2018, C-525/16, ECLI:EU:C:2018:270, paras. 37–38 ("A finding of such a 'competitive disadvantage' does not require proof of actual quantifiable deterioration in the competitive situation, but must be based on an analysis of all the relevant circumstances of the case leading to the conclusion that that behaviour has an effect on the costs, profits or any other relevant interest of one or more of those partners, so that that conduct is such as to affect that situation"). On this issue, see Van Bael & Bellis, *Competition Law*, 851; Eilmansberger & Bien, "Art. 102 AEUV," 1688, para. 434; Graef, "Differentiated Treatment," 466–68.

[49] See *infra* Part III, Chapter 8.

[50] See, e.g., OECD, *Data Portability, Interoperability and Competition*, 15–17, 19–22, 24–26 & 49; Ezrachi & Stucke, *Barons*, 50–54; Susskind, *Digital Republic*, 244; Akcigit et al., *Market Power*, 26, para. 45; Kades & Scott Morton, "Interoperability," 10–39; Falcon & Ragheb, "International Digital Competition" ("[C]reating open standards and allowing users to move their data around to different platforms shifts the market power away from companies and into the hands of consumers"); Guggenberger, "Platforms," 317–43; Hartmann, "Policy Developments in the USA," 111–13; Lemley, "Contradictions," 333–34; Becker, Holznagel & Müller, "Interoperability of Messenger Services," 124–25, 128–29 & 141; Philippon, *Reversal*, 275. Regarding Germany, see Bundesministerium für Wirtschaft und Klimaschutz, *Wettbewerbspolitische Agenda*, point 9.

[51] See, e.g., Bailey & Misra, "Interoperability," 9; Bourreau, Krämer & Buiten, *Interoperability*, 19.

[52] See, e.g., Bailey & Misra, "Interoperability," 18 & 33; Bourreau, Krämer & Buiten, *Interoperability*, 19.

effects in certain circumstances due to the coordination it implies,[53] or generate other difficulties with regard to privacy, for instance.[54]

Besides, remaining network effects, consumer inertia, data gravity, privacy, and property rights[55] as well as other factors,[56] such as the lack of suitable destination for user data[57] – although interoperability should in principle mitigate this last issue – or the absence of international interoperability and data portability standards,[58] may considerably attenuate this contribution. In any case, this book does not aim at predicting the magnitude of the deconcentration of power due to data access, portability, sharing, or interoperability obligations – if any. Indeed, any forward-looking analysis in this matter is highly speculative and, in fact, premature.[59] By way of comparison, the General Data Protection Regulation in the European Union has not weakened the large or, *a fortiori*, dominant digital platforms in Europe,[60] being noted that, in comparison with data access or interoperability, this regulation did not aim to foster competition in the first place.

The most salient issue due to the concentration of politico-economic power within the hands of a few digital firms relates to the possibility for a digital platform to influence – willfully or not – the electoral or democratic process and, *a fortiori*, the outcome of an election or a referendum. Distortions of this process lie at the cornerstone of the problem posed by digital platforms from a separation of powers' perspective. The lack of access to data is not necessarily problematic in this context, provided that the firm at stake refuses access to all candidates and parties. Moreover, data portability or sharing and interoperability do not seem to raise specific issues linked to politico-economic data or to political information and campaigns. They can concern all types of data.

By contrast, the power to – willfully or not, or effectively or not – distort the process or to discriminate between candidates in a way relevant for the outcome of an election is potentially of fundamental importance, especially for a firm whose

---

[53] See, e.g., Hovenkamp, "Interoperability," 4, 14 & 36; Yun, "Big Data," 241–42.

[54] See, e.g., OECD, *Data Portability, Interoperability and Competition*, 17–19, 22–24 & 49–50; Stucke, *Breaking Away*, 157–63; Fukuyama *et al.*, *Platform Scale*, 25–27. For an overview of these issues, see Lancieri & Sakowski, "Competition," 155–56.

[55] Fukuyama, "Internet Safe for Democracy," 41 ("For the platforms' purposes, the most important data that they hold is not personal data voluntarily surrendered to them by users, but the mountains of metadata created by the users' interaction with their platforms. It is legally not clear who owns metadata, and the platforms will fight to keep control over such data since this is the bedrock of their business models").

[56] See *supra* Part I, Chapter 4, Section 4.1.

[57] Hartmann, "Policy Developments in the USA," 113; see also Ball, *Metaverse*, 288.

[58] See Falcon & Ragheb, "International Digital Competition" (making the case for an international agreement on these issues).

[59] See, e.g., OECD, *Data Portability, Interoperability and Competition*, 49–50; see also Hovenkamp, "Interoperability," 35–36.

[60] See, e.g., Stucke, *Breaking Away*, 132 ("[D]ata-opolies are more powerful in Europe in 2021 than before the GDPR went into effect in 2018") & 139.

platform has become an important or, *a fortiori*, fundamental part of the electoral or democratic process and of the digital infrastructure of democracy. Whether existing or simply perceived or feared as significant, this power may be the most decisive one in a democracy. In other words, the political power of platforms also corresponds to their capacity to impact and, as the case may be, to distort the electoral or democratic process. A firm with such a power, if of significant magnitude, should be included in separation of powers' reflections. Before delving further into the analysis, it seems useful to illustrate this assertion.

Suppose that the access to products and services using data – prediction services especially[61] – is barred to third parties, such as political parties or candidates running for office, based on a decision of the social network in question. The person who controls the majority of the voting rights in the company that owns the social network, however, has access to these products and services in compliance with privacy or data protection and sector regulation laws. Assume that such a person decides to run for office, for instance in a presidential or a parliamentary election. That individual will benefit from additional "data power." This form of preferencing is very special, as the company and the person who controls it are different from a legal point-of-view. Nevertheless, they are closely interrelated and may see mutual advantages in the aforementioned hypothesis.

If election or other laws address this issue, then they will be relevant. Assume, however, that legislators have not yet anticipated this problem in many jurisdictions. Antitrust may then come into play, keeping in mind that self-preferencing or similar conduct still belongs to a very emerging field in antitrust.[62] Does such a case reflect an abuse of a dominant position within the meaning, for instance, of Article 102 TFEU? It is most probably not covered by the specific provisions of this Article. With no existing case law in this regard, an antitrust case would have to be built on the first section of Article 102 TFEU. The internal advantage granted to the person who controls the social network would hardly qualify as a behavior on a market relevant to antitrust and competition laws. Section 2 of the Sherman Act is also unlikely to cover this kind of behavior. In the United States, the conduct of a firm having a degree of dominance in a digital platform market that discriminates against sellers appears not to fall within the text of this statute, "[u]nless monopoly either exists in the secondary market or there is a dangerous probability that it will exist," as recalled by Herbert Hovenkamp.[63] Incidentally, one may wonder whether the high threshold of monopolization, as currently interpreted in the United States,[64] remains adequate.

---

[61] See Stucke, *Breaking Away*, 95 & 100.

[62] Regarding the issue of "self-preferencing" under EU competition law, see Crémer, de Montjoye & Schweitzer, *Competition Policy*, 67–68.

[63] Hovenkamp, "Monopolizing," 1719 (concluding, on p. 1755, that "a properly constrained 'abuse of dominance' standard would be superior").

[64] For a comparison between the United States and the European Union or other jurisdictions, see Weber Waller, "Isolation," 132–34; Keyte, "Divide," 116 ("'Dominance' is easier to show in the EU.");

In the European Union or in its Member States, the prospects for antitrust and regulatory proceedings are very uncertain in the abovementioned scenario. If a company is dominant in the European Union, and if access to data or to the related services and products is indispensable to compete effectively,[65] then antitrust may nevertheless come into play. However, the most salient problem as such is not only access to data or to the related services and products, but the discriminatory behavior of the company granting access to services and products only to its controlling shareholder or to certain individuals. Indeed, *discrimination* lies at the core of the most realistic hypotheses to be considered.[66] In this regard, the prohibition of favoring behaviors corresponding to active discriminations represents a more promising – albeit very steep – avenue, at least in some situations but probably not for the benefit of the controlling shareholder, as neither trading parties nor end users would, in principle, be subject to discrimination between themselves in such a case. The focus of the present analysis should therefore be put on abusive discriminatory behavior with respect to access to, or at least the use of, data and related services.

6.4 ABUSIVE DISCRIMINATION

Discrimination by a dominant firm may trigger the application of antitrust or competition laws especially or, depending on the applicable antitrust provision, only when it impacts trading parties (6.4.1). Further, a wide interpretation of key provisions of antitrust and competition laws may take account of positive obligations resulting from fundamental rights, principles, or values (6.4.2). According to circumstances, the conduct at stake may be exclusionary or exploitative (6.4.3) and provoke consumer harm that antitrust enforcement could address without

---

see also Ezrachi & Stucke, *Barons,* 170–71; Hovenkamp, "Monopolizing," 1681 (mentioning "decades of narrow construction [that] have led to most of the problems").

[65] Regarding EU competition law, see Crémer, de Montjoye & Schweitzer, *Competition Policy,* 98 & 107–8 ("If access is necessary to compete effectively on a neighbouring market, an interest balancing is nonetheless in place. If the data holder is a dominant platform, access to data requests may carry particular weight, provided that the platform's dominance is – as frequently – strongly entrenched and exclusive data control may reinforce such power and contribute to its further expansion" [quotation from pp. 107–8]); see also Stigler Committee, *Final Report,* 117; Bourreau & de Streel, *Digital Conglomerates,* 31 (2019) ("[A]pplying the [...] trade-off between short and long-term competition and innovation, the conditions to impose data sharing under competition law may in many instances be lower for data than for other products"). From a broader perspective, see World Economic Forum, *Competition Policy,* 11.

[66] See, for instance, Rahman, "New Utilities," 1670 ("The problem, therefore, is not just the possibility of self-interested manipulation of news, information, and search feeds by Google and Facebook themselves; it is also in the ways in which the emergent properties of the underlying algorithms might produce skewed results, favoring some kinds of media and content over others, or even creating patterns of discrimination in the absence of willful intent on the part of the programmers themselves" [footnote omitted]). From a broader perspective, see also, by analogy, Benkler, "Freedom, Power," 22 ("Regulation in a number of forms seems most likely to diffuse power; this will likely require a combination of utility regulation – interconnection and interoperability on nondiscriminatory terms – and net neutrality rules requiring nondiscrimination among applications and content").

facing either anticompetitive concerns or administrative hurdles in this context (6.4.4). Ultimately, antitrust may contribute to deconcentrate data or platform power and support some form of separation of powers from a politico-economic perspective (6.4.5).

6.4.1 *Discrimination between Trading Parties*

Suppose, as a first hypothesis, that the social network or the search engine of a dominant firm discriminates between political parties or candidates, for instance, against a candidate that promotes heavy regulation of social networks or even advocates for the breakup of this company. By way of example, a social network grants or sells access to services and products based on data to some political parties or candidates and not – or not to the same extent – to others; it thus distorts the political competition. Discrimination may concretely result from banning – prior to an election and for unfounded or weak security reasons – a candidate whose proposed policies actually represent a threat to a dominant digital firm's business model. In the future, the targeted access to citizens through digital platforms that owns, controls, or processes the data allowing the targeting may become an important or even indispensable tool, for instance, for elections or referenda.

Imagine now, as a second hypothesis, that a search engine firm, first and foremost, selects and presents negative or conspiracy websites and articles for some candidates and positive and supportive websites for others. This search engine may become the first and principal gateway to political information for a majority of citizens.[67]

In these two hypotheses, the firms at stake concentrate an immense amount of politico-economic power, potentially having an impact on all branches of government, especially when elections also matter for judicial appointments. Like it or not, it becomes a separation of powers' issue, at least when this principle is broadly envisaged.

These hypotheses raise two fundamental questions, especially regarding Article 102 Section 2(c) TFEU, according to which an abuse of a dominant position within the internal market or a substantial part of it may consist of "applying dissimilar conditions to equivalent transactions with other trading parties, thereby placing them at a competitive disadvantage." Are trading parties involved? Is there a competitive disadvantage? The focus is put on European competition law, as it seems more open on these issues than the laws in many other jurisdictions. A major development in the European Union may subsequently generate evolutions outside of its borders due to the so-called "Brussels Effect."[68] In the United States, non-price discrimination

---

[67] On this tendency, see Rieffel, *Révolution numérique*, 197–98. From a general perspective, see Stoller, *Goliath*, 449 ("One company [Google] controls roughly 90 percent of what we search for. And they also know what we think, because we tell them, through our searches").

[68] On the "Brussels Effect," see Bradford, *Effect*.

remains, for now, an undeveloped field of antitrust,[69] although a similar observation can also be made in the European Union.[70] Generally speaking, this area is still lightly affected, if not almost untouched, by competition law enforcement.[71] However, antitrust will have to evolve, notably with respect to zero monetary price products or services in multisided platforms. The French Competition Authority has already made a significant move out of pure price discrimination by condemning a discriminatory refusal of access to a database,[72] and its decision based on Article 102 TFEU was confirmed by the reviewing courts.[73] The European Commission has also applied the prohibition of discrimination to conduct that involved neither pricing nor the location of customers.[74]

In the first hypothesis at least, the social network could be considered as dealing with "trading parties" within the meaning of Article 102 Section 2(c) TFEU, possibly opening the door to an antitrust case in the European Union based on this provision of the Treaty, on the first Section of this Article or on the case law relating to refusal to deal.[75] The notion of "trading parties" should not be interpreted too restrictively[76] and, depending on the context, could include entities not in a direct contractual relationship with the dominant firm.[77] Candidates for an office trade data with Facebook or other social networks and, as soon as they have achieved significant visibility, bring traffic to social networks. They are not simply end consumers, who are not covered by Article 102 Section 2(c) TFEU according to many authors.[78]

---

[69] From a broad perspective, see, for instance, Werden, *Foundations*, 355 & 359 ("As a rule, U.S. antitrust law does not prescribe procompetitive or non-discriminatory behavior [...]. Reliably identifying anticompetitive conduct with an unpriced service [...] presents special challenges").

[70] See Mäihäniemi, *Competition Law*, 214–17; Graef, "Differentiated Treatment," 450 & 478–79; Ibáñez Colomo, "Discrimination," 142 ("Authorities and courts have not yet developed a coherent analytical framework clarifying why and in which circumstances exclusionary discrimination is an abuse within the meaning of Article 102 TFEU").

[71] See Kobel, Këllezi & Kilpatrick (eds.), *Competition Law*, 1–314. This first part of the book contains an international report and 12 national reports on Austria, Belgium, Brazil, France, Germany, Hungary, Italy, Japan, Spain, Switzerland, the United Kingdom, and Ukraine. The focus is clearly put on price discrimination, and there is virtually no discussion of non-price discrimination.

[72] Autorité de la concurrence (French Competition Authority), Decision No. 14-D-06 *(Cegedim)*, 8 July 2014, paras. 153–261. See, e.g., OECD, *Abuse of Dominance*, 27–28; Hutchinson, "Abuses," 458–59.

[73] Cour d'appel de Paris (Paris Court of Appeal), Judgment in Case No. 2014/17586, 24 September 2015; Cour de cassation (French Court of Cassation), Judgment No. 926 F-D, 21 June 2017.

[74] See Van Bael & Bellis, *Competition Law*, 855–56; see also OECD, *Abuse of Dominance*, 34–35.

[75] Regarding discrimination in the United States, see FTC, "Refusal to Deal" ("For instance, if the monopolist refuses to sell a product or service to a competitor that it makes available to others, or if the monopolist has done business with the competitor and then stops, the monopolist needs a legitimate business reason for its policies. Courts will continue to develop the law in this area").

[76] See, by analogy, Buchser, *Diskriminierungsverbot*, 198, para. 489 (regarding a provision of Swiss law, which was strongly influenced by Article 102 Section 2(c) TFEU).

[77] European Commission, *Deutsche Post AG – Interception of cross-border mail*, 25 July 2001, OJ 2001 L331/40, paras. 121–34. See Thompson, Brown & Gibson, "Article 102," 918–19; see also Huttenlauch, "Artikel 102 AEUV," 627–28, para. 209.

[78] On the scope of Article 102 TFEU in this respect, see Bulst, "Art. 102 AEUV," 685, para. 214; Fuchs, "Art. 102 AEUV," 751, para. 385; Schröter & Bartl, "Artikel 102 AEUV," 900, para. 271.

Incidentally, the justification usually brought to refuse to apply this provision to end consumers – they do not and cannot compete[79] – is not valid for candidates for an election. Finally, as previously mentioned, the concept of "competitive disadvantage" in European competition law can relate to "any other relevant interest"[80] and should not be interpreted too restrictively.[81] In other words, there is a narrow path for applying Article 102 Section 2(c) TFEU in the first hypothesis described above. Two creative steps are required. First, the notion of "trading parties" must be broadly understood. Second, noneconomic "competitive disadvantage" should not be automatically excluded. One should note that the definition of an economic neighboring or downstream market is not required by the text of Article 102 Section 2(c) TFEU. Only a competitive disadvantage – that is, an actual and measurable deterioration in the competition position[82] – between trading parties is needed.

In the second hypothesis, the search engine does not really deal with "trading parties,"[83] except if it sells more prominent placement to certain candidates running for office and not – or not to the same extent – to others.[84] Venturing down the anti-discrimination line of reasoning without "trading parties" most probably leads, for now, to a dead end in the European Union as far as Article 102 Section 2(c) TFEU is concerned[85] and, possibly, elsewhere. It is true that, in June 2017, the European Commission fined Google €2.42 billion for abusive dominance as a search engine, as it gave an illegal advantage to its own comparison shopping service. Rival comparison shopping services were not necessarily "trading partners" of Google. However, this case was not – at least not explicitly – based on Article 102 Section 2(c) TFEU, but related to Google's leveraging of its market dominance in general

---

[79] Bulst, "Art. 102 AEUV," 685, para. 214; Schröter & Bartl, "Artikel 102 AEUV," 900, para. 271; Persch, "Fundamental Rights," 560.

[80] See Court of Justice, *MEO – Serviços de Comunicações e Multimédia SA v Autoridade da Concorrência*, 19 April 2018, C-525/16, ECLI:EU:C:2018:270, paras. 37–38. On this issue, see Kirkwood, "Predation and Discrimination," 154–55; Van Bael & Bellis, *Competition Law*, 851; Eilmansberger & Bien, "Art. 102 AEUV," 1688, para. 434; Graef, "Differentiated Treatment," 466–68.

[81] See Eilmansberger & Bien, "Art. 102 AEUV," 1687, para. 432.

[82] Huttenlauch, "Artikel 102 AEUV," 625, para. 203; see also O'Donoghue & Padilla, *Article 102 TFEU*, 983.

[83] See, e.g., Akman, "Google Search," 329–31; Nazzini, "Google," 307 ("There is no trading relationship between a search engine and vertical search sites or any other site where information is obtained in order to respond to users' searches").

[84] From a general perspective, see Akman, "Google Search," 331–32.

[85] See Court of Justice, *MEO*, C-525/16, para. 27 ("It is only if the behaviour of the undertaking in a dominant position tends, having regard to the whole of the circumstances of the case, to lead to a distortion of competition between those business partners that the discrimination between trade partners which are in a competitive relationship may be regarded as abusive. In such a situation, it cannot, however, be required in addition that proof be adduced of an actual, quantifiable deterioration in the competitive position of the business partners taken individually [...]."). See also Eilmansberger & Bien, "Art. 102 AEUV," 1533, para. 416; Schröter & Bartl, "Artikel 102 AEUV," 884, para. 242. For an analysis based on the essential facilities doctrine, see Mäihäniemi, *Competition Law*, 213–49 (concluding that "one cannot claim that any essential facility can be, in fact, identified" [quotation from p. 248]).

internet searches into a separate market, comparison shopping.[86] Nevertheless, the Commission proceeded with an "equal treatment" remedy between its own and rival comparison-shopping products.[87] In November 2021, the General Court of the European Union dismissed, for the most part, the action brought by Google and Alphabet and upheld the fine imposed by the European Commission.[88] The General Court repeatedly mentioned the notion of discrimination[89] but referred to Article 102 overall[90] and did not analyze whether trading parties were at stake. Anyway, Google as such cannot become a candidate for a political office. Therefore, this decision is not directly relevant in our analysis.

An innovative approach toward the second hypothesis would rather be based on the idea that candidates actively or passively allowing Google to use their data are trading parties of this firm.[91] Indeed, they trade their data in order to be referenced by Google. This approach is engaging and is not without interest, or even relevance. It may nevertheless prove too innovative for competition agencies.

Finally, the first paragraph of Article 102 TFEU, which proscribes any abuse of a dominant position, may also come into play with respect to discrimination to end consumers or users not covered by the second paragraph,[92] but, for the time being, there is no case law with respect to the hypothesis at hand or analogical hypotheses. Fundamental rights, principles, or values may, however, bring new inputs to this debate.

6.4.2 *Fundamental Rights, Principles, or Values*

Antitrust and competition laws must be viewed and, in many jurisdictions, interpreted in the broader context of which they are part. Fundamental rights, principles, or values, especially, may influence the interpretation of laws. More concretely, laws

---

[86] See European Commission, *Google Search (Shopping)*, 27 June 2017, case AT.39740 https://ec.europa .eu/competition/antitrust/cases/dec_docs/39740/39740_14996_3.pdf.

[87] See Mäihäniemi, *Competition Law*, 263–66.

[88] General Court of the European Union, *Google and Alphabet v Commission (Google Shopping)*, 10 November 2021, T-612/17, ECLI:EU:T:2021:763.

[89] General Court of the European Union, *Google and Alphabet v Commission (Google Shopping)*, paras. 240 & 268–320.

[90] General Court of the European Union, *Google and Alphabet v Commission (Google Shopping)*, paras. 151–66, 234–48, 432–43 & 596. See Katsifis, "Google Shopping" ("[T]he GC confirmed that self-preferencing [which it referred to as 'favouring' and 'internal discrimination'] can constitute a distinct form of abuse under Article 102 TFEU [...]").

[91] From a general perspective on this issue, not related to elections, see O'Donoghue & Padilla, *Article 102 TFEU*, 1097.

[92] See Werner Berg, "Art. 102 AEUV" [Art. 102 TFEU], in Berg & Mäsch (eds.), *Kartellrecht*, 1361 & 1388, paras. 68 & 119; Bulst, "Art. 102 AEUV," 685, para. 214; Fuchs, "Art. 102 AEUV," 751, para. 385; Persch, "Fundamental Rights," 560. See, however, Eilmansberger & Bien, "Art. 102 AEUV," 1682–83, para. 418 (considering that discriminations of end consumers are covered neither by Section 1 nor by Section 2 of Article 102 TFEU).

must be interpreted in conformity with fundamental rights in many jurisdictions.[93] Accordingly, when a statutory provision can be interpreted in different ways, the interpretation that implements the relevant fundamental right or rights must, *ceteris paribus*, be privileged. Fundamental rights impose positive obligations or duties to take measures that protect and fulfill them, including through legislation, and produce a – at least indirect – horizontal effect in many jurisdictions, notably in Europe.[94] In the same vein, fundamental principles and values usually must radiate throughout the legal system and, therefore, may impact the interpretation of laws. That said, the discussion should not be limited to the horizontal effect of fundamental rights, as a new set of procedural and substantive rights may be necessary to fully address some main concerns raised by the activity of large or, *a fortiori*, dominant digital platforms.[95]

In most jurisdictions, private companies, even if dominant, are not directly bound by fundamental rights, principles, or values, except in special circumstances. They are, however, bound by antitrust and competition laws, which often use, in their key provisions, broad or even sweeping language that can be interpreted in several ways. This comment relates, for instance, to Article 102 TFEU or Section 2 of the Sherman Act.

In the European Union, as just seen, two quite uncertain and creative paths can cause some discriminations between candidates, parties, or movements in an election or in a referendum fall within the scope of Article 102 TFEU. One is through Section 2(c), the other through Section 1 of this Article. These two provisions contain unclear or indefinite legal terms such as "[a]ny abuse" or "a competitive disadvantage," potentially receptive to fundamental rights', principles', or values' influence. Democracy and nondiscrimination are among the fundamental values of the European Union, as stated in Article 2 of the Treaty on European Union (TEU):

> The Union is founded on the values of respect for human dignity, freedom, democracy, equality, the rule of law and respect for human rights, including the rights of persons belonging to minorities. These values are common to the Member States in a society in which pluralism, non-discrimination, tolerance, justice, solidarity, and equality between women and men prevail.

Furthermore, Article 6 of the Treaty on European Union is dedicated to fundamental rights. By virtue of its Section 1, the European Union recognizes the rights, freedoms, and principles set out in the Charter of Fundamental Rights of the European Union of 7 December 2000, as adapted on 12 December 2007. The Charter has the same legal value as the Treaties and, thus, ranks as EU primary law. All sub-primary

---

[93] Regarding the European context, see Besson, "Droit privé," 16–25. From a broader perspective, see also Bell, "Rights," 419.

[94] See, e.g., Peters, "Menschenrechtsfunktionen," 106–8; Pollicino, *Fundamental Rights*, 200–4; Pollicino & De Gregorio, "Constitutional Law," 16–24; Bayer, "Rights and Duties," 38–42; Callamard, "Human Rights Obligations," 210–12. Regarding Germany, see, e.g., Seyderhelm, *Grundrechtsbindung*, 55–230.

[95] See, e.g., Susskind, *Digital Republic*, 167–68; Cohen, *Homo numericus*, 180; Pollicino, *Fundamental Rights*, 188 & 205–7; Pollicino & De Gregorio, "Constitutional Law," 20–24.

provisions of EU law, such as EU regulations, must be interpreted in conformity
with the Charter, which prohibits, in its Article 21, discrimination based on, among
other things, political or any other opinion. The interpretation of the Digital Services
Act and the Digital Markets Act,[96] for instance, may indeed be influenced by the
Charter. By contrast, Article 21 and other provisions of the Charter do not enjoy
formal primacy over Article 102 TFEU.[97]

The tricky question is whether these values and fundamental rights may nevertheless influence the interpretation of Article 102 TFEU, which also belongs to EU primary law. Discrimination between candidates, parties, or movements in an election
or a referendum by a dominant digital firm raises fundamental issues in a democracy and distorts the electoral or democratic process, especially when the firm's platform has become an important or, *a fortiori*, fundamental part of this process and of
the digital infrastructure of democracy. Democracy as a value[98] and nondiscrimination as both a value[99] and a fundamental right[100] may help justify and solidify
an interpretation of Article 102 TFEU – whether its Section 2(c) or its Section 1 –
that could, in certain circumstances at least, tackle some cases of discrimination on
politico-economic grounds by a dominant firm. This would allow for a harmonized
interpretation of several articles of the EU Treaties and the Charter.[101]

Such circumstances may exist especially when a dominant firm has regulatory
power[102] and controls, through the social network or search engine it operates, a significant part of the digital infrastructure of democracy.[103] The firm may still justify its
actions by overriding general interest reasons such as the respect of privacy, the protection of security or the fight against false news.[104] Noteworthily and interestingly, the
European Court of Justice has already taken into account the "objectives of the Treaty"
(Article 3 TEU) when interpreting antitrust rules belonging to EU primary law.[105]

---

[96] See *infra* Part III, Chapter 8, Section 8.2.

[97] See, e.g., Persch, "Fundamental Rights," 547–48.

[98] See Robertson, "Antitrust, Big Tech, and Democracy," 264.

[99] See Persch, "Fundamental Rights," 550–51.

[100] See Persch, "Fundamental Rights," 558–66.

[101] On this interpretive approach, see, e.g., Hans D. Jarass, "Einleitung," in Jarass, *Charta*, para.
11 & "Verhältnis," 30–31; Eckhard Pache, "Art. 6 EUV" [Art. 6 TEU], in Pechstein, Nowak &
Häde (eds.), *Frankfurter Kommentar*, 269–70, para. 27; Dirk Ehlers, "§ 14 Allgemeine Lehren der
Unionsgrundrechte" [§ 14 General Doctrines of Fundamental Rights of the Union], in Ehlers (ed.),
Grundrechte und Grundfreiheiten, 513–80, 518, para. 9.

[102] Persch, "Fundamental Rights," 548–66 (focusing on regulatory power which "presupposes that an undertaking is able to make rules that are imposed or prescribed on other individuals and not merely on the
parties involved in a transaction with the undertaking" [quotation from p. 556; one footnote omitted]).

[103] See Persch, "Fundamental Rights," 547 ("Interpreting antitrust law in the light of fundamental rights
would, in principle, allow to take into account the role of social media platforms as public forums and
their paramount importance for freedom of expression in today's world").

[104] See Persch, "Fundamental Rights," 561–64 & 566.

[105] See already Court of Justice, *Europemballage Corporation and Continental Can Company Inc. v
Commission of the European Communities*, 21 February 1973, 6–72, ECLI:EU:C:1973:22, paras. 22–9.
See Persch, "Fundamental Rights," 550–51.

Considering European values in the interpretation of treaty provisions would be a logical and natural next step.[106] Of course, freedom to conduct a business is also guaranteed by the Charter of Fundamental Rights, in its Article 16. However, it cannot simply be said that Articles 16 and 21 neutralize each other. A firm in a dominant position is subject to special obligations, including with respect to discrimination, as set out in Article 102 TFEU. Furthermore, as already made clear by the European Court of Justice, a firm cannot simply invoke Article 16 of the Charter to avoid any obligation resulting from the prohibition of discrimination, noting that the latter resulted *in casu* from a directive.[107]

Finally, it should be noted that in jurisdictions where fundamental rights apply directly to private firms, or to some of them, like all or some digital platform firms,[108] the matter is largely dealt with by these rights. Article 21 Section 1 (nondiscrimination) of the EU Charter of Fundamental Rights is already deemed to produce horizontal direct effect according to the case law of the Court of Justice.[109] It remains to be seen how such an effect would operate in a dispute between, for instance, a candidate in an election or a political party and a large or a dominant digital platform.

[106] Persch, "Fundamental Rights," 551. On the influence of the EU values on the interpretation of EU law, see Christian Calliess, "Art. 2 EUV" [Art. 2 TEU], in Calliess & Ruffert, *Kommentar*, 38, para. 12; Marcus Klamert & Dimitry Kochenov, "Article 2 TEU," in Kellerbauer, Klamert & Tomkin (eds.), *EU Treaties and Charter*, 25, para. 7 ("Being programmatic values, they can give guidance for the interpretation and development of EU law"); Jürgen Schwarze & Nina Wunderlich, "Art. 2 EUV" [Art. 2 TEU], in Becker, Hatje, Schoo & Schwarze (eds.), *EU-Kommentar*, 52, para. 2; Potacs, "Wertkonforme Auslegung," 166–68, 170–72 & 175; see also Lenaerts & Gutiérrez-Fons, "Place of the Charter," 1721, para. 55.37.

[107] Court of Justice, *Samira Achbita and Centrum voor gelijkheid van kansen en voor racismebestrijding v G4S Secure Solutions NV*, 14 March 2017, C-157/15, ECLI:EU:C:2017:203, paras. 37–43. See Peters, "Menschenrechtsfunktionen," 108.

[108] See Peters, "Menschenrechtsfunktionen," 107 ("Relevant factors for the attribution of direct third-party effect are the dominant position, the orientation of the platform, the degree of dependence of the users, and the interests of the operator and third parties" [translation by the author of the present book]); see also Pollicino & De Gregorio, "Constitutional Law," 20; Pollicino, *Fundamental Rights*, 204 ("[A] potential initial answer to the new challenges for constitutional law in the age of new private powers could be found in the brave horizontal enforcement of fundamental rights, especially in the field of freedom of expression and privacy and data protection"). For a proposal in this respect, see Piketty, *Égalité*, 152, n. 1.

[109] Court of Justice (Grand Chamber), *Stadt Wuppertal v Bauer and Willmeroth v Broßonn*, 6 November 2018, C-569/16 and C-570/16, ECLI:EU:C:2018:871, para. 89 ("[T]he Court has, in particular, already held that the prohibition laid down in Article 21(1) of the Charter is sufficient in itself to confer on individuals a right which they may rely on as such in a dispute with another individual [...]." [reference omitted]); *Max-Planck-Gesellschaft zur Förderung der Wissenschaften e.V. v Shimizu*, 6 November 2018, C-684/16, ECLI:EU:C:2018:874, para. 78; *Egenberger v Evangelisches Werk für Diakonie und Entwicklung e.V.*, 17 April 2018, C-414/16, ECLI:EU:C:2018:257, para. 76. See, e.g., Matthias Rossi, "Art. 21 GRCh" [Art. 21 CFR], in Calliess & Ruffert, *Kommentar*, 2789, para. 5; Lenaerts & Gutiérrez-Fons, "Place of the Charter," 1719–20, para. 55.30-1; Pollicino, *Fundamental Rights*, 204; Emmanuelle Bribosia, Isabelle Rorive & Julien Hislaire, "Art. 21 CDF" [Art. 21 CFR], in Picod, Rizcallah & Van Drooghenbroeck (eds.), *Charte*, 586–87, para. 17; Tagaras, "Charte," 51–53. For a critical view on this evolution, see, e.g., Sven Hölscheidt, "Art. 21 GRCh" [Art. 21 CFR], in Meyer & Hölscheidt (eds.), *Charta*, 450–51, para. 34.

Moreover, since a specific provision of EU primary law – Article 102 Section 2(c) TFEU – deals with discrimination, it should probably be applied, with Article 21 Section 1 of the Charter then performing at least a supportive function. Anyway, this case law corroborates the aforementioned considerations, leading to the application of a nondiscrimination obligation to such platforms. The actual legal basis for such an obligation – Article 21 Section 1 of the EU Charter of Fundamental Rights, Article 102 Section 1 or Section 2(c) TFEU if the platform is deemed dominant on the relevant market, or a combination of all or some of these provisions – remains uncertain. Should Article 21 Section 1 of the EU Charter become the sole basis, then the following developments may lose all or most of their relevance, as far as EU law is concerned.

Reflection in this direction also exists in some countries. In Germany, for instance, the argument is made in favor of directly applying fundamental rights to a company such as Facebook.[110] This approach is based on the fact that Facebook qualifies as a public forum, is a powerful virtual social power, may significantly affect human rights, and that this matter is not covered by ordinary laws.[111] Notably, Facebook may be impacted by the right to equality before the law guaranteed by Article 3 Section 1 of the German Basic Law,[112] but the question remains controversial,[113] and the case law is not settled on this issue at this time.[114] The District Court *(Landgericht)* of Frankfurt am Main has rendered a decision stating that Facebook, although not directly bound by the German Basic Law, is obliged to respect the fundamental rights of the persons concerned.[115] In its famous Facebook decision, the Federal Court of Justice *(Bundesgerichtshof)* has stated that:

> Depending on the circumstances, especially when private companies [...] move into a dominant position and take over the provision of the framework conditions for communication themselves, the binding of private companies by fundamental rights may in fact be more similar or even equivalent to the binding of the State.[116]

By contrast, the state-action doctrine, or similar doctrines existing in many other jurisdictions, in principle prevent courts from directly enforcing fundamental

---

[110] See especially Seyderhelm, *Grundrechtsbindung*, 232–309.

[111] Seyderhelm, *Grundrechtsbindung*, 248–95 & 307–9; see also Peters, "Menschenrechtsfunktionen," 107.

[112] Seyderhelm, *Grundrechtsbindung*, 297–98; Persch, "Fundamental Rights," 546; see also Peters, "Menschenrechtsfunktionen," 107.

[113] See, e.g., Schliesky, "Digitalisierung," 699–701 (considering that fundamental rights do not directly apply to private parties and that the matter should be addressed through constitutional revisions); Lüdemann, "Grundrechtliche Vorgaben," 284 (considering that Article 3 Section 1 of the German Basic Law does not, in principle, directly bind social networks when they delete posts or other contributions).

[114] See Bayer, "Rights and Duties," 40.

[115] Landesgericht Frankfurt am Main, Case 2-03 310/18, 10 September 2018, para. 17, available in German at https://openjur.de/u/2188268.ppdf. See, e.g., Seyderhelm, *Grundrechtsbindung*, 298; Bayer, "Rights and Duties," 40.

[116] Bundesgerichtshof, Case KVR 69/19, 23 June 2020, para. 105 (English translation taken from Persch, "Fundamental Rights," 545); see, however, Bundesgerichtshof, Case III ZR 179/20, 29 July 2021, para. 59.

rights against private firms or individuals,[117] subject to special circumstances. Moreover, for example, in the United States, noneconomic considerations, such as free speech or the prohibition of discriminations on grounds of political opinion, are usually excluded from the scope of antitrust law,[118] at least for the time being.[119] Like Joseph Fishkin and William E. Forbath, one may also have a more systemic approach in that "[c]ourts ought to make self-conscious decisions about how to *interpret* such statutes and regulations [that aim to shape our political economy in a way that builds and preserves a democracy of opportunity] in light of their constitutionally significant purposes."[120] The historical objections that "the sacred sphere of freedom of contract and rights of property" should be preserved[121] do not fit in the relevant context here. The sacrifices imposed on dominant digital platforms regarding the nondiscriminatory treatment of political candidates or parties would indeed be very limited, if not nonexistent. Some evolution in the interpretation of Section 2 of the Sherman Act on this issue of discrimination by dominant digital platforms could create an antitrust bridge between the end or in the aftermath of the Gilded Age, a period in the U.S. history extending roughly from 1870 to 1900, and the current New Gilded Age. True, casting antitrust enforcement in explicitly democracy-reinforcing terms may raise constitutional difficulties, notably with respect to the First Amendment.[122] However, the focus would be put on nondiscrimination, with democracy potentially being positively impacted in turn.

Finally, such an evolution would also ensure that "the use of digital technologies reinforces, not weakens, democracy and respect for human rights," that "the Internet reinforces democratic principles and human rights and fundamental freedoms,"

---

[117] See, e.g., Susskind, *Digital Republic*, 165. Regarding the United States, see, for instance, a decision of a federal judge dismissing Donald J. Trump's lawsuit seeking to reinstate his Twitter account (United States District Court – Northern District of California, *Donald J. Trump, et al., v. Twitter Inc., et al.*, Case No. 21-cv-08378-JD, Order Re Motion To Dismiss, 6 May 2022, 13: "Overall, the amended complaint does not plausibly allege that Twitter acted as a government entity when it closed plaintiffs' accounts. This resolves the main thrust of plaintiffs' state action theory").

[118] See, e.g., Day, "Free Speech," 1321 ("So given antitrust's economic foundation, the modern view is that a firm may freely suppress ideas, speech, and expression without incurring antitrust liability").

[119] See Day, "Free Speech," 1363 ("[A]ntitrust should impose liability when a monopolist has unreasonably deprived consumers of commercial information and created a market failure of ideas").

[120] Fishkin & Forbath, *Constitution*, 29 (footnote omitted), 424 ("[W]e argue that constitutional political economy plays an essential role both in framing statutes and in statutory interpretation"), 428 & 442; see also Paul, "Antitrust" ("Fishkin and Forbath's constitutional arguments are a rich resource for deepening the arguments of advocates who are pushing back on both judicial and neoclassical economic supremacy in antitrust, in favor of an expanded role for the administrative state in implementing antitrust's broader egalitarian and democratic goals"); Foer, *World*, 203–4 (referring to the "health of our democracy" [quotation from p. 203]).

[121] From a historical perspective, see, regarding the United States, Fishkin & Forbath, *Constitution*, 213–14 & 225–26 (quotation from p. 214). From a contemporary perspective, see, e.g., Devlin, *Antitrust*, 172 ("[Antitrust] does not grant imprimatur to policymakers to reshape industries, inhibit free contract, or otherwise reconstitute markets to their liking").

[122] See Crane, "Instrument of Democracy," 30–31.

and that "safe and equitable use of the Internet for everyone, without discrimination based on […] political or any other opinion" is promoted, in alignment with the recent Declaration for the Future of the Internet.[123]

6.4.3 *Exclusionary or Exploitative Conducts*

If the company that discriminates between "trading parties" within the meaning of Article 102 Section 2(c) TFEU, or between candidates or parties that do not qualify as such but are nevertheless protected by Section 1 of this article, is dominant in the European Union, its conduct could be regarded as exclusionary or exploitative[124] and would need to be justified by legitimate business reasons. Since discrimination is actually at stake in the hypotheses considered here, the strict requirements relating to refusal to deal and "essential facilities," where and when applicable,[125] do not directly govern the analysis in our view.[126] The discriminations that are envisaged here could indeed lead to cases of differences in treatment or of favoring behaviors corresponding to active discrimination, to be distinguished from cases of refusal to deal or supply.[127]

In any event, the issue at stake does not really relate to "an indispensable input allowing the exclusion of all competition downstream."[128] The decisions relating to discriminatory access to products and services[129] or, eventually, to exclusive contracts

---

[123] *Declaration for the Future of the Internet*, 1st and 2nd paragraphs under "Our Vision" and 3rd bullet point under "Protection of Human Rights and Fundamental Freedoms."

[124] Coming from a different perspective but identifying the same risk for democracy, see Ezrachi & Stucke, "Antitrust Enforcement," 238.

[125] Regarding EU competition law, see Graef & Costa-Cabral, "Regulate," 26 ("The essential facilities doctrine can in principle be applied to open up datasets held by dominant firms, even if precedent has still not clarified how the conditions of the essential facilities doctrine will or should be applied to data" [footnote omitted]); see also Autorité de la concurrence & Bundeskartellamt, *Data*, 17–18. Regarding US antitrust, see, e.g., Guggenberger, "Platforms," 305–43 (concluding, on p. 343, that "[t]he essential facilities doctrine provides a crucial element of a comprehensive toolkit to rein in the gatekeeper power of Big Tech"); Abrahamson, "Data," 880 ("In the data context, the essential facilities doctrine captures suspect conduct and better withstands criticisms linked to ex ante incentives").

[126] See, by analogy, General Court of the European Union, *Google and Alphabet v Commission (Google Shopping)*, 10 November 2021, T-612/17, ECLI:EU:T:2021:763, paras. 199–249 (non-application of the criterion of indispensability to a case where a dominant undertaking favors the display of results from its own specialized search service). For an overview of the cases where no indispensability is currently required under EU competition law, see Graef, "Differentiated Treatment," 475–77 & 498. For a critical assessment of some or all of those cases, see Graef, "Essential Facilities," 56–63 & 72 (focusing on the essential facilities doctrine and regretting that, in certain decision of the European Commission, "essential facilities-alike remedies have been imposed under lower standards of tying and non-discrimination" [quotation from p. 56]); Nazzini, "Google," 308–10 & 313 (advocating, in foreclosure abuses, for a test based on indispensability); Ibáñez Colomo, "Discrimination," 148–49 & 157–62 (advocating for a uniform standard based on indispensability).

[127] On this distinction, see Katsifis, "Google Shopping." See also Autorité de la concurrence, Decision No. 14-D-06 *(Cogedim)*, 8 July 2014, paras. 192.

[128] For this definition of the essential facilities doctrine, see Graef & Costa-Cabral, "Regulate," 27.

[129] See Autorité de la concurrence, Decision No. 14-D-06 *(Cogedim)*, 8 July 2014, paras. 192.

are therefore relevant.[130] Should indispensability nevertheless be required,[131] or a milder form of it,[132] the difference would be one of degree. The analysis in the present section would thus remain valid, except that, to put it simply, the products and services would have to be considered as indispensable and not just important to compete.

Harm to economic competition may occur when a platform that discriminates among political candidates or parties and movements becomes more attractive – to powerful and well-funded candidates or parties, for instance – and thus benefits from an undue competitive and economic advantage,[133] such that the competitive process among platforms would be distorted. The behavior may thus provoke both primary-line injuries, as the dominant firm would obtain an advantage, strengthening its position on the market, as well as secondary-line injuries, as the downstream "market" – that is, the competitive political process or the "electoral market" – or, more exactly, the downstream competition would be distorted.[134] It may produce exploitative effects if discriminatory and unfair contractual terms and conditions are applied to political candidates or parties and movements using dominant firms' products and services as customers or as "trading parties" within the meaning of Article 102 Section 2(c) TFEU.

From a broader perspective, the platform or the search engine could benefit from the abuse not only in being possibly more attractive to powerful and well-funded candidates or parties and movements but also in facilitating the election of candidates who are sympathetic to their interests and will neither adopt legislation nor appoint persons who are detrimental to them. At the same time,[135] this behavior may also have exclusionary effects, as "dangerous" – from the dominant company's

---

[130] Regarding EU Law, see Nazzini, "Google," 308 ("[T]he case law on discrimination under Article 102(c) does not require that the dominant undertaking's input be indispensable" [footnote omitted]); Ibáñez Colomo, "Discrimination," 155–58. Regarding EU and French competition law, see Autorité de la concurrence & Bundeskartellamt, *Data*, 18–20.

[131] From a general perspective, see Ibáñez Colomo, "Discrimination," 148 & 157–62. Regarding Japan, see Japan Fair Trade Commission, *Exclusionary Private Monopolization*, 25–26.

[132] Regarding refusal to supply and margin squeeze under EU law, see European Commission, *Enforcement Priorities*, para. 83 ("[A]n input is indispensable where there is no actual or potential substitute on which competitors in the downstream market could rely so as to counter – at least in the long-term – the negative consequences of the refusal" [footnote omitted]).

[133] From a "classical" perspective regarding antitrust enforcement, see Shapiro, "Protecting Competition," 80 ("[T]he basic antitrust question for each tech titan is whether that company has engaged in practices that go beyond competition on the merits and are likely to (1) exclude its rivals and fortify its market position or (2) extend its power to adjacent markets"). One must qualify the hypotheses mentioned in this book as practices going beyond competition on the merits and fortifying market positions.

[134] On this distinction, see, e.g., Van Bael & Bellis, *Competition Law*, 849; Lemaire & Sevy, "Report," 27–34; Ibáñez Colomo, "Discrimination," 145; Akman, *Abuse*, 240–41. On "search neutrality" required from Google, see, from a general perspective, Newman, "Search," 450.

[135] On the double nature of Article 102 Section 2(c) TFEU (targeting exploitative abuses as well as exclusionary abuses), see, e.g., Schröter & Bartl, "Artikel 102 AEUV," 887–88, para. 249; see also Akman, *Abuse*, 265.

perspective – candidates running for office would be subject to discrimination in the competitive political process, be potentially excluded *de facto* from the latter and, in any event, see their "rivals' costs"[136] increase, as they would have to reach the citizens by other means, which would supposedly be very difficult, expensive, and inefficient.[137]

At first glance, it seems difficult to utilize the usual concept of rivals' cost[138] in this context, so it needs to be adapted. One may actually consider that candidates benefiting from the dominant firm are "affiliated" – the word is surely too strong – or, at least, connected with the latter, and that other – "dangerous" – candidates are their rivals. Since the "advantaged" candidates cannot be regarded as divisions of the dominant firm, the definition of the word "rivals" must remain elastic, which does not raise any insurmountable problems. Finally, this "dangerousness" may explain the discriminatory behavior of the dominant firm and answer the question as to why this firm discriminates between "customers" with whom it does not compete.[139]

6.4.4 *Consumer Harm and Absence of Major Anticompetitive Concerns or Administrative Hurdles*

Admittedly, consumer harm[140] may be contested in the cases considered here, as the harm is inflicted to voters rather than consumers.[141] But voters "consume" political information through social networks, search engines, and other platforms.[142]

---

[136] On this issue, see Ibáñez Colomo, "Discrimination," 146 & 155–58 ("Discriminatory conduct can be broadly defined [...] as any strategy implemented by an integrated firm that has the effect of raising the costs of rivals competing against an affiliated division on a neighbouring market" [quotation from p. 146]); see also Nazzini, *Foundations*, 394 & 400.

[137] Regarding Facebook, see, by analogy, Scott Morton & Dinielli, *Roadmap Facebook*, 25.

[138] See, e.g., David T. Scheffman & Richard S. Higgins, "Raising Rivals' Costs," in Blair & Sokol (eds.), *Antitrust Economics*, volume 2, 62–71.

[139] On this issue, see, e.g., Thompson, Brown & Gibson, "Article 102," 946; O'Donoghue & Padilla, *Article 102 TFEU*, 957 ("[I]n the case of discrimination between customers with whom the dominant firm does not compete – pure secondary-line injury – the dominant firm has no obvious interest in taking action that would affect the competitiveness of one customer when compared to another. It would gain no advantage in doing so and might even suffer a disadvantage through a reduction of its sales" [one footnote omitted]); see also, in the European Union, Opinion of Advocate General Wahl delivered on 20 December 2017 in *MEO – Serviços de Comunicações e Multimédia SA v Autoridade da Concorrência*, C-525/16, ECLI:EU:C:2017:1020, para. 79. For a more nuanced view on this issue, see Graef, "Differentiated Treatment," 456–58, 462 & 473.

[140] On this issue, see Mäihäniemi, *Competition Law*, 216 ("[T]he effects of the discrimination should be assessed on a case-by-case basis, and such a discrimination should only be anticompetitive where it leads to a decrease in consumer welfare"); Ohlhausen & Okuliar, "Competition," 153–55 (enjoining to "Focus on the Type of Harm"); Akman, *Abuse*, 265–66. From a broader perspective, see Hovenkamp, "Consumer Welfare Principle," 130.

[141] On an analogous issue (dissemination of populist or ideological views, including conspiracy theories), see Drexl, "Economic Efficiency," 260 ("A pure efficiency and consumer-welfare analysis would not take into account the broader implications of the information disseminated through such services for the democratic process").

[142] Regarding other digital markets, with a focus on Google and Facebook, see UK CMA, *Online Platforms*, 321 ("Consumers would directly benefit from more competition, which they will experience

As accurately put by Fiona M. Scott Morton and David C. Dinielli, consumers are "harmed by a reduction in the quality of their time on the open web."[143] Citizens also act as consumers, and vice versa.[144] From this perspective, consumer welfare and the competitive process[145] should not be ignored upfront.[146]

In this context, the access to data and the related services and products would not be granted to competitors of companies operating platforms; it would neither induce anticompetitive concerns, nor chill innovation and investment.[147] The sacrifice imposed on the dominant company would be of limited scope,[148] and the costs of false positives,[149] if any,[150] seem very limited. Further, this kind of case is unlikely

through more choice, better quality, innovative products and services and real control over how their data is used. We would also expect to see a range of other beneficial outcomes for society from more vibrant competition. In particular, we expect that improving the bargaining power of online news publishers will improve the health and sustainability of journalism in the UK, both nationally and regionally, and in turn contribute positively to the effectiveness and integrity of our democracy"); see also Stucke, "Data-opolies," 285–90. On 20 October 2020, the Department of Justice filed complaint against Google to restore competition in search and search advertising market, see www.justice.gov/opa/press-release/file/1328941/download, para. 167 ("By restricting competition in general search services, Google's conduct has harmed consumers by reducing the quality of general search services (including dimensions such as privacy, data protection, and use of consumer data), lessening choice in general search services, and impeding innovation").

[143] Scott Morton & Dinielli, *Roadmap Google*, 35; see also Robertson, "Antitrust, Big Tech, and Democracy," 275.

[144] On this point, see Beaton-Wells, "Antitrust's Neglected Question," 181–83 & 189–92.

[145] On the necessity that antitrust enforcement keeps protecting consumers and the competitive process, see, e.g., Shapiro, "Populism," 742 & 745–46 ("[T]he core principle guiding antitrust enforcement in the United States [...] has served us well for so many years: *antitrust is about protecting the competitive process so consumers receive the full benefits of vigorous competition*. None of the empirical evidence relating to growing concentration and growing corporate profits [...] provides a basis for abandoning this core principle").

[146] Sceptic in this respect, Drexl, "Economic Efficiency," 261–64 & 267 (focusing then on media law).

[147] On this risk, see, e.g., Kathuria & Globocnik, "Exclusionary Conduct," 521 & 533–34; Shapiro, "Protecting Competition," 86; Sokol & Comerford, "Antitrust," 301–3 & 313 ("Antitrust intervention over market forces threatens consumer welfare, especially in fast-moving markets, and proposed remedies, such as limiting the collection and use of Big Data or forcing large firms to share with rivals, are likely to harm competition and innovation, and in fact may raise privacy concerns" [quotation from p. 313]); Ibáñez Colomo, "Discrimination," 154; see also Furman, *Prepared Testimony*, 6; de Streel, "Antitrust," 3; OECD, *E-commerce*, 42 ("In the highly-dynamic digital context, where e-commerce is an important driver of ever-increasing innovation, it may be legitimately questioned whether a forced sharing policy that substantially decreases the return on investment is likely to enhance consumer welfare in the long term").

[148] From a general perspective, see de Streel, "Antitrust," 4 ("In any case, in the digital sector, behavioural access remedies are often preferable to structural separation remedies because the former keep the benefits of the economies of scope on the supply-side and ecosystem synergies on the demand-side"); Schweitzer, "Datenzugang," 580.

[149] On this issue, see, e.g., Akman, *Abuse*, 328.

[150] From a general perspective, see Alexiadis & de Streel, "Standard," 39 ("[I]f the market structure is concentrated and non-contestable and the digital platform under investigation is a digital gatekeeper, the[se] four commercial practices [...] (namely, bundling and envelopment strategies, refusals to provide access or interoperability to key inputs and innovation capabilities, discrimination/self-preferencing, and violations of key regulatory principles) have a high probability of having an

to present significant remedial difficulties.[151] The company would not have to assist its competitors,[152] and the discrimination would occur between parties other than itself.[153] No firm would be banned from the market.[154] Moreover, the issue at stake is most probably not addressed by consumer protection laws, eventually leaving more room for antitrust laws.[155]

Finally, the supervision should remain limited,[156] as the dominant firms would simply have to grant the same access to products and services, based on data, to various political competitors. Differences in monetary or data pricing may, however, exist and depend particularly on the volume or the intensity of use.[157] The possibility for a dominant firm to differentiate based on the negotiating skills of each trading party or counterpart – that is, each candidate running for office – should in principle be denied,[158] especially in this very sensitive context. Moreover, differences based on criteria "external to the trade relation between the platform and its customers" would be extremely suspicious.[159] Political considerations are external to this relation.

This approach may contribute to creating a level playing field for candidates running for office, even though it is not, as such, a goal of antitrust.[160] This does not

---

anti-competitive effect. Accordingly, Competition Authorities should prioritise investigations into such conduct, as the standard of proof for an antitrust infringement will often be met in such cases").

[151] See, by analogy, Hovenkamp, "Antitrust Duty to Deal," 1530–31.

[152] On this issue, see Mäihäniemi, *Competition Law*, 285 & 304; Nazzini, "Google," 307–10.

[153] On this issue, see Nazzini, "Google," 308.

[154] On this issue, see Wilson & Klovers, "Nostalgia," 29.

[155] On the relationship between consumer protection law and antitrust, see, e.g., Graef, "Differentiated Treatment," 464 ("Exploitative abuses are generally considered to be more adequately tackled under unfair trading or consumer protection law" [footnote omitted]); O'Donoghue & Padilla, *Article 102 TFEU*, 1031–33.

[156] On this issue, see, in the United States, *Verizon v. Trinko*, 540 U.S. 398, 414–15 (2004) (quoting Areeda, "Essential Facilities," 853); see also Wilson & Klovers, "Nostalgia," 14 & 26–9; Kathuria & Globocnik, "Exclusionary Conduct," 521–22 & 533–34; Digital Competition Expert Panel, *Digital Competition*, 76; Abrahamson, "Data," 877–78 ("[C]ourts may more easily administer access to data than to physical facilities" [quotation from p. 878]).

[157] See, e.g., Lemaire & Sevy, "Report," 41–42; O'Donoghue & Padilla, *Article 102 TFEU*, 1015–16 & 1018–20; see, however, Van Bael & Bellis, *Competition Law*, 857. In particular, no strict pricing rules across one sector would be imposed (on this issue, see Wilson & Klovers, "Nostalgia," 28–29).

[158] On this issue, see, e.g., O'Donoghue & Padilla, *Article 102 TFEU*, 995. See also Fuchs, "Art. 102 AEUV," 754, para. 390; Buchser, *Diskriminierungsverbot*, 303–5 (rejecting such a justification under Swiss competition law, which is based on EU law).

[159] Mandrescu, "Abusive Pricing Practices," 514.

[160] See Nazzini, "Google," 307–8; Ibáñez Colomo, "Discrimination," 153–55 & 161–63; Akman, *Abuse*, 262 ("[A]n outright ban on discrimination is not justified without a consideration of its effects on welfare"); see also Graef, "Essential Facilities," 60 & 66 ("[A] broad non-discrimination principle would go against the objective of competition law. It is the ability of firms to effectively compete against rivals that is protected under competition law, rather than to ensure that all players in the market are able to offer the same products under the same conditions" [quotation from p. 60, one footnote omitted]). The ability to effectively compete is at the core of the approach followed in the present book.

mean that a general prohibition of discrimination would be imposed on a dominant firm. A case-by-case approach that also considers the firm's strategy[161] would still prove appropriate.

6.4.5 Antitrust's Potential Contribution to Separation of Powers

Ultimately, antitrust may help separate or, at least, better distinguish data and platform power from actual or future political power and, *de facto* at least, deconcentrate data and platform power in making data and related services or products more accessible on a nondiscriminatory basis, if not completely open.[162] The politico-economic power of the affected dominant digital firms could thus be reduced, as candidates and political parties could not be discriminated against by these firms and would be able to use the same services under the same conditions, except in properly justified cases. This would diminish the leverage of these firms in elections and referenda, preventing them from acting as they wish and, for instance, pressuring candidates or political parties to follow their political agenda and be sympathetic to their business in order to receive ordinary or preferential treatment on the digital platforms. This would increase, *ceteris paribus*, the candidates' and parties' freedom toward these firms and, therefore, help reduce the political dimension of the latter's power. As elections matter for all branches of government in many countries, including the judicial one, the reduction of this leverage would contribute to the deconcentration of power and to the separation of powers in a broad sense. Otherwise, the actual or potential ability to freely impact the outcome of an election would translate into immense power to the digital firms, especially when this ability is widely perceived as real. In sum, checks and balances, as well as in this context transparency, are needed in a democracy.[163] The relevant digital firms should be included in any sensible model of separation of powers.

From this perspective, antitrust may have a place in the scheme of separation of powers, which would consider the ownership, control, or processing of – as well as the access to – politico-economic data by dominant firms whose platforms have become an important or, *a fortiori*, fundamental part of the electoral or democratic process and of the digital infrastructure of democracy. This may be the contribution – albeit indirect and quite limited – of antitrust *de lege lata* to a newly thought and, to a great extent, still prospective separation of powers.

---

[161] From a general perspective, see Ibáñez Colomo, "Discrimination," 154–55 (advocating for a case-by-case approach); see also Mäihäniemi, *Competition Law*, 216; Akman, *Abuse*, 245–46.

[162] On this last issue, see Persch, "Fundamental Rights," 560 ("Giving weight to Art. 21 (1) of the Charter [of Fundamental Rights] would indicate *platform neutrality* for dominant platforms with regulatory power and could ultimately for some platforms amount to a 'must-carry'-rule" [footnote omitted]); see also Tepper with Hearn, *Capitalism*, 245 ("Where tech companies have a monopoly, they must provide access to their services on fair, reasonable nondiscriminatory terms to all competitors").

[163] See, e.g., Foer, *World*, 193–94 & 203–4.

Of course, there may be other more appropriate tools, such as election, privacy, data protection, consumer, media, or platforms regulation laws, which would more accurately and specifically address the issues and protect the electoral and democratic process.[164] These tools may complement competition and antitrust laws,[165] be solely applicable or have primacy in a given case,[166] depending on the issue at stake. In other words, regulation is needed.[167] What happens, however, when such laws are missing and dominant digital platforms discriminate between candidates or parties and movements in order to influence the electoral and democratic process, with the ultimate goal to favor their own agenda and their business? Do they not abuse their powers? Is there no room for minimal protection by antitrust – for instance by Article 102 TFEU in the European Union – eventually limited to egregious cases involving trading parties to whom services are discriminatorily offered or sold? Some voices of competition law scholars, such as the ones of Ariel Ezrachi, Maurice E. Stucke, or Beata Mäihäniemi, are beginning to be heard on integrating nonexclusively economic considerations into the antitrust analysis:

> While differences may exist at the margin, ultimately, competition law worldwide can advance several common political, social and economic goals. One would hope that our common optimal goal will be to promote our welfare in an economy that is inclusive (that is, benefits many citizens, not just the wealthiest 1 per cent), protects the privacy interests of its citizens, promotes overall well-being, and promotes a healthy democracy.[168]
>
> [W]here the so-called information abuses can be identified, such as the self-preferencing of vertical content, biasing the quality of information or refusing access to it, and similar actions, this kind of behavior (in a particular context) may have a major social impact and may therefore invite social considerations such as fairness.[169]

---

[164] See *infra* Part III, Chapter 9, Section 9.2.

[165] See, e.g., Bostoen, "Digital Markets Act," 304–05; Parker, Petropoulos & Van Alstyne, "Platform Mergers," 1322–34; Salop, "Dominant Digital Platforms," 586 ("In light of the potential need to closely monitor the changing conduct of dominant digital networks over time, regulation may be necessary to supplement antitrust"); Klobuchar, *Antitrust,* 353; Simons & Ghosh, *Utilities for Democracy,* 7; Rahman, "New Utilities," 1678–80; Graef, "When Data Evolves into Market Power," 93–94; Stucke, "Data-opolies," 323 ("Antitrust enforcers must coordinate with privacy and consumer protection officials to ensure that the conditions for effective privacy competition are in place"); see also Dunne, "Pro-competition Regulation," 347 & 365–66. On the relationship between platform regulations and competition laws, see OECD, *Ex Ante Regulation,* 52.

[166] Regarding antitrust and data privacy laws, see Douglas, "Interface," 680–84 (advocating for an approach that "evaluates the importance of the interests at stake in each area of law with reference to the specific conduct and context of the case").

[167] From a general perspective, see, e.g., Podszun, Bongartz & Langenstein, "Digital Markets Act," 67 ("Freedom and fairness of markets are not based on the absence of regulation"); see also Ruschemeier, "State-Like Actors," 50 ("[S]olving the problems of the digital platform-sphere is a task for public law"); UNCTAD, *Digital Era,* 13–14.

[168] Ezrachi & Stucke, "Antitrust's Soul," 2.

[169] Mäihäniemi, *Competition Law,* 311.

Antitrust has at least three merits: it exists; it is adaptive due to, *inter alia*, the open formulation of its main material provisions[170]; and it is transversal, as it is not linked to a given economic sector or industry.[171] A fourth merit is also worth mentioning: antitrust would give way to specific legislation when and as wished by the legislature, as this will be explored in the third and last part of the book. In other words, democracy has the final say.[172]

---

[170] See, e.g., Crane, "Antitrust and Democracy," 8.

[171] From a global perspective, see, e.g., World Economic Forum, *Competition Policy*, 15; see also Hovenkamp, "Monopolizing," 1681–82 and "Antitrust and Platform Monopoly," 2049 ("Unlike legislative regulation, antitrust does not group classes of industries together for common treatment, but that also means it is less susceptible to regulatory capture"); Graef & Costa-Cabral, "Regulate," 29.

[172] See, e.g., Shoshana Zuboff, "The EU Has Fired the Starting Gun in the Fightback Against Big Tech," *Financial Times*, online edition, 2 May 2022, www.ft.com/content/31f49915-0f85-48b0-bf81-131960318967 ("Polling shows that people have lost faith in the tech giants and want lawmakers to act. And while democracy may be old and slow, it enjoys advantages that are difficult to rival. These include the ability to inspire hope in citizens and fear in adversaries. It teaches us that whatever has been made by people can also be unmade through democratic action. Only democracy retains the legitimate authority and power to make and enforce the rule of law, based on cherished values, ideas and principles").

PART III

Toward a New Separation of Powers

As seen in Part II of this book, antitrust may contribute to reduce the politico-economic power of certain dominant firms in the digital and artificial intelligence era. The perspective must now be broadened beyond antitrust, at least *de lege lata*, as the time may have come to elaborate upon a new scheme of separation of powers. Importantly, but generally ignored, separation of powers can be viewed from state-centered or power-centered approaches, the latter in particular implying a multidimensional perspective on this principle as outlined in Chapter 7. Recent or proposed pieces of legislation, examined in Chapter 8, may not have a significant impact on the separation of power viewed from a politico-economic perspective. Chapter 9 shows that a multidimensional approach to the separation of powers principle can justify several reforms of the existing laws, regulations, or practices. It is underpinned by the need to preserve independent and impartial decision making, to which Chapter 10 is mostly dedicated.

7

General Issues

Separation of powers is generally approached from a state-centered perspective (Section 7.1), but a power-centered perspective more easily allows for a multidimensional approach to this principle (Section 7.2).

7.1 STATE-CENTERED AND POWER-CENTERED APPROACHES

The separation of powers principle is usually state-centered and relates to the various branches of government or state functions.[1] However, it seems conceivable to broaden the perspective and to alternatively or cumulatively envisage a power-centered approach to this principle,[2] even if the latter raises a number of difficulties, notably, that of defining and delimiting the powers to be taken into account. As mentioned at the outset,[3] power is a multifactorial, multidimensional, contextual, and evolutive notion. What kind of powers should be considered in the search for a new separation of powers? The press or the media has, for instance, long been viewed as a "fourth power" but has not usually been conceptually incorporated in a model of separation of powers as normally understood.[4] Nevertheless, this shows that the focus, in institutional terms, on the branches of government can be considered as too restrictive.

A power-centered approach is also, at least implicitly, advocated for when political parties form the cornerstone of the reflection. The latter are not state bodies in a democracy, but their diversity, or the lack thereof – not only in numerical terms, but also with respect to the actual or potentially realistic chances of access to power, alone or in a coalition – helps determine the real separation of powers and checks and balances in a given country.[5] Lobbying, especially if it is very effective on the

---

[1] See *supra* Part I, Chapter 1, Section 1.3.
[2] Regarding various approaches to political economy, see, by analogy, Caporaso & Levine, *Political Economy*, 159–216 (distinguishing power-centered, state-centered, and justice-centered approaches).
[3] See *supra* Part I, Chapter 1, Section 1.1.
[4] See, however, Martenet, *Architecture des pouvoirs*, 173–75.
[5] Regarding Germany, see von Arnim, "Parteienstaat," 1215–17. Regarding the United States, see Levinson & Pildes, "Separation of Parties," 2347–86.

political branches of government, including on judicial nomination, must also be taken into account in a broad perspective on the separation of powers.[6]

The fact that a firm is dominant in a given market does not suffice to integrate it into a separation of powers model. However, firms whose platforms have become an important or, *a fortiori*, fundamental part of the electoral or democratic process and of the digital infrastructure of democracy should not be ignored.[7] This infrastructure may become non-pluralistic, not regarding the information it shares, but with respect to the fact that it is dominated by a few firms – some of them controlled by one or a few persons. There exists only one Google and one Facebook. There is only one Mark Zuckerberg. By contrast, various professional medias typically coexist in a democracy.[8]

More concretely, firms whose platforms have become an important or, *a fortiori*, fundamental part of the electoral or democratic process and of the digital infrastructure of democracy should be subject to checks and balances, both internally and externally. Antitrust clearly has a role to play here – though, a rather modest one – when the behavior of dominant firms is at stake.[9] Separation of powers and, more concretely, checks and balances – in this perspective and generally – should therefore be viewed and understood multidimensionally. Diverse types of checks and balances arguably coexist in a democracy.

7.2 INTERNAL, EXTERNAL, MULTILEVEL, INTERINSTITUTIONAL, AND TRANSVERSAL CHECKS AND BALANCES

Internal checks and balances contribute to avoiding abuses of power and reducing or suppressing the centralization of power in a few hands. This relates not only to branches of government, but also to firms whose platforms have become an important or, *a fortiori*, fundamental part of the electoral or democratic process and of the digital infrastructure of democracy. Corporate law and governance, regulations, and antitrust may impose checks and balances to these firms.[10] In other words, their organization may have to be adapted in order to deconcentrate power, at least within the firm or with respect to it.

Furthermore, the protection of whistleblowers may help avoid abuses of power within an administration, an institution, or a firm and should be considered when assessing existing or potential checks and balances.[11] It may even prove to be the most powerful internal–external mechanism of checks and balances for the largest

---

[6] On this issue, see *infra* Chapter 10, Section 10.3.
[7] See Nemitz & Pfeffer, "Future," 283–85 (using the notion of "separation of digital powers" and making a link with the principle of separation of powers).
[8] From a similar perspective, see Susskind, *Digital Republic*, 282.
[9] See *supra* Part II, Chapter 6.
[10] See *supra* Part II, Chapter 5.
[11] See, e.g., Martenet, *Architecture des pouvoirs*, 134–35 & 334.

firms in the digital industry, especially when their business model is based on algorithms that are difficult to check from the outside. The risk of internal whistleblowers revealing information about the firms' business externally may indeed help
prevent not only unlawful or unethical but also dangerous – from the perspective
of democracy – behaviors. This undoubtedly has a disciplining effect on the relevant firms, especially when they hire missionary, aspirational persons, as reported
by Nick Wingfield:

> Big tech companies are incredibly powerful now, so the potential stakes of their
> missteps are much bigger than in earlier eras, when whistleblowing was a rarity
> in the industry. A quote from one person I spoke to, a senior executive [of a tech
> company], stuck out to me. "We appeal to a certain kind of missionary, aspirational
> person," the person said. "You get all this energy from these people but when they
> feel disaffected or betrayed, they can turn on you."[12]

It is beyond the scope of this book to define the appropriate level and means of
whistleblower protection.[13] It will simply be noted that the protection of *democracy*
should be a valid reason for a whistleblower to report information through internal
or external channels or to make public disclosures in accordance with the applicable rules.[14] The danger for democracy can result from the excessive concentration
of power, leading to abuses. Frances Haugen, a former employee who disclosed tens
of thousands of Facebook's internal documents to the U.S. Securities and Exchange
Commission and *The Wall Street Journal* in 2021, notably came forward because of
democratic concerns.[15]

External checks and balances refer to the interactions between separate bodies or
entities. The pairing of separated powers, institutions, or functions with an intricate
system of checks and balances forms the core of the separation of powers as envisioned

[12] Nick Wingfield, "The Briefing: Whistleblowers' Moment in Tech," *The Information*, 8 October
2021, www.theinformation.com/articles/whistleblowers-moment-in-tech. See also Stucke, *Breaking
Away*, 256–7; Ariella Steinhorn & Amber Scorah, "Got Whistleblowers? Good," *The Information*, 9
December 2021, www.theinformation.com/articles/got-whistleblowers-good?utm_campaign=article_
email&utm_content=article-6785&utm_source=sg&utm_medium=email. On personality factors playing a motivating role for whistleblowing, see Anvari, Wenzel, Woodyatt & Haslam,
"Whistleblowing," 58–59; see also Thomas, "Whistleblowing," 853.
[13] Regarding the European Union, see Articles 19–24 of the Directive (EU) 2019/1937 of the European
Parliament and of the Council of 23 October 2019 on the Protection of Persons Who Report Breaches
of Union law (OJ L 305, 26 November 2019, 17–56).
[14] On the link between whistleblowing and democracy, see, e.g., Lochak, "Lanceurs d'alerte," 7–8.
On the distinction between internal and external reporting channels, see, in the European Union,
Articles 7–18 of Directive (EU) 2019/1937.
[15] See United States Senate Committee on Commerce, Science and Transportation – Sub-Committee
on Consumer Protection, Product Safety, and Data Security, Statement of Frances Haugen, 4
October 2021, available at: www.commerce.senate.gov/services/files/FC8A558E-824E-4914-BEDB-
3A7B1190BD49 ("The choices being made by Facebook's leadership are a huge problem – for children, for public safety, for democracy – that is why I came forward"). See also Ezrachi & Stucke,
Barons, 139.

by Montesquieu and brought to life by Jefferson, Madison, and others in the United States.[16] The need for external checks and balances also exists for firms whose platforms have become an important or, *a fortiori*, fundamental part of the electoral or democratic process and of the digital infrastructure of democracy. Antitrust and competition agencies, as well as courts, may check these firms, and the adoption – or the sole risk thereof – of laws and regulations, respectively, by the legislative or executive branches of government, constitutes some sort of balance of powers.

Checks and balances, as well as the separation of powers principle, should further be viewed more and more from a *multilevel* and *interinstitutional* approach.[17] Such an approach does not simply refer, for instance, to the relations and interactions between a federal state and its federated entities. It also relates to the interactions between institutions situated at different levels of power. Accordingly, this dimension of checks and balances is not just inter-level, but also interinstitutional.[18] By way of an example, the German Federal Constitutional Court – a federal institution in Germany – has become, indirectly or even directly to a certain extent, the main controller of the European Central Bank – a supranational institution belonging to the European Union.[19] As far as firms whose platforms have become an important or, *a fortiori*, fundamental part of the electoral or democratic process and of the digital infrastructure of democracy, checks may come from many different levels. Subnational authorities like the attorneys general of the states in the United States, national authorities, supranational authorities like the European Commission, and individuals or other private parties in civil actions may all come into play.

Transversal checks and balances mean that the matter is not simply left in public or private hands. Interactions between public bodies and private firms help built the infrastructure of democracy. Checks go both ways, as public bodies may check private firms, but the reverse is also true. Facebook or X/Twitter, for instance, may help disseminate pertinent and critical information about a given government and put pressure on the latter. This transversality is also expressed in the fact that public enforcement of competition laws or other laws can – and should – coexist with private enforcement.[20]

In sum, strong arguments plead for the integration, in a new scheme of separation of powers, of firms whose platforms have become an important or, *a fortiori*, fundamental part of the electoral or democratic process and of the digital infrastructure of democracy. These platforms may indeed play an important or even decisive role in elections or referenda when they serve as the main digital gatekeepers and gateways to political information and opinions, for instance on candidates or questions put in

---

[16] See *supra* Part I, Chapter 1, Section 1.3.

[17] See Martenet, *Architecture des pouvoirs*, 261–331.

[18] Martenet, *Architecture des pouvoirs*, 49–54.

[19] See, e.g., German Federal Constitutional Court, Judgment of the Second Senate of 5 May 2020, 2 BvR 859/15, www.bundesverfassungsgericht.de/e/rs20200505_2bvr085915en.html.

[20] See *infra* Chapter 10, Section 10.1.

referenda. In many democracies, elections matter for all branches of government, including for the judicial due to judicial appointments by elected bodies. From this perspective, the matter becomes a separation of powers' issue. The politico-economic power of the digital firms at stake cannot be left unregulated or even scarcely regulated. Indeed, several recent or proposed pieces of legislation try to restrain the power of some digital platforms.

8

Promises and Shortcomings of Recent
or Proposed Legislation

The digital economy raises important concerns relating to the concentration of economic-political power and, consequently, to the separation of powers in a broad sense, or more narrowly to checks and balances. Several recent or proposed pieces of legislation, especially in Australia (Section 8.1), the European Union (Section 8.2), Germany (Section 8.3), India (Section 8.4), Japan (Section 8.5), South Korea (Section 8.6), the United Kingdom (Section 8.7), and the United States (Section 8.8) aim at tackling some issues posed by large digital platforms. Do the solutions chosen really measure up to the stakes and challenges ultimately concerning, in a broad sense, the future of separation of powers and democracy (Section 8.9)?

8.1 AUSTRALIA

In February 2021, the Australian Parliament passed the News Media and Digital Platforms Mandatory Bargaining Code,[1] designed to have large digital platforms like Facebook and Google pay for making available or linking to local news content. The Code seeks to force designated digital corporations to enter negotiations with news producers for sharing ad revenues from content appearing on their platforms.

This Code deals with issues that are important for local news publishers. However, the concentration of politico-economic power in a few digital platforms is not addressed as such. It is even suggested that such a mechanism of collective bargaining does not solve the problem of increased concentration in the media ecosystem as it may "entrench the interests of incumbent media companies"[2] and even make "media *explicitly and statutorily* dependent on Facebook and Google."[3]

---

[1] Treasury Laws Amendment (News Media and Digital Platforms Mandatory Bargaining Code) Act 2021, No. 21, 2021, available at www.legislation.gov.au/Details/C2021A00021. See, e.g., Balasingham & Neilson, "Digital Platforms and Journalism," 297–301.
[2] Balasingham & Neilson, "Digital Platforms and Journalism," 317.
[3] Trendacosta & O'Brien, "Antitrust Exemption"; see also OECD, *News Media and Digital Platforms*, 32–33; Busch, Graef, Hofmann & Gawer, *Platform Power*, 23.

Finally, the concentration of power in the hands of firms whose platforms have become an important part of the electoral or democratic process and of the digital infrastructure of democracy is left unaddressed by recent or proposed legislation in Australia. The same can be said of the risk of distortion of this process by these firms.

8.2 EUROPEAN UNION

The Digital Services Act (DSA), proposed by the European Commission on 15 December 2020[4] and approved with numerous amendments by the European Parliament on 5 July 2022 and by the Council of the European Union on 4 October 2022,[5] aims at significantly improving the mechanisms for the removal of illegal content and for the effective protection of users' fundamental rights online. It also creates a stronger public oversight of online platforms, especially very large ones. Indeed, the DSA contains specific rules pertaining to the supervision, investigation, enforcement, and monitoring in respect of providers of very large online platforms and of very large online search engines.[6] It lists many due diligence obligations for a transparent and safe online environment,[7] with specific and additional obligations applicable to said providers.[8] Users have, for instance, access to an effective internal complaint-handling system enabling them to lodge complaints,[9] and transparency measures are imposed to online platforms, notably on algorithmic decision-making and human review.[10]

Providers of very large online platforms and of very large online search engines will have to assess, in-depth, the actual and foreseeable negative effects on democratic processes, civic discourse, and electoral processes, as well as public security.[11] Otherwise, the DSA does not regulate distortions of the electoral and democratic process through, or by, online platforms. It does not further provide adequate answers to fundamental questions such as:

> Why does harmful or illegal content spread so expansively on social media in the first place? What responsibility do online platforms' algorithms play in the

---

[4] Proposal for a Regulation of the European Parliament and the Council on a Single Market for Digital Services (Digital Services Act) and amending Directive 2000/31/EC, COM/2020/825 final, available at https://eur-lex.europa.eu/legal-content/en/TXT/?qid=1608117147218&uri=COM%3A2020%3A825%3AFIN.

[5] Regulation (EU) 2022/2065 of the European Parliament and of the Council of 19 October 2022 on a Single Market for Digital Services and amending Directive 2000/31/EC (Digital Services Act; OJ L 277, 27 October 2022, 1–102).

[6] Articles 64–83 DSA.

[7] Articles 11–48 DSA.

[8] Articles 33–43 DSA.

[9] Article 20 DSA.

[10] Article 14(1) DSA.

[11] Recital 82 and Article 34(1) para. 2(c) DSA ("democratic processes" are not explicitly mentioned in this provision).

distribution and promotion of online content? And what are the commercial incentives that guide the development of those algorithms?[12]

Moreover, the DSA does not deal with the concentration of power as such. On the contrary, it may even benefit large service providers and is not likely to affect their ability to dominate markets, notably given the economics of content moderation.[13]

The Digital Markets Act (DMA), proposed by the European Commission on 15 December 2020[14] and approved with numerous amendments by the European Parliament on 5 July 2022 and by the Council of the European Union on 18 July 2022,[15] establishes a set of narrowly defined objective criteria for qualifying a large online platform as a so-called "gatekeeper."[16] Identified gatekeepers would face specific obligations.[17] Practices known as self-preferencing are prevented, and a higher degree of data portability, interoperability, and access – for instance to performance measuring tools[18] – is imposed. Messaging services of Google, Meta Platforms, or Microsoft, for instance, are forced to interoperate with competing services from smaller competitors.[19] The interoperability obligations included in the DMA are, on a more general note, very demanding,[20] and are deemed to create a level playing field.[21] By contrast, interoperability for social media services is not included in the DMA.[22] Apple and Google must, for their part, allow rival app stores with equal functionality.[23] Time will tell how much competition these reforms will induce.[24] By way of illustration, Apple is already preparing to allow developers to sell their apps to iPhone or iPad users without going through its App Store,[25] but it also knows

[12] Becker Castellaro & Penfrat, "DSA."
[13] Buri & van Hoboken, "DSA," 12–14; see also Andriychuk, "New Modality of the Digital Markets," 266 & 284–85; Peukert, "DSA," 27; Ruschemeier, "State-Like Actors," 53–54.
[14] Proposal for a Regulation of the European Parliament and the Council on contestable and fair markets in the digital sector (Digital Markets Act), COM/2020/842 final, available at https://eur-lex.europa.eu/legal-content/en/TXT/?qid=1608116887159&uri=COM%3A2020%3A842%3AFIN.
[15] Regulation (EU) 2022/1925 of the European Parliament and of the Council of 14 September 2022 on Contestable and Fair Markets in the Digital Sector and amending Directives (EU) 2019/1937 and (EU) 2020/1828 (Digital Markets Act; OJ L 265, 12 October 2022, 1–66).
[16] Articles 3–4 DMA.
[17] Articles 5–15 DMA.
[18] See Article 6(8) DMA.
[19] Article 7(2) DMA.
[20] Articles 6(7) & 7 DMA. See Geradin, "Final Version of the DMA."
[21] See, e.g., Björn Herbers, "Art. 6(7)," in Podszun (ed.), *Digital Markets Act*, para. 143.
[22] See Scott Morton, "EU's New Law"; Natasha Lomas, "Europe Says Yes to Messaging Interoperability as It Agrees on Major New Regime for Big Tech," *The Crunch*, 25 March 2022, https://techcrunch.com/2022/03/24/dma-political-agreement/.
[23] See Article 6(4) DMA.
[24] Scott Morton, "EU's New Law."
[25] Mark Gurman, "Apple to Allow Outside App Stores in Overhaul Spurred by EU Laws," *Bloomberg*, 13 December 2022.

how to nudge users in its direction and to make other routes appear suboptimal, so that the change in the competitive landscape remains uncertain.[26]

The DMA deals with some risks associated with the concentration of powers by firms such as Google or Facebook. Like the DSA, however, it does not foresee measures to tackle the concentration or bigness as such,[27] as noted by various scholars, including John W. Cioffi, Martin F. Kenney, and John Zysman:

> [T]he DMA contains no substantive strengthening or other alteration of *merger review* procedures or standards. Consequently, the single most effective way in which platform firms achieve and perpetuate market dominance and expand their market power, and arguably the most injurious to competition and technological innovation, remains unaddressed. In addition, the DMA contains no provisions expanding the discretionary authority to impose structural remedies [...] beyond those already permitted by existing law.[28]

The DMA also does not regulate distortions of the electoral and democratic process.[29] Some nondiscriminatory obligations[30] may be of interest in this regard – especially the obligation for a gatekeeper to apply fair, reasonable, and nondiscriminatory general conditions of access for business users to its software application stores, online search engines, and online social networking services.[31] They may further ensure a level playing field for competition, and their scope is not limited to discriminatory treatments of trading partners.[32] However, they probably need to be further refined.[33] Moreover, the

---

[26] Jessica E. Lessin, "The Briefing: When It Comes to Apple, Watch the Fine Print," *The Information*, 13 December 2022, www.theinformation.com/articles/when-it-comes-to-apple-watch-the-fine-print.

[27] Heinemann & Meier, "DMA," 99. See, however, Zimmer, "DMA," 9, para. 33.

[28] Cioffi, Kenney & Zysman, "Platform Power," 828–29 (regarding the proposal of the European Commission). See also Budzinski & Mendelsohn, "Regulating Big Tech," 18–19 & 25–28; Podszun, "Regulierung," 59; Corporate Europe Observatory & LobbyControl, *Lobby Network*, 42–44; Monti, "Taming Digital Monopolies," 68 ("[T]here is a major gap in the European Union's current proposals, and this is the absence of merger rules to regulate the acquisition of nascent competitors" [footnote omitted]); Larouche & de Streel, "Digital Markets Act," 560 ("[The DMA] foresees mostly behavioural interventions leaving structural interventions for very exceptional circumstances"); Eifert, Metzger, Schweitzer & Wagner, "Taming the Giants," 994–95 ("[A]bsent a strict prohibition of vertical integration, the platforms might still be able to defend and extend their gatekeeper power, given the special characteristics of platform markets" [quotation from p. 995]) & 1024–28 ("[A] central problem of the DMA remains the ambiguity of its goals, and the fairness goal in particular [...]. The limitation of EU powers regarding the regulation of content poses serious problems with a view to the core obligation that the DSA defines for platforms" [quotation from p. 1025]); Geradin, "DMA" ("The DMA is not a general-purpose Regulation applying across the economy, nor can it solve all the problems in the digital markets"); Rodríguez de las Heras Ballell, "DMA," 76 ("In these gaps [of the DMA], Big Tech's power may continue to grow, whereas smaller actors may be hampered by uncertainty"); Franck & Peitz, "Big Tech," 86–88.

[29] From a broader perspective, see Persch, "Fundamental Rights," 565 ("[I]t should be noted that neither the DSA nor the DMA would regulate which content can or must be removed" [footnote omitted]).

[30] Article 6(5), (11) & (12) DMA.

[31] Article 6(12) DMA.

[32] Petit, "DMA," 537 & 540.

[33] See Akman, "Regulating Competition," 96–97, 101 & 110–13; Eifert, Metzger, Schweitzer & Wagner, "Taming the Giants," 1013.

provision on ranking and associated indexing or crawling relates especially to products and services[34] but not to candidates for an office, and fair, reasonable, and nondiscriminatory general conditions must be granted to "business users," as just seen, not to end users as such.[35] At the end of the day, implementation and enforcement will be crucial to ensuring the effectiveness of this new legislation,[36] whose impact on the concentration of politico-economic power remains highly uncertain.[37] Large digital firms are not without defenses.[38] Notably, they may challenge some provisions of the DMA in courts, with lengthy procedures to follow,[39] and secure some success or, at least, obtain the temporary suspension of these provisions and, more permanently, their narrow interpretation.[40] They may also choose to get actively involved in finding "reasonable" solutions, through dialogue, in the implementation of the DMA.[41]

Other recent or proposed acts could have some relevance on the concentration of power within the hands of a few digital firms. The Data Governance Act (DGA), formally adopted on 30 May 2022 and published in the EU Official Journal on 3 June 2022,[42] creates a framework facilitating data sharing. However, it does not include

---

[34] Article 6(5) DMA. See Silke Heinz, "Art. 6(5)," in Podszun (ed.), *Digital Markets Act*, paras. 90–91; Kalbhenn, "European Legislative Initiative," 68–69; Petit, "DMA," 537.

[35] Andreas Schwab, "Art. 6(12)," in Podszun (ed.), *Digital Markets Act*, para. 291.

[36] See Geradin, "The DMA Has Been Published"; Bania & Karanikioti, "Regulating Big Tech" ("The imminent entry into force of the DMA constitutes a significant step in the regulation of gatekeeper digital platforms, making the EU a frontrunner when it comes to digital regulation. As the countdown to the application of the DMA has started, big questions await their answers"); Akman, "Regulating Competition," 87–88 & 105–6; Renda, "Digital Economy," 351 & 354; Scott Morton, "EU's New Law"; Javier Espinoza, "How Big Tech Lost the Antitrust Battle with Europe," *Financial Times*, online edition, 21 March 2022, www.ft.com/content/cbb1fe40-860d-4013-bfcf-b75ee6e30206.

[37] See, e.g., Cennamo *et al.*, "Platforms," 51; Nick Wingfield, "The Briefing: Why Investors Shrugged Off Europe's Big Tech Rules," *The Information*, 25 March 2022, www.theinformation.com/articles/why-investors-shrugged-off-europe-s-big-tech-rules; Adam Satariano, "E.U. Takes Aim at Big Tech's Power with Landmark Digital Act," *New York Times*, online edition, 24 March 2022, www.nytimes.com/2022/03/24/technology/eu-regulation-apple-meta-google.html? ("Questions remain about how the new law will work in practice. Companies are expected to look for ways to diminish its impact through the courts. And regulators will need new funding to pay for their expanded oversight responsibilities, when budgets are under strain from the pandemic"); see also Bostoen, "Digital Markets Act," 289–91 & 304–05.

[38] Adam Satariano, "E.U. Takes Aim at Big Tech's Power with Landmark Digital Act," *New York Times*, online edition, 24 March 2022 (quoting Thomas Vinje, a veteran antitrust lawyer in Brussels).

[39] Budzinski & Mendelsohn, "Regulating Big Tech," 26; see also Anna Wolf-Posch, "Art. 6(11)," in Podszun (ed.), *Digital Markets Act*, para. 279.

[40] Tripp Mickle, "Big Tech Greets Markets' Slide with a Shrug," *New York Times*, 21 May 2022, A1 ("But the companies are expected to challenge the law in court, potentially tying up the legislation for years. The probability it gets bogged down leaves analysts sticking to their consensus: 'Big Tech is going to be more powerful. And what's being done about it? Nothing,' Mr. Kramer of Arete Research said"). On the challenges relation to the interpretation of the DMA, see d'Halluin, "DMA," 12–13, paras. 14–21; Brankin & Treacy, "DMA" 18–19, paras. 26–32.

[41] See Brankin & Treacy, "DMA," 21, para. 45; Larouche & de Streel, "Compass," 30, para. 17

[42] Regulation (EU) 2022/868 of the European Parliament and of the Council of 30 May 2022 on European Data Governance and Amending Regulation (EU) 2018/1724 (Data Governance Act; OJ L 152, 3 June 2022, 1–44).

obligations for digital platforms to share data. The Artificial Intelligence Act, proposed by the Commission on 21 April 2021,[43] does not specifically address issues raised by the concentration or the centralization of artificial intelligence.[44] This proposed regulation is subject to intense lobbying, and the initial proposal is already regarded as outdated,[45] showing the difficulty to concretely regulate this matter. Obligations to document, test, and take other safety measures would be imposed to programmers working on high-risk applications, and the European Parliament is poised to include in this category "AI systems intended to be used to influence the outcome of an election or referendum or the voting behaviour of natural persons in the exercise of their vote in elections or referenda."[46] This innovation could be promising, even if much will depend on its actual scope and the way these obligations are enforced.

The Regulation on the Transparency and Targeting of Political Advertising, proposed by the European Commission on 25 November 2021,[47] contains transparency obligations for political advertising services and specific requirements related to targeting and amplification. It addresses various issues on the distortions of the electoral and democratic process but does not provide for a full ban on microtargeting for political purposes nor does it prohibit targeted advertising based on pervasive tracking, for instance.[48] It is facing intense lobbying efforts from leading internet firms.[49] On 2 February 2023, the European Parliament adopted a long list of amendments on the proposed regulation, that would notably prohibit microtargeting for political adverstising.[50] That said, this regulation should not have much impact on the concentration of politico-economic power within the hands of the large digital platforms.

---

[43] Proposal for a Regulation of the European Parliament and of the Council Laying Down Harmonized Rules on Artificial Intelligence (Artificial Intelligence Act) and Amending Certain Union Legislative Acts, COM(2021) 206 final, available at https://eur-lex.europa.eu/resource.html?uri=cellar:e0649735-a372-11eb-9585-01aa75ed71a1.0001.02/DOC_1&format=PDF.

[44] See *infra* Chapter 9, Section 9.4.2.

[45] See Billy Perrigo, "Big Tech Is Already Lobbying to Water Down Europe's AI Rules," *Time*, online edition, 21 April 2023, https://time.com/6273694/ai-regulation-europe/#.

[46] European Parliament, *Draft Compromise Amendments on the Draft Report*, 14 June 2023, Recital 40a and Annex III, 8 (a) (aa); see also Hadrien Pouget, "Europe's AI Act Nears Finishing Line – Worrying Washington," *CEPA*, 1 May 2023, https://cepa.org/article/europes-ai-act-nears-finishing-line-worrying-washington.

[47] Proposal for a Regulation of the European Parliament and of the Council on the Transparency and Targeting of Political Advertising, COM(2021) 731 final, available at https://eur-lex.europa.eu/legal-content/EN/TXT/?uri=CELEX%3A52021PC0731.

[48] Summary of the Opinion of the European Data Protection Supervisor on the Proposal for Regulation on the Transparency and Targeting of Political Advertising, Brussels, 20 January 2022 (OJ, 1 April 2022, C 145/12), para. 51.

[49] Molly Killeen, "Big Tech Ramps Up Pressure to Curb Political Ads Regulation," *Euractiv*, 30 November 2022 (updated 1 December 2022), www.euractiv.com/section/digital/news/big-tech-ramps-up-pressure-to-curb-political-ads-regulation/.

[50] See Molly Killeen, "EU Parliament Adopts Position on Political Advertising Regulation," *Euractiv*, 2 February 2023 (updated 3 February 2023), www.euractiv.com/section/platforms/news/eu-parliament-adopts-position-on-political-advertising-regulation/.

The list of Commission proposals continues to grow steadily. On 23 February 2022, the European Commission proposed a Data Act,[51] which aims to make data sharing and use easier and ensure fairness in the digital environment, notably by setting up rules regarding the use of data generated by Internet of Things devices. Moreover, the Data Act seeks to ensure consistency between data access rights. It also lays down requirements relating to data interoperability. It remains to be seen how the Data Act will interact, for instance, with the DMA, the Data Governance Act or the General Data Protection Regulation[52]. In any event, the proposed Data Act neither addresses the concentration of politico-economic power within the hands of a few digital firms nor does it deal with issues relating to potential distortions of electoral and demo- cratic processes through large or, *a fortiori*, dominant digital platforms. On 24 March 2023, the Member States' representatives reached a common position allowing the Council of the European Union to enter negotiations with the European Parliament to clarify, for instance, the interplay between the Data Act and other acts or regula- tions, but not to address the concentration of power as such.[53]

Finally, the European Commission proposed, on 16 September 2022, a European Media Freedom Act.[54] It imposes a set of obligations on providers of very large online platforms.[55] However, the rules relating to the assessment of "media market concentrations"[56] suppose that "at least one media service provider" is involved,[57] and this last term does not cover, for instance, Facebook or X/Twitter.[58] This pro- posed act is even likely to exacerbate the regulatory asymmetries between service providers and online platforms.[59]

8.3 GERMANY

The Tenth Amendment to the Act against Restraints of Competition (ARC)[60] was approved by the German Bundestag on 14 January 2021 and came into force on 19 January 2021. It creates a regulatory framework for digital competition. The new

---

[51] Proposal for a Regulation of the European Parliament and of the Council on Harmonised Rules on Fair Access to and Use of Data (Data Act), COM(2022) 68 final, available at https://digital-strategy.ec .europa.eu/en/library/data-act-proposal-regulation-harmonised-rules-fair-access-and-use-data.

[52] See Karanikioti, "Data Act."

[53] Council of the EU, "Data Act: Member States Agree Common Position on Fair Access to and Use of Data," *Press Release*, 24 March 2023.

[54] Proposal for a Regulation of the European Parliament and of the Council establishing a Common Framework for Media Services in the Internal Market (European Media Freedom Act) and amending Directive 2010/13/EU, COM(2022) 457 final, available at https://eur-lex.europa.eu/legal-content/EN/ TXT/PDF/?uri=CELEX:52022PC0457&from=EN.

[55] Articles 17–19 of the proposed EMFA.

[56] Articles 21 of the proposed EMFA.

[57] Article 2(13) of the proposed EMFA.

[58] Bania, "Media Freedom Act Proposal."

[59] Bania, "Media Freedom Act Proposal."

[60] Gesetz zur Änderung des Gesetzes gegen Wettbewerbsbeschränkungen für ein fokussiertes, proak- tives und digitales Wettbewerbsrecht 4.0 und andere Bestimmungen (GWB-Digitalisierungsgesetz)

Section 19a ARC provides the Federal Cartel Office with additional powers of intervention toward "companies of paramount significance for competition across markets," that is, companies like Google/Alphabet,[61] Apple, Facebook/Meta Platforms,[62] Amazon,[63] and Microsoft.[64]

In addition to the general anti-abuse rules, the Federal Cartel Office can, for example, prohibit a company from giving preference to its own offerings or, under certain circumstances, from shifting market power to previously non-dominated markets through the use or linkage of data.[65] The provision on data access in Section 20(1a) ARC, in combination with the lowering of the intervention thresholds in the case of relative market power, is also worth mentioning. Finally, the essential facilities doctrine has been expanded by explicitly declaring unlawful a dominant undertaking's unjustified refusal to grant access to data, networks, or other infrastructure facilities that are necessary to compete on an upstream or downstream market.[66]

These changes are important and should not be underestimated. Companies regarded as gatekeepers are now subject to stricter rules. The Federal Cartel Office is able to intervene at an early stage in cases where digital companies of paramount significance for competition across markets threaten competition.[67] That said, the Tenth Amendment to the Act against Restraints of Competition does not tackle the concentration of power as such[68] and, notably, does not contain rules specifically regulating distortions of the electoral and democratic process.

In September 2022, the Ministry for Economic Affairs and Climate Action issued a draft of the Eleventh Amendment to the Act against Restraints of Competition.[69]

[Act Amending the Act Against Restraints of Competition for a Focused, Proactive and Digital Competition Law 4.0 and Other Provisions (GWB Digitization Act)], available at www.bgbl.de/xaver/bgbl/start.xav#__bgbl__%2F%2F*%5B%40attr_id%3D%27bgbl121s0002.pdf%27%5D__1629808324121.

[61] See Bundeskartellamt [Federal Cartel Office], Decision relating to Alphabet Inc., Case B7-61/21, 30 December 2021. On this decision, see Federal Cartel Office, "Alphabet/Google Subject to New Abuse Control Applicable to Large Digital Companies – Bundeskartellamt Determines 'Paramount Significance Across Markets,'" *Press Release*, 5 January 2022.

[62] See Bundeskartellamt [Federal Cartel Office], Decision relating to Meta Platforms Inc., Case B6-27/21, 2 May 2022. On this decision, see Federal Cartel Office, "New Rules Apply to Meta (Formerly Facebook) – Bundeskartellamt Determines its 'Paramount Significance for Competition Across Markets,'" *Press Release*, 4 May 2022.

[63] See Bundeskartellamt [Federal Cartel Office], Decision relating to Amazon.com, Inc., Case B2-55/21, 5 July 2022. On this decision, see Federal Cartel Office, "Amazon Now Subject to Stricter Regulations – Bundeskartellamt Determines its Paramount Significance for Competition across Markets (Section 19a GWB)," *Press Release*, 6 July 2022.

[64] See, e.g., Franck & Peitz, "Digital Platforms," 517; UNCTAD, *Digital Era*, 7–8.

[65] See, e.g., Robertson, "Digital Markets," 448; Franck & Peitz, "Digital Platforms," 519.

[66] Section 19(2, Number 4) ARC.

[67] See the press release of the Federal Cartel Office, dated 19 January 2021, available at www.bundeskartellamt.de/SharedDocs/Meldung/EN/Pressemitteilungen/2021/19_01_2021_GWB%20Novelle.html. See, e.g., Ezrachi & Stucke, *Barons*, 187.

[68] See, e.g., Podszun, "Regulierung," 59.

[69] See Bundesministerium für Wirtschaft und Klimaschutz, *Entwurf eines Gesetzes zur Verbesserung der Wettbewerbsstrukturen und zur Abschöpfung von Vorteilen aus Wettbewerbsverstößen* [Draft Law

Under this draft, the German Federal Cartel Office would carry out sector inquiries, notably to identify markets where a divestiture, regardless of a competition infringement, may remedy competition concerns.[70] Divestiture is meant as an *ultimate ratio* instrument.[71] On 5 April 2023, the German Government adopted a revised draft bill[72] that partly takes account of the critics raised by various stakeholders, including some of the largest business associations.[73] As *ultima ratio* and provided that there is a substantial and continuing disturbance of competition, the Federal Cartel Office would still be able to impose unbundling remedies on companies, but only to those with a dominant market position or with paramount significance for competition across markets according to Section 19a ARC.[74] This further requires that the measure is expected to eliminate or substantially lessen the disturbance.[75]

Moreover, the German Monopolies Commission has already recommended, with respect to the digital markets, to await the implementation of Section 19a ARC and of the DMA before considering further specific regulatory measures.[76] One may also wonder whether a decision of the German Cartel Office ordering Meta Platforms to divest Instagram or WhatsApp would be taken at the appropriate level. Finally, the German Cartel Office would, in any case, have to abide by the constitutional requirements, especially in relation to the guarantee of property.[77] To sum up, extreme caution and limited expectations are certainly required in this area.

8.4 INDIA

In India, the Information Technology (Intermediary Guidelines and Digital Media Ethics Code) Rules of 2021[78] regulates online intermediaries such as social

on the Improvement of Competition Structures and the Absorption of Benefits from Competition Violations], 15 September 2022.

[70] Proposed Section 32f ARC.

[71] Bundesministerium für Wirtschaft und Klimaschutz, *Entwurf*, 2, 15–16 & 26–28; see also Mendelsohn, "Unbundling."

[72] Bundesregierung [Federal Government], *Entwurf eines Gesetzes zur Änderung des Gesetzes gegen Wettbewerbsbeschränkungen und anderer Gesetze* [Draft Act Amending the Act against Restraints of Competition and Other Laws] (Berlin: Bundesregierung, 5 April 2023).

[73] Gibson Dunn, *Draft Amendment to German Competition Act Adopted by German Government – More Powers for the Bundeskartellamt* (Frankfurt & Munich: Gibson, Dunn & Crutcher LLP, 13 April 2023), 1, www.gibsondunn.com/draft-amendment-to-german-competition-act-adopted-by-german-government-more-powers-for-the-bundeskartellamt-part-ii/.

[74] Proposed Section 32f(4) ARC (draft of 5 April 2023).

[75] Proposed Section 32f(4), end of the 1st sentence, ARC (draft of 5 April 2023).

[76] Monopolkommission, *Wettbewerb 2022*, 200, para. 380.

[77] Article 14 of the German Basic Law. See Monopolkommission, *Wettbewerb 2022*, 200, para. 379; see also Zimmer, "Unbundling" ("[C]ompanies would have to be compensated for the net advantages they lose through the unbundling – even if the proceeds of the sale are taken into account. A lost return on investment and innovation efforts would thus have to be compensated"); Nettesheim & Thomas, *Entflechtung*, 85–139.

[78] For a critical analysis, see Ashwini, "Platform Regulation," 221–29.

media platforms and search engines, digital new organizations, over-the-top platforms, and other entities. On one hand, they aim to increase the accountability of social media platforms in order to prevent their misuse and abuse by providing the due diligence to be followed by intermediaries and other entities. On the other hand, they seek to empower users by establishing a redressal mechanism for efficient grievance resolution. However, their constitutionality is being challenged before courts.[79] The matter now rests with the latter, including the Supreme Court of India.[80]

On 28 October 2022, the Government of India notified Amendments to the Information Technology Rules 2021 "for an Open, Safe & Trusted and Accountable Internet."[81] Social media and other intermediaries "shall respect all the rights accorded to the citizens under the Constitution, including in the articles 14 [equality before the law], 19 [right to freedom] & 21 [protection of life and personal liberty]."[82] This reforms appears to make fundamental rights applicable to private parties, but the way it will be implemented and interpreted by courts "remains unclear."[83] Finally, on 6 April 2023, amendments to the Information Technology Rules 2021 were promulgated; they relate to online gaming and fake or false information about Central Government business.[84]

The Information Technology Rules of 2021, including its most recent amendments, do not address the issue of concentration of power as such and are criticized for being overbroad and disproportionately reducing the right to privacy or the freedom of expression.[85] From this perspective, it seems hard to see them as having an undisputable pro-competitive effect or as contributing to some deconcentration of platform power. They are actually focused on other questions.

---

[79] See Ashwini, "Platform Regulation," 228–29.

[80] See Nalini Sharma, "Legal Experts Raise Concern about Growing Govt Control over Social Media Content," *India Today*, 15 June 2022, www.indiatoday.in/law/story/legal-experts-government-it-rules-2021-amendments-social-media-content-1962515-2022-06-15.

[81] Ministry of Electronics & Information Technology, "Government notifies Amendments to the Information Technology (Intermediary Guidelines and Digital Media Ethics Code) Rules 2021 for an Open, Safe & Trusted and Accountable Internet," *Press Release*, 29 October 2022, www.pib.gov.in/PressReleasePage.aspx?PRID=1871840.

[82] Newly inserted Rule 3(1)(n).

[83] Rahul Matthan, Nikhil Narendran, Jyotsna Jayaram, Karishma Sundara, Thomas J. Vallianeth & Kuruvila M Jacob, "The Information Technology (Intermediary Guidelines and Digital Media Ethics Code) Amendment Rules, 2022," *Lexology*, 7 November 2022, www.lexology.com/library/detail.aspx?g=27a883ce-10ed-4ab9-8642-b7e2dc118ae0; see also Trishee Goyal, "Explained | The Amendments to the IT Rules, 2021," *The Hindu*, online edition, 31 October 2022 (updated 6 November 2022), www.thehindu.com/sci-tech/technology/explained-the-amendments-to-the-it-rules-2021/article66079214.ece.

[84] See Gazette Notification vide G.S.R. 275(E) dated 6.4.2023 regarding amendments to the IT (Intermediary Guidelines and Digital Media Ethics Code) Rules, 2021 in relation to online gaming and fake or false information about Central Government business.

[85] See Ashwini, "Platform Regulation," 228–29.

8.5 JAPAN

On 1 February 2021, the Japanese Act on Improving Transparency and Fairness of Digital Platforms came into force.[86] It aims at improving transparency and fairness in transactions whilst preserving digital innovation. According to Article 3 of this Act, measures should be primarily based on voluntary and proactive initiatives so that involvement by the Government or through other regulations should be kept to a minimum.[87]

The Act requires specified digital platforms to disclose their terms and conditions, as well as other relevant information, to create appropriate internal procedures in a voluntary manner to ensure the fairness of transactions or to settle disputes with users, and to submit a yearly report on the overview of measures that they have conducted, to which self-assessment results are attached.[88] In other words, "there is little room for strong enforcements but mostly voluntary actions," as emphasized by Izumi Aizu.[89] On 3 October 2022, the Japanese Ministry of Economy, Trade, and Industry designated the digital platform providers in the digital advertising sector subject to its specific regulations.[90]

This new Act does not address concentration of power as such and, to a certain degree, leaves it up to the voluntary effort of each platform operator to fulfill the purpose of the regulation. Moreover, it does not contain any rules relating to the electoral or democratic process, let alone to its distortion.

8.6 SOUTH KOREA

At the end of August 2021, the National Assembly of South Korea passed a bill requiring app stores like Google's Play Store or Apple's App Store to let users pay for in-app purchases through multiple payment systems.[91] This bill actually amends the country's Telecommunications Business Act.

This new bill addresses an important issue from users' perspectives and could have a large impact on how major app stores do business. It may reduce their economic power because in-app purchases will not necessarily flow through their payment

---

[86] See the key points of this Act prepared by the Ministry of Economy, Trade, and Industry (16 April 2021), www.meti.go.jp/english/policy/mono_info_service/information_economy/digital_platforms/tfdpa.html; see also UNCTAD, *Digital Era*, 9.

[87] UNCTAD, *Digital Era*, 9.

[88] See Ministry of Economy, Trade and Industry, Ordinance for Enforcement of the Act on Improving Transparency and Fairness of Digital Platforms, www.meti.go.jp/english/policy/mono_info_service/information_economy/digital_platforms/pdf/1012_001c.pdf.

[89] Aizu, "Platform Regulation," 204–5.

[90] Ministry of Economy, Trade, and Industry, "Designation of Digital Platform Providers Subject to Specific Regulations under the Act on Improving Transparency and Fairness of Digital Platforms," *Press Release*, 3 October 2022, www.meti.go.jp/english/press/2022/1003_005.html.

[91] See, e.g., Jin Yu Young, "South Korea Forces Google and Apple to Allow Third-party In-app Payments," *New York Times*, online edition, 31 August 2021, www.nytimes.com/2021/08/31/business/south-korea-google-apple.html.

systems. Furthermore, lower rates resulting from these new obligations imposed on Google or Apple may help app developers "invest in their businesses and workforce, and benefit consumers with greater innovation and more choice."[92]

The impact of this bill on Google or Apple ecosystems is quite uncertain, as both firms still plan to charge developers a service fee – albeit a reduced one – on purchases made through alternative payment systems.[93] However, they have been pushed to change their rules and practices regarding options for payment choices, not just in South Korea. In March 2022, Google and Spotify announced that the Google Play Store will allow a "dual billing option" in U.S. apps, starting with Spotify.[94] Notwithstanding these moves and further ones to come, the market may thus remain concentrated after all,[95] and while dual billing will not wipe Google's or Apple's related revenues out entirely,[96] the commission rates are now subject to downward pressure.[97] In any event, the new bill does not address the concentration of politico-economic power within the hands of such firms. Moreover, it does not deal with issues relating, for instance, to potential distortions of electoral and democratic processes through digital platforms since it is focused on another issue.

8.7 UNITED KINGDOM

In a consultation opened on 20 July 2021, the British Government set out its proposal for a new pro-competition regime for digital markets.[98] The consultation outcome was published on 6 May 2022,[99] and the Government has indicated a willingness to

---

[92] Coalition for App Fairness, "South Korea Makes History with World's First National Law Opening App Store Payments to Competition," *Press Release*, 3 September 2021, https://perma.cc/6ZR9-WHV3.

[93] See Kate Park, "Apple to Allow Third-Party App Payment Options in South Korea," *TechCrunch*, 11 January 2022, https://techcrunch.com/2022/01/10/apple-to-allow-third-party-app-payment-options-in-south-korea/. On this issue, see Geradin, "Korean Bill" ("If Apple's claim that IAP [Apple's in-app purchasing system] is the only way to collect its commission is true, then this commission should disappear – to the great relief of app developers in Korea. But I am confident than now that the mandatory use of IAP is banned in Korea, Apple will suddenly find another way to collect this commission. If they do so, their claim that the mandatory use of IAP is needed for them to collect their commission will lose any credibility").

[94] See "Expanded Payment Options: Spotify and Google Announce User Choice Billing," *For the Record*, 23 March 2022, https://newsroom.spotify.com/2022-03-23/spotify-and-google-announce-user-choice-billing/.

[95] See Kim, "Anti-Google Law," 125–34 (arguing that the new bill may make app developers even more beholden to dominant platforms than they are now); see also Ball, *Metaverse*, 203.

[96] See Martin Peers, "The Briefing: Apple Pressured by Google-Spotify Deal," *The Information*, 23 March 2022, www.theinformation.com/articles/apple-pressured-by-google-spotify-deal.

[97] See Geradin, "Billing."

[98] See www.gov.uk/government/consultations/a-new-pro-competition-regime-for-digital-markets.

[99] See the consultation outcome presented to Parliament by the Secretary of State for Digital, Culture, Media, and Sport and the Secretary of State for Business, Energy, and Industrial Strategy by Command of Her Majesty on 6 May 2022, www.gov.uk/government/consultations/a-new-pro-competition-regime-for-digital-markets/outcome/a-new-pro-competition-regime-for-digital-markets-government-response-to-consultation.

move toward legislation. In November 2022, it confirmed that the Digital Markets, Competition and Consumer Bill would be brought forward in 2023 "to provide the Competition and Markets Authority with new powers to promote and tackle anti-competitive practice in digital markets."[100] The new bill was introduced to the House of Commons on 25 April 2023.[101]

The Digital Markets Unit (DMU) within the Competition and Markets Authority (CMA) would be given the power to designate technology firms that hold substantial and entrenched market power and have a position of strategic significance in at least one digital activity with "Strategic Market Status."[102] Since April 2021, the DMU has been established on a non-statutory basis within the CMA.[103]

The DMU would be able to set tailored rules on how firms deemed to have this status in key digital services are expected to behave and operate.[104] Conduct requirements could be imposed if the DMU considers that it would be appropriate to do so for the purposes of fair dealing, open choices, trust and transparency.[105] The categories of permitted types of conduct requirement would be set out in legislation,[106] but each code of conduct would be tailored to each firm with Strategic Market Status.[107] The DMU would also have the power to make pro-competition interventions.[108] Moreover, companies with Strategic Market Status would be required to report their most significant transactions prior to completion.[109] Finally, changes include streamlined decision making and updating merger and fine thresholds.[110]

The proposed reform would establish a new regulatory regime for digital markets. New or clarified limits would apply to the conducts of firms with strategic market status. Ministers are facing intense lobbying from Big Tech firms, so that "the new

[100] HM Treasury, *Autumn Statement 2022*, CP 751 (London: HM Treasury, 2022), 35, para. 3.32. See, e.g., Smith, "Full Steam."
[101] Digital Markets, Competition and Consumers Bill, https://publications.parliament.uk/pa/bills/cbill/58-03/0294/220294.pdf.
[102] Sections 2(2), 5 & 6 of the proposed bill (25 April 2023).
[103] See, e.g., CMA, *Mobile Ecosystems*, 351.
[104] Department for Business and Trade, Department for Science, Innovation and Technology, Kevin Hollinrake MP, and Paul Scully MP, "New Bill to Crack Down on Rip-offs, Protect Consumer Cash Online and Boost Competition in Digital Markets," *Press Release*, 25 April 2023. See, e.g., Woods, "UK's Approach to Regulation," 339–40.
[105] Section 19(5) of the proposed bill (25 April 2023).
[106] Section 20 of the proposed bill (25 April 2023).
[107] Ashurst, "Digital Markets, Competition and Consumers Bill: Wide-ranging Reforms to UK Regulation," *Competition Law Update*, 26 April 2023, www.ashurst.com/en/news-and-insights/legal-updates/digital-markets-competition-and-consumers-bill---wide-ranging-reforms-to-uk-regulation/; Ashurst, "UK Government Update on Digital Markets, Competition and Consumer Bill," *Lexology*, 22 November 2022, www.lexology.com/library/detail.aspx?g=383f6cb2-6d8a-4abc-9564-430d4b376463.
[108] Section 55 of the proposed bill (25 April 2023).
[109] Section 44 of the proposed bill (25 April 2023).
[110] See, e.g., Herbert Smith Freehills LLP, "Digital Markets, Competition and Consumer Bill Introduced before Parliament," *Lexology*, 27 April 2023, www.lexology.com/library/detail.aspx?g=be3b19d5-5fd1-4b48-8b0b-ef9293734bcb; see also HM Treasury, *Autumn Statement 2022*, CP 751 (London: HM Treasury, 2022), 57, para. 5.71.

legislation could be watered down."[111] That said, the reform does not address concentration of power as such, nor does it deal with distortions of the electoral and democratic process, for instance.

8.8 UNITED STATES

In February 2021, the Competition and Antitrust Law Enforcement Reform Act was introduced in Congress.[112] It would apply a stricter standard for permissible mergers by prohibiting mergers that create an appreciable risk of materially lessening competition or unfairly lower the prices of goods or wages because of a lack of competition among buyers or employers. Additionally, for some large mergers or mergers that concentrate markets beyond a certain threshold, the burden of proof would be shifted to the merging parties to prove that the merger does not violate the law. The proposed Act also prohibits "exclusionary conduct that presents an appreciable risk of harming competition."[113] It could help avoid further concentration of economic power,[114] but it would not tackle the existing concentration as such. Moreover, the fate of this bill is highly uncertain.

In May 2021, the State Antitrust Enforcement Venue Act was introduced in Congress.[115] It would provide state attorneys general with the same venue selection rights as federal antitrust enforcers, without having to face delays or higher costs due to the transfer of state antitrust actions into a multidistrict litigation. This bill relates to procedural issues, which should not be underestimated, but do not affect the concentration of power as such. On 14 June 2022, it passed the Senate.

In June 2021, several bills aimed at overhauling antitrust were introduced in Congress. The proposed American Innovation and Choice Online Act[116] prevents digital platforms like Facebook, Google, or Amazon from highlighting their businesses over others in the online marketplace and thus from discriminating against other participants in their services. The proposed Ending Platform Monopolies Act[117] tackles potential conflicts of interest arising when a firm operates a platform and also uses it to sell its product, with the goal to avoid disadvantages to competitors in ways that undermine free and fair competition. The proposed

---

[111] Smith, "Fashionably Late" (mentioning "the current lobbying blitz"); Tom Bristow, "Big Tech Lobbyists Get Stuck in to UK's Landmark Competition Bill," *Politico*, 3 April 2023.

[112] S.225 – Competition and Antitrust Law Enforcement Reform Act, introduced 4 February 2021, available at www.congress.gov/bill/117th-congress/senate-bill/225.

[113] Section 9(a) amending the Clayton Act, 15 U.S.C. 12 et seq., section 26A(b)(1).

[114] See Silton, Davis & Spraggins, "Antitrust Bills," 30–32.

[115] H.R.3460 – State Antitrust Enforcement Venue Act, introduced 21 May 2021, available at www.congress.gov/bill/117th-congress/house-bill/3460.

[116] H.R.3816 – American Choice and Innovation Online Act, introduced 11 June 2021, available at www.congress.gov/bill/117th-congress/house-bill/3816.

[117] H.R.3825 – Ending Platform Monopolies Act, introduced 11 June 2021, available at www.congress.gov/bill/117th-congress/house-bill/3825.

Platform Competition and Opportunity Act[118] makes it more difficult to carry out certain acquisitions and especially prohibits acquisitions of competitive threats by dominant platforms that expand their market power. The Merger Filing Fee Modernization Act[119] requires companies to pay more to government agencies to review mergers and acquisitions. The proposed Augmenting Compatibility and Competition by Enabling Service Switching Act[120] requires platforms to make user data portable and interoperable with other services. The first and the last two bills may be the ones most likely to gain support in Congress, with the two others being harder to pass[121] and much more controversial.[122] On 29 September 2022, the Merger Filing Fee Modernization Act passed the House of Representatives.[123] On 22 and 23 December 2022, the Senate and the House of Representatives, respectively, passed the Merger Filing Fee Modernization Act of 2022 as a part of the Consolidated Appropriations Act of 2023. President Joe Biden signed this Act into law on 29 December 2022.

Unfortunately, the Ending Platform Monopolies Act[124] and the Platform Competition and Opportunity Act[125] are the most relevant from a separation of powers' or the avoidance of a further concentration of power's perspective. In any event, all these acts would or will be difficult to implement – except, probably, for the Merger Filing Fee Modernization Act – and do not address, for instance, issues relating to

---

[118] H.R.3826 – Platform Competition and Opportunity Act of 2021, introduced 11 June 2021, available at www.congress.gov/bill/117th-congress/house-bill/3826.

[119] H.R.3843 – Merger Filing Fee Modernization Act of 2021, introduced 11 June 2021, available at www.congress.gov/bill/117th-congress/house-bill/3843.

[120] H.R.3849 – ACCESS Act of 2021, introduced 11 June 2021, available at www.congress.gov/bill/117th-congress/house-bill/3849.

[121] See Cecilia Kang, "Lawmakers, Taking Aim at Big Tech, Push Sweeping Overhaul of Antitrust," *New York Times*, online edition, 11 June 2021, www.nytimes.com/2021/06/11/technology/big-tech-antitrust-bills.html; see also Greg Bensinger, "How Illinois Is Winning in the Fight Against Big Tech," *New York Times*, 31 May 2022, A16 ("With Congress's repeated failure to advance any meaningful legislation, it may be up to states to help consumers wrest back some control over their own data"); Adam Satariano, "E.U. Takes Aim at Big Tech's Power with Landmark Digital Act," *New York Times*, online edition, 24 March 2022, www.nytimes.com/2022/03/24/technology/eu-regulation-apple-meta-google.html?. See, however, Buck, "Antitrust Reform" ("Congress will likely pass three major antitrust bills – including the American Innovation and Choice Online Act, which would prohibit anticompetitive self-referencing – by the August [2022] recess").

[122] See Picker, "Antitrust Bills." Regarding the American Innovation and Choice Online Act, see, e.g., Gilbert, "Act" (concluding that "U.S. antitrust law should not mimic the European approach to unfair preferencing by a dominant platform").

[123] See Ken Buck, "Buck Announces House Passage of Historic Bills Taking on Big Tech's Unfettered Monopoly Power," *Press Release*, 29 September 2022, https://buck.house.gov/media-center/press-releases/buck-announces-house-passage-historic-bills-taking-big-techs-unfettered.

[124] See Silton, Davis & Spraggins, "Antitrust Bills," 28; Monti, "Taming Digital Monopolies," 66 ("[T]his Bill could at one stroke break up many of the present-day internet giants. If we consider past experiences with deconcentration, it is unlikely that this ambitious project will see the light of day" [footnote omitted]).

[125] See Ezrachi & Stucke, *Barons*, 193; Silton, Davis & Spraggins, "Antitrust Bills," 28; Monti, "Taming Digital Monopolies," 68, note 160.

distortions of the electoral and democratic process through or by large or, *a fortiori*, dominant digital platforms. Moreover, they would not tackle the existing concentration of power as such, except for the Ending Platform Monopolies Act, under which large digital platforms "could have to divest lines of business where their gatekeeper power allows them to favor their own services or disadvantage rivals."[126] At the end of the day, the few antitrust bills passed by the Senate or the House of Representatives in 2022 "make technical changes to antitrust processes but don't deliver the big reforms some lawmakers want."[127]

In August 2021, a bill intended to prohibit operators of app marketplaces like Apple and Google from requiring that app developers use their in-app payment system and to prevent these operators from self-preferencing was introduced in Congress.[128] The proposed Open App Markets Act would reduce the power of the aforementioned firms in their respective app ecosystem. However, it does not deal with issues relating, for instance, to the concentration of politico-economic power within the hands of such firms. Should this bill be adopted, it would impact Apple's and Google's app ecosystem with a scope that has yet to be determined.[129] Moreover, litigation relating to the Open App Markets Act and the American Innovation and Choice Online Act – if adopted – would be lengthy and likely very expensive.[130] The possibility for a platform to defend itself on multiple grounds[131] as well as the lack of forthrightness regarding the vision of competition embraced by the second act[132] could explain this.

[126] Pramila Jayapal, "Jayapal's Landmark Big Tech Legislation Passes House Judiciary Committee," *Press Release*, 24 June 2021. See also Silton, Davis & Spraggins, "Antitrust Bills," 28.

[127] Makenzie Holland, "Experts Torn on Impact of Antitrust Bills Passed by House," *TechTarget*, 7 October 2022, www.techtarget.com/searchcio/news/252525883/Experts-torn-on-impact-of-antitrust-bills-passed-by-House.

[128] S.2710 – Open App Markets Act, introduced 11 August 2021, available at www.congress.gov/bill/117th-congress/senate-bill/2710/titles.

[129] See Martin Peers, "The Briefing: Brits Target Apple's and Google's Mobile Power," *The Information*, 10 June 2022, www.theinformation.com/articles/brits-target-apple-s-and-google-s-mobile-power.

[130] Hovenkamp, "Self-Preferencing" ("Suppose a platform's own product appears first in the search results, but that the placement of competing products has not otherwise been degraded. This may or may not signal that the platform manipulated its algorithm to force its own product into the top spot. These are complicated algorithms that account for many different factors, so this is unlikely to be cut and dry. Under the proposed bills, a court would have to go through the algorithm in detail to determine whether it ranked the products in an unreasonable manner. Each side would introduce its own experts to argue why the algorithm is or isn't reasonable. But the judge, lacking any expertise in search algorithms, may well have a hard time evaluating these arguments. The litigation process would likely last years and cost tens of millions of dollars").

[131] Regarding the American Innovation and Online Choice Act, see Baer, "Amazon" ("Dominant online platforms possess enormous economic power, with the ability and demonstrated willingness to impede competition in ways that damage both competing sellers and consumers. We need tools to challenge abuses of that power. The American Innovation and Online Choice Act does that, but in a fashion that gives Amazon and other covered platforms the right to show that their actions are not harmful to competition or are otherwise needed to protect consumer privacy and our national and cyber-security").

[132] Picker, "Self-Preferencing."

Finally, in May 2022, a new federal bill that would force Alphabet, Meta Platforms, Amazon, and other digital advertising companies to divest major parts of their ad tech business was introduced into Congress.[133] Although the proposed Competition and Transparency in Digital Advertising Act[134] could present a fundamental challenge to the industry,[135] it would not directly deal, for instance, with distortions of the electoral or democratic process.

The states have also enacted pieces of legislation. For instance, on 9 September 2021, the Governor of Texas signed House Bill 20 into law, a law that "prevents social media companies with more than 50 million monthly users banning users simply based on their political viewpoints."[136] This law reflects the idea that social media platforms should be treated like "common carriers" or "public utilities" and be prevented from discriminating against users' viewpoints.[137] It remains to be seen how this law can and will be applied in practice. For the time being, it has been blocked by the U.S. Supreme Court after an emergency request from two trade associations that represent major digital platforms.[138] Moreover, its impact on the concentration of politico-economic power as such seems *prima facie* quite modest.

8.9 CRITICAL ASSESSMENT

These recent or proposed pieces of legislation all address important issues in the digital economy, and some of them could contribute to reduce entrenched market concentration,[139] however, to a degree that remains to be defined. The most comprehensive set of bills from this perspective was introduced in the U.S. Congress during the last two years. However, even in this country, the concentration of politico-economic power in a few firms and the control of the digital infrastructure

---

[133] Josh Sisco, "New Bill Could Break Up Google's Ad Tech Business," *The Information*, 19 May 2022, www.theinformation.com/briefings/new-bill-could-break-up-googles-ad-tech-business; Makena Kelly, "Senators Push to Break Up Google, Facebook Ads Businesses in New Bill," *The Verge*, 19 May 2022, www.theverge.com/2022/5/19/23130963/google-facebook-antitrust-digital-advertising-competition-bill-senate.

[134] H.R.7839 – Competition and Transparency in Digital Advertising Act of 2021, introduced 19 May 2022, available at www.congress.gov/bill/117th-congress/house-bill/7839.

[135] Martin Peers, "The Briefing: Google Breakup Bill Shows Real Threat Facing Tech," *The Information*, 19 May 2022, www.theinformation.com/articles/google-breakup-bill-shows-real-threat-facing-tech.

[136] Office of the Texas Governor, Greg Abbott, "Governor Abbott Signs Law Protecting Texans from Wrongful Social Media Censorship," *Press Release*, 9 September 2021.

[137] Cristiano Lima with Aaron Schaffer, "How the GOP Assault on Social Media Flipped Net Neutrality on its Head," *Washington Post*, online edition, 19 May 2022, www.washingtonpost.com/politics/2022/05/19/how-gop-assault-social-media-flipped-net-neutrality-its-head/?utm_content=article-7989&utm_source=sg&utm_medium=email&utm_campaign=article_email. On this issue, see, e.g., Candeub, "Bargaining for Free Speech," 429–33.

[138] Opinion Relating to Order (application to vacate stay), 31 May 2022, *Netchoice, LLC v. Paxton*, 596 U. S. ___ (2022). See, e.g., Adam Liptak, "Supreme Court Blocks a Texas Law Regulating Social Media Platforms," *New York Times*, 1 June 2022, A21.

[139] See Deutscher, "Reshaping Digital Competition," 312. Regarding the United States, see Silton, Davis & Spraggins, "Antitrust Bills," 26, 28 & 31–32.

of democracy by them would remain widely unregulated or, at least, insufficiently regulated, as in other countries,[140] should Congress pass the proposed bills, after having been reintroduced, or similar new ones.[141] In any case, the record of the 117th Congress in this regard is clearly poor.[142] Besides, Ariel Ezrachi and Maurice E. Stucke conclude that "[u]ltimately none of the current policy proposals seek to align the ecosystems' value chains with society's interests"[143] and emphasize that "[p]olicymakers must focus on the broader ecosystems, not just particular markets or platforms."[144]

Furthermore, no recent or proposed pieces of legislation significantly mitigate the risk of distortion of the electoral and democratic process.[145] The rules relating to discriminatory conducts proposed in the United States and in the European Union do not explicitly address the issue of political discrimination by, or on, a large or a dominant digital platform.[146] In the European Union, the proposed Artificial Intelligence Act, as amended by the European Parliament, is quite promising, and the proposed Regulation on the Transparency and Targeting of Political Advertising represents an important move to address these problems, but it needs significant improvements, especially with regard to microtargeting for political purposes or pervasive tracking.[147] The European Parliament has already sent reassuring signals in this matter.

These shortcomings call for deeper reforms, notably to better separate governmental and platform powers even though interactions will inevitably subsist, and to reduce or, at least, mitigate the power of firms whose platforms have become an important or, *a fortiori*, fundamental part of the electoral or democratic process and of the digital infrastructure of democracy. The reforms needed would bring about new politico-economic as well as institutional and individual axes of the separation of powers.

---

[140] See Dolata, "Platform Regulation," 473–74; see also Narula, *Society*, 207; Podszun, "Regulierung," 59.

[141] With respect to innovation, see Ezrachi & Stucke, *Barons*, 183–89 & 193–96 (concluding that "the changes are unlikely to eliminate the toxic innovation" [quotation from p. 189]).

[142] See, Fox, "Consumer Welfare" ("Famously, numerous antitrust bills were introduced into prior sessions of Congress. They did not have sufficient traction; they might be reintroduced. Almost all were specialized to specific conduct of big tech and would do nothing to change the general orientation of antitrust").

[143] Ezrachi & Stucke, *Barons*, 195.

[144] Ezrachi & Stucke, *Barons*, 197; see also Acemoglu & Johnson, *Power and Progress*, 406 ("[B]reakup and more broadly antitrust should be considered as a complementary tool to the more fundamental aim of redirecting technology away from automation, surveillance, data collection, and digital advertising").

[145] See OECD, *Ex Ante Regulation*, 24–48.

[146] For a comparative perspective on the US and EU proposals, see Schnitzer *et al.*, *International Coherence*, 13–20.

[147] See *supra* Section 8.2 in the present Chapter.

9

New Politico-Economic Axes of the Separation of Powers

Some major issues relating to the concentration of politico-economic power in the digital and artificial intelligence era are not addressed by recent or proposed pieces of legislation in many jurisdictions, as just seen. Furthermore, the contribution of antitrust *de lege lata* to the separation of powers is rather limited, as analyzed in Chapter 6. A role should nevertheless be granted to specific legislation, regulation, or practices and, possibly, antitrust *de lege ferenda* or, at least, fundamentally reinterpreted, especially with respect to the control of the digital infrastructure of democracy (Section 9.1), the prohibition of distortions of the electoral and democratic process (Section 9.2), the conclusion of certain governmental contracts with large or, *a fortiori*, dominant platforms (Section 9.3), as well as the regulation and deconcentration or decentralization of artificial intelligence (Section 9.4) and the metaverse (Section 9.5).

9.1 CONTROL OF THE DIGITAL INFRASTRUCTURE OF DEMOCRACY

As seen in the first part of this book, Montesquieu, Hayek, Aron, or the German Ordoliberals included commerce and powerful companies or organizations in their reflections on liberty and power but did not directly bridge them with their "separation of powers" theory. The U.S. Supreme Court has built a bridge, however, between antitrust laws and the Bill of Rights:

> Antitrust laws in general, and the Sherman Act in particular, are the Magna Carta of free enterprise. They are as important to the preservation of economic freedom and our free enterprise system as the Bill of Rights is to the protection of our fundamental personal freedoms.[1]

Influence by powerful private companies, trusts, or organizations on governments, elections, or referenda by no means constitutes a new phenomenon. The same can be said about the fact that an industry is dominated by one or a few companies or

---

[1]   *United States v. Topco Assocs., Inc.*, 405 U.S. 596, 610 (1972).

about the fact that some economic activities are performed by the state itself or by companies that closely interact with the government. The present era is witnessing, however, private social networks and search engines potentially playing a significant and, in the future, perhaps a decisive role in the coming to power or the staying in power of governments and officials.[2] This calls for transparency and possibly for sector regulation or the adaptation of election laws, which may, in turn, call for a strict separation between government and the relevant companies.

Recall Montesquieu's words: "a prince should not engage in commerce."[3] The modern version could state that a government should not engage in digital commerce, especially – for now at least – in social networks or search engines, whose platforms have come to play an important or, *a fortiori*, fundamental role in the electoral or democratic process and thus form a significant part of the digital infrastructure of democracy. This form of separation of powers must, however, be explained. A government can and, possibly, should use platforms to communicate transparently. However, in a democracy based on separation of powers, it should own shares neither in such social networks nor in such search engines. Otherwise, these meshing and concentration of powers would fundamentally alter any idea of separation of powers. The government in place would indeed control a platform playing a significant or, as the case may be, decisive role in the coming to power or the staying in power of governments and officials. From this perspective, governmental power and platform power should remain separated.[4] In this context, the notion of *separation of powers* seems adequate.

A public search alternative or alternative digital public spheres for electoral campaigns or, more broadly, for social interactions are sometimes advocated for.[5] Though these ideas are interesting and worth considering, they may prove chimeric and raise various difficulties.[6] Has the train not passed now, especially as far as search engines are concerned? Besides, "the appetite in many countries for state-owned social networks, search engines, or digital retailers, is quite reasonably somewhere between limited and non-existent," as realistically noted by Chris Pike and Gabriele Carovano.[7] Interestingly, Ganesh Sitaraman and Anne L. Alstott do not examine public options with regards to digital social networks or search engines in their book *The Public Option*.[8] This does not mean, however, that governments should remain passive;

---

[2]   See *supra* Part I, Chapter 4, Sections 4.2 & 4.3.
[3]   Montesquieu, *Spirit of the Laws*, 349 (see *supra* Part I, Chapter 2, Section 2.1). From a general and contemporaneous perspective, see, e.g., Obertone, *Game Over*, 122–24.
[4]   See, from a different but related perspective, Moore & Tambini, "Holistic Vision," 342 ("[W]ere the surveillance capabilities of a company like Google available and accessible to a national government, it would give that government unprecedented powers to control its citizens and curtail their freedoms").
[5]   Phillips & Mazzoli, "Public Search Alternative," 117–21; Moore, "Electoral Public Spheres," 225–30; see also Chavalarias, *Data*, 265–66; Fishkin & Forbath, *Constitution*, 475; Patino, *Civilisation*, 139–40.
[6]   See Balkin, "Regulate," 85–86.
[7]   Pike & Carovano, "Decentralised Blockchains," 115.
[8]   See Sitaraman & Alstott, *Public Option*; see also Sitaraman & Alstott (eds.), *Politics*.

they certainly have a role to play in the developments of digital platforms, not only as regulators but also as public developers, for instance, of apps in a given ecosystem.[9] In any event, the public search engine or alternative digital public spheres should be independent from governmental power in a democracy.[10] As it would be publicly funded, its governance may be extremely complicated. The proposal is, for instance, made by Angela Phillips and Eleonora Maria Mazzoli to create "a governing body composed of interested universities, independent research institutes, and public service media organizations," which "together [...] would have the necessary spread of expertise and experience to establish and drive such a venture."[11] It is not clear to which experience these authors are referencing. Furthermore, the functioning of this body may prove difficult if not impossible. Would such a body really be able to *drive* a public search platform? Doubt inevitably comes to mind. In the end, there is a significant risk that the cure turns out to be worse than the disease.

The control of the digital infrastructure of democracy is highly topical. Thus, the Chinese government, through Internet Investment Chinese (Beijing) Technology, bought, in late April 2021, a one percent stake of TikTok owner ByteDance's main Chinese subsidiary and obtained a seat board in this company.[12] This acquisition is highly problematic and troubling from a broader – politico-economic – separation of powers' perspective. This evolution should not be underestimated, as TikTok becomes an ever more popular online destination globally.[13] It remains to be seen whether people will increasingly turn to TikTok to search for a broad array of information, including political ones and, thus, put TikTok more directly in competition with Google and YouTube, Facebook and Instagram or Bing enhanced by OpenAI's ChatGPT.[14] The impressive growth – in terms of audience – of YouTube Shorts and Instagram Reels[15] will also have to be taken into account in this context. In any event, the Chinese government is engaged in digital commerce and has

---

[9] From a broader perspective, see van Dijck, Poell & de Waal, *Platform Society*, 154–62 ("For democracies to work in the age of platformization, they need the concerted effort of all actors – market, state, and civil society – to build a sustainable and trustworthy global platform ecosystem, a system that comes equipped with distributed responsibilities as well as with checks and balances" [quotation from p. 162]).

[10] Phillips & Mazzoli, "Public Search Alternative," 119–20; Moore, "Electoral Public Spheres," 230.

[11] Phillips & Mazzoli, "Public Search Alternative," 120.

[12] Jeanne Whalen, "Chinese Government Acquires Stake in Domestic Unit of TikTok Owner ByteDance in Another Sign of Tech Crackdown: Government Also Took One of Three Board Seats at the Subsidiary, Which Controls a Similar App Inside China," *Washington Post*, online edition, 17 August 2021, www.washingtonpost.com/technology/2021/08/17/chinese-government-bytedance-tiktok/.

[13] See João Tomé & Sofia Cardita, "In 2021, the Internet Went for TikTok, Space and Beyond, *Cloudflare*, 20 December 2021," https://blog.cloudflare.com/popular-domains-year-in-review-2021/?utm_source=sg&utm_medium=email&utm_campaign=article_email&utm_content=article-6884.

[14] See Martin Peers, "The Briefing: Why 2022 Will Be TikTok's Year," *The Information*, 22 December 2021, www.theinformation.com/articles/why-2022-will-be-tiktok-s-year.

[15] See Martin Peers, "The Briefing: TikTok's Oracle News Recalls Trump's War on the App," *The Information*, 17 June 2022, www.theinformation.com/articles/tiktok-s-oracle-news-recalls-trump-s-war-on-the-app.

directly undermined – if not destroyed – the idea of separating governmental and platform powers.

The control of the digital infrastructure of democracy by institutional or private investors also raises specific concerns about the concentration of power. Institutional investors have evolved to large or, even, the largest owners of many major corporations. This evolution raises important issues, including considerations under antitrust and competition laws.[16] The problem is particularly sensitive when the same institutional investor diversifies its holding within an industry.[17] Antitrust and competition laws may, at least partly, tackle it, but enforcement is widely lacking in this respect, as observed by Einer Elhauge.[18] Therefore, strict limits for this type of diversification have been argued for by him as well as by Eric Posner, Fiona Scott Morton, and Glen Weyl.[19] Their merits will not be examined here, as these questions fall outside the scope of this book, subject to the following. There is a special and quite convincing case for limits or thresholds with regard to firms whose platforms have come to play an important or, *a fortiori*, fundamental role in the electoral or democratic process and thus form a significant part of the digital infrastructure of democracy. Everything should be made to preserve some form of competition and to avoid risks of collusion or further concentration. Accordingly, restrictions could be imposed on institutional or private investors, preventing them from owning more than a fixed percentage of share in more than one of these firms, unless "the entity holding shares is a free-standing index fund that commits to being purely passive."[20] This may be deemed a democratic,[21] separation of powers, and antitrust concern, in the sense that the portfolio held by an institutional investor may lead to an excessive and unacceptable accumulation of power in a democracy. Of course, restrictions will have to comply with constitutional or other fundamental constraints resulting, for instance, from the First Amendment of the U.S. Constitution or from Article 16 (Freedom to conduct business) of the E.U. Charter of Fundamental Rights.

This first new politico-economic axis of separation of powers is, in principle, not a matter for antitrust,[22] except for the last point that has just been mentioned. That

---

[16] See, e.g., Posner & Weyl, *Radical Markets*, 180–204.

[17] See, e.g., Posner & Weyl, *Radical Markets*, 191–92 ("Because institutional investors appear to reduce competition among firms they own, they should not be permitted to own firms that are rivals within a single, concentrated industry – with exceptions where institutional investors are small or passive"). On this last point, one could prefer "small *and* passive."

[18] Regarding the United States and the European Union, see Elhauge, "How Horizontal Shareholding Harms Our Economy," 268–86 and "Horizontal Shareholding," 1301–16.

[19] See, e.g., Posner, Scott Morton & Weyl, "Institutional Investors," 708–21 ("No institutional investor or individual *holding* shares of more than a *single effective firm* in an *oligopoly* may *ultimately own* more than 1% the market share unless the entity holding shares is a free-standing index fund that commits to being *purely passive*" [quotation from p. 708]); see also Elhauge, "Causal Mechanisms," 73–75.

[20] See, by analogy, Posner, Scott Morton & Weyl, "Institutional Investors," 708.

[21] See Posner & Weyl, *Radical Markets*, 203 (making the link between democracy, antitrust and the excessive concentration of economic and political power due to "the rise of the institutional investor").

[22] From a similar perspective, see Susskind, *Future Politics*, 357–59.

said, a specific law or even a constitutional provision could be adopted to forbid the government from owning shares in private firms whose platforms have come to play an important or, *a fortiori*, fundamental role in the electoral or democratic process and thus form a significant part of the digital infrastructure of democracy. This limit could not apply to shares in these firms held, for instance, by the independent national bank or public pension funds, provided that they use their shareholders' rights independently from the government. The government may also simply abide by this limit, as long as these platforms could be significantly or, *a fortiori*, decisively relevant in the coming to power or the staying in power of governments and officials. The adoption of rules may therefore not even be necessary. As far as institutional or private investors are concerned, a specific law or a provision in an existing antitrust or other statute would bring some legal certainty and clarity.

9.2 PROHIBITION OF DISTORTIONS OF THE ELECTORAL AND DEMOCRATIC PROCESS

Distortions of the electoral and democratic process through digital platforms represent a major democratic issue in the digital and artificial intelligence era.[23] They may impact not only elections but also referenda, popular initiatives, or recalls. According to the recent Declaration for the Future of the Internet, trust in the digital ecosystem also supposes to "[r]efrain from using the Internet to undermine the electoral infrastructure, elections and political processes, including through covert information manipulation campaigns."[24] Additional checks and balances within a firm or outside of it are certainly justified in this respect. They may, however, prove insufficient.[25] Some distortions could qualify as abusive discriminations by a dominant firm between trading parties or consumers, but this area of antitrust is highly uncharted, as analyzed in Chapter 6.[26]

Unregulated or insufficiently regulated platforms may pose a threat to democracy,[27] which is not or only scarcely addressed by recent or proposed legislation in

---

[23] See, e.g., Ezrachi & Stucke, *Barons*, 129–34; Robertson, "Antitrust, Big Tech, and Democracy," 266 ("More and more evidence is surfacing that personal user data are being instrumentalized to shape political beliefs, reinforce one-sided thinking, and create filter bubbles or echo chambers"); Fukuyama, "Internet Safe for Democracy," 39 ("The real problem centers around the platforms' ability to either amplify or silence certain messages, and to do so at a scale that can alter major political outcomes"); Foer, *World*, 194.

[24] *Declaration for the Future of the Internet*, 6th bullet point under "Trust in the Digital Ecosystem."

[25] See *supra* Part II, Chapter 5, Sections 5.2.3, 5.3 & 5.4.

[26] See *supra* Part II, Chapter 6, Section 6.4.

[27] See, e.g., Balkin, "Regulate," 77–78 & 96 ("Social media perform their public functions well when they promote these three central values: political democracy, cultural democracy, and the growth and spread of knowledge. More generally, a healthy, well-functioning digital public sphere helps individuals and groups realize these three central values of free expression. A poorly functioning public sphere, by contrast, undermines political and cultural democracy, and hinders the growth and spread of knowledge" [quotation from p. 78]).

many jurisdictions, as seen in Chapter 8. Some digital platforms may accumulate too much concrete politico-economic power and have a significant or, *a fortiori*, decisive impact on the electoral and democratic process. As warned by Shoshana Zuboff, "power untamed by democracy can only lead to exile and despair."[28]

Such an evolution becomes a separation of powers' issue,[29] at least from a broad perspective. Indeed, the power of the largest digital platforms and the related artificial intelligence should be checked and balanced in order to prevent, detect, or correct distortions.[30] Otherwise, they could, willfully or not, distort the electoral and democratic process and gain some significant power over the branches of government, as elections matter for all of them in many democracies, including the judiciary due to the appointment of justices or judges by elected bodies. Such a concentration of power creates a risk of abuse and, above all, makes the separation of powers, as traditionally understood, somehow illusory. This threat calls for new laws and regulations or the revision of the current ones, if the latter do not address, for example, this question raised in the famous report of the Stigler Committee:

> Are we sure that Elizabeth Warren's posts on Facebook receive equal distribution when compared to other candidates? This is a major problem [...], and one that must be immediately addressed.[31]

Thereby, firms whose platforms have become an important or, *a fortiori*, fundamental part of the electoral or democratic process and of the digital infrastructure of democracy cannot be left unregulated.[32] Otherwise, they would concentrate too much politico-economic power in an untransparent and unchecked manner.[33] This is probably not a matter for only antitrust and its enforcing agencies.[34] At most, antitrust should be viewed as a legislation of last resort in this context, but it seems clear

---

[28] Zuboff, *Surveillance Capitalism*, 524.

[29] Fukuyama, "Internet Safe for Democracy," 39–40.

[30] See, e.g., Kissinger, Schmidt & Huttenlocher, *Age of AI*, 199–200 & 219–20; see also Kevin Roose, "AI Is Getting Good. What Happens Now?" *New York Times*, 25 August 2022, B1.

[31] Stigler Committee, *Final Report*, 15; see also Müller, *Democracy Rules*, 120–22 & 183. From a broader perspective, see Belgian Competition Authority, Authority for Consumers & Markets and Conseil de la concurrence, *Digital World*, 5–6 (proposing "to introduce an ex-ante intervention mechanism to prevent anti-competitive behaviour by dominant companies acting as gatekeeper to the relevant online ecosystem" with the ability to impose remedies "behavioural in nature" such as "platform access, data portability, data-sharing and non-discriminatory ranking"). On "data openness," see Digital Competition Expert Panel, *Digital Competition*, 74–76.

[32] See Nemitz & Pfeffer, "Future," 287–88; Susskind, *Digital Republic*, 294–304; Fukuyama, "Internet Safe for Democracy," 44 ("What we want [...] are public policies that prevent private actors from using their power to artificially amplify or suppress certain types of speech, and that maintain a level playing field on which ideas can compete").

[33] See, e.g., Fukuyama, "Loaded Weapon" ("These platforms control a great deal of the political speech that happens in the United States. They can amplify certain messages; they can suppress others; they can subtly guide people to certain views"); see also Stucke, *Breaking Away*, 79.

[34] See, e.g., Fukuyama et al., *Platform Scale*, 8–9 & 19–25; Fukuyama, "Loaded Weapon."

that it cannot address the complexity of the matter and solve all woes.[35] Specific laws and regulations,[36] complying with free speech requirements in the relevant jurisdictions,[37] as well as, possibly, the creation of a special agency or other independent body,[38] are the preferred path, notably for three main reasons.

First, the firms at stake should not obligatorily be dominant within the meaning of antitrust and competition laws. Some of them may be regarded as an important part of the electoral process and of the digital infrastructure of democracy without having a dominant position. This could, for instance, be the case of X/Twitter[39] – "the digital town square where matters vital to the future of humanity are debated," Elon Musk once tweeted[40] – depending on the way the relevant markets are defined. According to a survey of Pew Research Center, more than half of the adult Twitter users in the United States (55 and 53%) regularly got news on Twitter in 2021 and 2022.[41] The digital infrastructure of democracy or a similar notion should become the key concept in defining the scope of the new legislation. Once a firm is considered as a

---

[35] Regarding Article 102 TFEU, see O'Donoghue & Padilla, *Article 102 TFEU*, 1106.

[36] See, e.g., Rowbottom, "Obligations," 247 ([D]igital platforms should be subject to periodic public service reviews, in which a regulatory body examines how the services of the platform contribute to a fair electoral process and considers what changes should be made. Such a process would examine the algorithms and the systems of recommendation"); Shapiro, "Protecting Competition," 86 & 90 and "Populism," 744–46; Tambini & Moore, "Dominance," 401 ("The expectation that competition law will be able to deal with the social and political implications of digital dominance is based either on an underestimation of those implications or a misunderstanding of the intent and content of competition law"); Baker, *Antitrust Paradigm*, 61; Drexl, "Economic Efficiency," 259; Crémer, de Montjoye & Schweitzer, *Competition Policy*, 98, 107 & 109 ("Where a broader imposition of duties to grant access is found desirable, it may be expedient to draw upon a different [from Article 102 TFEU] legal basis" [quotation from p. 98]). See also Eifert, Metzger, Schweitzer & Wagner, "Taming the Giants," 991 ("[C]ommunications markets differ from the markets for goods and services and need particular regulation"); Khan, "Antitrust History," 1664 (arguing that "recognizing competition as one among several mechanisms for checking concentrated private power is especially critical" [footnote omitted]); Stigler Committee, *Final Report*, 19 ("[E]lectoral regulators must ensure that candidates who are criticizing companies like Facebook and Google receive equal treatment to candidates who support them).

[37] Regarding the United States, see, e.g., Persily, "Platform Power," 195–96 & 207–11 ("The First Amendment should be read as preventing many broad regulations of speech on the internet, but when it comes to regulating the large platforms themselves, the government should have much greater latitude […]. The law could prevent the large platforms from using their power to exclude one or another candidate" [quotation from p. 207]); Volokh, "Platforms," 445–52 ("The laws target a particular harm, though we can debate how much of a harm it is: they tackle large social media corporations' use of economic power to unduly influence political debate. They do so by equally protecting all speakers' viewpoints" [quotation from p. 451]). By contrast, Eugene Volokh considers that compelled recommendations are generally unconstitutional (451–52).

[38] From a broader perspective, see, e.g., Napoli, "Platforms as Public Trustees," 163; Wheeler, Verveer & Kimmelman, *New Digital Realities*, 19–21 (advocating for the creation of a Digital Platform Agency).

[39] See Fukuyama, "Loaded Weapon" ("Twitter is smaller in reach, but in a way, it's much more political [than Facebook and Google]"); Volokh, "Platforms," 401, 407–8 & 461 (speaking notwithstanding of "near-monopoly status" with respect to Twitter and Facebook).

[40] Words of Elon Musk in one of his tweets of 25 April 2022, https://twitter.com/elonmusk/status/1518677066325053441.

[41] Walker & Matsa, *News*, 5; Liedke & Matsa, *Social Media*, 3.

significant part of this infrastructure, it would have to comply with specific obligations aimed especially at avoiding the distortions of the electoral and democratic process and would be subject to the oversight of a dedicated independent agency. In other words, antitrust agencies would most probably not oversee this matter.

Second, the distortion of the electoral and democratic process would not necessarily suppose that some candidates or political parties are discriminated against by a digital firm compared to others. The notion of distortion is broader than the one of discrimination. For instance, untransparent microtargeting through Facebook and Google or other platforms can, depending on the circumstances, distort the electoral and democratic process,[42] but not discriminate against certain candidates or political parties. One can imagine that the tool would be proposed to all candidates and political parties by the platform, but that some of them would not use it for moral and democratic reasons.

Third, neither discriminations nor distortions between trading parties would be required. Mark Zuckerberg using Facebook's data to run for President of the United States would distort the electoral process but would, most probably, not be a trading party to Facebook in this context. The same can be said about Elon Musk with respect to X/Twitter. In other words, the citizens' perspective would be decisive. One of the most relevant questions should be worded along the following lines: Does the practice at stake distort the free formation of citizens' opinions in a democracy? Therefore, the citizen welfare or, from a general perspective, the democracy welfare – based on equality, liberty, and institutionalized uncertainty[43] – would be the goal of this new legislation and regulation. The latter's main contribution to the separation of powers in a broad – politico-economic – sense would lie in the obligations imposed to the firms concerned and the consequential reduction of their politico-economic power. This legislation would create a level playing field for candidates and political parties,[44] a goal which antitrust can, indirectly and in a quite limited way, contribute to but cannot achieve alone.[45]

9.3 GOVERNMENTAL CONTRACTS

Possibly significant in practice, the attribution of important governmental contracts to conglomerates or firms whose platforms have become an important or, *a fortiori*, fundamental part of the electoral or democratic process and of the digital

---

[42] See, e.g., Ezrachi & Stucke, *Barons*, 131–34; see also Bach & Kreuter, "Big Data," 128–30. From a broader perspective, see Ménissier, "Moment machiavélien," 72–73.

[43] On these principles and the need to "regulate in line with basis democratic principles," see Müller, *Democracy Rules*, 42–89 & 183 (quotation from this last page).

[44] For a proposal, see Fishkin & Forbath, *Constitution*, 439–40 ("Congress could […] requir[e] broadcasters and internet platforms to provide a floor of very inexpensive or even free advertising to political candidates").

[45] See *supra* Part II, Chapter 6, Section 6.4.

infrastructure of democracy is highly problematic. For instance, the attribution of a multi-billion cloud-computing governmental contract to companies such as Google or Facebook or other companies belonging to Alphabet or Meta Platforms – should these companies apply for such a contract in the future – would be extremely puzzling from a separation of powers perspective, at least in a broad sense. It would create major conflicts of interests, reduce effective checks and balances, and give decision-makers considerable power, as they may be advantaged on the digital platforms of the firms at stake which want to obtain a contract or have an existing one executed in their interests, prolonged, or renewed.

On 19 November 2021, the U.S. Department of Defense issued formal solicitations to Amazon Web Services, Inc., Google LLC, Microsoft Corporation and Oracle Corporation for a multi-billion dollar cloud-computing contract (commercial cloud service offerings and support services).[46] The attribution of such a contract to Google would have been very disconcerting, as this firm can reasonably be regarded as a gatekeeper or gateway to political information for many citizens and as a significant part of the digital infrastructure of democracy. This would further concentrate the politico-economic power in the hands of this firm. Fortunately, the Department of Defense has moved toward a multi-vendor approach, with possibly four cloud providers competing for task orders.[47] In other words, it relies on several cloud providers.[48] On 7 December 2022, the U.S. Department of Defense communicated its decision to award hybrid contracts to four cloud providers – Google Support Services LLC, Oracle America Inc., Amazon Web Services Inc. and Microsoft Corp. – with the funds totaling $ 9 billion being awarded "on individual orders as they are issued."[49] This means that the companies remain competitors for task orders throughout the contracts' lifecycle until 2028.[50] Still, one may wonder whether the government should select a firm that already has such an immense data and platform power impacting democracy itself.

Two solutions come to mind in this respect. The simpler – and cleaner – solution would consist of forbidding the government from passing major contracts with firms whose services and products related to the platforms they operate have come to play an important or, *a fortiori*, fundamental role in the electoral or democratic process

---

[46] See the contract opportunity, with formal solicitations, entitled "Joint Warfighting Cloud Capability (JWCC)" and updated on 19 November 2021, https://sam.gov/opp/dbc25be4a53746a19ecf7ed14863ffdd/view#general.

[47] See John D. McKinnon, "Pentagon Asks Tech Giants to Bid on Troubled Contract," *Wall Street Journal*, 20 November 2021 (online version: www.wsj.com/articles/pentagon-seeks-bids-from-four-tech-firms-for-jedi-replacement-11637338699?page=1).

[48] See Amanda Macias & Jordan Novet, "Pentagon Expects to Award Up to $9 billion in Cloud Contracts in December," CNBC, 29 March 2022, www.cnbc.com/2022/03/29/pentagon-will-award-up-to-9-billion-in-cloud-contracts-in-december.html.

[49] U.S. Department of Defense, "Contracts for Dec. 7, 2022," *Press Release*, www.defense.gov/News/Contracts/Contract/Article/3239197/.

[50] Makenzie Holland & Ed Scannell, "Amazon, Google, Microsoft, Oracle win JWCC Contract," *TechTarget*, 8 December 2022, www.techtarget.com/searchcloudcomputing/news/252528168/Amazon-Google-Microsoft-Oracle-win-JWCC-cloud-contract.

and which thus constitutes a significant part of the digital infrastructure of democracy. This first approach can lead a firm to split up or to spin off some of its activities. Such a decision would not be taken by an administrative agency or a court, but by the firm itself. In this respect, this is a more subtle way to deal with and tackle the concentration of power than the approach that consists of authorizing an agency or a court to break up a company or to unbundle its core activities. If the resulting firms are legally and economically independent from each other, one could apply to these governmental contracts, and the other possess or operate the platform at stake. The meshing of power and the risk of collusion between governmental power and platform power would, as a consequence, be reduced. One can go a step further and say that these two powers would be separated. Considering the amount of political power some platforms may have, this is a separation of powers' issue, at least in a broad sense.

A more complex solution would focus on regulation and the governance structure of the relevant digital firms and on the independence – from the political branches of government – of the bodies involved in the process to select firms obtaining such contracts. Moreover, such a solution would have to fully prevent the risks for the electoral or democratic process. This issue relates to the avoidance of conflicts of interests, to competition and to the separation of powers in a broad sense.

This third new politico-economic axis of the separation of powers is, in principle, no matter for antitrust. A specific law complying, of course, with constitutional requirements could and should be adopted. Legislation indeed seems necessary, as it would provide the basis for a general difference in treatment among firms, as only the ones whose platforms have become an important or, *a fortiori*, fundamental part of the electoral or democratic process and of the digital infrastructure of democracy would have to abide by the new prohibition or restrictions.

9.4 REGULATION AND DECONCENTRATION OR DECENTRALIZATION OF ARTIFICIAL INTELLIGENCE

Artificial intelligence possibly faces a cycle of concentration accentuating the need for regulation (9.4.1). Deconcentration or decentralization may be envisaged, imposed, or incentivized (9.4.2). Furthermore, limits are especially necessary when substantial autonomous powers are granted to forms of artificial intelligence (9.4.3).

9.4.1 *Concentration Tendency and Need for Regulation*

Artificial intelligence systems may enhance and strengthen economic or political power,[51] including from a geopolitical perspective.[52] In the words of Kate Crawford, they are

---

[51] See Crawford, *Atlas of AI*, 223; see also Hannes Bajohr, "Das Ende der menschlichen Politik" [The End of Human Politics], *Neue Zürcher Zeitung*, 25 April 2023, 18 ("Wer die Sprachmodelle beherrscht, beherrscht auch die Politik" [W]hoever masters the language models also masters politics]).

[52] See, e.g., "It's Worse Than You Think," and "China in your Hand," *The Economist*, 1 April 2023, 11 & 33–34.

"expressions of power that emerge from wider economic and political forces, created to increase profits and centralize control for those who wield them."[53] The development of artificial intelligence never stops and may prove inescapable[54] but remains full of uncertainties. AI technologies may become tools of empowerment or vehicles for abuse.[55]

Both governments and private or public firms are increasingly interested, for instance, in predictions of human behaviors through data analyses[56] and in generative artificial intelligence like large language models such as ChatGPT or Auto-GPT. Technology firms with the most data and the highest computing power – as well as deep pockets – will become ever more powerful in this respect.[57] Their predicative judgments are supposed, *ceteris paribus*, to be more accurate.[58] In this regard, "a cycle of concentration and advancement has defined AI," as observed, for instance, by Henry A. Kissinger, Eric Schmidt, and Daniel Huttenlocher.[59] The performance and utility of machine learning, including deep learning based on artificial neural networks, and other artificial intelligence systems are indeed linked to the quality and amount of available training data.[60] Interestingly, the current battle around AI-powered search engines and other tools pits notably tech giants such as Alphabet and Microsoft (in partnership with OpenAI) against each

---

[53] See Crawford, *Atlas of AI*, 211.

[54] Kissinger, Schmidt & Huttenlocher, *Age of AI*, 188 & 208.

[55] Andrew R. Chow, "Why the AI Explosion Has Huge Implications for the Metaverse," *Time*, online edition, 27 January 2023, https://time.com/6250249/chatgpt-metaverse/#.

[56] See, e.g., Kissinger, Schmidt & Huttenlocher, *Age of AI*, 105–14.

[57] See Kissinger, Schmidt & Huttenlocher, *Age of AI*, 85 & 91; Sejnowski, *Deep Learning*, 166 ("In machine learning, whoever has the most data wins, and Facebook has more data about more people's likes, friends, and photos than anyone else"); Jean, *Algorithmes*, 106; Benkler, "Freedom, Power," 19 & 23 ("Big data may ultimately allow a small number of companies – those large enough to control, access, and analyze sufficient data – to predict, shape, and 'nudge' the behaviors of hundreds of millions of people" [quotation from p. 19]); see also Jessica E. Lessin, "The Briefing: What's Google Cloud so Worried About?," *The Information*, 12 January 2023, www.theinformation.com/articles/what-s-google-cloud-so-worried-about ("Machine-learning models are getting bigger and using them to automate complex tasks isn't cheap"); Erin Griffith & Cade Metz, "Tech Slump Doesn't Slow New Boom In A.I. Field," *New York Times*, 7 January 2023, B1; Kevin Roose, "AI Is Getting Good. What Happens Now?" *New York Times*, 25 August 2022, B1 ("[B]igger models with more data and processing power behind them yield[s] slightly better results"). Regarding Facebook, Amazon, Google, and Alibaba, see Hoffman, *Forces*, 225–26. Steven S. Hoffman notes, however, that "[t]o compound the problem, there won't be a single, all-powerful AI that controls everything anytime in the near future," but "millions of independent AIs talking with one another, sharing data, and coordinating their activities" (*id.*, at 227). Regarding Google and Facebook, see Lee & Chen, *AI 2041*, 395.

[58] See, e.g., Stucke, *Breaking Away*, 9–11 ("The more personal data the platform collects, the better the platform can refine its algorithms [...]" [quotation from p. 9]) & 155–56; Hoffman, *Forces*, 153 ("And the more we use these algorithms, the more powerful and accurate they will become"); Zuboff, *Surveillance Capitalism*, 337–38; see also Chavalarias, *Data*, 237.

[59] Kissinger, Schmidt & Huttenlocher, *Age of AI*, 91 (quotation), 115–16 & 214; see also Santoni de Sio, "Ethics of AI," 50/2 & 5; Coeckelbergh, *AI Ethics*, 171; Nemitz, "Constitutional Democracy," 2–4.

[60] See, e.g., Acemoglu & Johnson, *Power and Progress*, 310; Massarotto, "Blockchain," 130 ("Data is the fuel that today runs machine-learning algorithms (MLA), which is the main application of Artificial Intelligence (AI), a business that all companies are now jumping into"); Nosthoff & Maschewski, "Big Data," 3–4. Regarding Google, see Ezrachi & Stucke, *Barons*, 70.

other, with AI-infrastructure firms such as Nvidia Corporation also playing an increasingly significant role in this field.[61]

The regulation or at least the framing of artificial intelligence by various rules and principles seems unavoidable.[62] A combination of – democratically legitimized – laws or regulations and ethical rules coming from various sources[63] is probably the appropriate path,[64] but identifying adequate rules and control mechanisms represent a Sisyphean task. Rules may rapidly become obsolete, which means that laws and regulations may consist of general principles and rules formulated in a technology-neutral – except for the issue of deconcentration or decentralization[65] – and future-oriented way.[66] The notion of "Constitutional AI" has already been coined.[67] Transparency is clearly an issue, here as well.[68] Antitrust, especially in cases of collusion, plays a role in this context, but it alone cannot cover the matter, and enforcement proves very challenging in this area.[69]

Further, no consensus exists on an appropriate level for the adoption of rules or norms relating to artificial intelligence. Yet, "[a]n international attempt to limit these risks is imperative," as noted by Henry A. Kissinger, Eric Schmidt, and Daniel Huttenlocher.[70] An international organization, such as the United Nations or another organization or special agency within the United Nations system, could, in theory, make sense as an organization in which to adopt rules, but a consensus would be extremely difficult to achieve at this level. Rules jointly elaborated by the

---

[61] See, e.g., Nico Grant, "Google's Fight to Stay Ahead of Bing's A.I.," *New York Times*, 17 April 2023, A1; Cade Metz & Karen Weise, "Microsoft Sets Off a Tech Race With Its A.I.-Assisted Search," *New York Times*, 8 February 2023, A1; see also "There's AI in Them Thar Hills", *The Economist*, 3 June 2023, 53–55; "Master the Machine," *The Economist*, 1 April 2023, 53–55 ("The tech giant have all they need – data, computing powers, billions of users – to thrive in the age of AI"); "The Battle for Search," and "Seeking Change," *The Economist*, 11 February 2023, 7 & 53–55 ("Alphabet retains formidable strengths. One is technology. [...] Google's other advantage is incumbency" [quotation from p. 55]).

[62] See, e.g., Russell, *Human Compatible*, 252–53; Lee & Chen, *AI 2041*, 23–25; Coeckelbergh, *AI Ethics*, 171; see also Kissinger, Schmidt & Huttenlocher, *Age of AI*, 113–14; Chavalarias, *Data*, 254. See also Renda, "Digital Economy," 351; Jean, *Algorithmes*, 115, 196–99, 204 & 213 (favoring the "framing" of algorithms, their regulation being "impossible" according to her); Kevin Roose, "AI Is Getting Good. What Happens Now?" *New York Times*, 25 August 2022, B1.

[63] See, e.g., Coeckelbergh, *AI Ethics*, 157 ("AI ethics policy is also not at all restricted to governments and their committees and bodies. Academics have also taken initiatives").

[64] See Nemitz, "Constitutional Democracy," 7–8

[65] See *infra* 9.4.2 & 9.4.3 in the present Section.

[66] Nemitz & Pfeffer, "Future," 285–86; see also Hoffman, *Impromptu*, 217 ("I hope that [...] we stay future-oriented and democratic in our AI-development approaches"); Ezrachi & Stucke, *Barons*, 190–93; "How to Worry Wisely About AI," and "How Generative Models Could Go Wrong," *The Economist*, 22 April 2023, 7–8 & 68–69 (quoting Samuel R. Bowman).

[67] Bai *et al.*, "Constitutional AI," 5; see also "How Generative Models Could Go Wrong," *The Economist*, 22 April 2023, 68–69 (quoting Samuel R. Bowman).

[68] See, e.g., Lee & Chen, *AI 2041*, 32 ("A great deal of research is currently under way that attempts to make AI more transparent, either by summarizing its complex logic, or by introducing new AI algorithms that are fundamentally more interpretable"); see also Dominique Nora, "Une régulation impossible ?" [An Impossible Regulation?], *L'Obs*, 2 February 2023, 34–35.

[69] See, e.g., Rab, "Artificial Intelligence," 150.

[70] Kissinger, Schmidt & Huttenlocher, *Age of AI*, 162; see also Jean, *Algorithmes*, 184–87 & 205–6.

European Union[71] and the United States could become global, but China could prefer other rules.[72] Professional societies like the Association for the Advancement of Artificial Intelligence (AAAI) or the Institute of Electrical and Electronics Engineers (IEEE) also come to mind and may adopt rules, but one may wonder whether this is the appropriate body for the adoption of fundamental norms regulating artificial intelligence.[73] At the end of the day, an international body, based on an international treaty or agreement and acting transparently,[74] with representatives from governments, academia, business, and civil society,[75] among others, could prove an interesting solution.[76] Equipped with sufficient and highly competent staff, it would develop global principles, rules or standards,[77] do safety research, and one of its departments could carry out controls and investigations.

However, control itself should not be concentrated in the hands of an international body. The setting of adequate control mechanisms also raises fundamental issues at the national level. Dedicated authorities or agencies that are independent, at least from the major firms at stake, would be required to apply and enforce public regulation – if any – and, more specifically, to monitor developments, mandate impact assessments, or publish recommendations and reports, among other tasks.[78] Internal control mechanisms and other measures are also important. In this regard,

---

[71] See, e.g., Jean, *Algorithmes*, 184–85. Regarding the European draft Act on Artificial Intelligence, see, however, Raposo, "Ex Machina," 108–9 ("A definition of standards to be adopted by the rest of the world – an expression of the so-called Brussels effects – may not be appropriate for the AI regulation, as most countries would prefer a model that is more balanced between fundamental rights and technological development. Ultimately, if the current proposal indeed becomes the new regulation, Europe may be inescapably relegated to the tail end of the digital revolution" [one footnote omitted]).

[72] See, e.g., Jean, *Algorithmes*, 185–86; Coeckelbergh, *AI Ethics*, 156–57.

[73] On this issue, see, e.g., Gasser & Schmitt, "Professional Norms," 157; see also Russell, *Human Compatible*, 250–51.

[74] See "How to Worry Wisely About AI," *The Economist*, 22 April 2023, 7–8 ("[G]overnments could form a body modelled on CERN" [quotation from p. 8]).

[75] On this last point, see, e.g., Mira Murati (Chief Technology Officer at OpenAI), "Keeping AI in Check," interview with John Simons, *Time*, 13 February 2023, 52–53 ([I]t's important that we bring in different voices, like philosophers, social scientists, artists, and people from humanities" [quotation from p. 53]); see also Future of Life Institute, *Policymaking*, 14 ("The path forward will require coordinated efforts by civil society, governments, academia, industry, and the public").

[76] See, e.g., Marcus, *Senate Testimony*, 16 May 2023, and "A.I. Future" ("What we need is something global, neutral, nonprofit, with governments and companies all part of it. We need to have coordinated efforts around building rules. [...] It's not even in the interest of the tech companies to have different policies everywhere. It is in their interest to have a coordinated and global response"); Sam Altman, *Written Testimony Before the U.S. Senate Committee on the Judiciary, Subcommittee on Privacy, Technology, & the Law*, 16 May 2023.

[77] See Cade Metz, "He Warns of Risks from A.I. He Helped Create," *New York Times*, 2 May 2023, A1 ("Dr. [Geoffrey] Hinton ['an artificial intelligence pioneer', 'The Godfather of A.I.'] believes that the race between Google and Microsoft and others will escalate into a global race that will not stop without some sort of global regulation")

[78] Bengio *et al.*, "Pause"; Future of Life Institute, *Policymaking*, 8–9; Korinek, "Agency"; Martenet, *Architecture des pouvoirs*, 252–53. See also "Posner," *Catastrophe*, 215; "How to Worry Wisely About AI," *The Economist*, 22 April 2023, 7–8.

the protection of whistleblowers,[79] notably within firms heavily involved in artificial intelligence developments,[80] could prove particularly necessary and potentially efficient to avoid unlawful or unethical conducts. Moreover, opportunities for members of civil society to participate in the development of artificial intelligence,[81] internal or external impact *ex ante* and *ex post* assessments, or other third-party auditing mechanisms[82] should make sure that the design of artificial intelligence is more inclusive and does not undermine or disregard but respects and ideally strengthens democracy, fundamental rights, and the rule of law,[83] in particular when this intelligence is used by platforms which have become an important or, *a fortiori*, fundamental part of the electoral or democratic process and of the digital infrastructure of democracy. This control and the related responsibility may contribute to the acceptance of artificial intelligence in society and the public trust therein.[84]

9.4.2 *Deconcentration or Decentralization*

Should artificial intelligence become an important or, *a fortiori*, central tool of governmental and corporate decision making,[85] and should it be somehow centralized in the sense that it would come from a few firms,[86] it would then affect the separation

---

[79] See *supra* Chapter 7, Section 8.2.

[80] See Global Privacy Assembly, Resolution on Accountability in the Development and Use of Artificial Intelligence, October 2020, 1(10).

[81] Hoffman, *Impromptu*, 217; Rossi *et al.*, *Future with AI*.

[82] Future of Life Institute, *Policymaking*, 6–7.

[83] Duberry, *Artificial Intelligence*, 231; Nemitz, "Constitutional Democracy," 12–3; see also Altman, *Written Testimony, supra* note 76 ("It is also essential that a technology as powerful as AI is developed with democratic values in mind"); Ezrachi & Stucke, *Barons*, 202–3; Susskind, *Digital Republic*, 141. Regarding the design of Internet in general and the role of academia, see Benkler, "Freedom, Power," 31 ("[T]he steady grind of policymaking and standards-setting mean that the values of a genuinely open Internet that diffuses and decentralizes power are often underrepresented where the future of power is designed and implemented. Thus, it falls to those primarily in the relatively independent domain of academia to pursue these values and insist on diagnosing design choices in terms of their effects on the distribution of power, as well as to develop and advocate design options that will preserve the possibility of decentralized, autonomous, and organically chosen collective action.") See, however, Coeckelbergh, *AI Ethics*, 172 ("[A]lbeit well-intended, ethics by design and responsible innovation have their own limitations. [...] methods such as value-sensitive design presuppose that we can articulate our values, and efforts to build moral machines assume that we can fully articulate our ethics").

[84] Nemitz, "Constitutional Democracy," 13.

[85] See, e.g., Hoffman, *Forces*, 133 & 225–28 ("AI, not machines, will be the major driver of automation moving forward. It will power everything from humanoid robots to the array of smart devices entering our homes, offices, factories, and bodies. Intelligent algorithms will also power the software used to manage our infrastructure, health care, finance, transportation, and government" [quotation from p. 133]). Steven S. Hoffman also notes that "[t]he more sophisticated these AIs become, the more deeply we will integrate them into our decision-making apparatus" (*id.*, at 226).

[86] For a fictional and prospective reflection in this direction, when the world's largest search engine/social media company merges the planet's dominant e-commerce site, see Eggers, *The Every*, 233–34, 470–71, 553–72 & 577.

of powers and probably democracy as well.[87] More concretely, it would shape the decisions and choices of bodies or entities that are supposed to control and limit each other, and could lead to some form of centralized surveillance over public bodies, private firms and individuals.[88] In other words, the system of checks and balances at the core of the separation of powers principle, as properly understood, would become quite inefficient, if not completely illusory. Artificial intelligence would form, so to speak, a conglomerate, or – the word inevitably comes up – a trust, progressively out of control and reach of governments and peoples.[89] It would thus weaken or even stifle democracy, as notably warned by Daron Acemoglu and Simon Johnson.[90] Should such an evolution occur or loom, then additional checks and balances will have to be safeguarded or put in place. A global, multilevel, and multidimensional strategy is required for addressing these issues.

Privacy and intellectual property rights may be viewed as answers, especially with respect to machine learning or other learning based on personal or business data. Strict rules would limit the type of activities that, for instance, large digital platforms intensively using artificial intelligence could perform and, hence, reduce the latter's politico-economic power. A note of caution is advisable here for several reasons. First, it seems difficult – if not impossible – and unrealistic to effectively prevent these platforms, only through privacy or intellectual property rules, from legally collecting a huge amount of personal or business data. Rather, much of the debate relates *inter alia* to data retention, use,[91] or transfer. Moreover, privacy and competition may conflict, and strict privacy protection may actually benefit large or dominant firms.[92] Indeed, "if companies are required to incorporate increasingly stringent data minimization policies, they will likely rely on these privacy policies to justify

---

[87] On the risk for the separation of powers principle, see Hoffman, *Forces*, 229 ("If we hope to avoid a despot leveraging technology to control us, we must put our efforts into making sure this type of scenario can never come about. This requires institutional safeguards that prevent the abuse of authority, well-conceived restrictions on the use of key technologies, and a separation of powers to keep tyrannical leaders in check. Unfortunately, most countries lack all three"). On the risk for democracy, see European Commission, Proposal for a Regulation of the European Parliament and of the Council Laying Down Harmonized Rules on Artificial Intelligence (Artificial Intelligence Act) and Amending Certain Union Legislative Acts, COM(2021) 206 final, available at https://eur-lex.europa.eu/resource .html?uri=cellar:e0649735-a372-11eb-9585-01aa75ed71a1.0001.02/DOC_1&format=PDF, recital 40 ("Certain AI systems intended for the administration of justice and democratic processes should be classified as high-risk, considering their potentially significant impact on democracy, rule of law, individual freedoms as well as the right to an effective remedy and to a fair trial"); Yeung, "Decision-Making," 41–45.

[88] See, e.g., Hoffman, *Forces*, 143 ("As we algorithmically automate our world, we won't just have police robots but also surveillance technology playing a central role in our security and commerce"); see also Stucke, *Breaking Away*, 210–45; Patino, *Civilisation*, 90. Steven S. Hoffman further notes, however, that "[i]n a world where smart devices are in the hands of everyone, the power of surveillance can act as a healthy counterbalance to surveillance" (*id.*, at 149).

[89] See, e.g., Hoffman, *Forces*, 154 ("[I]n the future, AI will become so powerful that its judgment will surpass our own in practically every way"); see also Santoni de Sio, "Ethics of AI," 50/2 & 5.

[90] Acemoglu & Johnson, *Power and Progress*, 31–33 & 392–96.

[91] See, e.g., Susskind, *Digital Republic*, 252.

[92] See, e.g., Fukuyama, "Internet Safe for Democracy," 41; see also Ezrachi & Stucke, *Barons*, 192.

their anticompetitive behavior," as noted by Maurice E. Stucke.[93] A ban on behavioral advertising and strict limits on profiling and amalgamating personal data or on personalized recommendations could help individuals regain their autonomy and privacy or have democracy be safeguarded,[94] but it would come under heavy criticism. Answers may exist for each of them.[95] The combination of the criticisms, the lack of consensus on appropriate measures, the highly evolving nature of the field, and the internationality of the issues – compared with the nationality or regionality of the answers[96] – suggest that societies should not limit themselves to these solutions for countering and reducing the power of large or, *a fortiori*, dominant platforms. In any case, one of the most fundamental issues – if not the squaring of the circle or the Holy Grail[97] – facing legislatures and governmental agencies actually consists in finding the appropriate balance and interaction, or even reciprocal reinforcement, between competition and privacy with respect to artificial intelligence based on personal data, again as convincingly emphasized by Maurice E. Stucke:

> Privacy can be a critical non-price component of competition. Competition along this parameter can deliver greater privacy protection (and better privacy technologies). Likewise, privacy policies can promote healthy competition.[98]

A solution can eventually be found by combining data openness policies with an obligation to de-identify data without the possibility to re-identify it.[99] Still, the appropriate mix between privacy and competition would be extremely difficult to find and would not solve all problems. Consequently, other avenues of reform must also be explored. In this respect, the tendency of concentration may lead governments to order, or, at least, to incentivize the deconcentration or decentralization of artificial intelligence, with the view of mitigating risks and of creating or reinstalling checks and balances on or within the intelligence.[100] As a footnote, deconcentration is distinguished from decentralization in French constitutional and administrative law. In the context here, deconcentration means the "reversal or diminution of concentration; spec. the dissolution of cartels or other large industrial groupings;

---

[93] Stucke, *Breaking Away*, 188 & 203 (quotation from p. 203).

[94] Stucke, *Breaking Away*, 211–12, 221–45 & 259.

[95] See Stucke, *Breaking Away*, 213–21.

[96] Susskind, *Digital Republic*, 207 ("[T]he digital republic is most likely to be realised at the national level, first and foremost – while working (as ever) to develop the international organisations, treaties and protocols that make international cooperation possible").

[97] Stucke, *Breaking Away*, 246; see also Akcigit *et al.*, *Market Power*, 26, para. 45.

[98] Stucke, *Breaking Away*, 171, 190–91 & 246 (quotation from p. 171).

[99] Stucke, *Breaking Away*, 252–54.

[100] Regarding the Internet, see, by analogy, Benkler, "Freedom, Power," 27 & 30–31 ("One of the core design targets of any future effort to keep the Internet open, decentralized, and resistant to control is to develop technically instantiated mechanisms to achieve user-owned and -shared capacity that offers no proprietary point of control for centralizing actors" [quotation from p. 27]); see also Lina M. Khan, "We Must Regulate A.I. Here's How," *New York Times*, online edition, 3 May 2023, www.nytimes.com/2023/05/03/opinion/ai-lina-khan-ftc-technology.html.

decentralization."[101] Federated learning[102] and fully decentralized learning (peer-to-peer) learning,[103] as well as interoperability or interconnectivity duties, constitute interesting avenues for innovation and competition as well as the deconcentration of data power, as analyzed by Peter Kairouz, H. Brendan McMahan *et al.*:

> Federated learning presents an opportunity to leverage uniquely diverse datasets by providing efficient decentralized training protocols along with privacy and non-identifiability guarantees for the resulting models. This means that federated learning enables training on multi-institutional datasets in many domains where this was previously not possible. This provides a practical opportunity to leverage larger, more diverse datasets and explore the generalizability of models which were previously limited to small populations. More importantly, it provides an opportunity to improve the fairness of these models by combining data across boundaries which are likely to have been correlated with sensitive attributes.[104]

Governments could adopt regulations imposing, in certain cases, these types of learning and other forms of decentralization or deconcentration, or create incentives in favor of these. Regulators may, for instance, authorize certain developments of artificial intelligence or, at least, provide a less stringent regime for these developments if the approach adopted is open-source, federated or fully decentralized and based on blockchain or another decentralized technology.[105] Unfortunately, in the European

---

[101] Oxford English Dictionary, under "deconcentration."

[102] See Kairouz, McMahan *et al.*, "Federated Learning," Chapter 1 *in initio* ("Federated learning (FL) is a machine learning setting where many clients (e.g., mobile devices or whole organizations) collaboratively train a model under the orchestration of a central server (e.g., service provider), while keeping the training data decentralized. It embodies the principles of focused collection and data minimization, and can mitigate many of the systemic privacy risks and costs resulting from traditional, centralized machine learning").

[103] See Kairouz, McMahan *et al.*, "Federated Learning," Chapter 2, Section 2.1 ("In federated learning, a central server orchestrates the training process and receives the contributions of all clients. The server is thus a central player which also potentially represents a single point of failure. While large companies or organizations can play this role in some application scenarios, a reliable and powerful central server may not always be available or desirable in more collaborative learning scenarios [...]. The key idea of fully decentralized learning is to replace communication with the server by peer-to-peer communication between individual clients [...]. It is worth noting that even in the decentralized setting outlined above, a central authority may still be in charge of setting up the learning task. Consider for instance the following questions: Who decides what is the model to be trained in the decentralized setting? What algorithm to use? What hyperparameters? Who is responsible for debugging when something does not work as expected? A certain degree of trust of the participating clients in a central authority would still be needed to answer these questions. Alternatively, the decisions could be taken by the client who proposes the learning task, or collaboratively through a consensus scheme [...]" [one footnote omitted]). However, see Ezrachi & Stucke, *Barons*, 192–93 (quoting Cecilia Rikap).

[104] See Kairouz, McMahan *et al.*, "Federated Learning," Chapter 6, Section 6.4. From a similar perspective, see, by analogy, Ezrachi & Stucke, *Barons*, 193; Nemitz & Pfeffer, "Future," 281–82 & 287–88 ("Correctly used edge technology could be one area in which technology companies and democracy can work together, namely when personal data no longer is transferred to central cloud data repositories of the platforms from the mobile phone and other devices under the control of the user" [quotation from p. 281]); Moore & Tambini, "Holistic Vision," 342.

[105] From a similar perspective, see Hoffman, *Forces*, 18 (regarding brain data); see also Schrepel, *Blockchain + Antitrust*, 248, 265–8 & 270–1 ("By removing ecosystems' gatekeepers, blockchains

Union, the proposed Artificial Intelligence Act[106] does not address this issue for now and, more generally, falls short of the goal to comprehensively regulate artificial intelligence.[107] Furthermore, decentralization, although desirable, is not a panacea in all cases.[108] Accordingly, incentives must therefore allow for some flexibility to maintain a few doses of centralization in areas that require it or for firms that do not reach certain thresholds.

Tax incentives, subsidies and direct funding may also come to mind,[109] in the sense that, for instance, profits resulting from activities performed in a federated or decentralized way would, *ceteris paribus*, receive a preferred tax treatment as compared to profits resulting from centralized activities. By way of an example, a service provider's profits based on its machine learning activities would be taxed at a higher level if the learning is centralized, at a medium level if it is federated, and at a lower level if it is fully decentralized. Of course, the lower level would not be inferior to the applicable rules fixing minimum tax, including the international ones. It is also conceivable that the service provider's clients receive some tax incentives if they privilege federated or decentralized forms of artificial intelligence. Specific tax deductibles or credits especially come to mind. These are some possible ideas that could indeed be contemplated, but a detailed analysis of these options falls beyond the scope of this book.

Additionally, more flexible data protection rules for federated or decentralized learning, as opposed to centralized learning, may create incentives to follow this path, but such rules are usually formulated in a technology-neutral way. Another possible path would be to consider the type of learning when applying general rules. In the European Union, the duty to carry out an assessment of the impact of the envisaged processing operations on the protection of personal data, when the processing is likely to result in a high risk to the rights and freedoms of natural persons,[110] can be relevant in this context. Concretely, federated or decentralized learning and data processing could be considered of limited risk and thus admissible. In the same vein, these types of learning and processing could be taken into account in the preparation of code of conducts and in the certification process foreseen, respectively, by Articles 40 and 42 GDPR. In any event, federated learning and an emerging field called "privacy computing" or "confidential computing" better protect personal data especially when they disallow the central AI owner to see the

---

eliminate de facto all anti-competitive practices they can engage in. This, once again, explains why blockchain and antitrust should work together" [quotation from p. 266]); Dixon, "Decentralization."

[106] European Commission, Proposal for a Regulation of the European Parliament and of the Council Laying Down Harmonized Rules on Artificial Intelligence (Artificial Intelligence Act) and Amending Certain Union Legislative Acts, COM(2021) 206 final, available at https://eur-lex.europa.eu/resource .html?uri=cellar:e0649735-a372-11eb-9585-01aa75ed71a1.0001.02/DOC_1&format=PDF.

[107] Raposo, "Ex Machina," 108.

[108] See, by analogy, Ball, *Metaverse*, 291 ("Decentralization, often seen as the solution to many of the problems created by the tech giants, will also make moderation more difficult, malcontents harder to stop, and illicit fundraising far less difficult").

[109] See Ezrachi & Stucke, *Barons*, 206–8.

[110] Article 35 GDPR.

data.[111] The centralization or decentralization of artificial intelligence systems could also play a role in the risk assessment required by existing or future regulation on artificial intelligence, or in the attribution of liability and the determination of damages on which legislation should also focus.

Finally, from an antitrust perspective, federated or fully decentralized machine learning and other artificial intelligence may be regarded, *ceteris paribus*, as less problematic than a system organized in a centralized way. This form of deconcentration or decentralization may be relevant in the appraisal of a behavior or a merger by an antitrust agency and impact the outcome of an inquiry or a market study.[112] Nevertheless, the fact remains that the choice in favor of deconcentration or decentralization does not remove all competition concerns, so that antitrust remains important in accompanying the transition to pro-competitive decentralized machine learning and artificial intelligence platforms.[113]

9.4.3 *Limits to Substantial Autonomous Powers*

A particularly sensitive issue is whether some forms of artificial intelligence will acquire or, more exactly, be given substantial autonomy, in the sense that it would develop and evolve without human intervention,[114] could not be safely controlled, and could have goals that may not align with those of their human creators.[115] It could become an autonomous power[116] – and, depending on the evolution, an algocracy – and so the principle of separation of powers should be considered in this context as well. As made clear by Montesquieu already,[117] this principle tries to prevent and avoid abuses. Prevention in this framework most probably means limiting and defining, precisely as well as controllably, the autonomy given to artificial intelligence

---

[111] Lee & Chen, *AI 2041*, 399 & 432; see also Eigenmann, "Enhanced Privacy," 29–35; Schrepel, *Blockchain + Antitrust*, 267.

[112] Regarding permission-less blockchains, see Pike & Carovano, "Decentralised Blockchains," 114–15 & 118 ("[T]the opportunity for competition agencies and policymakers to facilitate through market investigation remedies or sponsorship, the emergence of decentralised permission-less blockchains as part of a pro-competitive industrial policy is considerable. We encourage all agencies and policymakers to distinguish between the two types of blockchain, and to be pro-active and ambitious and make the most of the pro-competitive opportunity that the technology may offer" [quotation from p. 118]); see also Massarotto, "Blockchain," 131–32 & 136–37 (regarding distributed ledger technologies).

[113] Massarotto, "Blockchain," 132 & 137–50 ("Blockchain needs antitrust to succeed and antitrust needs to embrace blockchain technologies to be effective in today's data economy" [quotation from p. 150]).

[114] See, e.g., Hoffman, *Forces*, 202–5 & 225–35.

[115] See, e.g., Le Cun, *Machine*, 370–72; Hawking, *Brief Answers*, 184–90; "How to Worry Wisely About AI," and "How Generative Models Could Go Wrong," *The Economist*, 22 April 2023, 7–8 & 68–69.

[116] See, e.g., Rab, "Artificial Intelligence," 150 ("Ultimately enforcers, practitioners and businesses will have to confront the question of liability for the decisions or output of machine learning which are increasingly distanced from human intervention and which call into question traditional notions of antitrust liability").

[117] See *supra* Part I, Chapter 1, Section 1.3 & Chapter 2, Section 2.1.

systems.[118] Limits and control are of utmost importance when AI actions, notably through autonomous weapons, have potentially lethal effects.[119] Global and practicable rules would set the framework for this. Concentration of data power, general artificial intelligence or artificial superintelligence – possibly based on quantum computing – and autonomy[120] may not mix well,[121] which means that regulation and control mechanisms would be crucial[122] if such a combination nevertheless takes place. Here again, the tech giants are racing to dominate the field of quantum computing.[123]

Different control methods will probably coexist due to the many types of artificial intelligence systems and, within one type, the many challenges that may develop in the future.[124] According to the democratic participation principle of the Montreal Declaration for a Responsible Development of Artificial Intelligence, "[w]e must at all times be able to verify that [artificial intelligence systems] are doing what they were programed for and what they are used for."[125] In addition to multidimensional regulation and its effective implementation,[126] disclosure obligations and interpretability are key concerns in this context as well.[127]

As always, specific regulation may never come or arrive too late, but antitrust will most probably still exist, which means that antitrust may play a role with respect to this fourth new politico-economic axis of the separation of powers. Reflections on competition law and policy should address this issue preventively. This collusion, magma, or conglomerate of artificial intelligence could be regarded as dominant, including from an economic perspective, and its behaviors abusively exploitative or exclusionary. Some key concepts of competition or antitrust laws may obviously need to be stretched a bit, but the stakes would justify such an approach. Antitrust or competition agencies may therefore open proceedings to break up the

---

[118] See, e.g., Pasquale, *New Laws of Robotics*, 11–2. From a broader perspective, see Kissinger, Schmidt & Huttenlocher, *Age of AI*, 163, 199, 216–17 & 221 ("[T]o ensure human autonomy, core governmental decisions should be carved out of AI-imbued structures and limited to human administration and oversight" [quotation from p. 199]).

[119] Kissinger, Schmidt & Huttenlocher, *Age of AI*, 161, 171, 216 & 225; see also Cade Metz, "He Warns of Risks from A.I. He Helped Create," *New York Times*, 2 May 2023, A1 ("[Geoffrey Hinton] fears a day when truly autonomous weapons – those killer robots – become reality").

[120] On quantum computing and AI-enabled autonomous weapons, see Lee & Chen, *AI 2041*, 256 & 302–12 (describing these weapons as "the greatest danger from AI" and considering that they "may even become an existential threat to humankind" [quotation from p. 256]).

[121] On this issue, see Wheeler, "Autonomy," 355–56.

[122] See Russell, *Human Compatible*, 183 ("[C]ompeting to be the first to achieve human-level AI, without first solving the control problem, is a negative-sum game. The payoff for everyone is minus infinity"); see also Kissinger, Schmidt & Huttenlocher, *Age of AI*, 221–5; Cusumano, Gawer & Yoffie, *Business of Platforms*, 226–9. Regarding AI-enabled autonomous weapons, see Lee & Chen, *AI 2041*, 311–12.

[123] See, e.g., Charlie Campbell, "The Quantum Leap," *Time*, 13 February 2023, 46–51.

[124] See Le Cun, *Machine*, 370–72; Bostrom, *Superintelligence*, 127–58.

[125] *Montréal Declaration for a Responsible Development of Artificial Intelligence*, principle 5 ("Democratic participation principle"), para. 7.

[126] See *supra* 9.4.1 & 9.4.2 in the present Section.

[127] See, e.g., "How to Worry Wisely about AI," and "How Generative Models Could Go Wrong," *The Economist*, 22 April 2023, 7–8 & 68–69.

conglomerate, to separate various artificial intelligence tools, forbid some behaviors, or impose remedies. By doing so, they would embark on a very difficult crusade to restore competition, separate or limit powers and, at the same time, rescue human-kind.[128] They may have no choice. The stakes are high, as observed by Stephen Hawking or Kai-Fu Lee and Qiufan Chen:

> [T]he advent of super-intelligent AI would be either the best or the worst thing ever to happen to humanity.[129]
>
> In the story of AI and humans, if we get the dance between artificial intelligence and human society right, it would unquestionably be the single greatest achieve-ment in human history.[130]

And antitrust may be part of this – hopefully not last – dance…

9.5 REGULATION AND DECONCENTRATION OR DECENTRALIZATION OF THE METAVERSE

The metaverse may reshape society, politics, and economy around the globe in the future. It may, or may not, concentrate power in the hands of a few firms (9.5.1). From an antitrust perspective, the metaverse poses at least two main issues: antitrust on the metaverse (9.5.2) and antitrust in the metaverse (9.5.3).

9.5.1 *The Metaverse between Centralization and Decentralization*

In colloquial use, a metaverse – a combination of "meta" and "universe" – refers to a "network of 3D virtual worlds focused on social and economic connection."[131] Due to interoperability, portability, and cross-platforms interactions *inter alia*,[132] various networks or, more precisely, subnetworks could actually form one single, universal, and immersive virtual world called the metaverse, a term which was coined by Neal Stephenson[133] and is defined as follows by Matthew Ball:

> A massively scaled and interoperable network of real-time rendered 3D virtual worlds that can be experienced synchronously and persistently by an effec-tively unlimited number of users with an individual sense of presence, and with

---

[128] On this issue, see, e.g., Geoffrey Hinton *et al.*, *Statement on AI Risk*, Center for AI Safety, May 2023 ("Mitigating the risk of extinction from AI should be a global priority alongside other societal-scale risks such as pandemics and nuclear war"); Hoffman, *Forces*, 235.

[129] Hawking, *Brief Answers*, 188.

[130] Lee & Chen, *AI 2041*, 438; see also Kanaan, *T-Minus AI*, 232–33.

[131] Wikipedia, *Metaverse*, https://en.wikipedia.org/wiki/Metaverse (28 June 2023).

[132] See Ball, *Metaverse*, 37–42, 121–40, 245–46 & 306–7 (referring, among other things, to cross-platform gaming); Terry & Keeney, *Metaverse*, 140–7; Mystakidis, "Metaverse," 492–93; Parisi, "Metaverse" ("*Rule #4: The Metaverse is open. It is built upon interoperable technologies and tools, connected via rigorously defined and broadly agreed-upon free and open communications standards*").

[133] Stephenson, *Snow Crash*, 244 ("The Metaverse is a fictional structure made out of code. And code is just a form of speech – the form that computers understand").

continuity of data, such as identity, history, entitlements, objects, communications, and payments.[134]

The metaverse may become "the future form of Internet evolution, realizing a solution to break the gap between virtual and reality," as foreseen by Steven S. Hoffman,[135] or even "the future of human experience," as predicted by Herman Narula.[136] It could "eat TV."[137] It should be noted at the outset that "it is being pioneered and built by private businesses."[138] Accordingly, the firm or firms that would control some of its powering technologies, engines, operating systems, constitutive parts, must-have devices, standards, payment rails, or other decisive features would concentrate enormous economic, social, and political power and may feel entitled, for instance, to dictate the content of the metaverse.[139] In 2016, Tim Sweeney, founder and CEO of Epic Games, warned about the risks of such a concentration:

> This Metaverse is going to be far more pervasive and powerful than anything else. If one central company gains control of this, they will become more powerful than any government and be a god on Earth. What we want is not a company but a protocol, that anyone can implement.[140]

The metaverse will probably remain decentralized to various extents,[141] notably with the coexistence of several popular virtual worlds or virtual world platforms[142] or the use of blockchains or blockchain-like technologies,[143] but one or a few firms

---

[134] Ball, *Metaverse*, 29–59 (quotation from p. 29). For other definitions, see Narula, *Society*, 120, 126–27, 226 & 231("A metaverse is a network of consequences and meaning between multiple worlds in which people are simultaneously engaged and invested" [quotation from p. 120]); Mystakidis, "Metaverse," 486 ("The Metaverse is the post-reality universe, a perpetual and persistent multiuser environment merging physical reality with digital virtuality. It is based on the convergence of technologies that enable multisensory interactions with virtual environments, digital objects and people such as virtual reality (VR) and augmented reality (AR)").

[135] Hoffman, *Forces*, 21–24; see also Narula, *Society*, xii; "Opportunities and Risks Behind the Vision of Metaverse," *iNEWS*, 24 January 2022, https://inf.news/en/economy/3ad49037bc7ddfff107210b48c79 a4b1.html. From a general perspective, see Kissinger, Schmidt & Huttenlocher, *Age of AI*, 102.

[136] Narula, *Society*, xv, 72, 78–80 & 216 (quotation from p. xv).

[137] Andrew R. Chow, "What Mark Zuckerberg Revealed about His Metaverse Plans," *Time*, online edition, 1 September 2022, https://time.com/6210005/mark-zuckerberg-metaverse-future-joe-rogan/ (quoting Mark Zuckerberg).

[138] Matthew Ball, "The Coming Worlds," *Time*, 8 & 15 August 2022 (double issue), 36–40, 40.

[139] Narula, *Society*, 137.

[140] Dean Takahashi, "The DeanBeat: Epic Graphics Guru Tim Sweeney Foretells How We Can Create the Open Metaverse," *Venture Beat*, 9 December 2016, https://venturebeat.com/games/the-deanbeat-epic-boss-tim-sweeney-makes-the-case-for-the-open-metaverse/. See also Narula, *Society*, 209; Ball, *Metaverse*, 14–17 & 289.

[141] See Ball, *Metaverse*, 58–59 & 63; see also Parisi, "Metaverse" ("Rule #3: Nobody controls the Metaverse. It is the universal commons for digital communication and commerce, intermediated as needs dictate, governed as required for the common interest, toward the greatest good for the greatest number").

[142] See Ball, *Metaverse*, 119–20.

[143] See Ball, *Metaverse*, 207–35, 245 & 306–7 (concluding that "one of the central lessons of the computing era is that the platforms that best serve developers and users will win" and adding that "[b]

may still concentrate an enormous amount of power.[144] For Herman Narula, "[b]lockchain-like systems can incentivize transparency while disempowering corporate tyrants."[145]

In other words, the metaverse will oscillate between centralization and decentralization[146] to eventually find some middle ground[147] thanks, among others, to regulation and antitrust. One of the most fundamental questions relating to centralization consists of determining what these decisive powering technologies, engines, operating systems, constitutive parts, must-have devices,[148] standards, payment rails,[149] or other features, such as the control of data not "on chain,"[150] will be. New gatekeepers, possibly dominant from an antitrust perspective, may emerge,[151] perhaps coming from the gaming industry, like Roblox Corporation, Epic Games, Unity Software Inc. (doing business as Unity Technologies)[152] or Tencent Holdings Ltd.,[153] or from graphics-based computing, like Nvidia Corporation.[154] Of course, firms such as Alphabet Inc., Amazon.com, Inc., Apple Inc., Meta Platforms, Inc., Microsoft Corporation – especially if it can successfully close its acquisition of Activision Blizzard, Inc. announced on 18 January 2022 but challenged by the FTC[155] and blocked by the CMA,[156] but cleared, subject to conditions, by the European

---

lockchains have a long way to go, but many see their immutability and transparency as the best way to ensure the interests of these two constituencies remain prioritized as the Metaverse economy grows" [quotation from p. 235]); see also Narula, *Society*, 152–53 & 204–5; Terry & Keeney, *Metaverse*, 149.

[144] From a similar perspective, see Ball, *Metaverse*, 306.

[145] Narula, *Society*, 205.

[146] See Ball, *Metaverse*, 283–89 & 291 ("What matters is where the Metaverse falls between the two poles, why, and how its position shifts over time" [quotation from pp. 283–84]).

[147] See Narula, *Society*, 149–50.

[148] Ball, *Metaverse*, 163 ("The more important the device – and the more devices that connect to it – the greater the control afforded to the company which makes it").

[149] See Ball, *Metaverse*, 164–206.

[150] Ball, *Metaverse*, 233.

[151] See Matthew Ball, "The Coming Worlds," *Time*, 8 & 15 August 2022 (double issue), 36–40, 40 ("[T]he companies that control these virtual worlds and their virtual atoms will be more dominant than those that lead in today's digital economy").

[152] See Ball, *Metaverse*, 213–14, 275–83 & 299–300 ("Though their valuations, revenues, and operational scale are modest compared to GAFAM, [companies such as Epic Games, Unity, and Roblox Corporation] have the player networks, the developer networks, the virtual worlds, and the 'virtual plumbing' to be real leaders in the Metaverse" [quotation from p. 275]); see also Narula, *Society*, 145–46; Terry & Keeney, *Metaverse*, 78–82.

[153] See Ball, *Metaverse*, 303–4 ("No other company [than Tencent] is better positioned to facilitate the interoperation of user data, virtual worlds, identity, and payments, nor influence Metaverse standards" [quotation from p. 304]).

[154] Ball, *Metaverse*, 282 ("We may never wear Nvidia-branded headsets nor play Nvidia-published games, but at least in 2022, it looks likely that we live in a Metaverse powered in large part by Nvidia").

[155] FTC, "FTC Seeks to Block Microsoft Corp.'s Acquisition of Activision Blizzard, Inc.," *Press Release*, 8 December 2022, www.ftc.gov/news-events/news/press-releases/2022/12/ftc-seeks-block-microsoft-corps-acquisition-activision-blizzard-inc.

[156] CMA, *Anticipated Acquisition by Microsoft of Activision Blizzard, Inc. – Final Report*, 26 April 2023, 415 ("We have decided that prohibition of the Merger would be an effective and proportionate remedy to address the [significant lessening of competition] in the market for cloud gaming services in

Commission[157] – or Sony Group Corporation should not by any means be left out of the picture.[158] Meta, for instance, seems to be well aware of the importance of games to its nascent ecosystem around its metaverse projects,[159] even though it has recently reduced its investments in the latter. Furthermore, the combination of a deep library of games with cloud computing could give a company such as Microsoft a very significant competitive advantage over game-streaming competitors.[160]

The analysis performed here does not relate only to Meta Platforms, but to the metaverse in general. It seems extremely difficult to predict how the latter will evolve, notably whether one network will prevail or several independent networks will coexist in the medium or long term.[161] There will undoubtedly be delays and project abandonments, but the creation and the development of virtual worlds, not limited to the gaming industry, remain highly probable.[162] Matthew Ball, among others, convincingly comes to the conclusion that the metaverse in singular is the appropriate notion – "Many Virtual Platforms and Engines, Not Many Metaverses."[163] Herman Narula uses the plural, but still envisages that "[t]here will probably also be a metaverse of metaverses – a *mega*verse, perhaps – that connects the various metaverses together."[164] Nevertheless, this last new politico-economic axis of separation of powers is highly prospective, even speculative, as put by Matthew Ball:

> Eventually, a thing that seems trivial – a mobile phone, a touchscreen, a video game – becomes essential, and ends up changing the world in ways both predicted and never even considered.[165]

---

the UK and its resulting adverse effects"). See, e.g., Tom Warren, "The UK Doesn't Want Microsoft's Activision Blizzard Deal, so What Happens Next?," *The Verge*, 1 May 2023, www.theverge.com/2023/5/1/23702716/microsoft-activision-blizzard-uk-deal-what-happens-next ("Microsoft will have to file a notice with the Competition Appeal Tribunal (CAT), a process that can take months. It will have to convince a panel of judges that the CMA acted irrationally, illegally, or with procedural impropriety or unfairness. And the chances of winning are slim")

[157] European Commission, *Press Release*, 15 May 2023.

[158] See Ball, *Metaverse*, 273–83 ("How Today's Tech Giants Are Positioned for the Metaverse"); Ezrachi & Stucke, *Barons*, 4 & 121–22 ("As the digital economy expands to new industries and the metaverse, so will the Tech Barons' power" [quotation from p. 4]); Boris Manenti & Dominique Nora, "Comment vivrons-nous dans le métavers?" [How Will We Live in the Metaverse?], *L'Obs*, 11 August 2022, 38–45, 44–45 (quoting Laurent Chrétien, Laurence Devillers & Jean Barrère).

[159] Andrew R. Chow, "A Year Ago, Facebook Pivoted to the Metaverse. Was It Worth It?" *Time*, online edition, 27 October 2022, https://time.com/6225617/facebook-metaverse-anniversary-vr/.

[160] See David McCabe & Karen Weise, "Can Big Tech Get Bigger?" *New York Times*, 21 November 2022, B1.

[161] On various view on this question, see Ball, *Metaverse*, 21, 119–20 & 302–4 (predicting that "[g]iven the pace of change, level of technical difficulty, and the diversity of potential applications, it's likely that we will end up with dozens of popular virtual worlds and virtual world platforms, with many more underlying technology providers" [quotation from p. 119]).

[162] See, e.g., Dominik Erhard, "Métavers – Le meilleur des mondes ?" [Metaverse: The Best of All Worlds ?], translated by Octave Larmagny-Mahteron, *Philosophie Magazine*, April 2023, 28–33.

[163] Ball, *Metaverse*, 113–20; see also Mystakidis, "Metaverse," 493; Parisi, "Metaverse" ("*Rule #1. There is only one Metaverse. It is the sum total of all publicly accessible virtual worlds, real-time 3D content and related media that are connected on an open global network, controlled by none and accessible to all*").

[164] Narula, *Society*, 108.

[165] Ball, *Metaverse*, 309.

Due notably to the many risks that the metaverse poses, regulation is certainly needed.[166] As some of these risks relate to the concentration of economic power and the related issues, antitrust also comes to play.

9.5.2 *Antitrust on the Metaverse*

Firms building, developing, managing or, ultimately, controlling some decisive aspects of the metaverse will certainly be subject to antitrust and competition laws. Power *on* the metaverse will probably constitute a major issue for the next years or decades, as the metaverse will become an economic force.[167] New markets may appear and possibly disappear. As just seen, centralized phases may follow decentralized ones raising antitrust concerns, including (eco)systemic ones, opening the door to what could be called *meta-antitrust* – the prefix "meta" denoting transformation and meaning here "at a higher level," rather than "beyond"[168]:

> [A]s an emerging digital ecology that contains the integration of cutting-edge technologies, the technical characteristics and development forms of Metaverse have initially proposed some potential risks and challenges. The first is the challenge of industrial hegemony. Although Metaverse has the characteristics of "decentralization," similar to the previous cutting-edge technology and digital ecology, long-term industry evolution can easily eventually form "centralized" giants and countries. The top companies that enter the market early will gain huge advantages through technological research and development and capital accumulation, and show superior position advantages on the track. These monopolistic giants will then have more comprehensive information and data [...].[169]

If a firm is dominant on the relevant market or markets, it will have to comply with the anti-abuse obligations foreseen by these laws. For instance, firms building the most popular devices necessary for users to connect to the metaverse could be considered gatekeepers[170] and, depending on their market shares and other criteria,

---

[166] Narula, *Society*, 185–86, 193–94 & 209–14; Ball, *Metaverse*, 300–1; Ezrachi & Stucke, *Barons*, 115 & 121–22; Boris Manenti & Dominique Nora, "Comment vivrons-nous dans le métavers?" [How Will We Live in the Metaverse?], *L'Obs*, 11 August 2022, 38–45, 45 (quoting Dominique Boullier, Isabelle Djian & Jean Barrère).

[167] See Narula, *Society*, 104, 128–29 & 134.

[168] See Oxford English Dictionary, first two meanings of "meta-" as a prefix.

[169] "Opportunities and Risks Behind the Vision of Metaverse," *iNEWS*, 24 January 2022; see also Stucke, *Breaking Away*, 55 ("By quickly colonizing these next-generation ecosystems [metaverse platforms], the data-opolies can leverage their monopoly power, and use the economies of scale and network effects offensively to improve the odds that they remain on top, widen their data and attention advantage over rivals, and hedge against potential dynamic disruption" [one footnote omitted]) & 186; Sheldon, "Metaverse"("[B]ig business and governments have dominated online activities and governance with ruthless effectiveness. I doubt the metaverse will be any different"); Gavin Guerrette, Simona Hausleitner, Sarah Feng, Anabel Moore & Zack Hauptman, "Welcome to the Metaverse," *Yale Daily News Magazine*, February 2022, 4–8, 6–7 (quoting Charles Hodgson).

[170] Mackenzie, Goeteyn, Mantine & Westrup, "Metaverse."

have a dominant position on the relevant market or markets. In the same vein, games have become a path toward more immersive online worlds, and currently very large technology companies already have significant stakes or projects in the gaming world.[171] A given game, or several games of the same firm or conglomerate, could become main gateways to the metaverse. Besides, should a firm have control over, for instance, the operating system, the decisive powering technologies, engines, or other elements of the "virtual plumbing"[172] of the metaverse, it may qualify as dominant within the meaning of antitrust and competition laws. The focus is put here on the infrastructure of the metaverse and its key players, if any. The behavior of firms in the metaverse will be addressed in the next subsection (9.5.3).

The prohibition of discrimination[173] may prove of special importance in this context as well. Furthermore, these firms may issue private regulation setting standards for the whole industry and even for society in general. Besides, the metaverse may become an important or even fundamental part of the digital infrastructure of democracy.[174] These evolutions would raise challenge on the organization of these firms and the appropriate internal and external checks and balances.[175] In the words of Herman Narula, the metaverse may have "to be conducted on democratic principles and invite democratic engagements."[176] Moreover, specific regulations,[177] complementary to antitrust and competitions laws, and incentives or obligations to decentralize a given metaverse platform, as just seen with respect to artificial intelligence,[178] may be needed to avoid too high of a concentration of politico-economic power.[179] On a general note, some of the issues raised by the metaverse are linked to those related to artificial intelligence.[180]

---

[171] Richard Waters & Leo Lewis, "Why Gaming Is the New Big Tech Battleground," *Financial Times*, online edition, 21 January 2022, www.ft.com/content/2d446160-08cb-489f-90c8-853b3d88780d ("Some of the biggest tech companies already have significant stakes in the gaming world, even if they haven't pushed far into trying to produce games themselves. These include the Apple and Google mobile app stores, which act as the main shop front for the single largest segment of the gaming market. Amazon's Twitch and Google's YouTube attract mass audiences for viewing video games. And through its Oculus headsets, Facebook holds the lion's share of the nascent virtual reality market").

[172] Ball, *Metaverse*, 275.

[173] See *supra* Part II, Chapter 6, Section 6.4.

[174] See "Opportunities and Risks behind the Vision of Metaverse," *iNEWS*, 24 January 2022.

[175] See *supra* Part II, Chapter 5.

[176] Narula, *Society*, 126 & 155 (quotation from p. 126). For past experiences, see, however, Chalmers, *Reality+*, 351–52 & 358–59.

[177] See, e.g., Santesteban, "Metaverse"; "Opportunities and Risks behind the Vision of Metaverse," *iNEWS*, 24 January 2022.

[178] See *supra* Section 9.4.2 in the present Chapter, by analogy.

[179] See Chalmers, "Virtual Reality," 51 ("One major question that comes up right now is the role of corporations in setting up virtual societies […]. Do we really want Facebook or its descendants to be controlling every aspect of our reality when we're in virtual worlds? It's not as if I have a replacement model in mind, but I think the corporate metaverse is something we should try to resist […]. I kind of hope, at the end of the day, there's going to be a cornucopia of virtual worlds run on many different models that people will be able to choose their virtual world with some autonomy").

[180] Andrew R. Chow, "Why the AI Explosion Has Huge Implications for the Metaverse," *Time*, online edition, 27 January 2023, https://time.com/6250249/chatgpt-metaverse/#.

9.5.3 *Antitrust in the Metaverse and Separation of Powers*

Virtual activities *in* the metaverse would also have to be regarded as relevant from an antitrust perspective. A notion of virtual antitrust comes to mind. The starting point of the reflection must be found in the importance that the metaverse could gain for each person, firm or even state: "When the Metaverse really comes, it may be the moment when the digital life of human beings is greater than the physical life."[181] In the words of David Chalmers, virtual reality may become, or is already, "as real as physical reality, but just different,"[182] and "virtual realities are genuine realities."[183] He even considers that "life in virtual worlds in the long term may approach or exceed the quality of life in nonvirtual worlds."[184] At a later stage, humankind could migrate to a largely or even fully simulated and stimulated existence where human brains would be plugged into the Internet and begin sharing thoughts, emotions or memories,[185] leading to some "human-computer symbiosis."[186] Additionally, the metaverse or, more broadly, virtual environments may be "far more engaging and richer than anything we can experience in our everyday lives," as envisaged by Steven S. Hoffman[187] or by Herman Norula.[188]

From this more or less distant perspective, it is not impossible that a firm or a few firms could gain an individual or collective dominant position in the relevant market or markets *in* the metaverse.[189] By way of an example, suppose that a firm becomes the main purveyor of political, economic, or societal information in a dominant metaverse platform for a given country or for several countries. Most of the avatars corresponding to persons coming from it or them would consult the information provided by this firm. Suppose further that these persons are mostly or exclusively informed through this platform. This leads to a concentration of power issue. Depending on how the market would be defined and on the behaviors of this information firm, antitrust may come to play. Data portability and interoperability[190] could help decentralize

---

[181] "Opportunities and Risks behind the Vision of Metaverse," *iNEWS*, 24 January 2022; see also Terry & Keeney, *Metaverse*, 20–1; Zoe Weinberg, "The Metaverse Is Coming, and the World Is Not Ready for It," *New York Times*, online edition, 2 December 2021, www.nytimes.com/2021/12/02/opinion/metaverse-politics-disinformation-society.html.

[182] Chalmers, "Virtual Reality," 50–51

[183] Chalmers, *Reality+*, xvii; see also Narula, *Society*, 65 ("Virtual experiences are real experiences").

[184] Chalmers, *Reality+*, 361.

[185] Hoffman, *Forces*, 242–47 & 260–61; see also Narula, *Society*, 218 & 222–25.

[186] Narula, *Society*, 225.

[187] Hoffman, *Forces*, 253 (quotation).

[188] Narula, *Society*, xv, 72, 78–80 & 216.

[189] See Samuel Stolton, "Vestager: Metaverse Poses New Competition Challenges," *Politico*, 18 January 2022, www.politico.eu/article/metaverse-new-competition-challenges-margrethe-vestager/ (quoting Margrethe Vestager, Executive Vice-President of the European Commission for a Europe fit for the Digital Age and Commissioner for Competition).

[190] See Ball, *Metaverse*, 37–42, 121–40, 245–46 & 306–7; Terry & Keeney, *Metaverse*, 140–47; Andrew Bosworth & Nick Clegg, "Building the Metaverse Responsibly," *Meta Newsroom*, 27 September 2021, updated on 2 November 2021, https://about.fb.com/news/2021/09/building-the-metaverse-responsibly/

a metaverse platform and reduce the concentration of power and the risk of abuses linked to it, but the risk for the separation of powers, in a broad sense, remains.

In this context, one of the most difficult questions relates to the antitrust liability. If a metaverse platform is deemed as a veil, the firm or firms controlling it may be deemed liable and it would then be up to it or them to impose appropriate obligations on commercial and end users. Antitrust and competition agencies or private claimants may also decide to pierce the metaverse veil and enforce antitrust and competition laws directly against the firms – the information company in the aforementioned example – active on a metaverse platform. This raises fundamental separation of powers questions, as also envisaged by Matthew Ball:

> What is clear [...] is that one of the larger challenges facing the Metaverse is that it lacks governing bodies beyond virtual world platform operators and service providers [...]. The Metaverse presents an opportunity not just for users, developers, and platforms, but for new rules, standards, and governing bodies, as well as new expectations for those governing bodies.[191]

Should the economic control of a major or dominant metaverse platform not be – partly, at least – separated from the ability to adopt rules for this platform and to enforce them? In particular, who shall enforce the rules designed to prevent abuse of power in the metaverse? A firm like Meta Platforms if it controls the main or, *a fortiori*, dominant metaverse platform or substantial parts of it? National or international agencies? Private parties? Decentralized autonomous organizations[192] based on blockchain technology? Non-profit organizations acting as oversight bodies?[193] A combination of all or most of these, probably and ideally,[194] provided that some general coherence can be found. The "multistakeholder system of Internet governance," recently promoted by the Declaration for the Future of the Internet,[195] should also prevail with regard to the metaverse. The governance structure must be flexible and forward-thinking, as disparate groups of people, many societies, many worlds, possibly run according to different principles, will form the metaverse.[196]

("We'll work with experts in government, industry and academia to think through issues and opportunities in the metaverse. For instance, its success depends on building robust interoperability across services, so different companies' experiences can work together. We also need to involve the human rights and civil rights communities from the start to ensure these technologies are built in a way that's inclusive and empowering"); see also Samuel Stolton, "Vestager: Metaverse Poses New Competition Challenges," *Politico*, 18 January 2022; Mackenzie, Goeteyn, Mantine & Westrup, "Metaverse."

[191] Ball, *Metaverse*, 295–96.

[192] See Zoe Weinberg, "The Metaverse Is Coming, and the World Is Not Ready for It," *New York Times*, online edition, 2 December 2021, www.nytimes.com/2021/12/02/opinion/metaverse-politics-disinformation-society.html.

[193] Earn, *Metaverse*, 14–5; Parisi, "Metaverse."

[194] From a similar perspective, see Ball, *Metaverse*, 304.

[195] *Declaration for the Future of the Internet*, 1st paragraph under "Reclaiming the Promise of the Internet" and 1st paragraph under "Our Vision."

[196] Chalmers, *Reality+*, 360; Narula, *Society*, 236.

For now, one thing seems quite obvious: a private monopoly for the adoption of the rules governing the virtual life in the main or, *a fortiori*, dominant metaverse platform and, subsequently, for their enforcement, would lead to a too dangerous, definitive, and irreversible concentration of powers.[197] As emphasized by Herman Narula, "we'll need transparent and ethical governance guaranteed by democratic principles."[198]

The time has come to conduct a prospective and in-depth reflection on the architecture of powers within the metaverse to avoid *fait accompli* and irreversible situations. Public legislation and regulation will be needed[199] and is likely to coexist with private regulation; governmental and regulatory bodies are likely to coexist with private bodies, including non-profit organizations. One or several oversight boards, as well as one or several metaverse assemblies or parliaments come to mind.[200] *Users-citizens* may demand some – political – power to organize their virtual societies.[201]

If not a partnership, at least a public-private architecture constitutes an interesting and, actually, unavoidable avenue. Ultimately, there must be some separation of powers and checks and balances in the metaverse, and antitrust may help define it by placing limits on the behavior of companies of *and* in the metaverse.

Finally, the metaverse may, at some point, become a seamless extension of real life, and the distinction between the latter and virtual life will grow meaningless.[202] From this perspective, antitrust both in and on the metaverse will not be distinguishable from one other, instead forming a fluid continuum, even a kind of unity.

---

[197] See, by analogy, Narula, *Society*, 194 ("It would be a folly to leave the governance and supervision of this prospective future to the companies that have abdicated these responsibilities thus far"); Caplan, "Private Speech Governance," 186 ("[G]iven variations and significant limitations in developing and enforcing rules, the current model of private governance by platforms is perhaps the most problematic").

[198] Narula, *Society*, 213.

[199] See Ball, *Metaverse*, 300–1; Lee & Chen, *AI 2041*, 209 ("If we learned anything from the recent concerns about the externalities of social networks and AI, we should start thinking early about how to address the inevitable issues when these externalities multiply with XR [immersive simulation technologies known generally as X reality, or XR]. In the short term, extending laws may be the most expedient solution. In the longer term, we will need to draw on an array of solutions, including new regulations, broader digital literacy, and inventing new technologies to harness technological issues").

[200] For a similar perspective, see Narula, *Society*, 212–14. See, by analogy, *supra* Part II, Chapter 5, Section 5.3.2.

[201] Chalmers, *Reality+*, 360.

[202] See Narula, *Society*, 104–5, 116, 222 & 230.

10

New Institutional and Individual Axes
of the Separation of Powers

Separation of powers or, more exactly, the rule of law, due process or, in Europe, the right to a fair trial influence the institutional setting of antitrust or regulatory authorities and law enforcement, as alluded to above in the Introduction. An increased role given to specific regulation or antitrust in order to tackle some fundamental issues posed by the concentration of economic-political power does not go without independent and impartial decision-making from an institutional and procedural (Section 10.1), a personal (Section 10.2), or a financial and lobbying (Section 10.3) perspective.

10.1 INSTITUTIONAL AND PROCEDURAL SETTINGS

Firms whose platforms have become an important or, *a fortiori*, fundamental part of the electoral or democratic process and of the digital infrastructure of democracy raise fundamental issues relating to the independence of antitrust or regulatory agencies. The politico-economic power of these platforms renders this independence particularly sensitive to avoid or, at least, reduce major conflicts of interest for elected officials and their subordinates. It has become a fundamental question of separation of powers. The collusion between governmental power and platform power must be avoided to prevent too high of a concentration of politico-economic power undermining the separation of powers and, possibly, the proper functioning of democracy. This speaks for the institutional independence of antitrust or regulatory agencies in charge of these platforms and, of course, of the courts. As digital markets pose many challenges to which antitrust cannot fully and effectively respond, the creation of an independent regulator or of a specific unit or branch within an existing agency or commission – the Digital (Markets) and Artificial Intelligence Agency, Authority, Commission, Unit or Branch – in charge of overseeing digital markets or digital and artificial intelligence platforms specifically – should be considered seriously.[1] The powers of a new, independent regulator – if

---

[1]   See, e.g., UK CMA, *Online Platforms*, 327; Australian Competition & Consumer Commission, *Digital Platforms*, 141; Stigler Committee, *Final Report*, 100–6; Digital Competition Expert Panel, *Digital Competition*, 55–56; Akcigit *et al.*, *Market Power*, 26–27, para. 46; Fukuyama *et al.*, *Platform Scale*, 38–39; Fukuyama, "Loaded Weapon." For an overview, see Lancieri & Sakowski, "Competition," 164.

one is created – would complement and not supersede those notably of antitrust or data protection agencies, for instance.[2]

Generally speaking, the independence – probably not fully comparable to that of one of the courts – of antitrust and at least some regulatory agencies has become a major issue for an effective and, at the same time, fair enforcement of applicable laws in concrete cases.[3] Independence with respect to this adjudicatory role or other similar roles is particularly justified.[4] When policymaking power is at stake, however, the question is much more debated.[5] In the European Union, the various powers of the European Commission – a political body composed of twenty-seven Commissioners – with respect to competition law raises significant separation of powers' concerns, even though several provisions of the EU treaties emphasize the Commission's duty to serve the general interest of the Union and to act independently.[6] The creation of an independent European agency is advisable in this context.[7] The independence of courts deciding in antitrust matters or reviewing challenged decisions, though fundamental,[8] is not sufficient considering the issues at stake. Agencies – and not courts – decide, for instance, to launch investigations or to sue companies. When political considerations influence such a decision, the risk of underenforcement or, on the opposite, of overenforcement may *ceteris paribus* increase. Composed of independent specialists, agencies may more freely and adequately decide or renounce to launch investigations or market inquiries.

A more difficult question concerns the independence of the political executive branch toward antitrust or competition agencies. In jurisdictions such as France,[9] Germany,[10] Italy,[11] Spain,[12] Switzerland,[13] or the United Kingdom,[14] mergers and

---

[2]   Lancieri & Sakowski, "Competition," 164.

[3]   Regarding the Member States of the European Union – but not the European Union itself! –, see Directive (EU) 2019/1 of the European Parliament and of the Council of 11 December 2018 to empower the competition authorities of the Member States to be more effective enforcers and to ensure the proper functioning of the internal market (OJ L 11, 14 January 2019, 3–33), Article 4. See, e.g., Bernatt, *Populism and Antitrust*, 229–30; Wiggers, Struijlaart & Dibbits, *Digital Competition Law*, 141; Philippon, *Reversal*, 132–34 & 202–3.

[4]   See, e.g., Rose-Ackerman, *Democracy*, 87.

[5]   See, e.g., Rose-Ackerman, *Democracy*, 88–90 & 119–21.

[6]   See Articles 17(1), 17(3) TUE, 245 and 298(1) TFUE.

[7]   See Martenet, *Pacte européen*, 66–67 & 147–48; Amato, *Antitrust*, 122–24. See also Deffains, d'Ormesson & Perroud, *Politique*, 40 (raising the question); Gaulard, *Pleine juridiction*, 307–10 (considering, without further analysis, that the creation of a European competition agency with normative power is not desirable).

[8]   See, e.g., Bernatt, *Populism and Antitrust*, 233–34.

[9]   Code du Commerce [Code of Commerce], Article L. 430-7-1.

[10]   Section 42 GWB.

[11]   Legge 10 ottobre 1990, n. 287 – Norme per la tutela della concorrenza e del mercato [Act of October 10, 1990, n. 287 – Rules for the Protection of Competition and the Market], Article 25.

[12]   Ley de Defensa de la Competencia [Competition Defense Law], Article 60.

[13]   Swiss Federal Act on Cartels and other Restraints of Competition, Article 11, translation available at www.fedlex.admin.ch/eli/cc/1996/546_546_546/en.

[14]   Enterprise Act, Section 42.

acquisitions blocked by the antitrust agencies may receive an exceptional ministerial authorization by the Minister of Economic Affairs, the Council of Ministers, or
a similar governmental body.[15] Such a system is based on the idea that said agencies
should only take competition considerations into account and are not supposed
to balance various public interests. It may function and even be regarded as a sensible way to allocate decision-making power in a democracy, as noted by Andreas
Heinemann,[16] since the task of balancing public interests typically belongs to a political body.[17] It seems that no jurisdiction provides for an executive or legislative interdiction which would follow an authorization by the relevant competition authority.
This form of political independence toward administrative agencies may come to
mind, especially when a merger poses a threat to democracy but is not blocked in
the merger review process. However, it is a very sensitive issue, and the decision
should not be taken by one person such as the Minister of Economic Affairs, the
Prime Minister, or the Head of State. It should have stronger legitimacy. A proposal
could come from the executive branch and would be sent to the legislative branch
for approval,[18] eventually with a qualified majority. In any event, political bodies
should decide within a tight timeframe, not least to avoid an unacceptable uncertainty for the merging parties. Of course, such a reform could politicize merger
control, which could be caught in partisan fights, and lead the parliament of a given
country to block a merger for political but non-democratic reasons, for instance to
protect the "national or European champion."[19] After careful analysis, it may present more risks than guarantees for democracy, but the idea is worth examining in
the context prevailing in each jurisdiction.

Besides, criteria on the notion of democracy are quite elusive. Defining them is a
difficult, but not necessarily impossible, task. It should, at least partly, be performed
in advance to bring more legal certainty. In this context, some form of judicial review
of the prohibition of a merger due to democratic concerns may create some appropriate checks and balances, even if it would be on limited grounds, as courts should
not – fully – review the democratic appraisal itself made by the competent political
body. At least some judicial self-restraint would be warranted in this assessment.

A comparison with the national security review through the Committee on
Foreign Investment in the United States (CFIUS) may highlight this issue. Civil

[15] See Bien, "Autorisation," 5–6.
[16] Heinemann, "Demokratie," 126; see also Kühling, "Herausforderungen," 526 (noting, however, the
risks posed by lobbying).
[17] See Bien, "Autorisation," 6; see also Bechtold, "Ministererlaubnis," 118–19. Regarding Germany in
particular, see Fries, *Berücksichtigung*, 82–83 & 264–65.
[18] Regarding a possible reform of the German ministerial authorization procedure, see, by analogy,
Bundesministerium für Wirtschaft und Klimaschutz, *Wettbewerbspolitische Agenda*, point 2 (envisag-
ing the involvement of the German *Bundestag*). See, however, Fries, *Berücksichtigung*, 256–63 (showing great scepticism about the involvement of the Bundestag or the federal government as a whole in
this procedure).
[19] On this issue, see Kühling, "Herausforderungen," 525–26.

actions challenging CFIUS actions and decision may be brought before the U.S. Court of Appeals for the District of Columbia. In certain circumstances, CFIUS may refer a transaction to the President for decision.[20] Presidential actions and findings resulting from CFIUS are not subject to judicial review, although the process by which the disposition of a transaction is determined can be challenged on constitutional grounds.[21] That said, rules on foreign investment control could not be the sole framework for implementing a more democracy-oriented mechanism of merger control, as it should not be limited to foreign investments. Furthermore, transparency and judicial review would anyway need to be improved.

A final institutional and procedural question relates to the independence between public enforcement and private enforcement in antitrust and in some regulatory matters. In abuse of dominance cases especially, private enforcement often takes the form of follow-on actions.[22] In other words, these are *de facto* dependent upon public enforcement,[23] which itself depends on many factors, including, for instance, limited resources and the setting of priorities.[24] However, the politico-economic power accumulated by some firms justifies opening or reinforcing an independent civil front against abuses and their consequences.[25] In the words of Jamie Susskind, "[a] digital republic needs citizens ready to stand on their rights *and* public authorities ready to protect the republic as a whole."[26] Private enforcement can indeed contribute to check and balance economic *and* state power, as underlined by Peter Picht:

> By engaging in rule enforcement, individuals and companies help to confine key market players' (unlawful use of) economic power. And by taking such enforcement in their own hands, they counterbalance a tendency for state agencies to become the sole decision makers on when and how to sanction what they consider undue conduct. Balancing state as well as corporate power looms particularly large in the digital realm as its technologies – and potentially the control market players or the state exercise through them – increasingly permeate all parts of life and society.[27]

It would go well beyond the purpose of this book to propose concrete reforms in this regard such as early-on remedies, rules on burden of proof and information

---

[20] See Section 6(c) of Executive Order 11858, as amended, and 31 C.F.R. (Code of Federal Regulations) § 800.508 and § 802.508.

[21] *Ralls Corp. v. Committee on Foreign Investment in the United States*, 758 F.3d 296 (D.C. Cir. 2014). See, e.g., Mir, Laciak & Melanson, "CFIUS," 81.

[22] Regarding competition law in general, see Picht, "Private Enforcement," 100.

[23] See Picht, "Private Enforcement," 100–1.

[24] See, e.g., Picht, "Private Enforcement," 98–99.

[25] Podszun, "Private Enforcement," 95–97; Picht, "Private Enforcement," 99–102. Regarding Germany, see Bundesministerium für Wirtschaft und Klimaschutz, *Wettbewerbspolitische Agenda*, point 2 ("[w]e also want to strengthen private enforcement, particularly in the digital area" [unofficial translation]).

[26] Susskind, *Digital Republic*, 187.

[27] Picht, "Private Enforcement," 102.

access, reasonable limitation periods, the possibility to bundle individual claims by a third party agent or the creation of specialized alternative dispute resolution bodies.[28] The only point made here is that private enforcement should be taken very seriously, for instance in Europe, in order to create independent and effective checks and balances toward not only the firms at stake but also, at least as far balancing is concerned, public enforcement. Such an approach affects the way private enforcement is institutionally and procedurally conceptualized, as made clear by Rupprecht Podszun:

> Private parties should be able to claim injunctive relief or prohibition orders against infringements by gatekeepers. This would mean that enforcement could become independent from the European Commission. An alternative path to enforce the obligations of the DMA [Digital Markets Act] would open up.[29]

10.2 PERSONNEL

The separation of powers also has a personal or even individual dimension. Independence goes with appropriate human and budgetary resources, which may notably mean paying public servants at rates more comparable with the private sector to reduce the revolving door dynamic,[30] or providing for cooling-off periods in order to prevent conflicts of interest. This type of independence relates to agencies[31] as well as courts and seeks to avoid too great of an asymmetry of information and expertise between them and firms, leading to a dependence toward the latter. Appearances with regard to independence also matter in this context. Concretely, agencies should hire persons with diverse backgrounds, appropriate expertise, and prior experiences,[32] capable of in-depth analysis of the relevant markets, as noted by Lina M. Khan, chair of the U.S. Federal Trade Commission:

> [W]e should broaden our institutional skillsets to ensure we are fully grasping market realities, especially as the economy becomes increasingly digitized. Bringing on additional technologists, data analysts, financial analysts, and experts from outside disciplines will build on our existing talent and position us to analyze conduct, assess remedies, and pursue market studies with greater rigor.[33]

---

[28] Picht, "Private Enforcement," 101.

[29] Podszun, "Private Enforcement," 96.

[30] Barrett, Moy, Ohm & Soltani, "Illusory Conflicts," 832.

[31] Regarding the Member States of the European Union, see Directive (EU) 2019/1, Article 5.

[32] Rose-Ackerman, *Democracy*, 267; Barrett, Moy, Ohm & Soltani, "Illusory Conflicts," 832; Guggenberger, "Platforms," 342–43; see also de Streel *et al.*, "DMA" (making the following comment regarding the enforcement of the DMA: "The [EU] Commission will also have to develop the knowledge and technical capability to understand data and algorithms, which are the foundation of all the newly-regulated digital services"); Wiggers, Struijlaart & Dibbits, *Digital Competition Law*, 131–32.

[33] Memorandum from Chair Lina M. Khan to Commission Staff and Commissioners Regarding the Vision and Priorities for the FTC, Washington D.C., 22 September 2021, 4. Regarding the federal agencies in the United States, see Devlin, *Antitrust*, 301.

Courts, usually composed of generalists, should also have sufficient *de iure* and *de facto* independence toward agencies. This supposes, here also, appropriate expertise in economic or technological fields,[34] and the possibility to appoint court experts. By the way, the political branches of government also need such an expertise to appropriately legislate and regulate in the digital and artificial intelligence era.[35]

As has just been pointed out, another concern relates to the revolving doors practice, for instance as it exists in the United States. By contrast, it is less common in Europe, both at the level of the European Union and at the level of national competition authorities.[36] This practice has been analyzed from multiple perspectives. It produces positive and negative effects, which will not be addressed here, as they fall outside the scope of this book.

The focus will be put on the doors between antitrust, regulatory, or other agencies and firms whose platforms have become an important or, *a fortiori*, fundamental part of the electoral or democratic process and of the digital infrastructure of democracy. Persons going, or planning of going, through these doors, when they hold a significant position or have access to sensitive information, may face important conflicts of interest and gain too much politico-economic power, blurring the separation between state and economic powers or, in other words, between governmental and platform powers in a way detrimental to public interest and democracy.[37] In this context, the following recommendation is made in the European Union by two non-governmental organizations, Corporate Europe Observatory and LobbyControl:

> Block the revolving door between EU institutions and Big Tech firms by strengthening revolving door rules and setting up an independent ethics committee that is able to launch investigations and implement sanctions.[38]

---

[34] See, e.g., Summers, "Policy" ("I think it's important for the judiciary to have antitrust expertise. I think that often the merits of antitrust cases depend upon quite subtle and sophisticated economic analysis that is desirable to have [...]. But I certainly hope that over time, there would come to be a growing number of experts in market analysis and the like who would come to serve as the judiciary").

[35] See, e.g., Narula, *Society*, 207; Jean, *Algorithmes*, 143–44 & 203.

[36] See, e.g., Philippon, *Reversal*, 200–2; Coen & Vannoni, "Sliding Doors," 817–22.

[37] OECD, *Post-Public Employment*, 18–9 ("[C]oncern about post-public employment is part of a broader concern in countries around the world about integrity of public officials and, in particular, about bias resulting from conflict of interest in public decision making [...]. A significant concern about post-public employment offences, like conflict of interest in general, is that they could significantly undermine public trust in government. In democratic societies, potential decline of citizens' trust in public institutions and confidence in public decision making justify strong and concerted actions to promote good public governance"); see also Dayen, *Monopolized*, 282–85.

[38] Corporate Europe Observatory & LobbyControl, *Lobby Network*, 43; see also Frischhut, *IEB*, 86–119; Josh Hawley, *Overhauling the Federal Trade Commission*, Proposal, 10 February 2020 (considering, with regard to the FTC and the Antitrust Division of the Department of Justice, that "Congress could add ethics laws that ban senior officials from working for very large companies at all for a few years"); Public Citizen, "The FTC's Big Tech Revolving Door Problem," *Citizen.org*, 23 May 2019, www .citizen.org/article/ftc-big-tech-revolving-door-problem-report/ ("Public Citizen supports the creation

Anti-revolving-door laws,[39] appropriately tailored cooling-off periods,[40] full transparency,[41] and other measures, such as control or monitoring by an independent ethics committee,[42] may be especially required in these cases. However, it is a very difficult matter,[43] and the purpose of this book does not consist of determining what kind of rules would be most appropriate. In any event, the context prevailing in each country should be considered, likely leading to different rules in different jurisdictions. Two points are made here. First, this issue is relevant from a separation of powers' perspective, considering the politico-power detained by firms whose platforms have become an important or, *a fortiori*, fundamental part of the electoral or democratic process and of the digital infrastructure of democracy. Restrictions may help avoid an additional increase of their power and their influence on public decision-makers. Second, the politico-economic power of these firms may justify special rules specifically applicable to them. Incidentally, laws and regulations imposing specific obligations to some digital firms are not unknown and are due to the gatekeeping function exercised by these platforms.[44] The functions the latter performed in a democracy are also relevant in this context and could also justify specific rules.

of a new data protection agency with a mission to enforce privacy protections and secure digital rights. If new authority is to be lodged at the FTC, then, at minimum, tighter restrictions should be placed on the FTC-tech sector revolving door").

[39] Regarding anti-revolving door laws in the United States, see Hasen, "Lobbying," 198 ("Lobbying laws that make it more difficult for interest groups to purchase access – such as anti-revolving-door laws and laws that make it harder for lobbyists to ingratiate themselves with elected officials by engaging in fundraising activities on the officials' be- half – should lead to a decrease in the total amount of inefficient legislation, and for this reason such restrictions have a good chance of passing constitutional scrutiny under the national economic welfare rationale"); see also Tepper with Hearn, *Capitalism*, 245.

[40] On this issue, see OECD, *Lobbying*, 98–102 ("Ensuring integrity in the policy-making process and lobbying activities also involves establishing both rules of procedure for joining the public sector from the private sector and vice versa, as well as cooling-off periods tailored to the level of seniority" [quotation from p. 98]) and *Post-Public Employment*, 67–71 ("The restrictions, in particular the length of time limits imposed on the activities of former public officials, are proportionate to the gravity of the post-public employment conflict of interest threat that officials pose" [quotation from p. 67]); Blanes i Vidal, Draca & Fons-Rosen, "Lobbyists," 3746; Chari, Hogan, Murphy & Crepaz, *Regulating Lobbying*, 199.

[41] See, e.g., Barrett, Moy, Ohm & Soltani, "Illusory Conflicts," 831; see also Rose-Ackerman, *Democracy*, 268.

[42] Regarding the European Union, see the Commission decision of 31 January 2018 on a Code of Conduct for the Members of the European Commission (2018/C 65/06; OJ C 65, 2 February 2018, 7–20), especially Articles 11 and 12.

[43] See, e.g., Lapira & Thomas, *Lobbying*, 192 ("The consequence of adding new restrictions on top of old definitions has been to drive lobbying into the shadows") & 195–96 ("Most importantly, however, restrictions on employment opportunities on either side of the revolving door actually alter the need for interest groups to seek out legitimate lobbying services from those with previous government experience. Trying to stop the flow of expertise, knowledge, and skills between public service and the private sector is futile if the fundamental problems that interest groups need to solve remain the same [...]. We should not continue to expand cooling-off periods despite evidence that they do not work. We should give good people a reason to stay in public service to begin with"); see also Devlin, *Antitrust*, 302.

[44] See *supra* Chapter 8, Sections 8.2 & 8.3, regarding the European Union and Germany. On this issue, see Geradin, "DMA" ("[T]he DMA rightly proposes to impose on such gatekeepers [a small number

Due to individual fundamental rights *inter alia*, it may be difficult to impose special obligations to persons joining or coming from firms whose platforms have become an important or, *a fortiori*, fundamental part of the electoral or democratic process and of the digital infrastructure of democracy. Furthermore, the exact delimitation of the firms covered by these obligations may prove uncertain. This issue may even raise constitutional concerns, especially with respect to the equal protection of the laws. To avoid the latter difficulty, the scope of all these measures may need to be widened or even generalized[45] if permitted by the constitution of the country where rules are adopted.

10.3 CAMPAIGN FINANCE, LOBBYING, AND ANTI-CORRUPTION LAWS AND REGULATIONS

Finally, campaign finance, lobbying, and corruption can distort the electoral or democratic process and the decision-making of the executive or legislative branches of government. They share institutional and individual dimensions which are interrelated.[46]

Actual or potential influences of the economic sector on elections, on referenda or on executive or legislative decisions are usual in a democracy and are not necessarily antithetical to it. The separation of powers principle is normally not interpreted as preventing them. Regulation is certainly needed with the aim of assuring the proper functioning of democracy and independent decision-making. For instance, an inclusive and transparent policy-making process, conducted with integrity, may *ceteris paribus* lead to better policies.[47] This concern will not be discussed here, as it falls outside the scope of this book, except as to the following matters.

Issues relating to influences of the economic sector on elections, on referenda or on executive or legislative decisions are intrinsically linked to the prohibition of distortions of the electoral and democratic process. However, the prohibition examined in the previous chapter, entitled "New politico-economic axes of the separation

---

of large digital platforms] a series of obligations to protect the contestability of the core platform services concerned, as well as to prevent them from adopting unfair behaviour vis-à-vis the business or end users that are dependent on these services. The DMA proposal does so by providing for a mechanism to designate gatekeepers (using a combination of qualitative and quantitative criteria) and laying down a list of obligations in Articles 5 and 6"); OECD, *Ex Ante Regulation*, 24–29; Persily, "Platform Power," 195–96 & 207–11; Bayer, Holznagel, Korpisaari & Woods, "Regulatory Responses," 570 ("The significant difference in power between small and large platforms justifies the differentiated treatment of large platforms, as it is envisaged in the draft Digital Services Act").

45 Regarding the Member States of the European Union, see Directive (EU) 2019/1, Article 4 Sect. 2/c (duty for the Member States to adopt procedures ensuring that, for a reasonable period after leaving office, staff and persons who take decision exercising certain powers in national administrative authorities "refrain from dealing with enforcement proceedings that could give rise to conflicts of interest").

46 Regarding political corruption, see Ceva & Ferretti, *Political Corruption*, 45–79 (concluding, on p. 78, that "[o]ur continuity-based approach to political corruption has shown how political corruption is rooted in the corrupt conduct of individual officeholders, interconnected through their institutional roles").

47 OECD, *Lobbying*, 29–125; see also Kühling, "Herausforderungen," 524 & 529.

of powers," covers digital platforms and, through them, the relations, contacts and information between candidates, office holders or political parties and citizens especially.[48] Campaign finance, lobbying, and anti-corruption laws and regulations are focused on the behaviors of firms or individuals toward political or administrative actual or future public office and, more specifically, power holders,[49] and vice versa. They, therefore, belong to the new institutional and individual axes of the separation of powers, bearing in mind that these two axes interact and cover common or related concerns. In other words, they are by no means rigidly separated.

When firms whose platforms have become an important or, *a fortiori*, fundamental part of the electoral or democratic process and of the digital infrastructure of democracy finance political campaign or lobby – or, *a fortiori*, corrupt – the government, they use their politico-economic power. In such a case, they affect democracy in several ways, especially through influence *and* infrastructure, as the same firm importantly contributes to set the digital infrastructure of democracy, finances political campaigns, and influences – or tries to influence – persons elected, their staff, or their cabinet.[50] Their power, which notably derives from "their reach, their ubiquity, their [artificial] intelligence,"[51] is both infrastructural[52] and influential. It is worth noting, *en passant*, that lobbying seems to increase[53] and to be more able to influence the political system[54] when an industry becomes more concentrated, at least until a certain point,[55] and that major firms of the digital economy are likely to lobby the government on many fronts,[56] principally with respect to bills important for them or the political institutions.[57] The digital industry and, notably, large

---

[48] See *supra* Chapter 9, Section 9.2.

[49] See Chari, Hogan, Murphy & Crepaz, *Regulating Lobbying*, 197–98 ("When government departments formulate lobbying laws, they need to think carefully *where power lies*" [quotation from p. 197]).

[50] See Nemitz, "Constitutional Democracy," 3–4; see also Fukuyama, *Liberalism*, 37; Susskind, *Digital Republic*, 238.

[51] O'Mara, *Code*, 404.

[52] See Dolata, "Platform Regulation," 466.

[53] See Cowgill, Prat & Valletti, "Power," 37–41 ("Our data from the U.S. suggests that firms increase lobbying after mergers" [quotation from p. 41]).

[54] See Zingales, "Political Theory," 124–27. See, however, McCarty & Shahshahani, "Political Antitrust," 64 ("The story of West Coast tech firms starting off as Washington-shy but gradually shedding their shyness to become lobbying powerhouses holds up for Amazon, Google, and Facebook. It does not hold up for Apple and Twitter, which have been relatively indifferent to lobbying in the years under study [1999–2017]"); Hovenkamp, "Monopolists or Cartels."

[55] See Callander, Foarta & Sugaya, "Market Competition and Political Influence," 2746 (highlighting "a more subtle relationship between technology levels and government protection, generating a nonmonotonicity in which the leader stops lobbying and loses political protection at its maximum technology level, albeit precisely when competition has disappeared and political protection is no longer valuable").

[56] Stucke, "Data-opolies," 291. From a historical perspective, see, regarding the United States, Fishkin & Forbath, *Constitution*, 230–35, 246 & 252–55.

[57] Regarding the United States, see, e.g., Lapira & Thomas, *Lobbying*, 175 ("If party leaders in Congress or the White House determine that a bill is important and simply must pass, chances are revolving door lobbyists will be all over it"); see also Fox, Scott Morton & Kimmelman, "Fighting"; Callander, Foarta & Sugaya, "Market Competition and Political Influence," 2746.

digital platforms have immense lobbying firepower in the European Union,[58] in the United States,[59] and elsewhere. From a general perspective, total lobbying spending in the United States is much higher now than in the early 2000s.[60]

Lobbying may prove particularly persuasive in this context due to mutual interests, as "[c]ompanies need things from the government" and "governments often want access to data," as rightfully put by Maurice E. Stucke.[61] Of course, the exchange theory of lobbying – that is the idea that lobbying thrives due to the existence of mutual interests – is not specific to the digital sector. However, these interests are especially strong when data, artificial intelligence, and the related services are useful for election or policy purposes. Moreover, firms whose platforms have become an important or, *a fortiori*, fundamental part of the electoral or democratic process and of the digital infrastructure of democracy may have the "ability to affect the public debate and public's perception of right and wrong,"[62] making them particularly influential for instance toward governments and especially elected officials. This power does not guarantee, however, a favorable result for its holders, as recently seen in the European Union, where new landmark legislation to tackle the power of digital gate-keepers has been adopted.[63] In the United States, the proposed American Innovation and Choice Online Act[64] contains prohibitions that would apply only to platforms deemed "critical trading partners."[65] It has been subject to intense lobbying.

The combination of these elements and this concentration of power call not only for the complement between antitrust, lobbying regulation and campaign finance regulation,[66] but also for leveling the playing field with respect to access to decision-makers or for reducing the dependence – if any – of the latter toward firms whose platforms have become an important or, *a fortiori*, fundamental part of the electoral or democratic process and of the digital infrastructure of democracy. In the words of Jürgen Kühling, Chairman of the German Monopolies Commission (*Monopolkommission*), "[g]ood lobbying regulation is thus just as important for increasing welfare as a functioning competition regime."[67]

---

[58] Corporate Europe Observatory & LobbyControl, *Lobby Network*, 10–7 & 42; see also Kühling, "Herausforderungen," 524.

[59] See, e.g., Ezrachi & Stucke, *Barons*, 188; Buck, "Antitrust Reform" ("There's a lot of money that is trying to stifle whatever progress we can make"); Philippon, *Reversal*, 260–62; Foer, *World*, 198. For an example, see Cristiano Lima, "A Multimillion-dollar Campaign is Pushing Dems to Ditch Antitrust Reform," *Washington Post*, online edition, 6 June 2022.

[60] Open Secrets, *Lobbying Data Summary*, www.opensecrets.org/federal-lobbying (consulted on 1 December 2022).

[61] Stucke, *Breaking Away*, 243 and "Data-opolies," 291 (quotation) & 313–15.

[62] Stucke, "Data-opolies," 315.

[63] See Javier Espinoza, "How Big Tech Lost the Antitrust Battle with Europe," *Financial Times*, online edition, 21 March 2022, www.ft.com/content/cbb1fe40-860d-4013-bfcf-b75ee6e30206.

[64] See *supra* Chapter 8, Section 8.8.

[65] See Scott Morton, Salop & Dinielli, "American Innovation and Choice Online Act."

[66] See, for instance, Kühling, "Herausforderungen," 524; Teachout, "Monopoly," 57–9.

[67] Kühling, "Herausforderungen," 524.

Neither lobbying nor other means of influence on decision-makers should necessarily be prohibited or heavily restricted, as such measures would most likely raise serious constitutional difficulties in most jurisdictions, but the system must preserve some independence in the decision-making and address the risk of capture.[68] The relation between independence and risk of capture is, by the way, complex and not necessarily concordant. In other words, political, administrative, and economic context matters in this respect, as observed by Susan Rose-Ackerman:

> The puzzle of how to combine expertise with political accountability is particularly acute for regulatory agencies where the regulated industry is politically powerful. The industry may lobby for a body that is not dependent on the cabinet, believing that it will be better off dealing with a regulator that is not beholden to politicians. In other situations, firms may prefer a politically dependent agency that will bow to the wishes of politicians who benefit from industry payoffs — bribes, future employment, or campaign contributions.[69]

In any event, the decision-makers must decide themselves based on their analysis and own convictions. This supposes some form of separation or, more exactly, distance between governmental power – be it political or administrative – on one side, and private or platform power on the other side. Considering the amount of politico-economic power retained by a few firms in the digital and artificial intelligence era and the risks associated to this concentration of power, rules safeguarding this distance can now be deemed to contribute to the separation of powers in a broad sense. Indeed, the influence *and* infrastructure of these firms – coupled with, and resulting from, their data, computing and artificial intelligence power – may impact all the branches of government. The institutional implications of this form of separation of powers will likely differ depending on whether one is looking at the executive branch or the legislative branch, not to mention the judiciary branch.

The risks that some firms in the digital and artificial intelligence era pose to the integrity of democratic decision-making processes and, to some extent, to democracy itself[70] could justify a differential treatment between them and other firms, even dominant ones. The politico-economic power of firms whose platforms form a significant part of the digital infrastructure of democracy may indeed be of such magnitude that specific restrictions on them or some measures in favor of other stakeholders could be envisaged in order to preserve, in reality, equal opportunities for the latter to inform and shape public policies.[71] Here again, additional

---

[68] See, e.g., Robertson, "Antitrust, Big Tech, and Democracy," 270; Rose-Ackerman, *Democracy*, 87–88, 120 & 252–54, Zingales, "Political Theory," 128–29; Philippon, *Reversal*, 201. See also Callander, Foarta & Sugaya, "Market Competition and Political Influence," 2750–51; Foarta, Callander & Sugaya, "Market Dominance and Political Influence."

[69] Rose-Ackerman, *Democracy*, 254.

[70] Corporate Europe Observatory & LobbyControl, *Lobby Network*, 5–9 & 42–44.

[71] On this issue, see OECD, *Lobbying*, 118–21. From a general perspective, see Acemoglu & Johnson, *Power and Progress*, 29.

requirements and limitations that specifically target and apply to certain firms only could be challenged on constitutional grounds. Therefore, the first path – specific restrictions or prohibitions – is a difficult one and may raise fundamental and insurmountable constitutional issues in several jurisdictions. Equal protection and even freedom of speech may prevent the adoption of laws imposing limits on lobbying activities or campaign finance to certain firms only or to all of them, like in the United States.[72] The second path – measures benefitting certain stakeholders, at least *de facto* – seems softer and more promising from this perspective, as it would not limit speech but favor it. It would imply facilitating access to decision-makers for stakeholders such as start-ups, small and medium enterprises, consumer and other organizations or citizens that are not in the same situation and, *de facto*, do not have the same power to influence decision-makers as, for instance, the largest firms in the digital and artificial intelligence era. Consultations or notice-and-comment procedures by political or administrative bodies, for instance, could become more proactive, inclusive and effective.[73] Extensive transparency requirements may be adopted.[74] Many proposals come into play.[75] The following one is, for instance, made in the European Union by two non-governmental organizations, Corporate Europe Observatory and LobbyControl:

> EU officials and policy-makers should proactively seek out the voices of those that have less resources: SMEs, independent academics, civil society groups, local groups.[76]

This kind of proposal would make some differences in treatment – but not adopt specific restrictions – justified by different situations. Distances or proximities between political or administrative bodies on one side, and private actors on the other side, would not be uniformized but would be equalized or, at least, become less disparate. Constitutional difficulties in terms of equality may nevertheless subsist in certain jurisdictions; a way to circumvent them would then be to widen or even to

---

[72] See *Citizens United v. Federal Election Commission*, 558 U.S. 310 (2010) (holding that the free speech clause of the First Amendment to the United States Constitution prohibits the government from restricting independent expenditures for political campaigns by corporations, wealthy individuals, and committees established for the purpose of fundraising). See, however, Fishkin & Forbath, *Constitution*, 436–37.

[73] Regarding the European Commission's consultations in connection with the European Climate Law, see, by analogy, Ammann & Boussat, "Participation," 245–51.

[74] On this issue, see Clothilde Goujard, "Big Tech Accused of Shady Lobbying in EU Parliament: Lawmakers File Complaints Against 8 Companies and Trade Groups over Alleged Shadow Lobbying," *Politico*, 14 October 2022, www.politico.eu/article/big-tech-companies-face-potential-eu-lobbying-ban/; see also Kühling, "Herausforderungen," 524.

[75] Regarding the European Union, see Alemanno, "Playing Field," 124–34 (making several recommendations to redesign public consultations in light of the principle of political equality, among them diversifying consultation via deliberative mechanisms, equalizing resources or investing in participatory capacity-building through, for instance, "lobbying aid").

[76] Corporate Europe Observatory & LobbyControl, *Lobby Network*, 43.

generalize stricter policies on campaign finance, lobbying, and anti-corruption to create or maintain a level playing field with respect to access to decision-makers. The equality or level playing field argument[77] may, however, not suffice in some jurisdictions like the United States[78]; it could be completed or replaced by an argument relating to the potentially corrupting dependence of decision-makers[79] toward firms whose platforms have become an important or, *a fortiori*, fundamental part of the electoral or democratic process and of the digital infrastructure of democracy. Determining which reform is appropriate falls outside the scope of this book, but the argument is made here that these firms have gained a politico-economic power of such magnitude and play such a salient role in democracy in the digital and artificial intelligence era, that some corrective measures in the name of equality, fair competition, efficient government,[80] or anti-corruptive dependence are necessary.

Campaign finance, lobbying, and anti-corruption laws and regulations should certainly coexist with antitrust and competition laws. As antitrust and competition agencies normally only enforce the latter, specific independent agencies or other bodies[81] may be appropriate. In the end, taking care of this last new institutional and individual axis of the separations of powers is actually everyone's responsibility, so that, in the words of Luigi Zingales, "the single most important remedy may be broader public awareness."[82]

---

[77] Regarding the European Union, see Alemanno, "Playing Field," 118–24; Ammann, "Transparency," 263–64.

[78] For a critical account and appraisal of the caselaw (*Citizens United* case in particular), see Fishkin & Forbath, *Constitution*, 436–37; Hasen, "Fixing Washington," 569 & 575; Lessig, "Reply to Hasen," 62–64.

[79] On "dependence corruption" in the United States, see Lessig, "Reply to Hasen," 65–71 (noting, on p. 68, that "[t]he dynamic of representative government – in which representatives are responsive to all citizens – has been undermined by a system that makes representatives responsive to funders first, and only then to citizens").

[80] On this argument, see Hasen, "Fixing Washington," 569 and 574 ("In short, the problem is not that lobbyists are corrupt. It is that the private system lobbyist-arbitrageurs distorts politics and that distortion in turn leads public policy public's important interest" [quotation from p. 574]).

[81] Regarding lobbying regulation, see Chari, Hogan, Murphy & Crepaz, *Regulating Lobbying*, 204–7 & 212 ("A critical principle of lobbying regulation is that it be overseen by an independent regulatory authority who can implement the law without political interference" [quotation from p. 212]).

[82] Zingales, "Political Theory," 129.

Conclusion

Separation of powers and antitrust share common ground. They are both focused on power and the risks arising from the concentration of it in one or a few hands. One relates first and foremost to state power and the other to economic power. The distinction between these two types of power, however, is not clear-cut and is, to a certain extent, blurred in a digital economy and society, as seen throughout this book.

Antitrust does not aim to preserve separation of powers between the branches of government. In any event, antitrust agencies do not bear this responsibility in a democracy. The interactions between separation of powers and antitrust are to be sought elsewhere. The concentration of power in one company, including the power to adopt principles, community standards, codes of conduct, guidelines, or other rules that have a broad impact on society and can distort economic or political competition, raises questions not unlike some at the heart of the separation of powers principle. *Private regulation* having such an impact raises fundamental issues in a democracy, some of them being tackled by antitrust laws and policy. Indeed, antitrust may establish some requirements for checks and balances within or for a firm.[1] The latter may even have to abandon the control over the content of important principles, rules, or codes. The idea of platform assemblies or parliaments has been, for instance, raised in this book.[2]

The concentration of power in a few firms whose social networks or search engines are part of the electoral and democratic process and of the *digital infrastructure of democracy*, as well as the growing importance of data and artificial intelligence in this respect, also leads to a partial rethinking of the separation of powers principle. Data access, portability, sharing, and interoperability on one hand and nondiscrimination on the other become important issues, just like the relationship between data and political powers or, put another way, and actually more accurately, between platform and governmental powers.[3] "Open up or break up"[4] may become the alternative for these firms. The potential contribution of antitrust to this issue is quite limited but not insignificant, as the latter may render data, artificial intelligence, and related services or products more accessible on a nondiscriminatory basis,[5] if not completely open.

---

[1] See *supra* Part II, Chapter 5.
[2] See *supra* Part II, Chapter 5, Section 5.3.2.
[3] See *supra* Part II, Chapter 6.
[4] Tambini & Moore, "Dominance," 405–6.
[5] See *supra* Part II, Chapter 6, Section 6.4.

In sum, private regulation by dominant firms and the digital infrastructure of democracy controlled by some firms constitute the areas where the separation of powers principle, envisaged in a broad sense, and antitrust may share much common ground. A single dominant digital firm may adopt private regulation affecting an entire industry and even society at large, be an important part of the digital infrastructure of democracy and, through many means including lobbying, exercise a significant influence on public decision-makers. Such a firm concentrates an immense amount of politico-economic powers. At the same time, it is subject to antitrust laws and relevant from a contemporary and prospective separation of powers' viewpoint.

The challenge posed by the largest digital platforms and their related ecosystems goes beyond competition law and antitrust alone. Antitrust is no Swiss Army knife.[6] A new and broader – politico-economic – separation of powers should deal especially with the control of the digital infrastructure of democracy, the prohibition of distortions of the electoral and democratic process, the conclusion of certain governmental contracts with firms owning and operating large or, *a fortiori*, dominant platforms, and the regulation of artificial intelligence or metaverse platforms.[7] Moreover, particular attention should be paid to independent and impartial decision-making of antitrust and relevant regulatory agencies, as well as courts, from an institutional, procedural, personal, financial, or lobbying perspective.[8] The risk of capture of political or administrative bodies by a firm or an industry is of special concern. At the end of the day, political or administrative decision-making should not be privatized.[9]

Public enforcement should certainly continue to coexist with private enforcement, with some reinforced independence between them being desirable in order to increase the chances that major or, *a fortiori*, dominant platforms are effectively checked. Multilevel and multidimensional antitrust and regulatory enforcement constitutes a key component of a sound and viable architecture of powers in the digital and artificial intelligence era. In other words, multi-type, multilevel, and multidimensional checks and balances should be placed on these platforms. This need will only increase if certain companies acquire immense power in artificial intelligence or in the metaverse. Checks and balances on, within, and by artificial intelligence are indeed needed. On this last, seemingly contradictory aspect, it may be justified to paraphrase Montesquieu and argue that, by the arrangement of things, artificial intelligence also must check artificial intellingence.[10]

---

[6] See "Antitrust Redux," *The Economist*, Special report on "The New Interventionism," 15 January 2022, 7–9, 8, ("White House staff look on antitrust as a 'Swiss-army knife': a tool to fix lots of different problems, including such ills as inflation"); see also Devlin, *Antitrust*, 172 ("In its modern conception, antitrust does not serve as a catch-all device for economic regulation or industrial policy").

[7] See *supra* Part III, Chapter 9.

[8] See *supra* Part III, Chapter 10.

[9] From a similar perspective, see Ménissier, *Philosophie de la corruption*, 163.

[10] See Montesquieu, *Spirit of the Laws*, 155 ("So that one cannot abuse power, power must check power by the arrangement of things").

Furthermore, the "digital platform neutrality" of laws and regulations – that is, their application to all digital platforms – should be questioned and reassessed. There is certainly a case for rules applying to certain digital platforms only, as recently witnessed in the European Union or Germany.[11] Hence, those which form an important or, *a fortiori*, fundamental part of the electoral or democratic process and of the digital infrastructure of democracy should face specific obligations as well as checks and balances.

While the debate is broader and some needed reforms are not relevant to antitrust, the latter may nevertheless play a role in this respect, especially in some cases when a dominant firm discriminates between political parties or candidates,[12] or, in the future, if artificial intelligence or metaverse developments leads to an immense concentration of power generating collusive or abusive behaviors.[13] A treatise entitled *The Spirit of Algorithms* would certainly contain one or several chapters on antitrust…

Thus, antitrust can help preserve or rebuild some trust within society[14] and in democracy,[15] though this should be considered as one of its rather indirect goals.[16] Now, Shoshana Zuboff warns us that "shared trust is the only real protection from uncertainty"[17] and – one could add – also, possibly, a shield against undemocratic tendencies and endeavors. Some separation between governmental power and platform power may, for instance, result from the involvement of antitrust agencies. In the same vein, checks and balances are needed for democracies to work in the digital and artificial intelligence era dominated by a few platforms.[18] The time for platform democracy – not to mention democratic artificial intelligence – has probably not come yet, but it could be looming in the not-so-distant future. The call for platform democracy may become ever more insistent as, in the words of Francis Fukuyama, "the diminution of platform power is critical for the survival of democracy around the world."[19] True, antitrust is not meant to answer it but may help to partly address some related concerns. As aptly put by Daniel A. Crane, "[a] well-functioning antitrust system serves as an instrument of democracy without antitrust decision-makers directly attempting to promote democracy in the way that other political and legal actors […] might do."[20] Antitrust could, in the end, contribute to democracy, to the separation of powers in the digital and artificial intelligence era and, ultimately, to trust. *Antitrust for trust,* or the ultimate apparent antitrust paradox.

---

[11]   See *supra* Part III, Chapter 8, Sections 8.2 & 8.3.

[12]   See *supra* Part II, Chapter 6, Section 6.4.

[13]   See *supra* Part III, Chapter 9, Sections 9.4 & 9.5.

[14]   On this issue, see, e.g., Stucke, "Data-opolies," 301–2; van Dijck, Poell & de Waal, *Platform Society*, 161–62.

[15]   On this issue, see, e.g., Bradshaw & Howard, *Global Disinformation Order*, 21 ("Social media, which was once heralded as a force for freedom and democracy, has come under increasing scrutiny for its role in amplifying disinformation, inciting violence, and lowering levels of trust in media and democratic institutions").

[16]   See, however, Robertson, "Antitrust, Big Tech, and Democracy," 278 ("Once antitrust's soul-searching concludes, the hope is that democracy will be among one of its aims" [footnote omitted]); see also Ezrachi & Stucke, "Antitrust's Soul," 2.

[17]   Zuboff, *Surveillance Capitalism*, 524.

[18]   From a similar perspective, see van Dijck, Poell & de Waal, *Platform Society*, 162.

[19]   Fukuyama, "Internet Safe for Democracy," 44; see also Durand, *Techno-féodalisme*, 234 (calling for the advent of a "true economic democracy").

[20]   Crane, "Instrument of Democracy," 23.

Bibliography

Zachary Abrahamson, 'Essential Data', 124 *Yale Law Journal* 867–81 (2014)

Daron Acemoglu & James A. Robinson, 'Persistence of Power, Elites, and Institutions', 98 *American Economic Review* 267–93 (2008)

Daron Acemoglu & Simon Johnson, *Power and Progress: Our Thousand-Year Struggle Over Technology and Prosperity* (London: Basic Books, 2023)

Bruce Ackerman, 'The New Separation of Powers', 113 *Harvard Law Review* 633–729 (2000)

Izumi Aizu, 'Digital Platform Regulation in Japan – Does the Soft Approach Work?', in Bayer, Holznagel, Korpisaari & Woods (eds.), *Perspectives on Platform Regulation*, 187–213

Ufuk Akcigit, Wenjie Chen, Federico J. Diez, Romain A. Duval, Philipp Engler, Jiayue Fan, Chiara Maggi, Marina Mendes Tavares, Daniel A. Schwarz, Ippei Shibata & Carolina Villegas-Sánchez, *Rising Corporate Market Power: Emerging Policy Issues* (Washington: IMF Staff Discussion Note, 2021)

Pınar Akman, 'Searching for the Long-Lost Soul of Article 82 EC', 29 *Oxford Journal of Legal Studies* 267–303 (2009)

Pınar Akman, *The Concept of Abuse in EU Competition Law: Law and Economic Approaches* (Oxford/Portland: Hart, 2012, 2015 for the paperback edition)

Pınar Akman, 'The Role of "Freedom" in EU Competition Law', 34 *Legal Studies* 183–213 (2014)

Pınar Akman, 'The Theory of Abuse in *Google Search*: A Positive and Normative Assessment under EU Competition Law', 2 *Journal of Law, Technology and Policy* 301–74 (2017)

Pınar Akman, 'Regulating Competition in Digital Platform Markets: A Critical Assessment of the Framework and Approach of the EU Digital Markets Act', 47 *European Law Review* 85–114 (2022)

Pınar Akman, Or Brook & Konstantinos Stylianou (eds.), *Research Handbook on Abuse of Dominance and Monopolization* (Cheltenham: Edward Elgar, 2023)

Alberto Alemanno, 'Levelling the EU Participatory Playing Field: A Legal and Policy Analysis of the Commission's Public Consultations in Light of the Principle of Political Equality', 26 *European Law Journal* 114–35 (2020)

Peter Alexiadis & Alexandre de Streel, 'Designing an EU Intervention Standard for Digital Platforms', *EUI Working paper* (Florence: European University Institute, 2020)

Trevor R. S. Allan, 'The Rule of Law', in Dyzenhaus & Thorburn (eds.), *Constitutional Law*, 201–20

Akhil Reed Amar, *America's Constitution: A Biography* (New York: Random House, 2005)

Giuliano Amato, *Antitrust and the Bounds of Power: The Dilemma of Liberal Democracy in the History of the Market* (Oxford: Hart, 1997)

Odile Ammann, 'Transparency at the Expense of Equality and Integrity: Present and Future Directions of Lobby Regulation in the European Parliament', 6/1 *European Papers* 239–68 (2021)

Odile Ammann & Audrey Boussat, 'The Participation of Civil Society in European Union Environmental Law-Making Processes: A Critical Assessment of the European Commission's Consultations in Connection with the European Climate Law', 14 *European Journal of Risk Regulation* 235–52 (2023)

Oles Andriychuk, *The Normative Foundations of European Competition Law: Assessing the Goals of Antitrust through the Lens of Legal Philosophy* (Cheltenham: Edward Elgar, 2017)

Oles Andriychuk, 'Shaping the New Modality of the Digital Markets: The Impact of the DSA/DMA Proposals on Inter-Platform Competition', 44 *World Competition* 261–86 (2021)

Farid Anvari, Michael Wenzel, Lydia Woodyatt & S. Alexander Haslam, 'The Social Psychology of Whistleblowing: An Integrated Model', 9 *Organizational Psychology Review* 41–67 (2019)

Philip E. Areeda, 'Antitrust Laws and Public Utility Regulation', 3 *The Bell Journal of Economics and Management Science* 42–57 (1972)

Philip E. Areeda, 'Essential Facilities: An Epithet in Need of Limiting Principles', 58 *Antitrust Law Journal* 841–53 (1990)

Philip E. Areeda & Herbert Hovenkamp, *Antitrust Law: An Analysis of Antitrust Principles and Their Application*, 5th edn (Alphen aan den Rijn: Wolters Kluwer, 2020)

Hans-Herbert von Arnim, 'Parteienstaat oder Parteiendemokratie?' [Party State or Party Democracy?], 131 *Deutsches Verwaltungsblatt* [German Administrative Gazette] 1213–18 (2016)

Raymond Aron, *Democracy and Totalitarianism* (Valence Ionescu trans., London: Weidenfeld and Nicolson, 1968, first published in France in 1965 under the title *Démocratie et totalitarisme*, by Éditions Gallimard, Paris)

Raymond Aron, *Introduction à la philosophie politique : Démocratie et révolution* [Introduction to Political Philosophy: Democracy and Revolution] (Paris: Le livre de poche, 1997, book based on a course given in 1952 at the French National School of Administration)

Raymond Aron, *La lutte de classes – Nouvelles leçons sur les sociétés industrielles* [Class Struggle – New Lessons on Industrial Societies], in Raymond Aron, (ed.), *Penser la liberté, penser la démocratie* [Thinking Freedom, Thinking Democracy], 991–1216 (Paris: Éditions Gallimard, 2005, first published in France in 1964 by Éditions Gallimard, Paris)

Siwal Ashwini, 'Social Media Platform Regulation in India – A Special Reference to the Information Technology (Intermediary Guidelines and Digital Media Ethics Code) Rules, 2021', in Bayer, Holznagel, Korpisaari & Woods (eds.), *Perspectives on Platform Regulation*, 215–31

Serge Audier, 'A Machiavellian Conception of Democracy? Democracy and Conflict', in Colen & Dutartre-Michaut (eds.), *Aron*, 149–62

Australian Competition & Consumer Commission, *Digital Platforms Inquiry: Final Report* (Canberra: ACCC, 2019)

Autorité de la concurrence [French Competition Authority], *Contribution au débat sur la politique de concurrence et les enjeux numériques* [Contribution to the Debate on Competition Policy and Digital Issues] (Paris: Autorité de la concurrence, 19 February 2020)

Autorité de la concurrence [French Competition Authority] & Bundeskartellamt [German Federal Cartel Office], *Competition Law and Data* (Paris & Bonn: Autorité de la concurrence & Bundeskartellamt, 10 May 2016)

Ruben Bach & Frauke Kreuter, 'Big Data in einer digitalisierten, datengestützten Demokratie' [Big Data in a Digitalized, Data-Driven Democracy], in Spiecker gen. Döhmann, Westland & Campos (eds.), *Demokratie*, 127–48

Bill Baer, 'Why Amazon Is Wrong about the American Innovation and Online Choice Act', *Brookings Institution* (14 June 2022)

Vicente Bagnoli, 'Digital Platforms as Public Utilities', 51 *International Review of Intellectual Property and Competition Law* 903–5 (2020)

Yuntao Bai *et al.*, 'Constitutional AI: Harmlesness from AI Feedback', Unpublished manuscript, https://arxiv.org/abs/2212.08073 (December 2022)

Rishab Bailey & Prakhar Misra, 'Interoperability of Social Media: An Appraisal of the Regulatory and Technical Ecosystem', 1–39, *SSRN*: https://papers.ssrn.com/sol3/papers.cfm?abstract_id=4095312 (February 2022)

Donald I. Baker & William S. Comanor, 'A U.S. Antitrust Agenda for the Dominant Information Platforms', 35 *Antitrust Magazine* 66–71 (2021)

Jonathan B. Baker, *Market Power in the U.S. Economy Today* (Washington: Washington Center for Equitable Growth, March 2017)

Jonathan B. Baker, *The Antitrust Paradigm: Restoring a Competitive Economy* (Cambridge: Harvard University Press, 2019)

Jonathan B. Baker, 'Finding Common Ground among Antitrust Reformers', 84 *Antitrust Law Journal* 705–51 (2022)

Baskaran Balasingham & Tai Neilson, 'Digital Platforms and Journalism in Australia: Analysing the Role of Competition Law', 45 *World Competition* 295–318 (2022)

Jack M. Balkin, 'How to Regulate (and Not Regulate) Social Media', 1 *Journal of Free Speech Law* 71–96 (2021)

Matthew Ball, *The Metaverse: And How It Will Revolutionize Everything* (New York: Liveright, 2022)

Konstantina Bania, 'Unravelling the Media Freedom Act Proposal: Ambitious Yet Underwhelming?', *The Platform Law Blog*, 23 September 2022, https://theplatformlaw.blog/2022/09/23/unravelling-the-media-freedom-act-proposal-ambitious-yet-underwhelming/

Konstantina Bania & Theano Karanikioti, 'Regulating Big Tech Raises Big Implementation Questions', *The Platform Law Blog*, 19 July 2022, https://theplatformlaw.blog/2022/07/19/regulating-big-tech-raises-big-implementation-questions/

Mauro Barberis, 'La séparation des pouvoirs' [The Separation of Powers] (Isabelle Boucobza trans.), in Troper & Chagnollaud (eds.), *Droit constitutionnel*, 705–32

Lindsey Barrett, Laura Moy, Paul Ohm & Ashkan Soltani, 'Illusory Conflicts: Post-Employment Clearance Procedures and the FTC's Technological Expertise', 35 *Berkeley Technology Law Journal* 793–833 (2020)

Sandrine Baume & Biancamaria Fontana (eds.), *Les usages de la séparation des pouvoirs – The Uses of the Separation of Powers* (Paris: Houdiard, 2008)

Judit Bayer, 'Rights and Duties of Online Platforms', in Bayer, Holznagel, Korpisaari & Woods (eds.), *Perspectives on Platform Regulation*, 25–45

Judit Bayer, Bernd Holznagel, Päivi Korpisaari & Lorna Woods (eds.), *Perspectives on Platform Regulation: Concepts and Models of Social Media Governance across the Globe* (Baden-Baden: Nomos, 2021)

Judit Bayer, Bernd Holznagel, Päivi Korpisaari & Lorna Woods, 'Conclusions: Regulatory Responses to Communication Platforms: Models and Limits', in Bayer, Holznagel, Korpisaari & Woods (eds.), *Perspectives on Platform Regulation*, 565–84

Caron Beaton-Wells, 'Antitrust's Neglected Question: Who Is "The Consumer"?', 65 *Antitrust Bulletin* 173–93 (2020)

Olivier Beaud, 'La multiplication des pouvoirs' [The Multiplication of Powers], 143 *Pouvoirs* [Powers] 47–59 (2012)

Rainer Bechtold, 'Ministererlaubnis in Brüssel?' [Ministerial Authorization in Brussels?], 7 *Neue Zeitschrift für Kartellrecht* [New Journal of Competition Law] 118–19 (2019)

Jörg Becker, Bernd Holznagel & Kilian Müller, 'Interoperability of Messenger Services. Possibilities for a Consumer-Friendly Approach', in Bayer, Holznagel, Korpisaari & Woods (eds.), *Perspectives on Platform Regulation*, 119–43

Sebastian Becker Castellaro & Jan Penfrat, 'The DSA Fails to Reign in the Most Harmful Digital Platform Businesses – But It Is Still Useful', *Verfassungsblog* (8 November 2022)

Ulrich Becker, Armin Hatje, Johann Schoo & Jürgen Schwarze (eds.), *EU-Kommentar* [EU-Commentary], 4th edn (Baden-Baden, Vienna & Basel: Nomos, Facultas & Helbing, 2019)

David Beetham, *The Legitimation of Power*, 2nd edn (Basingstoke: Palgrave Macmillan, 2013)

Belgian Competition Authority, Authority for Consumers & Markets (Netherlands) and Conseil de la concurrence (Luxemburg), *Joint Memorandum of the Belgian, Dutch and Luxembourg Competition Authorities on Challenges Faced by Competition Authorities in a Digital World* (Brussels, The Hague and Luxembourg, 2 October 2019)

John Bell, 'Comparative Law and Fundamental Rights', in John Bell & Marie-Luce Paris (eds.), *Rights-Based Constitutional Review: Constitutional Courts in a Changing Landscape* (Cheltenham: Edward Elgar, 2016), 409–29

Richard Bellamy & Graham Child (David Bailey & Laura Elizabeth John, eds.), *European Union Law of Competition*, 8th edn (Oxford/New York: Oxford University Press, 2018)

Yoshua Bengio *et al.*, 'Pause Giant AI Experiments: An Open Letter', *Future of Life Institute* (22 March 2023)

Yochai Benkler, 'Degrees of Freedom, Dimensions of Power', 145 *Dædalus* 18–32 (2016)

Karim Benyekhlef, 'Droit global : un défi pour la démocratie' [Global Law: A Challenge for Democracy], 353 *Revue Projet* [Project Review] 14–22 (2016/4)

Werner Berg & Gerald Mäsch (eds.), *Deutsches und Europäisches Kartellrecht: Kommentar* [German and European Competition Law: Commentary], 4th edn (Hürth: Wolters Kluwer, 2022)

Gerald Berk, *Louis D. Brandeis and the Making of Regulated Competition, 1900–1932* (Cambridge: Cambridge University Press, 2009, 2011 for the paperback edition)

Maciej Bernatt, *Populism and Antitrust: The Illiberal Influence of Populist Government on the Competition Law System* (Cambridge: Cambridge University Press, 2022)

Lea Bernhardt & Paul Voges, 'Kartellrechtsdurchsetzung in Plattformmärkten: Strukturelle und funktionale Entflechtung von Plattformen' [Antitrust Enforcement in Platform Markets: Structural and Functional Unbundling of Platforms], 72 *Wirtschaft und Wettbewerb* [Economy and Competition] 651–59 (2022)

Lucy Bernholz, Hélène Landemore & Rob Reich (eds.), *Digital Technology and Democratic Theory* (Chicago: The University of Chicago Press, 2021)

Valérie Bertrand, 'La conception du commerce dans l'*Esprit des Lois* de Montesquieu' [The Conception of Commerce in Montesquieu's *Spirit of the Laws*], 269–70 *Annales historiques de la Révolution française* [The Historical Annals of the French Revolution] 266–90 (1987)

Samantha Besson, 'Comment unifier le droit privé sans commodifier les droits de l'homme' [How to Unify Private Law without Commodifying Human Rights], in Franz Werro (ed.), *Droit civil et Convention européenne des droits de l'homme* [Civil Law and the European Convention on Human Rights] (Zurich: Schulthess, 2006), 14–26

Andrew Scott Bibby, *Montesquieu's Political Economy* (New York/Basingstoke: Palgrave Macmillan, 2016)

Florian Bien, 'Vers une autorisation "ministérielle" dans la procédure européenne de contrôle des fusions ? Un point de vue allemand' [Towards a 'Ministerial' Authorization in the European Merger Control Procedure? A German Point of View], 2–2019 *Concurrences* 2–7

Tom Bingham, *The Rule of Law* (London: Penguin, 2011)

William Blackstone, *Commentaries on the Laws of England in Four Books*, 9th edn (London: W. Strahan, T. Cadell & D. Prince, 1783)

Roger D. Blair & D. Daniel Sokol (eds.), *The Oxford Handbook of International Antitrust Economics*, 2 volumes (Oxford/New York: Oxford University Press, 2015)

Roger D. Blair & D. Daniel Sokol (eds.), *The Cambridge Handbook of Antitrust, Intellectual Property, and High Tech* (Cambridge: Cambridge University Press, 2017)

Jordi Blanes i Vidal, Mirko Draca & Christian Fons-Rosen, 'Revolving Door Lobbyists', 102 *American Economic Review* 3731–48 (2012)

Alexander Bogner, Michael Decker, Michael Nentwich & Constanze Scherz (eds.), *Digitalisierung und die Zukunft der Demokratie* [Digitalization and the Future of Democracy] (Baden-Baden: Nomos, 2022)

Franz Böhm, 'Das Problem der privaten Macht: Ein Beitrag zur Monopolfrage' [The Problem of Private Power: A Contribution to the Monopoly Question], in Goldschmidt & Wohlgemuth (eds.), *Grundtexte*, 49–67 (first published in 1928)

Franz Böhm, 'Democracy and Economic Power in Cartel and Monopoly in Modern Law', in Crane & Hovenkamp (eds.), *Competition Policy*, 264–81 (first published in 1961)

Carles Boix, *Democratic Capitalism at the Crossroads: Technological Change and the Future of Politics* (Princeton: Princeton University Press, 2019)

Lee C. Bollinger & Geoffrey R. Stone (eds.), *Social Media, Freedom of Speech, and the Future of Our Democracy* (Oxford/New York: Oxford University Press, 2022)

Napoléon Bonaparte, *Maximes et pensées recueillies par Jean-Louis Gaudy jeune* [Maxims and Thoughts Collected by Jean-Louis Gaudy, the Young] (Paris: A. Barbier – P. Baudouin, 1838)

Frank Bönker & Hans-Jürgen Wagener, 'Hayek and Eucken on the State and Market Economy', in Labrousse & Weisz (eds.), *Institutional Economics*, 183–99

Robert H. Bork, *The Antitrust Paradox: A Policy at War with Itself*, 2nd edn (New York: Free Press, 1993, first published in 1978)

Friso Bostoen, 'Understanding the Digital Markets Act', 68 *Antitrust Bulletin* 263–306 (2023)

Nick Bostrom, *Superintelligence: Paths, Dangers, Strategies* (Oxford/New York: Oxford University Press, 2014, 2017 [reprint with corrections])

Marco Botta & Klause Wiedemann, 'Exploitative Conducts in Digital Markets: Time for a Discussion after the Facebook Decision', 10 *Journal of European Competition Law & Practice* 465–78 (2019)

Marc Bourreau & Alexandre de Streel, *Digital Conglomerates and EU Competition Policy* (Paris & Namur: Telecom ParisTech & University of Namur, 2019)

Marc Bourreau, Jan Krämer & Miriam Buiten, *Interoperability in Digital Markets* (Brussels: Centre on Regulation in Europe, 2022)

Robert Boyer, 'Joining a Century-Long Process or Imagining a Revolution', 19 *Socio-Economic Review* 1201–7 (2021)

Anu Bradford, *The Brussels Effect: How the European Union Rules the World* (Oxford/New York: Oxford University Press, 2020)

Samantha Bradshaw & Philip N. Howard, *The Global Disinformation Order: 2019 Global Inventory of Organised Social Media Manipulation* (Oxford: Oxford Internet Institute, 2019), https://comprop.oii.ox.ac.uk/wp-content/uploads/sites/93/2019/09/Cyber Troop-Report19.pdf

Louis D. Brandeis, 'The Regulation of Competition against the Regulation of Monopoly', An Address to the Economic Club of New York on 1 November 1912, in Fraenkel (ed.), *Curse of Bigness*, 109–11

Louis D. Brandeis, *Other People's Money and How the Bankers Use It* (New York: Stokes, 1914)

Sean-Paul Brankin & Pat Treacy, 'The DMA: Challenges for the Regulator as Well as the Regulated', 2022/3 *Concurrences | On-Topic* 15–21

Johannes Buchmann, 'Demokratie und Öffentlichkeit im Digitalen Zeitalter' [Democracy and the Public Sphere in the Digital Age], in Spiecker gen. Döhmann, Westland & Campos (eds.), *Demokratie*, 15–39

Lydia Patrizia Buchser, *Kartellrechtliches Diskriminierungsverbot* [Prohibition of Discrimination under Competition Law] (Zurich: Schulhess, 2022)

Ken Buck, 'Rep. Ken Buck on the Need for Antitrust Reform: "Big Corporate America Scares People"', Interview with Asher Schechter, *ProMarket* (26 April 2022)

Oliver Budzinski & Juliane Mendelsohn, 'Regulating Big Tech: From Competition Policy to Sector Regulation?', 1–35, *SSRN*: https://papers.ssrn.com/sol3/papers.cfm?abstract_id=3938167 (October 2021), 71 *ORDO* (forthcoming 2023)

Oliver Budzinski & Annika Stöhr, 'Competition Policy Reform in Europe and Germany: Institutional Change in the Light of Digitalization', 15 *European Competition Journal* 15–54 (2019)

Friedrich Wenzel Bulst, 'Art. 102 AEUV' [Art. 102 TFEU], in Bunte (ed.), *Kartellrecht 2*, 613–745

Bundesministerium für Wirtschaft und Klimaschutz (BMWK; German Federal Ministry for Economic Affairs and Climate Action), *Wettbewerbspolitische Agenda des BMWK bis 2025: 10 Punkte für nachhaltigen Wettbewerb als Grundpfeiler der sozialökologischen Marktwirtschaft* [Competition Policy Agenda of the BMWK until 2025: 10 Points for Sustainable Competition as a Cornerstone of the Social-ecological Market Economy] (Berlin: BMWK, 21 February 2022; English translation: www.d-kart.de/en/blog/2022/02/21/die-wettbewerbspolitische-agenda-der-bundesregierung/)

Hermann-Josef Bunte (ed.), *Kartellrecht: Kommentar* [Competition Law: Commentary], *Band 1: Deutsches Kartellrecht* [Volume 1: German Competition Law], 14th edn (Hürth: Wolters Kluwer, 2022)

Hermann-Josef Bunte (ed.), *Kartellrecht: Kommentar* [Competition Law: Commentary], *Band 2: Europäisches Kartellrecht* [Volume 2: European Competition Law], 14th edn (Hürth: Wolters Kluwer, 2022)

Ilaria Buri & Joris van Hoboken, 'The DSA Proposal's Impact on Digital Dominance', in Richter, Straub & Tuchtfeld (eds.), *Big Tech*, 10–5

Léonard Burnand, *Benjamin Constant* (Paris: Perrin, 2022)

Christoph Busch, 'Self-Regulation and Regulatory Intermediation in the Platform Economy', in Marta Cantero Gamito & Hans-Wolfgang Micklitz (eds.), *The Role of the EU in Transnational Legal Ordering: Standards, Contracts and Codes* (Cheltenham: Edward Elgar, 2020), 115–34

Christoph Busch, Inge Graef, Jeanette Hofmann & Annabelle Gawer, *Uncovering Blindspots in the Policy Debate on Platform Power: Final Report* (Brussels: European Commission, 2021)

Cuihong Cai & Tianchan Wang, 'Moving toward a "Middle Ground"? – The Governance of Platforms in the United States and China', 14 *Policy & Internet* 243–62 (2022)

Agnès Callamard, 'The Human Rights Obligations of Non-State Actors', in Jørgensen (ed.), *Human Rights*, 191–225

Steven Callander, Dana Foarta & Takuo Sugaya, 'Market Competition and Political Influence: An Integrated Approach', 90 *Econometrica* 2723–53 (2022)

Christian Calliess & Matthias Ruffert, *EUV & AEUV mit Europäischer Grudrechtecharta: Kommentar* [TEU & TFEU with European Charter of Fundamental Rights: Commentary], 6th edn (Munich: Beck, 2022)

Adam Candeub, 'Bargaining for Free Speech: Common Carriage, Network Neutrality, and Section 230', 22 *Yale Journal of Law & Technology* 391–433 (2020)

Robyn Caplan, 'The Artisan and the Decision Factory: The Organizational Dynamics of Private Speech Governance', in Bernholz, Landemore & Reich (eds.), *Digital Technology and Democratic Theory*, 167–90

James A. Caporaso & David P. Levine, *Theories of Political Economy* (Cambridge: Cambridge University Press, 1992)

Eoin Carolan, *The New Separation of Powers: A Theory for the Modern State* (Oxford/New York: Oxford University Press, 2009)

David W. Carrithers, Michael A. Mosher & Paul A. Rahe (eds.), *Montesquieu's Science of Politics: Essays on The Spirit of Laws* (Lanham: Rowman & Littlefield, 2001)

Ramon Casadesus-Masanell & Andres Hervas-Drane, 'Competing with Privacy', 61 *Management Science* 229–46 (2015)

Cristiano Castelfranchi, 'The Micro-Macro Constitution of Power', 18/19 *ProtoSociology* 208–65 (2003)

Carmelo Cennamo *et al.*, 'Digital Platforms Regulation: An Innovation-Centric View of the EU's Digital Markets Act', 14 *Journal of European Competition Law & Practice* 44–51 (2023)

Emanuela Ceva & Maria Paola Ferretti, *Political Corruption: The Internal Enemy of Public Institutions* (Oxford/New York: Oxford University Press, 2021)

David J. Chalmers, 'What Can Virtual Reality Tell Us about Real Reality and the Nature of Existence? David Chalmers Reveals All to Richard Webb', Interview with Richard Webb, *New Scientist* 48–51 (29 January 2022)

David J. Chalmers, *Reality+: Virtual Worlds and the Problems of Philosophy* (New York: W. W. Norton, 2022)

Raj Chari, John Hogan, Gary Murphy & Michele Crepaz, *Regulating Lobbying: A Global Comparison*, 2nd edn (Manchester: Manchester University Press, 2019)

Gwendal Châton, *Introduction à Raymond Aron* [Introduction to Raymond Aron] (Paris: La Découverte, 2017)

David Chavalarias, *Toxic Data : Comment les reseaux manipulent nos opinions* [Toxic Data: How Networks Manipulate Our Opinions] (Paris: Flammarion, 2022)

John W. Cioffi, Martin F. Kenney & John Zysman, 'Platform Power and Regulatory Politics: Polanyi for the Twenty-First Century', 27 *New Political Economy* 820–36 (2022)

Mark Coeckelbergh, *AI Ethics* (Cambridge: MIT Press, 2020)

David Coen & Matia Vannoni, 'Sliding Doors in Brussels: A Career Path Analysis of EU Affairs Managers', 55 *European Journal of Political Research* 811–26 (2016)

Cary Coglianese, 'Legitimacy and Corporate Governance', 32 *Delaware Journal of Corporate Law* 159–67 (2007)

Daniel Cohen, *Homo numericus: La 'civilization' qui vient* [Homo Numericus: The Civilization That Is Coming] (Paris: Albin Michel, 2022)

Joshua Cohen & Archon Fung, 'Democracy and the Digital Public Sphere', in Bernholz, Landemore & Reich (eds.), *Digital Technology and Democratic Theory*, 23–61

Giuseppe Colangelo & Oscar Borgogno, 'Is It Better to Address the Apple-Google App Store Duopoly through Antitrust or Regulation?', *ProMarket* (7 April 2022)

Stephen Coleman, 'Digital Democracy', in Mazzoleni (ed.-in-chief), *Political Communication*, volume I, 306–17

José Colen & Elisabeth Dutartre-Michaut (eds.), *The Companion to Raymond Aron* (New York/Basingstoke: Palgrave Macmillan, 2015)

William S. Comanor & Donald I. Baker, 'The Issue of Consumer Welfare in the Government Complaints against Google & Facebook', 67 *Antitrust Bulletin* 12–22 (2022)

Emmanuel Combe, *La concurrence* [Competition], 2nd edn (Paris: P.U.F., 2022)

Benjamin Constant, *Principles of Politics Applicable to All Representative Governments*, in *Political Writings* 169–305 (Biancamaria Fontana trans. & ed., Cambridge: Cambridge University Press, 1988, first published in French in 1815)

James C. Cooper, 'Antitrust and Privacy', in Global Antitrust Institute, *Digital Economy*, 1188–222

Corporate Europe Observatory & LobbyControl, *The Lobby Network: Big Tech's Web of Influence in the EU* (Brussels and Cologne: Corporate Europe Observatory & LobbyControl e.V., August 2021)

Bo Cowgill, Andrea Prat & Tommaso M. Valletti, 'Political Power and Market Power', *CEPR Discussion Paper No. DP17178*, SSRN: https://papers.ssrn.com/sol3/papers.cfm?abstract_id=4390776 (May 2023)

Diane Coyle, 'Platform Dominance: The Shortcomings of Antitrust Policy', in Moore & Tambini (eds.), *Digital Dominance*, 50–70

Daniel A. Crane, 'Antitrust's Unconventional Politics', 104 *Virginia Law Review Online* 118–55 (2018)

Daniel A. Crane, 'Fascism and Monopoly', 118 *Michigan Law Review* 1315–70 (2020)

Daniel A. Crane, 'Antitrust and Democracy', *Investigaciones CeCo* 1–9 (2021)

Daniel A. Crane, 'Antitrust as an Instrument of Democracy', 72 *Duke Law Journal Online* 21–40 (2022)

Daniel A. Crane & Herbert Hovenkamp (eds.), *The Making of Competition Policy: Legal and Economic Sources* (Oxford/New York: Oxford University Press, 2013)

Kate Crawford, *Atlas of AI: Powers, Politics, and the Planetary Costs of Artificial Intelligence* (New Haven: Yale University Press, 2021)

Jacques Crémer, Yves-Alexandre de Montjoye & Heike Schweitzer, *Competition Policy for the Digital Era* (Brussels: European Commission, 2019)

Colleen Cunningham, Florian Ederer & Song Ma, 'Killer Acquisitions', 129 *Journal of Political Economy* 649–702 (2021)

Michael A. Cusumano, Annabelle Gawer & David B. Yoffie, *The Business of Platforms: Strategy in the Age of Digital Competition, Innovation, and Power* (New York: HarperCollins, 2019)

Michael A. Cusumano, Annabelle Gawer & David B. Yoffie, 'Can Self-Regulation Save Digital Platforms?', 30 *Industrial and Corporate Change* 1259–85 (2021)

Robert A. Dahl, 'The Concept of Power', 2 *Behavioral Science* 201–15 (1957)

Dorothe Dalheimer, Christoph T. Feddersen & Gerald Miersch, *EU-Kartellverfahrensverordnung: Kommentar zur VO 1/2003* [EU Cartel Procedure Regulation: Commentary on Regulation 1/2003] (Munich: Beck, 2005)

Gregory Day, 'Monopolizing Free Speech', 88 *Fordham Law Review* 1315–64 (2020)

David Dayen, *Monopolized: Life in the Age of Corporate Power* (New York: The New Press, 2020)

Simon Deakin, 'The Corporation as Commons: Rethinking Property Rights, Governance and Sustainability in the Business Enterprise', 37 *Queen's Law Journal* 339–81 (2011)

Declaration for the Future of the Internet, available at www.whitehouse.gov/wp-content/uploads/2022/04/Declaration-for-the-Future-for-the-Internet_Launch-Event-Signing-Version_FINAL.pdf (2022)

Bruno Deffains, Olivier d'Ormesson & Thomas Perroud, *Politique de concurrence et politique industrielle : pour une réforme du droit européen* [Competition Policy and Industrial Policy: For a Reform of European Law] (Paris: Fondation Robert Schuman, January 2020)

Giovanni De Gregorio & Oreste Pollicino, 'The European Constitutional Road to Address Platform Power', in Richter, Straub & Tuchtfeld (eds.), *Big Tech*, 16–21

Elias Deutscher, 'How to Measure Privacy-Related Consumer Harm in Merger Analysis? A Critical Reassessment of the European Commission's Merger Control in Data-Driven Markets', in Lundqvist & Gal (eds.), *Competition Law*, 173–211

Elias Deutscher, 'Reshaping Digital Competition: The New Platform Regulations and the Future of Modern Antitrust', 67 *Antitrust Bulletin* 302–40 (2022)

Elias Deutscher & Stavros Makris, 'Exploring the Ordoliberal Paradigm: The Competition-Democracy Nexus', 11 *Competition Law Review* 181–214 (2016)

Alan J. Devlin, *Reforming Antitrust* (Cambridge: Cambridge University Press, 2021)

Albert V. Dicey, *Introduction to the Study of the Law of the Constitution*, 8th edn (London: Macmillan, 1915)

Digital Competition Expert Panel, *Unlocking Digital Competition* (London: HM Treasury, March 2019)

Fabiana Di Porto & Rupprecht Podszun (eds.), *Abusive Practices in Competition Law* (Cheltenham: Edward Elgar, 2018)

Chris Dixon, 'Why Decentralization Matters', *OneZero*, 18 February 2018

Marie-Laure Djelic, *Exporting the American Model: The Postwar Transformation of European Business* (Oxford/New York: Oxford University Press, 2001)

Virginia Doellgast, 'Labor Power and Solidarity in Economic Bicameralism', 19 *Socio-Economic Review* 1207–11 (2021)

Ulrich Dolata, 'Platform Regulation: Coordination of Markets and Curation of Sociality on the Internet', in Kurz, Schütz, Strohmaier & Zilian (eds.), *Smart Technologies*, 457–77

Erika M. Douglas, 'The New Antitrust/Data Privacy Law Interface', *Yale Law Journal Forum*, 18 January 2021, 647–84

Michael W. Dowdle, John Gillespie & Imelda Maher (eds.), *Asian Capitalism and the Regulation of Competition: Towards a Regulatory Geography of Global Competition Law* (Cambridge: Cambridge University Press, 2013)

Josef Drexl, 'Economic Efficiency versus Democracy: On the Potential Role of Competition Policy in Regulating Digital Markets in Times of Post-Truth Politics', in Gerard & Lianos (eds.), *Efficiency and Equity*, 242–67

Markus D. Dubber, Frank Pasquale & Sunit Das (eds.), *The Oxford Handbook of Ethics of AI* (Oxford/New York: Oxford University Press, 2020)

Jérôme Duberry, *Artificial Intelligence and Democracy: Risks and Promises of AI-Mediated Citizen-Government Relations* (Cheltenham: Edward Elgar, 2022)

Niamh Dunne, 'Pro-competition Regulation in the Digital Economy: The United Kingdom's Digital Markets Unit', 67 *Antitrust Bulletin* 341–66 (2022)

Cédric Durand, *Techno-féodalisme – Critique de l'économie numérique* [Techno-feudalism: Critique of the Digital Economy] (Paris: Zones, 2020)

Cédric Durand, 'Musk s'inscrit dans une logique techno-féodale' [Musk Is Part of a Techno-feudal Logic], Interview with Pascal Riché, *L'Obs*, 12 January 2023, 28–31

David Dyzenhaus & Malcolm Thorburn (eds.), *Philosophical Foundations of Constitutional Law* (Oxford/New York: Oxford University Press, 2016)

Jonathan Earn, *The Metaverse: What You Need to Know about the Metaverse, Virtual Reality, Augmented Reality and Extended Reality* (independently published, 2022)

Magali Eben & Viktoria H.S.E. Robertson, 'Digital Market Definition in the European Union, United States, and Brazil: Past, Present, and Future', 18 *Journal of Competition Law & Economics* 417–55 (2022)

Economic Security Project, *From Moment to Movement: The Antimonopoly Fund* (Washington: Economic Security Project, 2022)

Dave Eggers, *The Every* (London: Hamish Hamilton, 2021)

Dirk Ehlers (ed.), *Europäische Grundrechte und Grundfreiheiten* [European Fundamental Rights and Fundamental Freedoms], 4th edn (Berlin: de Gruyter, 2014)

Martin Eifert, Axel Metzger, Heike Schweitzer & Gerhard Wagner, 'Taming the Giants: The DMA/DSA Package', 58 *Common Market Law Review* 987–1028 (2021)

Matthias Eigenmann, 'Enhanced Privacy for Data Analytics', 5 *Life Science Recht* [Life Science Law] 27–35 (2022)

Thomas Eilmansberger & Florian Bien, 'Art. 102 AEUV' [Art. 102 TFEU], in Säcker, Bien, Meier-Beck & Montag (eds.), *Wettbewerbsrecht 1*, 1533–815

Einer Elhauge, 'Horizontal Shareholding', 129 *Harvard Law Review* 1267–317 (2016)

Einer Elhauge, 'How Horizontal Shareholding Harms Our Economy – And Why Antitrust Law Can Fix It', 10 *Harvard Business Law Review* 207–86 (2020)

Einer Elhauge, 'The Causal Mechanisms Horizontal Shareholding', 82 *Ohio State Law Journal* 1–75 (2021)

Luca Enriques, Henry Hansmann, Reinier Kraakman & Mariana Pargendler, 'The Basic Governance Structure: Minority Shareholders and Non-Shareholder Constituencies', in Kraakman *et al.*, *Corporate Law*, 79–108

Robert Epstein, 'Manipulating Minds: The Power of Search Engines to Influence Votes and Opinions', in Moore & Tambini (eds.), *Digital Dominance*, 294–319

Samson Y. Esayas, 'Data Privacy in European Merger Control: Critical Analysis of Commission Decisions Regarding Privacy as a Non-price Competition', 40 *European Competition Law Review* 166–81 (2019)

William N. Eskridge Jr. & John Ferejohn, *A Republic of Statutes: The New American Constitution* (New Haven: Yale University Press, 2010)

Walter Eucken, *Grundsätze der Wirtschaftspolitik* [Principles of Economic Policy], 7th edn (Stuttgart: UTB, 2004, first published in 1952)

European Commission, *Guidance on the Commission's Enforcement Priorities in Applying Article 82 of the EC Treaty* [now Article 102 TFEU] to Abusive Exclusionary Conduct by Dominant Undertakings (OJ C 45, 24 February 2009, 7–20)

European Commission, *Evaluation of the Commission Notice on the Definition of Relevant Market for the Purposes of Community Competition Law of 9 December 1997*, Commission Staff Working Document (Brussels: European Commission, 12 July 2021)

Ariel Ezrachi & Maurice E. Stucke, *Virtual Competition: The Promise and Perils of the Algorithm-Driven Economy* (Cambridge: Harvard University Press, 2016)

Ariel Ezrachi & Maurice E. Stucke, 'The Fight over Antitrust's Soul', 9 *Journal of European Competition Law & Practice* 1–2 (2018)

Ariel Ezrachi & Maurice E. Stucke, 'Antitrust Enforcement and Market Power in the Digital Age: Is Your Digital Assistant Devious?', in Gerard & Lianos (eds.), *Efficiency and Equity*, 222–41

Ariel Ezrachi & Maurice E. Stucke, *How Big-Tech Barons Smash Innovation–and How to Strike Back* (New York: Harper Business, 2022)

Ernesto Falcon & Suzi Ragheb, 'What about International Digital Competition?', *Electronic Frontier Foundation Blog*, 26 October 2021, www.eff.org/fr/deeplinks/2021/10/what-about-international-digital-competition

Henry Farrell & Melissa Schwartzberg, 'The Democratic Consequences of the New Public Sphere', in Bernholz, Landemore & Reich (eds.), *Digital Technology and Democratic Theory*, 191–218

Federal Trade Commission (FTC), 'Refusal to Deal', in *Guide to Antitrust Laws*, www.ftc.gov/tips-advice/competition-guidance/guide-antitrust-laws/single-firm-conduct/refusal-deal

Niall Ferguson, *The Square and the Tower: Networks, Hierarchies and the Struggle for Global Power* (London: Allen Lane, 2017)

Isabelle Ferreras, *Firms as Political Entities: Saving Democracy through Economic Bicameralism* (Cambridge: Cambridge University Press, 2017)

Edward Feser (ed.), *The Cambridge Companion to Hayek* (Cambridge: Cambridge University Press, 2006)

Harry First & Spencer Weber Waller, 'Antitrust's Democracy Deficit', 81 *Fordham Law Review* 2543–74 (2013)

Joseph Fishkin & William E. Forbath, *The Anti-Oligarchy Constitution: Reconstructing the Economic Foundations of American Democracy* (Cambridge: Harvard University Press, 2022)

Dana Foarta, Steven Callander & Takuo Sugaya, 'The Understated Relationship between Market Dominance and Political Influence', *ProMarket* (21 July 2022)

Franklin Foer, *World without Mind: The Existential Threat of Big Tech* (New York: Penguin, 2017)

Rana Foroohar, *Don't Be Evil: The Case Against Big Tech* (London: Allen Lane, 2019)

Brooke Fox, Fiona Scott Morton & Gene Kimmelman, 'Fighting New Antitrust Rules Is a Bad Move for Big Tech', *ProMarket* (26 October 2022)

Eleanor M. Fox, 'The Battle for the Soul of Antitrust', 75 *California Law Review* 917–23 (1987)

Eleanor M. Fox, 'Against Goals', 81 *Fordham Law Review* 2157–61 (2013)

Eleanor M. Fox, 'Antitrust and Democracy: How Markets Protect Democracy, Democracy Protects Markets, and Illiberal Politics Threatens to Hijack Both', 46 *Legal Issues of Economic Integration* 317–28 (2019)

Eleanor M. Fox, '"Consumer Welfare" and the Real Battle for the Soul of Antitrust', *ProMarket* (19 April 2023)

Osmond K. Fraenkel (ed.), *The Curse of Bigness: Miscellaneous Papers of Louis D. Brandeis* (New York: Viking Press, 1935)

Jens-Uwe Franck & Martin Peitz, 'How to Challenge Big Tech', in Richter, Straub & Tuchtfeld (eds.), *Big Tech*, 84–9

Jens-Uwe Franck & Martin Peitz, 'Digital Platforms and the New 19a Tool in the German Competition Act', 12 *Journal of European Competition Law & Practice* 513–28 (2021)

Ellen Frankel Paul, 'Hayek on Monopoly and Antitrust in the Crucible of *United States v. Microsoft*', 1 *New York University Journal of Law & Liberty* 167–204 (2005)

Sheera Frenkel & Cecilia Kang, *An Ugly Truth: Inside Facebook's Battle for Domination* (New York: HarperCollins, 2021)

Milton Friedman, 'Capitalism and Freedom', 1 *New Individualist Review* 3–10 (1961)

Milton Friedman, *Capitalism and Freedom* (Chicago: The University of Chicago Press, 1962, 40th Anniversary Edition, 2002)

Milton & Rose Friedman, *Free to Choose: A Personal Statement* (New York: Harcourt, 1980, 1990)

Carl J. Friedrich & Zbigniew K. Brzezinski, *Totalitarian Dictatorship and Autocracy*, 2nd edn revised by Carl J. Friedrich (Cambridge: Harvard University Press, 1965, first edition published in 1956)

Lukas Fries, *Die Berücksichtigung außerwettbewerblicher Interessen in der Fusionskontrolle* [The Consideration of Non-Competitive Interests in Merger Control] (Baden-Baden: Nomos, 2020)

Markus Frischhut, *Strengthening Transparency and Integrity via the New 'Independent Ethics Body' (IEB)* (Brussels: Policy Department for Citizens' Rights and Constitutional Affairs, European Parliament, 2020)

Benoît Frydman, 'Droit global et régulation : Quels points de contrôle pour une régulation de l'économie de marché ?' [Regulating Global Law: Finding the Levers to Regulate Market Economy], 14 *Revue d'études benthamiennes* [Journal of Benthamian Studies] 14–20 (2018)

Andreas Fuchs, 'Art. 102 AEUV' [Art. 102 TFEU], in Immenga & Mestmäcker (Körber, Schweitzer & Zimmer, eds.), *Wettbewerbsrecht 1*, 550–774

Francis Fukuyama, '"A Loaded Weapon": Francis Fukuyama on the Political Power of Digital Platforms', Interview with Asher Schechter & Filippo Lancieri, *ProMarket* (4 December 2020)

Francis Fukuyama, 'Making the Internet Safe for Democracy', 32 *Journal of Democracy* 37–44 (2021)

Francis Fukuyama, *Liberalism and Its Discontents* (London: Profile Books, 2022)

Francis Fukuyama, Barak Richman & Ashish Goel, 'How to Save Democracy from Technology', 100 *Foreign Affairs* 98–104 & 106–10 (2021)

Francis Fukuyama, Barak Richman, Ashish Goel, Roberta R. Katz, A. Douglas Melamed & Marietje Schaake, *Report of the Working Group on Platform Scale* (Stanford: Stanford University, 2020)

Jason Furman, *Prepared Testimony for the Hearing 'Online Platforms and Market Power, Part 3: The Role of Data and Privacy in Competition'* (Washington: U.S. House of Representatives, Committee on the Judiciary, Subcommittee on Antitrust, Commercial and Administrative Law, 18 October 2019)

Future of Life Institute, *Policymaking in the Pause: What Can Policymakers Do Now to Combat Risks from Advanced AI Systems?* (Cambridge: Future of Life Institute, 2023)

John Kenneth Galbraith, *The Anatomy of Power* (Boston: Houghton Mifflin, 1983)

Andrew Gamble, 'Hayek on Knowledge, Economics, and Society', in Feser (ed.), *Hayek*, 111–31

Urs Gasser & Carolyn Schmitt, 'The Role of Professional Norms in the Governance of Artificial Intelligence', in Dubber, Pasquale & Das (eds.), *Ethics of AI*, 141–59

Géraldine Gaulard, *La pleine juridiction du juge de l'Union européenne en droit de la concurrence : Contrôle et compétence sur les amendes* [The Full Jurisdiction of the European Union Judge in Competition Law: Control and Jurisdiction over Fines] (Brussels: Bruylant, 2020)

Damien Geradin, 'Korean Bill Banning Apple and Google from Mandating their In-app Payment Solutions Moves Forward', *The Platform Law Blog*, 1 September 2021, https://theplatformlaw.blog/2021/09/01/korean-bill-banning-apple-and-google-from-mandating-their-in-app-payment-solutions-moves-forward/

Damien Geradin, 'The DMA Should Stay True to Its Principles, or It Could Fail', *The Platform Law Blog*, 8 November 2021, https://theplatformlaw.blog/2021/11/08/the-dma-should-stay-true-to-its-principles-or-it-could-fail/

Damien Geradin, 'Spotify and Google Announce User Choice Billing: A Preliminary Assessment', *The Platform Law Blog*, 24 March 2022, https://theplatformlaw.blog/2022/03/24/spotify-and-google-announce-user-choice-billing-a-preliminary-assessment/

Damien Geradin, 'The Leaked "Final" Version of the Digital Markets Act: A Summary in Ten Points', *The Platform Law Blog*, 19 April 2022, https://theplatformlaw.blog/2022/04/19/the-leaked-final-version-of-the-digital-markets-act-a-summary-in-ten-points/

Damien Geradin, 'The DMA Has Been Published: Now the Real Challenges Start', *The Platform Law Blog*, 12 October 2022, https://theplatformlaw.blog/2022/10/12/the-dma-has-been-published-now-the-real-challenges-start/

Damien Geradin & Dimitrios Katsifis, 'The Antitrust Case against the Apple App Store', 17 *Journal of Competition Law & Economics* 503–85 (2021)

Damien Geradin, Dimitrios Katsifis & Theano Karanikioti, 'Google as *de facto* Privacy Regulator: Analysing the Privacy Sandbox from an Antitrust Perspective', 17 *European Competition Journal* 617–81 (2021)

Damien Gerard & Ioannis Lianos (eds.), *Reconciling Efficiency and Equity: A Global Challenge for Competition Policy* (Cambridge: Cambridge University Press, 2019)

David J. Gerber, *Law and Competition in Twentieth Century Europe: Protecting Prometheus* (Oxford/New York: Oxford University Press, 1998)

David J. Gerber, *Global Competition: Law, Markets, and Globalization* (Oxford/New York: Oxford University Press, 2010)

David J. Gerber, 'Prisms of Distance and Power: Viewing the U.S. Regulatory Tradition', 93 *Business History Review* 781–99 (2019)

David J. Gerber, *Competition Law and Antitrust: A Global Guide* (Oxford/New York: Oxford University Press, 2020)

Anna Gerbrandy, 'Rethinking Competition Law within the European Economic Constitution', 57 *Journal of Common Market Studies* 127–42 (2019)

Dipayan Ghosh, 'Don't Break Up Facebook – Treat It Like a Utility', *Harvard Business Review*, 30 May 2019, https://hbr.org/2019/05/dont-break-up-facebook-treat-it-like-a-utility

Richard J. Gilbert, 'The American Innovation and Choice Online Act: Lessons from the 1950 Celler-Kevaufer Amendment', *Concurrentialiste*, 27 January 2022

Global Antitrust Institute, *Report on the Digital Economy* (Arlington: Global Antitrust Institute, 2020)

Ebru Gökçe Dessemond, 'Restoring Competition in "Winner-Took-All" Digital Platform Markets', *UNCTAD Research Paper* No. 40 (December 2019)

Nils Goldschmidt & Michael Wohlgemuth (eds.), *Grundtexte zur Freiburger Tradition der Ordnungsökomik* [Basic Texts on the Freiburg Tradition of Constitutional Economics] (Tübingen: Mohr Siebeck, 2008)

H. Stephen Grace Jr., S. Lawrence Prendergast & Susan Koski-Grafer, 'Board Oversight and Governance: From Tone at the Top to Substantive Checks and Balances', *American Bar Association, Business Law Today* (14 February 2019)

Inge Graef, 'Market Definition and Market Power in Data: The Case of Online Platforms', 38 *World Competition* 473–505 (2015)

Inge Graef, 'When Data Evolves into Market Power – Data Concentration and Data Abuse under Competition Law', in Moore & Tambini (eds.), *Digital Dominance*, 71–97

Inge Graef, 'Rethinking the Essential Facilities Doctrine for the EU Digital Economy', 53 *Revue juridique Thémis de l'Université de Montréal* [Thémis Law Review of the University of Montreal] 33–72 (2019)

Inge Graef, 'Differentiated Treatment in Platform-to-Business Relations: EU Competition Law and Economic Dependence', 38 *Yearbook of European Law* 448–99 (2019)

Inge Graef & Francisco Costa-Cabral, 'To Regulate or not to Regulate Big Tech', 2020 *Concurrences* 24–9

Edward M. Graham & J. David Richardson (eds.), *Global Competition Policy* (New York: Columbia University Press, 1997)

Kent Greenfield, 'Reclaiming Corporate Law in a New Gilded Age', 2 *Harvard Law & Policy Review* 1–32 (2008)

Dieter Grimm, Anne Peters & Dan Wielsch, *Grundrechtsfunktionen jenseits des Staates* [Fundamental Rights Functions Beyond the State] (Tübingen: Mohr Siebeck, 2021)

Nikolas Guggenberger, 'Essential Platforms', 24 *Stanford Technology Law Review* 237–343 (2021)

Jürgen Habermas, *Ein neuer Strukturwandel der Öffentlichkeit und die deliberative Politik* [A New Structural Transformation of the Public Sphere and Deliberative Politics] (Berlin: Suhrkamp, 2022)

John O. Haley, *Antitrust in Germany and Japan: The First Fifty Years, 1947–1998* (Seattle: University of Washington Press, 2001)

Martin d'Halluin, 'The DMA: An Ambitious Act with Countless Challenges', 2022/3 *Concurrences | On-Topic* 10–4

Alexander Hamilton, James Madison & John Jay, *The Federalist Papers* (Lawrence Goldman ed., Oxford/New York: Oxford University Press, 2008, first published as a series of eighty-five essays in the winter of 1787–88)

Yuval Noah Harari, *21 Lessons for the 21st Century* (London: Jonathan Cape, 2018)

Sarah Hartmann, 'Policy Developments in the USA to Address Platform Information Disorders', in Bayer, Holznagel, Korpisaari & Woods (eds.), *Perspectives on Platform Regulation*, 99–117

Richard L. Hasen, 'Lobbying, Rent-Seeking, and the Constitution', 64 *Stanford Law Review* 191–253 (2012)

Richard L. Hasen, 'Fixing Washington', 126 *Harvard Law Review* 550–85 (2012)

Maurice Hauriou, *Principes de droit public* [Principles of Public Law], 2nd edn (Paris: Sirey, 1916)

Barry E. Hawk, *Monopoly in America* (Huntington: Juris, 2022)

Stephen Hawking, *Brief Answers to the Big Questions* (London: Murray, 2018)

Josh Hawley, *The Tyranny of Big Tech* (Washington: Regnery, 2021)

Friedrich A. von Hayek, *The Road to Serfdom* (London: Routledge, 2005 [reprint], first published in 1944)

Friedrich A. von Hayek, *The Constitution of Liberty* (Ronald Hamowy ed., Chicago: The University of Chicago Press, 2011, first published in 1960)

Friedrich A. von Hayek, *Law, Legislation and Liberty* (London: Routledge, 1982, reprinted in 1998)

Friedrich A. von Hayek, *Political Order of a Free People*, volume 3 of Law, Legislation and Liberty (London: Routledge, 1982, reprinted in 1998, volume 3 first published in 1979 by The University of Chicago Press)

Jonathan Hearn, *Theorizing Power* (Basingstoke: Palgrave Macmillan, 2012)

Andreas Heinemann, 'Demokratie und Marktwirtschaft: Direkte und indirekte Formen dezentraler Organisation' [Democracy and Market Economy: Direct and Indirect Forms of Decentralized Organization], in Andreas Good & Bettina Platipodis (eds.), *Direkte Demokratie: Herausforderungen zwischen Politik und Recht, Festschrift für Andreas Auer zum 65. Geburtstag* [Direct Democracy: Challenges between Politics and Law, Festschrift for Andreas Auer on the Occasion of his 65th Birthday] (Bern: Stämpfli, 2013), 121–34

Andreas Heinemann & Giulia Mara Meier, 'Der Digital Markets Act (DMA): Neues "Plattformrecht" für mehr Wettbewerb in der digitalen Wirtschaft' ['The Digital Markets Act (DMA): New "Platform Law" for More Competition in the Digital Economy'], 23 *Zeitschrift für Europarecht* [*Journal of European Law*] 86–101 (2021)

Natali Helberger, 'The Political Power of Platforms: How Current Attempts to Regulate Misinformation Amplify Opinion Power', 8 *Digital Journalism* 842–54 (2020)

Horst J. Helle, 'Soziologie der Konkurrenz – Sociology of Competition by Georg Simmel', 33 *Canadian Journal of Sociology* 945–56 (2008)

Ignacio Herrera Anchustegui, 'Competition Law through an Ordoliberal Lens', 2 *Oslo Law Review* 139–74 (2015)

Jennifer G. Hill & Randall S. Thomas (eds.), *Research Handbook on Shareholder Power* (Cheltenham: Edward Elgar, 2015)

Reid Hoffman with GPT-4, *Impromptu: Amplifying Our Humanity Through AI* (Anacortes: Dallepedia, 2023)

Steven S. Hoffman, *The Five Forces That Change Everything: How Technology Is Shaping Our Future* (Dallas: Matt Holt, 2021)

Thomas J. Horton, 'Restoring Antitrust's Lost Values', 16 *University of New Hampshire Law Review* 179–242 (2018)

Erik Hovenkamp, 'Platform Antitrust', 44 *The Journal of Corporation Law* 713–52 (2019)

Erik Hovenkamp, 'The Antitrust Duty to Deal in the Age of Big Tech', 131 *Yale Law Journal* 1483–558 (2022)

Erik Hovenkamp, 'Big Tech "Self-Preferencing" Bills May Hurt – Not Help – Antitrust Reform', *ProMarket* (8 June 2022)

Herbert Hovenkamp, *Federal Antitrust Policy: The Law of Competition and Its Practice*, 5th edn (St. Paul: West Academic Publishing, 2015)

Herbert Hovenkamp, 'Is Antitrust's Consumer Welfare Principle Imperiled?', 45 *The Journal of Corporation Law* 101–30 (2019)

Herbert Hovenkamp, *Principles of Antitrust*, 2nd edn (St. Paul: West Academic Publishing, 2021)

Herbert Hovenkamp, 'Antitrust and Platform Monopoly', 130 *Yale Law Journal* 1952–2050 (2021)

Herbert Hovenkamp, 'The Sherman Act and Abuse of Dominance in the Age of Networks', *ProMarket* (20 December 2021)

Herbert Hovenkamp, 'President Biden's Executive Order on Competition: An Antitrust Analysis', 64 *Arizona Law Review* 383–416 (2022)

Herbert Hovenkamp, 'Are Monopolists or Cartels the True Source of Anticompetitive US Political Power?', *ProMarket* (3 August 2022)

Herbert Hovenkamp, 'Antitrust Interoperability Remedies', 123 *Columbia Law Review Forum* 1–36 (2023)

Herbert Hovenkamp, 'Monopolizing Digital Commerce', 64 *William & Mary Law Review* 1677–755 (2023)

Herbert Hovenkamp, 'The Slogans and Goals of Antitrust Law', 1–89, SSRN: https://papers .ssrn.com/sol3/papers.cfm?abstract_id=4121866# (May 2023), *New York University Journal of Legislation and Public Policy* (forthcoming 2023)

Herbert Hovenkamp, 'The Antitrust Text', 1–94, SSRN: https://papers.ssrn.com/sol3/papers .cfm?abstract_id=4277914 (May 2023), *Indiana Law Journal* (forthcoming 2023 or 2024)

Christophe Samuel Hutchinson, 'Potential Abuses of Dominance by Big Tech through Their Use of Big Data and AI', 10 *Journal of Antitrust Enforcement* 443–68 (2022)

Anna Blume Huttenlauch, 'Artikel 102 AEUV' [Article 102 TFEU], in Loewenheim, Meessen, Riesenkampff, Kersting & Meyer-Lindemann (eds.), *Kartellrecht*, 611–88, paras. 178–314

Pablo Ibáñez Colomo, 'Exclusionary Discrimination under Article 102 TFEU', 51 *Common Market Law Review* 141–63 (2014)

Ulrich Immenga & Ernst-Joachim Mestmäcker (Torsten Körber, Heike Schweitzer & Daniel Zimmer, eds.), *Wettbewerbsrecht* [Competition Law], *Band 1. EU: Kommentar zum Europäischen Kartellrecht* [Volume 1. UE – Commentary on European Competition Law], 6th edn (Munich: Beck, 2019)

Ulrich Immenga & Ernst-Joachim Mestmäcker (Torsten Körber, Heike Schweitzer & Daniel Zimmer, eds.), *Wettbewerbsrecht* [Competition Law], *Band 2. GWB: Kommentar zum Deutschen Kartellrecht* [Volume 2. ARC – Commentary on German Competition Law], 6th edn (Munich: Beck, 2020)

Hiroshi Iyori, 'A Comparison of U.S.-Japan Antitrust Law: Looking at the International Harmonization of Competition Law', 4 *Pacific Rim Law & Policy Journal* 59–91 (1995)

Japan Fair Trade Commission, *Guidelines Concerning Companies Which Constitute an Excessive Concentration of Economic Power* (Tokyo: JFTC, 12 November 2002)

Japan Fair Trade Commission, *Guidelines for Exclusionary Private Monopolization under the Antimonopoly Act* (Tokyo: JFTC, 28 October 2009, revised 25 December 2020)

Hans D. Jarass, 'Zum Verhältnis von Grundrechtecharta und sonstigem Recht' [On the Relationship between the Charter of Fundamental Rights and Other Law], 48 *Europarecht* [European Law] 29–44 (2013)

Hans D. Jarass, *Charta der Grundrechte der Europäischen Union: Kommentar* [Charter of Fundamental Rights of the European Union: Commentary], 4th edn (Munich: Beck, 2021)

Aurélie Jean, *Les algorithmes font-ils la loi ?* [Do Algorithms Make the Law?] (Paris: L'Observatoire, 2021)

Frédéric Jenny, 'Competition Law and Digital Ecosystems: Learning to Walk Before We Run', 30 *Industrial and Corporate Change* 1143–67 (2021)

Colin P. A. Jones & Frank S. Ravitch, *The Japanese Legal System* (St Paul: West Academic Publishing, 2019)

Rikke Frank Jørgensen (ed.), *Human Rights in the Age of Platforms* (Cambridge: MIT Press, 2019)

Michael Kades & Fiona M. Scott Morton, 'Interoperability as a Competition Remedy for Digital Networks', 1–39, SSRN: https://ssrn.com/abstract=3808372 (February 2021)

Daniel Kahneman, Olivier Sibony & Cass R. Sunstein, *Noise: A Flaw in Human Judgment* (London: William Collins, 2021, 2022 for the paperback edition)

Peter Kairouz, H. Brendan McMahan *et al.*, 'Advances and Open Problems in Federated Learning', 14/1–2 *Foundations and Trends® in Machine Learning* 1–210 (23 June 2021)

Jan Christopher Kalbhenn, 'European Legislative Initiative for Very Large Communication Platforms', in Bayer, Holznagel, Korpisaari & Woods (eds.), *Perspectives on Platform Regulation*, 47–76

Michael Kanaan, *T-Minus AI: Humanity's Countdown to Artificial Intelligence and the New Pursuit of Global Power* (Dallas: BenBella, 2020)

Immanuel Kant, *The Metaphysics of Morals* (Lara Denis ed. & Mary Gregor ed. & trans., 2nd edn, Cambridge: Cambridge University Press, 2018, first published in German in 1797)

Louis Kaplow, 'On the Relevance of Market Power', 130 *Harvard Law Review* 1303–407 (2017)

Theano Karanikioti, 'The EU Data Act – The Commission's Latest Legislative Initiative', *The Platform Law Blog*, 25 February 2022, https://theplatformlaw.blog/2022/02/25/the-eu-data-act-the-commissions-latest-legislative-initiative/amp/

Vikas Kathuria & Jure Globocnik, 'Exclusionary Conduct in Data-driven Markets: Limitations of Data Sharing Remedy', 8 *Journal of Antitrust Enforcement* 511–34 (2020)

Dimitrios Katsifis, 'General Court of the EU Delivers Landmark Google Shopping Judgment (Google and Alphabet v Commission, T-612/17)', *The Platform Law Blog*, 15 November 2021, https://theplatformlaw.blog/2021/11/15/general-court-of-the-eu-delivers-landmark-google-shopping-judgment-google-and-alphabet-v-commission-t-612–17/

Ariel Katz, 'The Chicago School and the Forgotten Political Dimension of Antitrust Law', 87 *University of Chicago Law Review* 413–58 (2020)

Aileen Kavanagh, 'The Constitutional Separation of Powers', in Dyzenhaus & Thorburn (eds.), *Constitutional Law*, 221–39

Carl Kaysen & Donald F. Turner, *Antitrust Policy: An Economic and Legal Analysis* (Cambridge: Harvard University Press, 1959)

Manuel Kellerbauer, Marcus Klamert & Jonathan Tomkin (eds.), *The EU Treaties and the Charter of Fundamental Rights: A Commentary* (Oxford/New York: Oxford University Press, 2019)

Pranvera Këllezi, *Les mesures correctives dans les cas de concentrations d'entreprises et d'abus de position dominante* [Corrective Remedies in Merger and Abuse of Dominance Cases] (Bern, Paris & Brussels: Stämpfli, L.G.D.J. & Bruylant, 2010)

Raymond M. Kethledge, 'Hayek and the Rule of Law: Implications for Unenumerated Rights and the Administrative State', 13 *New York University Journal of Law & Liberty* 193–219 (2020)

Matthias C. Kettemann & Martin Fertmann, *Platform-Proofing Democracy: Social Media Councils as Tools to Increase the Public Accountability of Online Platforms* (Potsdam-Babelsberg: Friedrich Naumann Foundation for Freedom, May 2021)

John Maynard Keynes, *The General Theory of Employment, Interest, and Money* (London: Macmillan, 1936)

James Keyte, 'Why the Atlantic Divide on Monopoly/Dominance Law and Enforcement Is So Difficult to Bridge', 33 *Antitrust* 113–19 (2018)

Lina M. Khan, 'Amazon's Antitrust Paradox', Note, 126 *Yale Law Journal* 710–805 (2017)

Lina M. Khan, 'The New Brandeis Movement: America's Antimonopoly Debate', 9 *Journal of European Competition Law & Practice* 131–32 (2018)

Lina M. Khan, 'The Separation of Platforms and Commerce', 119 *Columbia Law Review* 973–1098 (2019)

Lina M. Khan, 'The End of Antitrust History Revisited', 133 *Harvard Law Review* 1655–82 (2020)

Lina M. Khan, 'The Word "Efficiency" Doesn't Appear Anywhere in the Antitrust Statutes', Interview with Guy Rolnik, *ProMarket* (3 June 2022)

Lina M. Khan & Sandeep Vaheesan, 'Market Power and Inequality: The Antitrust Counterrevolution and Its Discontents', 11 *Harvard Law & Policy Review* 235–94 (2017)

Yunsieg P. Kim, 'Does the Anti-Google Law Actually Help Google and Hurt Startups?', 110 *Georgetown Law Journal Online* 120–34 (2021)

John B. Kirkwood, 'Predation and Discrimination', in Akman, Brook & Stylianou (eds.), *Abuse*, 140–61

Henry A. Kissinger, Eric Schmidt & Daniel Huttenlocher, *The Age of AI: And Our Human Future* (London: John Murray, 2021)

Trine M. Kjeldahl, 'Defence of a Concept: Raymond Aron and Totalitarianism', 2 *Totalitarian Movements and Political Religions* 121–41 (2001)

Amy Klobuchar, *Antitrust: Taking on Monopoly Power from the Gilded Age to the Digital Age* (New York: Alfred A. Knopf, 2021)

Kate Klonick, 'The Facebook Oversight Board: Creating an Independent Institution to Adjudicate Online Free Expression', 129 *Yale Law Journal* 2418–99 (2020)

Rainer Klump & Manuel Wörsdörfer, 'An Ordoliberal Interpretation of Adam Smith', 61 *ORDO – Jahrbuch für die Ordnung von Wirtschaft und Gesellschaft* [Ordo – Yearbook of Economic and Social Order] 29–52 (2010)

Pierre Kobel, Pranvera Këllezi & Bruce Kilpatrick (eds.), *Competition Law Analysis of Price and Non-price Discrimination & Abusive IP Based Legal Proceedings* (Cham: Springer, 2021)

Anton Korinek, 'Why We Need a New Agency to Regulate Advanced Artificial Intelligence: Lessons on AI Control from the Facebook Files', *Report, Brookings Institution* (2021)

William E. Kovacic, 'Failed Expectations: The Troubled Past and Uncertain Future of the Sherman Act as a Tool for Deconcentration', 74 *Iowa Law Review* 1105–50 (1989)

Reinier Kraakman, John Armour, Paul Davies, Luca Enriques, Henry Hansmann, Gerard Hertig, Klaus Hopt, Hideki Kanda, Mariana Pargendler, Wolf-Georg Ringe & Edward Rock, *The Anatomy of Corporate Law: A Comparative and Functional Approach*, 3rd edn (Oxford/New York: Oxford University Press, 2017)

Sharon Krause, 'Despotism in *The Spirit of Laws*', in Carrithers, Mosher & Rahe (eds.), *Montesquieu's Science of Politics*, 231–71

Jürgen Kühling, 'Die sieben Herausforderungen für eine wettbewerbliche Ordnung' [Seven Challenges for the Competition Regime], 72 *Wirtschaft und Wettbewerb* [Economy and Competition] 522–29 (2022)

Timothy K. Kuhner, 'The Separation of Business and State', 95 *California Law Review* 2353–91 (2007)

Adrian Künzler, 'Economic Content of Competition Law: The Point of Regulating Preferences', in Zimmer (ed.), *Goals*, 182–213

Heinz D. Kurz, Marlies Schütz, Rita Strohmaier & Stella S. Zilian (eds.), *The Routledge Handbook of Smart Technologies: An Economic and Social Perspective* (London: Routledge, 2022)

Shigeki Kusunoki, 'Hayek and Antitrust', 61 *History of Economics Review* 57–68 (2015)

John Kwoka & Tommaso Valletti, 'Unscrambling the Eggs: Breaking Up Consummated Mergers and Dominant Firms', 30 *Industrial and Corporate Change* 1286–306 (2021)

Agnès Labrousse & Jean-Daniel Weisz (eds.), *Institutional Economics in France and Germany: German Ordoliberalism versus the French Regulation School* (Berlin/Heidelberg: Springer, 2001)

Genevieve Lakier, *The Limits of Antimonopoly Law as a Solution to the Problems of the Platform Public Sphere* (New York: Knight First Amendment Institute, 2020)

Naomi R. Lamoreaux, 'The Problem of Bigness: From Standard Oil to Google', 33 *Journal of Economic Perspectives* 94–117 (2019)

Filippo Lancieri & Patricia Morita Sakowski, 'Competition in Digital Markets: A Review of Expert Reports', 26 *Stanford Journal of Law, Business & Finance* 65–170 (2021)

Hélène Landemore, *Open Democracy: Reinventing Popular Rule for the Twenty-First Century* (Princeton: Princeton University Press, 2020)

Hélène Landemore, 'Open Democracy and Digital Technologies', in Bernholz, Landemore & Reich (eds.), *Digital Technology and Democratic Theory*, 62–89

Ganaele Langlois & Greg Elmer, 'Impersonal Subjectivation from Platforms to Infrastructures', 41 *Media, Culture & Society* 236–51 (2019)

Timothy M. LaPira & Herschel F. Thomas, *Revolving Door Lobbying: Public Service, Private Influence, and the Unequal Representation of Interests* (Lawrence: University Press of Kansas, 2017)

Pierre Larouche & Alexandre de Streel, 'The European Digital Markets Act: A Revolution Grounded on Traditions', 12 *Journal of European Competition Law & Practice* 542–60 (2021)

Pierre Larouche & Alexandre de Streel, 'A Compass on the Journey to Successful DMA Implementation', 2022/3 *Concurrences | On-Topic* 26–30

Catherine Larrère, 'Montesquieu on Economics and Commerce', in Carrithers, Mosher & Rahe (eds.), *Montesquieu's Science of Politics*, 335–73

Yann Le Cun, *Quand la machine apprend – La révolution des neurones artificiels et de l'apprentissage profond* [When Machines Learn: The Revolution of Artificial Neurons and Deep Learning] (Paris: Odile Jacob, 2019)

Kai-Fu Lee & Qiufan Chen, *AI 2041: Ten Visions for Our Future* (New York: Currency, 2021)

Christophe Lemaire & David Sevy, 'International Report', in Kobel, Këllezi & Kilpatrick (eds.), *Competition Law*, 3–54

Mark A. Lemley, 'The Contradictions of Platform Regulation', 1 *Journal of Free Speech Law* 303–36 (2021)

Koen Lenaerts & José Antonio Gutiérrez-Fons, 'The Place of the Charter in the European Legal Space', in Peers, Hervey, Kenner & Ward (eds.), *Charter*, 1711–34

Lawrence Lessig, 'A Reply to Professor Hasen', 126 *Harvard Law Review Forum* 61–74 (2013)

Lawrence Lessig, *They Don't Represent Us: Reclaiming Our Democracy* (New York: Dey Street Books, 2019)

François Lévêque, *Les entreprises hyperpuissantes – Géants et Titans, la fin du modèle global?* [Hyperpowerful Companies: Giants and Titans, the End of the Global Model?] (Paris: Odile Jacob, 2021)

Daryl J. Levinson & Richard H. Pildes, 'Separation of Parties, Not Powers', 119 *Harvard Law Review* 2311–86 (2006)

Jacob Liedke & Katerina Eva Matsa, *Social Media and News Fact Sheet* (Washington: Pew Research Center, 2022)

Danièle Lochak, 'Les lanceurs d'alerte et les droits de l'homme : réflexions conclusives' [Whistleblowers and Human Rights: Concluding Thoughts], 10 *La Revue des droits de l'homme* [The Human Rights Review] 1–22 (2016)

John Locke, *Second Treatise of Government: An Essay Concerning the True Original, Extent and End of Civil Government* (London: Awnsham Churchill, 1689)

Ulrich Loewenheim, Karl M. Meessen, Alexander Riesenkampff, Christian Kersting & Hans-Jürgen Meyer-Lindemann (eds.), *Kartellrecht: Kommentar zum Deutschen und Europäischen Recht* [Competition Law: Commentary on German and European Law], 4th edn (Munich: Beck, 2020)

Liza Lovdahl Gormsen, 'Algorithmic Antitrust and Consumer Choice', in Portuese (ed.), *Algorithmic Antitrust*, 65–86

Jörn Lüdemann, 'Grundrechtliche Vorgaben für die Löschung von Beiträgen in sozialen Netzwerken' [Fundamental Rights Requirements for the Deletion of Contributions on Social Networks], 22 *Multimedia und Recht – Zeitschrift für IT-Recht und Recht der Digitalisierung* [Multimedia and Law – Journal for IT Law and Digitalization Law] 279–84 (2019)

Steven Lukes, 'Robert Dahl on Power', 8 *Journal of Political Power* 261–71 (2015)

Steven Lukes, 'Power and Economics', in Robert Skidelsky & Nan Craig (eds.), *Who Runs the Economy? The Role of Power in Economics* (London: Palgrave Macmillan, 2016), 17–25

Björn Lundqvist & Michal S. Gal (eds.), *Competition Law for the Digital Economy* (Cheltenham: Edward Elgar, 2019)

Yotam Lurie & David A. Frenkel, 'Corporate Governance: Separation of Powers and Checks and Balances in Israeli Corporate Law', 12 *Business Ethics: A European Review* 275–83 (2003)

Ross Mackenzie, Geert Goeteyn, Michelle Mantine & Michaela Westrup, 'Competition Law in the Metaverse: Preparing for the New Regulatory Frontier', *Competition Law Insight*, 12 July 2021

Imelda Maher, 'Re-imagining the Story of European Competition Law', 20 *Oxford Journal of Legal Studies* 155–66 (2000)

Daniel J. Mahoney, 'The Totalitarian Negation of Man: Raymond Aron on Ideology and Totalitarianism', in Colen & Dutartre-Michaut (eds.), *Aron*, 137–48

Frank Maier-Rigaud, 'On the Normative Foundations of Competition Law – Efficiency, Political Freedom and the Freedom to Compete', in Zimmer (ed.), *Goals*, 132–68

Beata Mäihäniemi, *Competition Law and Big Data: Imposing Access to Information in Digital Markets* (Cheltenham: Edward Elgar, 2020)

Daniel Mandrescu, 'Abusive Pricing Practices by Online Platforms: A Framework Review of Article 102 TFEU for Future Cases', 10 *Journal of Antitrust Enforcement* 469–517 (2022)

John F. Manning, 'Separation of Powers and Ordinary Interpretation', 124 *Harvard Law Review* 1939–2040 (2011)

Sandra Marco Colino, 'The Incursion of Antitrust into China's Platform Economy', 67 *Antitrust Bulletin* 237–58 (2022)

Gary Marcus, 'How Do We Ensure an A.I. Future That Allows for Human Thriving?', Interview with David Marchese, *New York Times*, online edition, www.nytimes.com/interactive/2023/05/02/magazine/ai-gary-marcus.html (1 May 2023)

Vincent Martenet, 'Les autorités de la concurrence et la liberté économique' [Competition Authorities and Economic Freedom], 17 *Pratique juridique actuelle* [Current Legal Practice] 963–82 (2008)

Vincent Martenet, *Architecture des pouvoirs : Enjeux et perspectives pour un État, une union d'États et les Nations Unies* [Architecture of Powers: Challenges and Perspectives for a State, A Union of States and The United Nations] (Geneva/Zurich & Paris: Schulthess & L.G.D.J., 2016)

Vincent Martenet, *Pour un Pacte européen* [For a European Pact] (Geneva/Zurich & Paris: Schulthess & L.G.D.J., 2017)

Vincent Martenet, 'La séparation des pouvoirs' [Separation of Powers], in Oliver Diggelmann, Maya Hertig Randall & Benjamin Schindler (eds.), *Verfassungsrecht der Schweiz – Droit constitutionnel suisse* [Swiss Constitutional Law] (Zurich/Geneva: Schulthess, 2020), 999–1023

Frédéric Marty, 'Politiques européennes de concurrence et économie sociale de marché' [European Competition Policies and Social Market Economy], in Potvin-Solis (ed.), *Valeurs communes*, 341–77

Giovanna Massarotto, 'Can Antitrust Trust Blockchain?', in Portuese (ed.), *Algorithmic Antitrust*, 121–54

Roger Masterman & Robert Schütze (eds.), *The Cambridge Companion to Comparative Constitutional Law* (Cambridge: Cambridge University Press, 2019)

Shigenori Matsui, 'The Principle of Separation of Powers in Japan', 5 *Journal of International and Comparative Law* 387–410 (2018)

Mitsuo Matsushita, 'The Antimonopoly Law of Japan', in Graham & Richardson (eds.), *Global Competition Policy*, 151–97

Gianpietro Mazzoleni (ed.-in-chief), *The International Encyclopedia of Political Communication*, 3 volumes (Chichester: Wiley Blackwell, 2016)

Mariana Mazzucato, *Mission Economy: A Moonshot Guide to Changing Capitalism* (London: Allen Lane, 2021)

Mariana Mazzucato, Josh Entsminger & Rainer Kattel, 'Reshaping Platform-Driven Digital Markets', in Moore & Tambini (eds.), *Regulating Big Tech*, 17–34

Nolan McCarty & Sepehr Shahshahani, 'Testing Political Antitrust', 1–75, SSRN: https://papers.ssrn.com/sol3/papers.cfm?abstract_id=4363447 (March 2023), 98 *New York University Law Review* (forthcoming 2023)

Ewan McGaughey, 'The Codetermination Bargains: The History of German Corporate and Labor Law', 23 *Columbia Journal of European Law* 135–76 (2016)

Françoise Mélonio & Charlotte Manzini (textes choisis par) [Texts Chosen by], *L'abécédaire d'Alexis de Tocqueville* [The Primer on Alexis de Tocqueville] (Paris: Éditions de l'Observatoire, 2021)

Juliane Mendelsohn, 'Agenda 2025: Hello, Mandated Unbundling, My Old Friend', *D'Kart – Antitrust Blog* (22 April 2022)

Thierry Ménissier, *Philosophie de la corruption* [Philosophy of Corruption] (Paris: Hermann, 2018)

Thierry Ménissier, 'Un "moment machiavélien" pour l'intelligence artificielle? La Déclaration de Montréal pour un développement responsable de l'IA' [A 'Machiavellian Moment' for Artificial Intelligence? The Montreal Declaration for a Responsible Development of AI], 77 *Raisons politiques* [Political Reasons] 67–81 (2020)

Thierry Ménissier, 'Les Nouvelles figures du Prince' [The New Figures of the Prince], Interview with Sven Ortoli & Edern Pollet-Bourdaloue, *Philosophie Magazine hors-série* 'Machiavel: Comment le pouvoir se prend, se garde ou se perd' [Philosophy Magazine special issue 'Machiavelli: How Power Is Taken, Kept or Lost'] 96–102 (2022)

Ernst-Joachim Mestmäcker, 'Private Macht – Grundsatzfragen in Recht, Wirtschaft und Gesellschaft' [Private Power – Fundamental Issues in Law, Economy and Society], in Möslein (ed.), *Macht*, 25–45

Jürgen Meyer & Sven Hölscheidt (eds.), *Charta der Grundrechte der Europäischen Union* [Charter of Fundamental Rights of the European Union], 5th edn (Baden-Baden, Bern & Basel: Nomos, Stämpfli & Facultas, 2019)

Denise Meyerson, 'The Rule of Law and the Separation of Powers', 4 *Macquarie Law Journal* 1–6 (2004)

Hans-W. Micklitz, Oreste Pollicino, Amnon Reichman, Andrea Simoncini, Giovanni Sartor & Giovanni De Gregorio (eds.), *Constitutional Challenges in the Algorithmic Society* (Cambridge: Cambridge University Press, 2022)

David Millon, 'The Sherman Act and the Balance of Power', 61 *Southern California Law Review* 1219–92 (1988)

Aimen Mir, Christine Laciak & Sarah Melanson, 'United States: CFIUS Review', *Global Competition Review's Americas Antitrust Review* 2022 68–85

Christoph Möllers, *The Three Branches: A Comparative Model of Separation of Powers* (Oxford/New York: Oxford University Press, 2013)

Christoph Möllers, 'Separation of Powers', in Masterman & Schütze (eds.), *Comparative Constitutional Law*, 230–57

Monopolkommission, *Wettbewerb 2020 – XXIII. Hauptgutachten der Monopolkommission gemäß § 44 Abs. 1 Satz 1 GWB* [Competition 2020 – XXIII. Biennial Report by the Monopolies Commission in Accordance with Section 44 Paragraph 1 Sentence 1 of the German Act against Restraints of Competition] (Bonn: Monopolkommission, 2020)

Monopolkommission, *Wettbewerb 2022 – XXIV. Hauptgutachten der Monopolkommission gemäß § 44 Abs. 1 Satz 1 GWB* [Competition 2022 – XXIV. Biennial Report by the Monopolies Commission in Accordance with Section 44 Paragraph 1 Sentence 1 of the German Act against Restraints of Competition] (Bonn: Monopolkommission, 2022)

Charles Louis de Secondat, Baron de La Brède et de Montesquieu, *The Spirit of the Laws* (Anne M. Cohler, Basia Carolyn Miller & Harold Samuel Stone eds. & trans., Cambridge: Cambridge University Press, 1989, first published in French in 1748 under the title *L'esprit des lois*)

Charles Louis de Secondat, Baron de La Brède et de Montesquieu, *The Spirit of Law* (Philip Steward trans., Lyon: E.N.S., 2018, last updated on 1 October 2021, a new translation of *L'esprit des lois*, http://montesquieu.ens-lyon.fr/spip.php?rubrique186)

Giorgio Monti, 'Taming Digital Monopolies: A Comparative Account of the Evolution of Antitrust and Regulation in the European Union and the United States', 67 *Antitrust Bulletin* 40–68 (2022)

Montreal Declaration for a Responsible Development of Artificial Intelligence (2018)

Martin Moore, 'Creating New Electoral Public Spheres', in Moore & Tambini (eds.), *Regulating Big Tech*, 221–34

Martin Moore & Damian Tambini (eds.), *Digital Dominance: The Power of Google, Amazon, Facebook, and Apple* (Oxford/New York: Oxford University Press, 2018)

Martin Moore & Damian Tambini (eds.), *Regulating Big Tech: Policy Responses to Digital Dominance* (Oxford/New York: Oxford University Press, 2021)

Martin Moore & Damian Tambini (eds.), 'Conclusion: Without a Holistic Vision, Democratic Media Reforms May Fail', in Moore & Tambini (eds.), *Regulating Big Tech*, 338–47

Peter Morriss, *Power: A Philosophical Analysis*, 2nd edn (Manchester: Manchester University Press, 2002)

Peter Morriss, 'A Response to Pamela Pansardi', 5 *Journal of Political Power* 91–99 (2012)

Wernhard Möschel, 'Competition Policy from an Ordo Point of View', in Alan Peacock & Hans Willgerodt (eds.), *German Neo-Liberals and the Social Market Economy* (London: Palgrave Macmillan, 1989), 142–59

Florian Möslein (ed.), *Private Macht* [Private Power] (Tübingen: Mohr Siebeck, 2016)

Jan-Werner Müller, 'Democracy's Critical Infrastructure: Rethinking Intermediary Powers', 47/3 *Philosophy & Social Criticism* 269–82 (2021)

Jan-Werner Müller, *Democracy Rules* (London: Allen Lane, 2021)

Stylianos Mystakidis, 'Metaverse', 2 *Encyclopedia* 486–97 (2022)

Thomas B. Nachbar, 'The Antitrust Constitution', 99 *Iowa Law Review* 57–114 (2013)

Philip M. Napoli, 'Treating Dominant Digital Platforms as Public Trustees', in Moore & Tambini (eds.), *Regulating Big Tech*, 151–68

Herman Narula, *Virtual Society: The Metaverse and the New Frontiers of Human Experience* (New York: Currency, 2022)

John Naughton, 'Platform Power and Responsibility in the Attention Economy', in Moore & Tambini (eds.), *Digital Dominance*, 371–95

Renato Nazzini, *The Foundations of European Union Competition Law: The Objective and Principles of Article 102* (Oxford/New York: Oxford University Press, 2011)

Renato Nazzini, '*Google* and the (Ever-stretching) Boundaries of Article 102 TFEU', 6 *Journal of European Competition Law & Practice* 301–14 (2015)

Paul Nemitz, 'Constitutional Democracy and Technology in the Age of Artificial Intelligence', 376 *Philosophical Transactions of the Royal Society* A 1–14 (2018)

Paul Nemitz & Matthias Pfeffer, 'Determining Our Technological and Democratic Future', in Moore & Tambini (eds.), *Regulating Big Tech*, 280–98

Martin Nettesheim & Stefan Thomas, *Entflechtung im deutschen Kartellrecht: Wettbewerbspolitik, Verfassungsrecht, Wettbewerbsrecht* [Deconcentration in German Cartel Law: Competition Policy, Constitutional Law, Competition Law] (Tübingen: Mohr Siebeck, 2011)

John M. Newman, 'Antitrust in Digital Markets', 72 *Vanderbilt Law Review* 1497–561 (2019)

Nathan Newman, 'Search, Antitrust, and the Economics of the Control of User Data', 31 *Yale Journal on Regulation* 401–54 (2014)

Paul Nihoul & Tadeusz Skoczny (eds.), *Procedural Fairness in Competition Proceedings* (Cheltenham: Edward Elgar, 2015)

Anna-Verena Nosthoff & Felix Maschewski, 'Big Data and the Platform Economy: On Infrastructural Power', *Presentation for the United Nations Expert Group Meeting on Population, Food Security, Nutrition, and Sustainable Development*, 1–8 www.academia .edu/44424738/Big_Data_and_the_Platform_Economy_On_Infrastructural_Power_ Presentation_at_United_Nations_Expert_Meeting_Oct_29th_2020 (29 October 2020)

Laurent Obertone, *Game Over: La révolution antipolitique* [Game Over: The Anti-political Revolution] (Paris: Magnus, 2022)

Robert O'Donoghue & Jorge Padilla, *The Law and Economics of Article 102 TFEU*, 3rd edn (Oxford: Hart, 2020)

OECD, *Post-Public Employment: Good Practices for Preventing Conflict of Interest* (Paris: OECD Publishing, 2010)

OECD, *Guidelines for Multinational Enterprises* (Paris: OECD Publishing, 2011)

OECD, *Procedural Fairness and Transparency: Key Points* (Paris: OECD Publishing, 2012)

OECD, *Quality Considerations in Digital Zero-Price Markets* (Paris: OECD Publishing, 2018)

OECD, *Implications of E-commerce for Competition Policy* (Paris: OECD Publishing, 2019)

OECD, *The Standard of Review by Courts in Competition Cases*, Background Note by the Secretariat (Paris: OECD, 14 May 2019)

OECD, *Abuse of Dominance in Digital Markets* (Paris: OECD Publishing, 2020)

OECD, *Start-ups, Killer Acquisitions and Merger Control* (Paris: OECD Publishing, 2020)

OECD, *Lobbying in the 21st Century: Transparency, Integrity and Access* (Paris: OECD Publishing, 2021)

OECD, *Ex Ante Regulation and Competition in Digital Markets* (Paris: OECD Publishing, 2021)

OECD, *Data Portability, Interoperability and Digital Platform Competition* (Paris: OECD Publishing, 2021)

OECD, *Competition Issues Concerning News Media and Digital Platforms* (Paris: OECD Publishing, 2021)

OECD, *Handbook on Competition Policy in the Digital Age* (Paris: OECD Publishing, 2022)

Yoshio Ohara, 'International Application of the Japanese Antimonopoly Act', 10 *World Competition* 5–40 (1986)

Maureen K. Ohlhausen & Alexander P. Okuliar, 'Competition, Consumer Protection, and the Right [Approach] to Privacy', 80 *Antitrust Law Journal* 121–56 (2015)

Margaret O'Mara, *The Code: Silicon Valley and the Remaking of America* (New York: Penguin, 2019)

Oxera, *Market Power in Digital Platforms*, Paper prepared for European Commission (Oxford: Oxera, 30 September 2018)

Pamela Pansardi, '*Power To* and *Power Over*: Two Distinct Concepts of Power?', 5 *Journal of Political Power* 73–89 (2012)

Pamela Pansardi, 'On Abilities and Power Again: A Reply to Peter Morriss', 5 *Journal of Political Power* 493–97 (2012)

Tony Parisi, 'The Seven Rules of the Metaverse: A Framework for the Coming Immersive Reality', *Medium* (22 October 2021)

Geoffrey G. Parker, Georgios Petropoulos & Marshall Van Alstyne, 'Platform Mergers and Antitrust', 30 *Industrial and Corporate Change* 1307–36 (2021)

Geoffrey G. Parker, Marshall W. Van Alstyne & Sangeet Paul Choudary, *Platform Revolution: How Networked Markets Are Transforming the Economy – And How to Make Them Work for You* (New York: W. W. Norton, 2016)

Frank Pasquale, *New Laws of Robotics: Defending Human Expertise in the Age of AI* (Cambridge: Harvard University Press, 2020)

Kiran Klaus Patel & Heike Schweitzer (eds.), *The Historical Foundations of EU Competition Law* (Oxford/New York: Oxford University Press, 2013)

Kiran Klaus Patel & Heike Schweitzer (eds.), 'Introduction', in Patel & Schweitzer (eds.), *Foundations*, 1–18

Bruno Patino, *La civilisation du poisson rouge : Petit traité sur le marché de l'attention* [The Goldfish Civilization: A Short Treatise on the Attention Market] (Paris: Grasset, 2019; Paris: Livre de Poche, 2022)

Sanjukta Paul, 'Beyond Neoliberal Antitrust', *Boston Review* (23 June 2022)

Matthias Pechstein, Carsten Nowak & Ulrich Häde (eds.), *Frankfurter Kommentar zu EUV, GRC und AEUV, Band I* [Frankfurt Commentary on TEU, CFR and TFEU], volume I (Tübingen: Mohr Siebeck, 2017)

Steve Peers, Tamara Hervey, Jeff Kenner & Angela Ward (eds.), *The EU Charter of Fundamental Rights*, 2nd edn (Oxford: Hart, 2021)

Johannes Persch, 'The Role of Fundamental Rights in Antitrust Law – A Special Responsibility for Undertakings with Regulatory Power under Art. 102 TFEU?', 17 *European Competition Journal* 542–66 (2021)

Nathaniel Persily, 'Platform Power, Online Speech, and the Search for New Constitutional Categories', in Bollinger & Stone (eds.), *Social Media*, 193–211

Anne Peters, 'Menschenrechtsfunktionen jenseits des Staates' [Human Rights Functions Beyond the State], in Grimm, Peters & Wielsch, *Grundrechtsfunktionen*, 73–117

Niels Petersen, 'Antitrust Law and the Promotion of Democracy and Economic Growth', 9 *Journal of Competition Law & Economics* 593–636 (2013)

Nicolas Petit, *Droit européen de la concurrence* [European Competition Law], 3rd edn (Paris: L.G.D.J., 2020)

Nicolas Petit, *Big Tech and the Digital Economy: The Moligopoly Scenario* (Oxford/New York: Oxford University Press, 2020)

Nicolas Petit, 'The Proposed Digital Markets Act (DMA): A Legal and Policy Review', 12 *Journal of European Competition Law & Practice* 529–41 (2021)

Alexander Peukert, 'Five Reasons to be Skeptical about the DSA', in Richter, Straub & Tuchtfeld (eds.), *Big Tech*, 22–28

Thomas Philippon, *The Great Reversal: How America Gave Up on Free Markets* (Cambridge: Harvard University Press, 2019, 2021 for the paperback edition)

Angela Phillips & Eleonora Maria Mazzoli, 'Minimizing Data-Driven Targeting and Providing a Public Search Alternative', in Moore & Tambini (eds.), *Regulating Big Tech*, 110–26

Peter Picht, 'Private Enforcement for the DSA/DGA/DMA Package', in Richter, Straub & Tuchtfeld (eds.), *Big Tech*, 98–102

Randy Picker, 'The House's Recent Spate of Antitrust Bills Would Change Big Tech as We Know It', *ProMarket* (29 June 2021)

Randy Picker, 'How Would the Big Tech Self-Preferencing Bill Affect Users?', *ProMarket* (16 June 2022)

Fabrice Picod, Cecilia Rizcallah & Sébastien Van Drooghenbroeck (eds.), *Charte des droits fondamentaux de l'Union européenne : Commentaire article par article* [Charter of Fundamental Rights of the European Union: Article-by-Article Commentary], 2nd edn (Brussels: Bruylant, 2020)

Chris Pike & Gabriele Carovano, 'Reasons to Be Cheerful: The Benevolent Market Power of Decentralised Blockchains', in Portuese (ed.), *Algorithmic Antitrust*, 107–20

Thomas Piketty, *Capital and Ideology* (Arthur Goldhammer trans., Cambridge: Harvard University Press, 2020)

Thomas Piketty, *Une brève histoire de l'égalité* [A Brief History of Equality] (Paris: Seuil, 2021)

Robert Pitofsky, 'The Political Content of Antitrust', 127 *University of Pennsylvania Law Review* 1051–75 (1979)

Rupprecht Podszun, 'The Pitfalls of Market Definition: Towards an Open and Evolutionary Concept', in Di Porto & Podszun (eds.), *Abusive Practices*, 68–90

Rupprecht Podszun, 'Private Enforcement and the Digital Markets Act', in Richter, Straub & Tuchtfeld (eds.), *Big Tech*, 92–97

Rupprecht Podszun, 'Empfiehlt sich eine stärkere Regulierung von Online-Plattformen und anderen Digitalunternehmen?' [Is Stronger Regulation of Online Platforms and Other Digital Companies Recommended?], 2022 *Neue Juristische Wochenschrift* [New Legal Weekly Journal], *Beilage 2* [Supplement 2] 56–60

Rupprecht Podszun, 'Agenda 2025: "Taking Ordnungspolitik Seriously"', *D'Kart – Antitrust Blog* (12 April 2022)

Rupprecht Podszun (ed.), *Digital Markets Act – Handkommentar* [Commentary] (Baden-Baden: Nomos, 2023)

Rupprecht Podszun, Philipp Bongartz & Sarah Langenstein, 'The Digital Markets Act: Moving from Competition Law to Regulation for Large Gatekeepers', 10 *Journal of European Consumer and Market Law* 60–67 (2021)

Rupprecht Podszun & Benjamin Franz, 'Was ist ein Markt? – Unentgeltliche Leistungsbeziehungen im Kartellrecht' [What Is a Market? – Free of Charge Services in Competition Law], 3 *Neue Zeitschrift für Kartellrecht* [New Journal of Competition Law] 121–27 (2015)

Julia Pohle & Daniel Voelsen, 'Centrality and Power. The Struggle over the Techno-political Configuration of the Internet and the Global Digital Order', 14 *Policy & Internet* 13–27 (2022)

Oreste Pollicino, *Judicial Protection of Fundamental Rights on the Internet: A Road towards Digital Constitutionalism?* (Oxford: Hart, 2021)

Oreste Pollicino & Giovanni De Gregorio, 'Constitutional Law in the Algorithmic Society', in Micklitz *et al.*, (eds.), *Algorithmic Society*, 3–24

Heinrich Popitz, *Phenomena of Power: Authority, Domination, and Violence* (Gianfranco Poggi trans., Andreas Göttlich & Jochen Dreher eds., New York: Columbia University Press, 2017, first published in German in 1986, translation based on the 2nd edn of 1992)

Aurelien Portuese, 'Beyond Antitrust Populism: Towards Robust Antitrust', 40 *Economic Affairs* 237–58 (2020)

Aurelien Portuese (ed.), *Algorithmic Antitrust* (Cham: Springer, 2022)

Eric A. Posner, Fiona M. Scott Morton & E. Glen Weyl, 'A Proposal to Limit the Anticompetitive Power of Institutional Investors', 81 *Antitrust Law Journal* 669–728 (2017)

Eric A. Posner & E. Glen Weyl, *Radical Markets: Uprooting Capitalism and Democracy for a Just Society* (Princeton: Princeton University Press, 2018)

Richard A. Posner, *Antitrust Law*, 2nd edn (Chicago: The University of Chicago Press, 2001)

Richard A. Posner, *Catastrophe: Risk and Response* (Oxford/New York: Oxford University Press, 2004)

Michael Potacs, 'Wertkonforme Auslegung des Unionsrechts?' [Interpretation of Union Law in Conformity with Values], 51 *Europarecht* [European Law] 164–75 (2016)

Laurence Potvin-Solis (ed.), *Les valeurs communes dans l'Union européenne* [Common Values in the European Union] (Brussels: Bruylant, 2014)

George L. Priest, 'What to Do about the Big Tech Monopolies?', *Concurrentialiste*, 17 May 2021

Suzanne Rab, 'Artificial Intelligence, Algorithms and Antitrust', 18 *Competition Law Journal* 141–50 (2019)

K. Sabeel Rahman, 'From Economic Inequality to Economic Freedom: Constitutional Political Economy in the New Gilded Age', 35 *Yale Law & Policy Review* 321–36 (2016)

K. Sabeel Rahman, 'The New Utilities: Private Power, Social Infrastructure, and the Revival of the Public Utility Concept', 39 *Cardozo Law Review* 1621–89 (2018)

K. Sabeel Rahman & Kathleen Thelen, 'The Rise of the Platform Business Model and the Transformation of Twenty-First-Century Capitalism', 47 *Politics & Society* 177–204 (2019)

Vera Lúcia Raposo, 'Ex Machina: Preliminary Critical Assessment of the European Draft Act on Artificial Intelligence', 30 *International Journal of Law and Information Technology* 88–109 (2022)

Max Read, 'The Crypting Point: The Role of Chaos in Contemporary Political and Economic Thought', *Bookforum Magazine* (June, July & August 2022)

Antoine Rebérioux, 'Worker Involvement in Decision-Making: Bicameralism, Code-termination and Co-management', 19 *Socio-Economic Review* 1211–15 (2021)

Andrea Renda, 'Making the Digital Economy "Fit for Europe"', 26 *European Law Journal* 345–54 (2022)

Heiko Richter, Marlene Straub & Erik Tuchtfeld (eds.), *To Break Up or Regulate Big Tech? Avenues to Constrain Private Power in the DSA/DMA Package* (Munich: Max Planck Institute for Innovation and Competition, 2021)

Rémy Rieffel, *Révolution numérique, révolution culturelle ?* [Digital Revolution, Cultural Revolution?] (Paris: Éditions Gallimard, 2014)

Viktoria H. S. E. Robertson, 'Antitrust, Big Tech, and Democracy: A Research Agenda', 67 *Antitrust Bulletin* 259–79 (2022)

Viktoria H. S. E. Robertson, 'Antitrust Law and Digital Markets', in Kurz, Schütz, Strohmaier & Zilian (eds.), *Smart Technologies*, 432–56

Teresa Rodríguez de las Heras Ballell, 'The Scope of the DMA', in Richter, Straub & Tuchtfeld (eds.), *Big Tech*, 72–77

Susan Rose-Ackerman, *Democracy and Executive Power: Policymaking Accountability in the US, the UK, Germany, and France* (New Haven: Yale University Press, 2021)

Francesca Rossi *et al.*, *Working Together on our Future with AI* (Washington: Association for the Advancement of Artificial Intelligence, 2023)

Luc Rouban, *La démocratie représentative est-elle en crise ?* [Is Representative Democracy in Crisis?] (Paris: La documentation française, 2018)

Jacob Rowbottom, 'Transposing Public Service Media Obligations to Dominant Platforms', in Moore & Tambini (eds.), *Regulating Big Tech*, 235–51

Daniel L. Rubinfeld & Michal S. Gal, 'Access Barriers to Big Data', 59 *Arizona Law Review* 339–81 (2017)

Marco Ruediger & Amaro Grassi, 'Polarization Presidentialism. How Social Media Reshaped Brazilian Politics: A Case Study on the 2018 Elections', in Spiecker gen. Döhmann, Westland & Campos (eds.), *Demokratie*, 283–98

Hannah Ruschemeier, 'Re-Subjecting State-Like Actors to the State', in Richter, Straub & Tuchtfeld (eds.), *Big Tech*, 49–54

Stuart Russell, *Human Compatible: Artificial Intelligence and the Problem of Control* (New York: Viking, 2019)

Franz Jürgen Säcker, Florian Bien, Peter Meier-Beck & Frank Montag (eds.), *Münchener Kommentar zum Wettbewerbsrecht* [Munich Commentary on Competition Law], *Band 1: Europäisches Wettbewerbsrecht* [Volume 1: European Competition Law], 3rd edn (Munich: Beck, 2020)

Franz Jürgen Säcker & Peter Meier-Beck (eds.), *Münchener Kommentar zum Wettbewerbsrecht* [Munich Commentary on Competition Law], *Band 2: Deutsches Wettbewerbsrecht* [Volume 2: German Competition Law], 3rd edn (Munich: Beck, 2020)

Hillary A. Sale, 'The New "Public" Corporation', 74 *Law and Contemporary Problems* 137–48 (2011)

Razeen Sally, *Classical Liberalism and International Economic Order: Studies in Theory and Intellectual History* (London: Routledge, 1998, 2002 for the paperback edition)

Steven C. Salop, 'Dominant Digital Platforms: Is Antitrust Up to the Task?', *Yale Law Journal Forum*, 18 January 2021, 563–87

Cristian Santesteban, 'How to Prevent Big Tech from Hindering Pathbreaking Innovation in the Metaverse', *ProMarket* (17 March 2022)

Filippo Santoni de Sio, 'Ethics of AI: The Philosophical Challenges', 27 *Science and Engineering Ethics* 50/1–6 (2021)

Mike S. Schäfer, 'Digital Public Sphere', in Mazzoleni (ed.-in-chief), *Political Communication*, volume I, 322–28

Peter D. Schapiro, 'The German Law against Restraints of Competition – Comparative and International Aspects: Part One', 62 *Columbia Law Review* 1–48 (1962)

Frank Schimmelfennig, Thomas Winzen, Tobias Lenz, Jofre Rocabert, Loriana Crasnic, Cristina Gherasimov, Jana Lipps, and Densua Mumford, *The Rise of International Parliaments: Strategic Legitimation in International Organizations* (Oxford/New York: Oxford University Press, 2021)

Utz Schliesky, 'Digitalisierung – Herausforderung für den demokratischen Verfassungsstaat' [Digitalization – Challenge for the Democratic Constitutional State], 38 *Neue Zeitschrift für Verwaltungsrecht* [New Journal for Administrative Law] 693–702 (2019)

Ingo Schmidt & Justus Haucap, *Wettbewerbspolitik und Kartellrecht: Eine interdisziplinäre Einführung* [Competition Policy and Cartel Law: An Interdisciplinary Introduction], 10th edn (Munich: Oldenbourg, 2013)

Monika Schnitzer, Jacques Crémer, David Dinielli, Amelia Fletcher, Paul Heidhues, Fiona M. Scott Morton & Katja Seim, *International Coherence in Digital Platform Regulation: An Economic Perspective on the US and EU Proposals* (New Haven: Yale Tobin Center for Economic Policy, Digital Regulation Project, Policy Discussion Paper No. 5, 9 August 2021)

Jan-Felix Schrape, 'Plattformöffentlichkeit' [Platform Public Sphere], in Bogner, Decker, Nentwich & Scherz (eds.), *Digitalisierung*, 117–30

Thibault Schrepel, 'Friedrich Hayek's Contribution to Antitrust Law and Its Modern Application', 7 *Global Antitrust Review* 199–216 (2014)

Thibault Schrepel, 'Antitrust without Romance', 13 *New York University Journal of Law & Liberty* 326–431 (2020)

Thibault Schrepel, 'Platforms or Aggregators: Implications for Digital Antitrust Law', 12 *Journal of European Competition Law & Practice* 1–3 (2021)

Thibault Schrepel, *Blockchain + Antitrust: The Decentralization Formula* (Cheltenham: Edward Elgar, 2021)

Helmuth Schröter & Ulrich Bartl, 'Artikel 102 AEUV' [Article 102 TFEU], in Schröter, Jakob, Klotz & Mederer (eds.), *Europäisches Wettbewerbsrecht*, 744–941

Helmuth Schröter, Thinam Jakob, Robert Klotz & Wolfgang Mederer (eds.), *Europäisches Wettbewerbsrecht: Kommentar* [European Competition Law: Commentary], 2nd edn (Baden-Baden: Nomos, 2014)

Joseph A. Schumpeter, *History of Economic Analysis* (8th printing 1972, first published in London in 1954 by Allen & Unwin)

Heike Schweitzer, 'Efficiency, Political Freedom and the Freedom to Compete – Comment on Maier-Rigaud', in Zimmer (ed.), *Goals*, 169–81

Heike Schweitzer, 'Wettbewerbsrecht und das Problem privater Macht' [Competition Law and the Problem of Private Power], in Möslein (ed.), *Macht*, 447–73

Heike Schweitzer, 'Datenzugang in der Datenökonomie: Eckpfeiler einer neuen Informationsordnung' [Access to Data in the Data Economy: Cornerstone of a New Information Order], 121 *GRUR: Gewerblicher Rechtsschutz und Urheberrecht* [Intellectual Property and Copyright Law] 569–80 (2019)

Heike Schweitzer, 'Digitale Plattformen als private Gesetzgeber: Ein Perspektivwechsel für die europäische "Plattform-Regulierung"' [Digital Platforms as Private Regulators: A Change of Perspective for European 'Platform Regulation'], 27 *Zeitschrift für Europäisches Privatrecht* [Journal of European Private Law] 1–12 (2019)

Heike Schweitzer, 'Missbrauch von Marktmacht durch Datenzugriff: Kartellrechtliche Vorgaben für den Umgang digitaler Plattformen mit Nutzerdaten' [Abuse of Market Power through Data Access: Antitrust Requirements for the Handling of User Data by Digital Platforms], 77 *JuristenZeitung* [Lawyers Journal] 16–27 (2022)

Heike Schweitzer, Justus Haucap, Wolfgang Kerber & Robert Welker, *Modernisierung der Missbrauchsaufsicht für marktmächtige Unternehmen* [Modernization of Abuse Control for Companies with Market Power] (Baden-Baden: Nomos, 2018)

Fiona M. Scott Morton, 'Will the EU's New Law Remake Big Tech?', *Yale Insights*, 4 April 2022

Fiona M. Scott Morton & David C. Dinielli, *Roadmap for a Digital Advertising Monopolization Case against Google* (Redwood City: Omidyar Network, May 2020)

Fiona M. Scott Morton & David C. Dinielli, *Roadmap for an Antitrust Case against Facebook* (Redwood City: Omidyar Network, June 2020)

Fiona M. Scott Morton, Steven C. Salop & David C. Dinielli, 'Why Congress Should Pass the American Innovation and Choice Online Act', *ProMarket* (8 July 2022)

Terrence J. Sejnowski, *The Deep Learning Revolution: Artificial Intelligence Meets Human Intelligence* (Cambridge: MIT Press, 2018)

Maximilian Seyderhelm, *Grundrechtsbindung Privater* [Binding of Private Parties to Fundamental Rights] (Baden-Baden: Nomos, 2021)

Carl Shapiro, 'Antitrust in a Time of Populism', 61 *International Journal of Industrial Organization* 714–48 (2018)

Carl Shapiro, 'Protecting Competition in the American Economy: Merger Control, Tech Titans, Labor Markets', 33 *Journal of Economic Perspectives* 69–93 (2019)

Carl Shapiro, 'Antitrust: What Went Wrong and How to Fix It', 35 *Antitrust Magazine* 33–45 (2021)

John B. Sheldon, 'The Rise of the Metaverse', *Engelsberg Ideas*, 17 September 2021

Heidi M. Silton, Craig S. Davis & Halli Spraggins, 'Congressional Antitrust Bills Seek to Regulate a New Internet Era', 36 *Antitrust Magazine* 26–33 (2022)

Georg Simmel, 'Sociology of Competition', 33 *Canadian Journal of Sociology* 957–78 (2008) (Horst J. Helle trans., first published in Germany under the title *Soziologie der Konkurrenz, Neue Deutsche Rundschau* XIV, 1009–23 [1903])

Andrea Simoncini & Erik Longo, 'Fundamental Rights and the Rule of Law in the Algorithmic Society', in Micklitz *et al.*, (eds.), *Algorithmic Society*, 27–41

Josh Simons & Dipayan Ghosh, *Utilities for Democracy: Why and How the Algorithmic Infrastructure of Facebook and Google Must Be Regulated* (Washington: Foreign Policy at Brookings, August 2020)

Ganesh Sitaraman, 'The Regulation of Foreign Platforms', 74 *Stanford Law Review* 1073–152 (2022)

Ganesh Sitaraman & Anne L. Alstott, *The Public Option: How to Expand Freedom, Increase Opportunity, and Promote Equality* (Cambridge: Harvard University Press, 2019)

Ganesh Sitaraman & Anne L. Alstott (eds.), *Politics, Policy, and Public Options* (Cambridge: Cambridge University Press, 2021)

Adam Smith, *An Inquiry into the Nature and Causes of the Wealth of Nations* (Oxford/New York: Oxford University Press, 1976, first published in 1776)

Tom Smith, 'Meta/Giphy Court Judgment: The CMA's Controversial Merger Analysis Survives, but Its Procedures Don't', *The Platform Law Blog*, 20 June 2022, https://theplatformlaw.blog/2022/06/20/meta-giphy-court-judgment-the-cmas-controversial-merger-analysis-survives-but-its-procedures-dont/

Tom Smith, 'Full Steam Ahead for the UK Digital Markets Unit', *The Platform Law Blog*, 17 November 2022, https://theplatformlaw.blog/2022/11/17/full-steam-ahead-for-the-uk-digital-markets-unit/

Tom Smith, 'Fashionably Late: The UK Digital Markets Legislation Starts Its Passage through Parliament', *The Platform Law Blog*, 27 April 2023, https://theplatformlaw.blog/2023/04/27/better-late-than-never-the-uk-digital-markets-legislation-starts-its-passage-through-parliament/

D. Daniel Sokol & Roisin Comerford, 'Does Antitrust Have a Role to Play in Regulating Big Data?', in Blair & Sokol (eds.), *Antitrust, Intellectual Property, and High Tech*, 293–316

D. Daniel Sokol & Andrew T. Guzman (eds.), *Antitrust Procedural Fairness* (Oxford/New York: Oxford University Press, 2019)

Céline Spector, *Montesquieu et l'émergence de l'économie politique* [Montesquieu and the Emergence of Political Economy] (Paris: Honoré Champion, 2006)

Céline Spector, 'Commerce' (Philipp Stewart trans.), in Volpilhac-Auger (ed.), *Dictionnaire Montesquieu*, September 2013, http://dictionnaire-montesquieu.ens-lyon.fr/fr/article/1378153189/en/

Indra Spiecker gen. Döhmann, Michael Westland & Ricardo Campos (eds.), *Demokratie und Öffentlichkeit im 21. Jahrhundert – zur Macht des Digitalen* [Democracy and the Public Sphere in the 21st Century – On the Power of the Digital] (Baden-Baden: Nomos, 2022)

John C. Stedman, 'The German Decartelization Program – The Law in Repose', 17 *University of Chicago Law Review* 441–57 (1950)

Marshall Steinbaum, 'Establishing Market and Monopoly Power in Tech Platform Antitrust Cases', 67 *Antitrust Bulletin* 130–45 (2022)

Marshall Steinbaum & Maurice E. Stucke, 'The Effective Competition Standard: A New Standard for Antitrust', 86 *University of Chicago Law Review* 595–623 (2019)

Neal Stephenson, *Snow Crash* (New York: Bantam Books, 1992)

Stigler Committee on Digital Platforms, *Final Report* (Chicago: Stigler Center for the Study of the Economy and the State, 2019)

Matt Stoller, *Goliath: The 100-Year War between Monopoly Power and Democracy* (New York: Simon and Schuster, 2019)

Alexandre de Streel, 'Should Digital Antitrust Be Ordoliberal?', 2020 *Concurrences* 2–4

Alexandre de Streel, Fiona Scott Morton, Jacques Crémer, Amelia Fletcher, Paul Heidhues, Giorgio Monti, Rupprecht Podszun & Monika Schnitzer, 'How Europe Can Enforce the Digital Markets Act Effectively', *ProMarket* (11 May 2022)

Maurice E. Stucke, 'Reconsidering Antitrust's Goals', 53 *Boston College Law Review* 551–629 (2012)

Maurice E. Stucke, 'Should We Be Concerned about Data-Opolies?', 2 *Georgetown Law Technology Review* 275–324 (2018)

Maurice E. Stucke, 'Why Competition Alone Won't Bring about a More Inclusive Digital Economy', *ProMarket* (31 March 2022)

Maurice E. Stucke, *Breaking Away: How to Regain Control over Our Data, Privacy, and Autonomy* (Oxford/New York: Oxford University Press, 2022)

Maurice E. Stucke, 'The Relationship between Privacy and Antitrust', 1–17, SSRN: https://papers.ssrn.com/sol3/papers.cfm?abstract_id=4042262 (June 2022), *Notre Dame Law Review* (forthcoming 2023)

Maurice E. Stucke & Allen P. Grunes, *Big Data and Competition Policy* (Oxford/New York: Oxford University Press, 2016)

Richard Sturn, 'Digital Transformation and the Sovereignty of Nation States', in Kurz, Schütz, Strohmaier & Zilian (eds.), *Smart Technologies*, 409–31

Larry Summers, 'Larry Summers Cautions Antitrust Regulators against Broad-Brush Policy', Interview with Brooke Fox, *ProMarket* (6 June 2022)

Jamie Susskind, *Future Politics: Living Together in a World Transformed by Tech* (Oxford/New York: Oxford University Press, 2018)

Jamie Susskind, *The Digital Republic: On Freedom and Democracy in the 21st Century* (London: Bloomsbury, 2022)

Haris Tagaras, 'La valeur ajoutée de la Charte des droits fondamentaux: Une tentative de bilan à l'approche du dixième anniversaire de son application' [The Added Value of the Charter of Fundamental Rights: An Attempt to Take Stock as We Approach the Tenth Anniversary of Its Application] 55 *Cahiers de droit européen* [European Law Notebooks] 33–90 (2019)

Conor Talbot, 'Ordoliberalism and Balancing Competition Goals in the Development of the European Union', 61 *Antitrust Bulletin* 264–89 (2016)

Damian Tambini, 'Social Media Power and Election Legitimacy', in Moore & Tambini (eds.), *Digital Dominance*, 265–93

Damian Tambini & Martin Moore, 'Dominance, the Citizen Interest and the Consumer Interest', in Moore & Tambini (eds.), *Digital Dominance*, 396–407

Maren Tamke, 'Big Data and Competition Law', 15 *Zeitschrift für Wettbewerbsrecht* [Competition Law Review] 358–85 (2017)

Ida M. Tarbell, *The History of the Standard Oil Company* (briefer version edited by David M. Chalmers; Mineola: Dover, 2003, first published in 1966 by Harper & Row, New York)

Pierre-Henri Tavoillot, *Comment gouverner un peuple-roi ? Traité nouveau d'art politique* [How to Govern a People-King? A New Treatise on the Art of Politics] (Paris: Odile Jacob, 2019)

Zephyr Teachout, *Corruption in America: From Benjamin Franklin's Snuff Box to Citizen United* (Cambridge: Harvard University Press, 2016)

Zephyr Teachout, 'Monopoly Versus Democracy: How to End a Gilded Age', 100 *Foreign Affairs* 52–59 (2021)

Zephyr Teachout & Lina Khan, 'Market Structure and Political Law: A Taxonomy of Power', 9 *Duke Journal of Constitutional Law & Public Policy* 37–74 (2014)

Jonathan Tepper with Denise Hearn, *The Myth of Capitalism: Monopolies and the Death of Competition* (Hoboken: Wiley, 2019)

QuHarrison Terry & Scott 'DJ Skee' Keeney, *The Metaverse Handbook: Innovating for the Internet's Next Tectonic Shift* (Hoboken: Wiley, 2022)

R. Guy Thomas, 'Whistleblowing and Power: A Network Perspective', 29 *Business Ethics: A European Review* 842–55 (2020)

Rhodri Thompson, Christopher Brown & Nicholas Gibson, 'Article 102', in Bellamy & Child (Bailey & John, eds.), *Competition*, 859–970

Robert B. Thompson, 'The Power of Shareholders in the United States', in Hill & Thomas (eds.), *Shareholder Power*, 441–58

Robert B. Thompson, 'Anti-Primacy: Sharing Power in American Corporations', 71 *Business Lawyer* 381–425 (2016)

Zhao Tingyang, 'A Feasible Smart Democracy', published online in the Beijing Cultural Review (16 May 2021), introduction and translation by David Ownby, www.readingthechinadream.com/zhao-tingyang-on-democracy.html

Jean Tirole, 'Why Google and Facebook Can't Be Broken Up Like a Utility', 2018 *Eccles Prize and Speaker Forum* (New York: Columbia Business School, 2018), www8.gsb.columbia.edu/articles/chazen-global-insights/why-google-and-facebook-can-t-be-broken-utility

Alexis de Tocqueville, *Democracy in America* (Harvey C. Mansfield & Delba Winthrop eds. & trans., Chicago: The University of Chicago Press, 2002, first published in French in 1835)

Katharine Trendacosta & Danny O'Brien, 'An Antitrust Exemption for News Media Won't Take Us Back to the Time Before Big Tech', *Electronic Frontier Foundation Blog*, 17 March 2021, www.eff.org/fr/deeplinks/2021/03/antitrust-exemption-news-media-wont-take-us-back-time-big-tech

Michel Troper, *La séparation des pouvoirs et l'histoire constitutionnelle française* [Separation of Powers and French Constitutional History] (Paris: L.G.D.J., 1980)

Michel Troper, 'Les nouvelles séparations des pouvoirs' [The New Separations of Powers], in Baume & Fontana (eds.), *Usages de la séparation des pouvoirs*, 17–37

Michel Troper, 'Separation of Powers' (Philipp Stewart trans.), in Volpilhac-Auger (ed.), *Dictionnaire Montesquieu*, September 2013, http://dictionnaire-montesquieu.ens-lyon.fr/fr/article/1376427308/en/

Michel Troper & Dominique Chagnollaud (eds.), *Traité international de droit constitutionnel* [International Treatise of Constitutional Law], 3 volumes (Paris: Dalloz, 2012)

Paul Tucker, 'Antitrust and Rule by Judges', *ProMarket* (27 June 2022)

UK Competition & Markets Authority (CMA), *Online Platforms and Digital Advertising* (London: CMA, 1 July 2020)

UK Competition & Markets Authority (CMA), *Mobile Ecosystems: Market Study Final Report* (London: CMA, 10 June 2022)

United Nations – Office of the High Commissioner for Human Rights, *Guiding Principles on Business and Human Rights* (New York & Geneva: United Nations, 2011)

United Nations Conference on Trade and Development (UNCTAD), *Competition Issues in the Digital Economy*, Note by the Secretariat (Geneva: United Nations, 1 May 2019)

United Nations Conference on Trade and Development (UNCTAD), *Competition Law, Policy and Regulation in the Digital Era*, Note by the Secretariat (Geneva: United Nations, 28 April 2021)

The U.S. Department of State, *Germany 1947–1949: The Story in Documents* (Washington: Office of Public Affairs, 1950)

The U.S. House of Representatives – Subcommittee on Antitrust, Commercial and Administrative Law of the Committee on the Judiciary, *Investigation of Competition in Digital Markets*, Majority Staff Report and Recommendations (Washington, 2020)

Maham Usman, 'Breaking Up Big Tech: Lessons from AT&T', 170 *University of Pennsylvania Law Review* 523–48 (2022)

Van Bael & Bellis, *Competition Law of the European Union*, 6th edn (Alphen aan den Rijn: Wolters Kluwer, 2021)

Simon Vande Walle, 'Competition and Competition Law in Japan: Between Scepticism and Embrace', in Dowdle, Gillespie & Maher (eds.), *Asian Capitalism*, 123–43

José van Dijck, Thomas Poell & Martijn de Waal, *The Platform Society* (Oxford/New York: Oxford University Press, 2018)

José van Dijck, David Nieborg & Thomas Poell, 'Reframing Platform Power', 8/2 *Internet Policy Review* 1–18 (2019)

Rory Van Loo, 'In Defense of Breakups: Administering a "Radical" Remedy', 105 *Cornell Law Review* 1955–2021 (2020)

Cento Veljanovski, 'Algorithmic Antitrust: A Critical Overview', in Portuese (ed.), *Algorithmic Antitrust*, 39–64

Maurice J. C. Vile, *Constitutionalism and the Separation of Powers*, 2nd edn (Oxford/New York: Oxford University Press, 1967; Indianapolis: Liberty Fund, 1998)

Eugene Volokh, 'Treating Social Media Platforms Like Common Carriers?', 1 *Journal of Free Speech Law* 377–462 (2021)

Catherine Volpilhac-Auger (ed.), *Dictionnaire Montesquieu* [Montesquieu Dictionary] (Lyon: E.N.S., 2013)

Ben Wagner, 'Free Expression? Dominant Information Intermediaries as Arbiters of Internet Speech', in Moore & Tambini (eds.), *Digital Dominance*, 219–40

Masako Wakui, *Antimonopoly Law: Competition Law and Policy in Japan*, 2nd edn (Independently published, 2018)

Jeremy Waldron, 'Separation of Powers in Thought and Practice', 54 *Boston College Law Review* 433–68 (2013)

Mason Walker & Katerina Eva Matsa, *News Consumption Across Social Media in 2021* (Washington: Pew Research Center, 2021)

Spencer Weber Waller, 'Antitrust and Democracy', 46 *Florida State University Law Review* 807–60 (2019)

Spencer Weber Waller, 'The Omega Man or the Isolation of U.S. Antitrust Law', 52 *Connecticut Law Review* 123–212 (2020)

Spencer Weber Waller & Jacob E. Morse, 'The Political Face of Antitrust', 15 *Brooklyn Journal of Corporate, Financial & Commercial Law* 75–95 (2020)

Tim Ward, James Bourke & Milan Kristof, 'Enforcement and Procedure', in Bellamy & Child (Bailey & John, eds.), *Competition*, 1123–250

We Are Social/Hootsuite, *Digital 2022 Global Overview Report* (New York & Vancouver: We Are Social & Hootsuite, 2022)

We Are Social/Meltwater, *Digital 2023 Global Overview Report* (New York & San Francisco: We Are Social & Meltwater, 2023)

Gregory J. Werden, *The Foundations of Antitrust* (Durham: Carolina Academic Press, 2020)

Michael Wheeler, 'Autonomy', in Dubber, Pasquale & Das (eds.), *Ethics of AI*, 343–57

Tom Wheeler, Phil Verveer & Gene Kimmelman, *New Digital Realities; New Oversight Solutions in the U.S.: The Case for a Digital Platform Agency and a New Approach to Regulatory Oversight* (Cambridge: Harvard Kennedy School, The Shorenstein Center on Media, Politics and Public Policy, August 2020)

Richard Whish & David Bailey, *Competition Law*, 10th edn (Oxford/New York: Oxford University Press, 2021)

D. M. White, 'The Problem of Power', 2 *British Journal of Political Science* 479–90 (1972)

Marc Ph. M. Wiggers, Robin A. Struijlaart & Johannes W. Dibbits, *Digital Competition Law in Europe: A Concise Guide* (Alphen aan den Rijn: Wolters Kluwer, 2019)

Christine S. Wilson & Keith Klovers, 'The Growing Nostalgia for Past Regulatory Misadventures and the Risk of Repeating These Mistakes with Big Tech', 8 *Journal of Antitrust Enforcement* 10–29 (2020)

Clifford Winston, 'Back to the Good – or Were They the Bad – Old Days of Antitrust? A Review Essay of Jonathan B. Baker's *The Antitrust Paradigm: Restoring a Competitive Economy*', 59 *Journal of Economic Literature* 265–84 (2021)

Anne C. Witt, 'Taming Tech Giants', 67 *Antitrust Bulletin* 187–9 (2022)

Anne C. Witt, 'Who's Afraid of Conglomerate Mergers?', 67 *Antitrust Bulletin* 208–36 (2022)

Anne C. Witt, 'Platform Regulation in Europe – *per se* Rules to the Rescue?', 18 *Journal of Competition Law & Economics* 670–708 (2022)

Lorna Woods, 'The UK's Approach to Regulation of Digital Platforms', in Bayer, Holznagel, Korpisaari & Woods (eds.), *Perspectives on Platform Regulation*, 329–50

World Economic Forum (WEF), *Competition Policy in a Globalized, Digitalized Economy*, White paper prepared by Pınar Akman (Cologny/Geneva: WEF, December 2019)

Dennis H. Wrong, *Power: Its Forms, Bases, and Uses*, 3rd edn (London: Routledge, 2017)

Tim Wu, *The Curse of Bigness: Antitrust in the New Gilded Age* (New York: Columbia Global Reports, 2018)

Karen Yeung, 'Why Worry about Decision-Making by Machine?', in Yeung & Lodge (eds.), *Regulation*, 21–48

Karen Yeung & Martin Lodge (eds.), *Algorithmic Regulation* (Oxford/New York: Oxford University Press, 2019)

John M. Yun, 'The Role of Big Data in Antitrust', in Global Antitrust Institute, *Digital Economy*, 220–42

John M. Yun, 'Potential Competition, Nascent Competitors, and Killer Acquisitions', in Global Antitrust Institute, *Digital Economy*, 652–78

Bai Yuntao *et al.*, 'Constitutional AI: Harmlessness from AI Feedback', Unpublished manuscript, https://arxiv.org/abs/2212.08073 (December 2022)

Daniel Zimmer (ed.), *The Goals of Competition Law* (Cheltenham: Edward Elgar, 2012)

Daniel Zimmer (ed.), 'Agenda 2025: Abuse-Independent Unbundling in the Competition Policy Agenda of the BMWK', *D'Kart – Antitrust Blog* (3 May 2022)

Daniel Zimmer (ed.), 'The DMA: An *ex ante* Evaluation', 2022/3 *Concurrences| On-Topic* 4–9

Luigi Zingales, *A Capitalism for the People: Recapturing the Lost Genius of American Prosperity* (New York: Basic Books, 2012, 2014 for the paperback edition)

Luigi Zingales, 'Towards a Political Theory of the Firm', 31 *Journal of Economic Perspectives* 113–30 (2017)

Shoshana Zuboff, *The Age of Surveillance Capitalism: The Fight for a Human Future at the New Frontier of Power* (New York: PublicAffairs, 2019)

Ethan Zuckerman, *What Is Digital Public Infrastructure?* (Washington: Center for Journalism & Liberty, November 2020)

Index

Index

Regulation on the Transparency and Targeting of Political Advertising (European Union), 127, 139
remedies, 74–84, 100, 125, 130, 160, 172–73, 181
Responsible Business Conduct, 58
revolving doors, 173–75
rivals' cost, 108, 137
Robertson, Viktoria H.S.E., 89
Roblox, 163
Roosevelt, Franklin D., 24
Rose-Ackerman, Susan, 179
rule of law, 4, 11, 15, 18, 35, 38, 64, 71, 101, 153, 169
rule of reason, 22, 81
Russia, 20, 50

sanction, 13, 57, 172, 174
Sarbanes-Oxley Act (USA), 58
satellite, 50
Saudi Arabia, 20
Schmidt, Eric, 150–51
Schumpeter, Joseph, 25
Schweitzer, Heike, 69
Scott Morton, Fiona M., 109, 143
search, 41, 46, 51, 88, 100. *See also* search engine
search engine, 48, 86, 97, 99, 102, 107–08, 123, 125, 131, 141–42, 150, 182
self-preferencing, 95, 112, 124, 135, 137
self-restraint, 171
separation of powers. *See also* checks and balances
    antitrust in, 85–113
    in antitrust, 57–84
    history, 13–18
    multilevel, 120
    new axes, 140–81
    notion, 13–18, 182–84
    power-centered, 117–21
    in separation of powers, 85–113
Shapiro, Carl, 64
shareholder, 43–44, 57, 61, 77, 80–91, 83, 96, 144. *See also* General Meeting of Shareholders
Sherman, John, 11, 32
Sherman Act (USA), 4, 19, 22–23, 31–34, 72, 77, 95, 101, 105, 140
Sibony, Olivier, 71
Simmel, Georg, 30
Simoncini, Andrea, 68
Simons, Josh, 45, 53, 76
Sitaraman, Ganesh, 141
small but significant and non-transitory decrease in privacy (SSNDP), 89–91
small but significant and non-transitory decrease in quality (SSNDQ), 89–91

small but significant and non-transitory increase in price (SSNIP), 89
smartphones, 41
SMEs, small and medium enterprises, 180
Smith, Adam, 25, 41
social justice, 15, 79, 101
social media, 41, 43, 46, 52, 76–77, 123–24, 131, 138
social media council, 76–77
social networks, 24, 41, 48, 85–86, 88, 95, 97–98, 102, 108, 125, 141, 182
society
    civil, 17, 80, 152–53, 180
    information, 47, 49–54, 75, 182–83
    virtual, 104, 168
Sony, 162–63
South Africa, 20
SpaceX, 50
Spain, 20–21, 170
Spotify, 133
Standard Oil, 33, 92
standards, 40, 67–68, 77, 94, 125, 152, 161–62, 165, 167, 182. *See also* community standards
Starlink, 50
start-up, 12, 65, 90, 180
State Antitrust Enforcement Venue Act (USA), 135
Statement of Objections, 61, 66
statute
    antitrust, 19–23, 34, 72, 77, 95, 101, 105, 128–30, 133–38, 140, 144
    interpretation, 34, 105
    varia, 79, 122–23, 130–33, 144
Stephenson, Neal, 160
Stigler Committee, 145
Stucke, Maurice E., 112, 139, 154–55, 178
subsidiarity of antitrust and competition laws, 48–49, 145
Sunstein, Cass R., 71
Supreme Court (India), 131
Supreme Court (USA), 21–22, 138, 140
surveillance, 79, 154
Susskind, Jamie, 5, 79, 172
Sweeney, Tim, 161
Switzerland, 170

talent, 40, 173
Tambini, Damian, 68
tax, 28, 157
Telecommunications Business Act (South Korea), 132–33
Tencent, 3, 66, 69–70, 78, 162
Tesla, 47

Printed in the USA
CPSIA information can be obtained
at www.ICGtesting.com
LVHW020935301023
762437LV00005B/106